A History of Union Theological Seminary in New York

Union Theological Seminary in New York

A History
of Union Theological
Seminary
in New York

Robert T. Handy

COLUMBIA UNIVERSITY PRESS
NEW YORK

Columbia University Press
New York   Guildford, Surrey
Copyright © 1987 Columbia University Press
All rights reserved

Printed in the United States of America

Library of Congress Cataloging-in-Publication Data

Handy, Robert T.
  A history of Union Theological Seminary in New York.

  Bibliography: p.
  Includes index.
  1. Union Theological Seminary (New York, N.Y.)—
History.   I. Title.
BV4070.U66H18   1987   207'.7471   86–20702
ISBN 0–231–06454-3

This book is Smyth-sewn.
Book design by J.S. Roberts

To my colleagues and students at Union,
1950–1986

Contents

Preface   ix

Acknowledgments   xiii

1. Embodying a Vision (1836–1850)   1

2. Strengthening the Seminary's Identity
   (1850–1870)   25

3. Union as a Denominational Seminary
   (1870–1890)   47

4. The Trials of Charles Briggs
   (1891–1893)   69

5. Liberal Evangelicalism Faces Twentieth-Century
   Realities (1894–1908)   95

6. A Shift of Emphasis: The Scholarly Dimensions
   of Theological Education (1908–1926)   121

7. Advance Through Storm: The Coffin Years
   (1926–1945)   159

8. Ecumenicity and Expansion in the Van Dusen
   Era (1945–1963)   211

9. Turmoil and Transition (1963–1975)   259

10. Reaffirmation in a Time of Testing
    (1975–)   315

CONTENTS

Notes	351
Bibliographical Note	367
Index	371

Preface

The Presbyterian founders of New York's Union Theological Seminary in 1836 originally had in mind an institution for ministerial students living in the area, though they left the door open to those of other places and other denominations. To their surprise, Union soon became the third largest seminary in the country at the time. The determination of the school's leaders to hold together high academic standards, sincere Christian piety, and enlightened practical experience in an atmosphere of freedom attracted attention and got results, and Union became widely known. Backed by an earnest group of lay supporters, the seminary was able through the years to gather a faculty studded with eminent Christian scholars and to draw a steady stream of talented students. Among them were those from other countries, and as numbers of Union graduates fulfilled their ministries overseas, the seminary became well-known in the wider Christian world. Because of its stands on certain theological and social issues, its history has been marked by sharp controversies. As it grew it moved twice into larger quarters, settling into its present quadrangle on Morningside Heights halfway through the century and a half of history that is recounted here.

As Union's 150th anniversary approached, the value of a comprehensive history of the seminary, with its important roles in church, ecumenical, and educational history, became apparent. George L. Prentiss' two volumes covering the first sixty years of Union's his-

tory have been long out of print, as has Henry Sloane Coffin's more
recent "informal history," which continued the story for another half
century. Invited as a church historian to deal not just with the four
decades since Coffin but to retell the whole story, I soon rediscovered
what I already knew—that no two persons would interpret a complex
history in quite the same way. Though I have tried to be faithful to
the voluminous but uneven archival and published materials about
Union, I know well that in identifying themes and selecting materials
I have made hard choices and passed by things that someone else
would emphasize more strongly.

      When Donald W. Shriver Jr. was inaugurated as Union's
thirteenth president early in 1976, he improved on Emerson's obser-
vation that an institution is one person's lengthened shadow to say
that an institution with any history in it is the overlapping shadow of
many people. Many persons do indeed march through these pages.
If members of the seminary's faculty and board predominate in the
text, it is partly because they were related to the school over long
periods and played central roles in its direction, and partly because
there are permanent records of what they said and did. Yet by far the
largest number of persons related to Union have been its students
and its graduates. Even brief mention of their lives and contributions
would fill a book far longer than this one. A fitting tribute to them
was paid by James A. Joseph when he gave the commencement address in 1979: "Union Theological Seminary is respected throughout
the world because its historic commitment to the pursuit of excellence has never been permitted to extinguish its concern with equity.
Union graduates have not only the capacity for theological reflection
but the ability to share another person's burden and feel another person's pain."

      In various ways Union students and graduates across a
century and a half have sought to keep together a rigorous concern
for truth and freedom with a commitment to the love of God and
humanity. Hence the story of their seminary, with its passion for
holding in creative tension things that so easily come apart, is worth
retelling, even those hard places in the account where Union fell
below its own principles and standards. Though the seminary has
gone through various changes and has reflected many shifting aspects
of the religious and educational culture of which it is a part, there

remain certain continuities during the 150 years. What may at first appear to have been great changes often later show themselves to be but fresh expressions of recurring unities in Union's history. Throughout the story, Union students and faculty, graduates, and directors were striving to express a historic faith in timely terms and to transmit it in a living way. Such efforts have many times attracted wide attention—at one extreme highly commendatory, at another sharply critical. An anniversary provides an opportunity to look ahead from the perspective that a renewed understanding of the past can provide. To that end this history has been undertaken.

> Robert T. Handy
> Henry Sloane Coffin Professor
> of Church History

Union Theological Seminary, New York
November 19, 1986

Acknowledgments

Many persons have been helpful in the preparation of this book. Not infrequently a casual remark or question by a colleague, student, director, or graduate has put me on to something that has found its way into these pages. Of particular help have been Robert Wood Lynn, who shared generously his perceptions of Union and of the history of theological education, and Margaret M. McGuinness, who assisted with the research. Both read the early draft with meticulous care and helped me to say better what I had in mind. Others who read the typescript chapter by chapter and provided useful comments and encouragement were Donald W. Shriver Jr., Milton McCormick Gatch Jr., and Staley Hitchcock. Persons I interviewed who also read certain chapters or sections of the work as it developed were John C. Bennett, Beverly Wildung Harrison, David W. Lotz, Glenn T. Miller, J. Brooke Mosley, and Roger L. Shinn. Among others interviewed were Anne McGrew Bennett, Blanche M. Britton, Beverly Roberts Gaventa, Elizabeth Jones, Lawrence N. Jones, Arthur C. McGiffert Jr., Louise Richardson, Sidney D. Skirvin, A. Hildegard Ross, Carl Hermann Voss, and Barbara G. Wheeler. Gatherings of alumni/ae that I have addressed have responded thoughtfully to questions I have asked, and informal group interviews followed. Besides a number of such occasions in New York, those in Columbus, Dallas, Denver, Detroit, and Rochester have been illuminating.

        Much of the research has been done in the Burke Library of Union Theological Seminary. Members of the library staff, especially Richard D. Spoor, Betty C. Bolden, Paul A. Byrnes, John Cox, Seth E. Kasten, Kirk A. Moll, Ruthmary Pollack, and Robert H. Schroeder, have been unfailingly cooperative. Others of the seminary's staff who have been particularly helpful in this effort have been Mary Cox, James A. Hayes, Karen Leahy, Mildred B. Stoerker, and Joyce Williams. I am grateful for the advice and assistance of Maureen MacGrogan, Leslie Bialler, and Jennifer Roberts of Columbia University Press. Though they died before this project was begun, my late colleagues Cyril C. Richardson and William Walker Rockwell originally interested me in Union's history and from them I learned much.

A History of Union Theological Seminary in New York

CHAPTER ONE

Embodying a Vision
(1836–1850)

O n October 10, 1835, nine Presbyterians—five laymen and
four ministers—met at the home of Knowles Taylor, a prominent New York merchant and a ruling elder at the Bleecker Street
Presbyterian Church. He was called to the chair, and his pastor, Erskine Mason, was appointed secretary. After discussion, the group
unanimously resolved "That it is expedient, depending on the blessing of God, to attempt to establish a Theological Seminary in this
city."[1] In so acting, they were in the mainstream of an important
educational development of their time. Many seminaries were founded
in nineteenth-century America to prepare leaders for the burgeoning
denominations.

American evangelical Protestantism in the middle of the
fourth decade of the nineteenth century was a thriving, confident,
steadily growing movement. The opportunities were immense, for
continuing immigration implemented the natural increase of population to provide a growing pool of persons to be won to the cause of
Christ. The country's frontiers were pressing toward the West, opening extensive areas where there were few Christian institutions of any
kind. In most of the denominations the theology and practice of the
revival, developed through the excitements of the First Great Awakening of the eighteenth century and the Second of the nineteenth,

provided both motivation and methods for serious effort not only to win persons to Christ, but to reform the nation so that it would more closely approximate the Christian ideal. Erskine Mason exclaimed in one of his sermons, "Nothing, my brethren, is great in this world but the kingdom of Jesus Christ; nothing but that, to a spiritual eye, has an air of permanency."[2] To extend that kingdom meant both winning individuals and then organizing them for mission to others and for the Christianizing of the nation.

The lines between denominations were then rather sharply drawn. Even those groups that shared much in common—those stemming primarily from the specific historical background of the British Protestant tradition (such as Baptists, Congregationalists, Disciples, Episcopalians, Methodists, and Presbyterians)—were quite certain that their doctrines and polity were closest to the teaching of the Bible, and they were determined to win converts to their particular ways. They formed various denominational agencies for such causes as evangelism, home and foreign missions, education, publication, and reform.

The overall task of Christianization confronting them was so great, however, that many of them looked for allies in their effort. Presbyterians and Congregationalists were sufficiently close theologically in their devotion to the Westminster Confession that they could work out a formal Plan of Union for work in the developing states and territories to the west of New England.[3] The plan was initially an agreement made in 1801 between the General Assembly of the Presbyterian Church in the United States of America and the Congregational General Association of Connecticut; by 1830, it had been accepted by the Congregational associations of the other five New England states. It provided ways for the two communions to merge their forces in forming congregations in new settlements.

That was a unique arrangement made possible by the confessional closeness of these two Calvinist bodies. As they searched for allies in the work of extending the gospel and winning the nation, many evangelicals recognized that there were true followers of Christ in other denominations. Even as they were loyal to their own denominational standards, as individuals they could work with other Christians and form with them voluntary societies for the carrying out of agreed tasks of mission and reform. So they developed a network of voluntary agencies for evangelizing and Christianizing America and the world. The balance between denominational loyalty and cooperation on an individual and voluntary basis with others was not easy to maintain. The tension was implicit in a passage of a Presbyterian Pastoral Letter of 1817: "Endeavour to maintain A SPIRIT OF HARMONY WITH ALL DENOMINATIONS OF CHRISTIANS. While you *contend earnestly for the faith once delivered to the saints,* and bear a faithful testimony to the Apostolic doctrine and order, which we profess to receive; let no bigotry, or prejudice, no party rancour or offensive crimination, pollute your testimony."[4] Despite the difficulties in maintaining such a stance, however, by the 1830s the national gatherings of the denominations were paralleled by the annual meetings of the national voluntary societies, with many of the same persons participating in both. The whole system depended on the local congregations across the land to provide able leaders, convinced followers, and adequate financial support.

To maintain such a system required many well-prepared leaders both for the local churches and for the denominations and societies. Before the nineteenth century, future ministers were educated largely by serving as apprentices to a well-established pastor, by remaining after college graduation for a period of further study with the president or professor of divinity, or by engaging in denominationally sponsored educational, reading, and examination programs (some of which later matured into seminaries).

Early in the nineteenth century a new development in ministerial education emerged to meet growing opportunities and demands—the theological seminary, an independent educational institution with a resident faculty of three or more conducting a three-year academic program. They were designed primarily for college graduates, but those with varying levels of preparation were also admitted. The prototypical seminaries which set the standards were the Congregational seminary founded at Andover, Massachusetts in 1808 and the Presbyterian institution established at Princeton, New Jersey, four years later. The value of this new approach was quickly recognized, and by the time that small Presbyterian group met in New York in the middle of the fourth decade more than twenty-five seminaries had opened their doors. The curricula (entirely prescribed) that were developed by the early seminaries were normally devoted to the four divisions of theological seminary that had by then become standard: exegetical, historical, systematic, and practical theology, the latter embracing such topics as sacred rhetoric, homiletics, church government, and pastoral work.[5]

Most seminaries founded in this period were not only denominational in nature, but represented the interest of a particular region or theological party. With their commitment to both theological regularity and a learned ministry, Presbyterians were especially active in establishing seminaries. The largest body, the Presbyterian Church in the United States of America, harbored six by 1835—in addition to Princeton, Auburn in New York State, Western in Pennsylvania, Lane in Ohio, Columbia in South Carolina, and the school founded in Indiana which moved to Chicago and eventually became McCormick.

The denomination itself was torn by the Old School/New School controversy, for there were sharp differences between these parties. Though there were significant exceptions, the Old School found its strength among the Scottish and Scotch-Irish elements which stressed the "objective" side of the tradition, the New School among Presbyterians from England, Wales, and New England who had been influenced by evangelical Puritan teachings and paid greater attention to the experiential, "subjective" aspects of their Calvinist inheritance. Theologically, the Old School adhered to a stricter interpretation of the Westminster Confession, particularly of its doctrine of original sin. The New School, many of whose members had originally been Congregationalists who came into Presbyterianism through the workings of the Plan of Union, tended to hold milder views on the doctrine of human depravity. The New School was more favorable to revivalism; the Old School sharply criticized what was regarded as the excesses and extremism of the "New Measures" revivalism of Charles G. Finney, who in 1835 left the Presbyterian fold for the Congregational. In matters of polity, the Old School granted greater authority to the church courts. It was increasingly dissatisfied with the way the nondenominational voluntary societies not under the control of their judicatories were influencing the life of the denomination. There was also tension over the slavery issue between the two parties; the New School had its center of strength primarily in New

York and other northern states and was inclined to be more receptive
to the antislavery movement, while the Old School was more evenly
distributed across the nation, and hence had many members in the
South, among whom were some prominent proslavery leaders.

The bitterness between these two parties as they struggled
for control of the one church was intense. It was displayed in some
bitter heresy trials, two of which took place in 1835. In Cincinnati
the president of Lane, Lyman Beecher, a former Congregationalist
who had once led the orthodox Calvinists in their struggle against the
Unitarians, found himself among Old Schoolers who held staunchly
to the Westminster Confession. As one scholar has aptly put it, "they
loved the document, covers and all." He was brought up on charges
before presbytery, but he won, arguing that to show people their true
situation before God ecclesiastical symbols might have to be reinter-
preted, for "the language never stands still."[6] Much closer to those
who were seeking to found a seminary in New York was the case of
the pastor of the First Church of Philadelphia, Albert Barnes. He
had previously been charged with heresy by the Presbytery of Philadelphia and the matter went before the General Assembly of 1831,
where his call was sustained by a New School majority. In 1835 the
publication of his new commentary on Romans provided an opening
for his opponents to try again as they pressed charges against him
from presbytery to synod, so that when the seminary founders first
met in October 1835 in New York his right to preach had been suspended. The atmosphere of mistrust was deeply resented by those
who longed for the cooperation of the faithful in the tasks of evangelizing and Christianizing.

The members of the group that met in New York on
October 10, 1835 with the intention of founding a seminary primarily to serve the thriving cities of New York and Brooklyn (which would
remain separate cities until 1898) were predominantly New School
in their sympathies. When they met again nine days later there were
five more lay representatives. Knowles Taylor continued to preside;
he had long been interested in theological education and had contributed liberally to the endowment of Union Theological Seminary
in Virginia and served as treasurer of one of the important national
voluntary agencies, the American Home Missionary Society. A staunch

supporter of the new venture was another prominent merchant, Richard T. Haines, who later was to serve for thirty years as president of its Board of Directors.

The best known of the four clerical members was Absalom Peters, a determined believer in the voluntary societies and himself a founder and early secretary (today we would say executive secretary) of the American Home Missionary Society. Another prominent figure was William Patton, who had been the founding pastor of Central Presbyterian Church in New York. At the time of Union's origins, he was the secretary of the Central American Education Society (an auxiliary of the American Education Society concerned with the "central" region of New York and Pennsylvania), a voluntary society in which the New School influence was strong. In that role he vigorously promoted the cause of ministerial education, and apparently was the first to suggest that a seminary be planted in the great city and convinced Peters that such a plan was feasible. The other two were then serving pastorates in the city, Henry White at the Allen Street Presbyterian Church, and Erskine Mason, a young man of 31, at the Bleecker Street Church. With the other ministers and one layman, the latter was placed on a committee to draft an exhibit of the reasons for a new seminary, and to prepare an outline of the plan of instruction. He was the principal author of the Preamble to the Constitution, so important in giving shape and direction to the fledgling institution, as he participated in the preparation of the documents necessary to the founding.

As the meetings progressed, others were invited to join the group, including Thomas McAuley, pastor of the Murray Street Presbyterian Church. Twenty-four persons, fourteen from the laity and ten of the clergy, were chosen to be the first Board of Directors. Plans for raising money were proceeding well when a calamity occurred—a devastating fire on the night of December 16, 1835 destroyed more than five hundred buildings in the wealthiest section of the city, making it difficult for some to fulfill their pledges. But the founders determined to go ahead; meeting early in January 1836 they adopted the Constitution, and on January 18 in the building of the American Tract Society the Board of Directors met for the first time.

Thomas McAuley was elected president of both board and seminary. A graduate of Union College in 1804, he taught there for some eighteen years before entering the pastorate. The church on Murray Street was his third; he added his new responsibilities on a part-time basis, continuing to serve his congregation. The new institution was named "The New York Theological Seminary." On that same eventful evening, the board also adopted the carefully prepared Preamble to the Constitution. It was so significant in giving lasting direction to the institution that it follows in full as it was originally written, with some parenthetical observations inserted.

That the design of the founders of this Institution may be fully known to all whom it may concern, and be sacredly regarded by the Directors, Professors, and Students it is judged proper to make the following preliminary statements:

1. A number of Christians, Clergymen and Laymen, in the cities of New York and Brooklyn, deeply impressed with the claims of the world upon the church of Christ to furnish a competent supply of well-educated and pious ministers of correct principles to preach the Gospel to every creature; impressed also with the inadequacy of all existing means for this purpose; and believing that large cities furnish many peculiar facilities and advantages for conducting Theological education, after several meetings for consultation and prayer,

Resolved, unanimously, in humble dependence on the grace of God, to attempt the establishment of a Theological Seminary in the city of New York.

(What the predominantly New School founders meant by "correct principles" can be discerned in the pledge originally required of professors: "I believe the Scriptures of the Old and New Testament to be the word of God, the only infallible rule of faith and practice; and I do now, in the presence of God and the Directors of this Seminary, solemnly and sincerely receive the Westminster Confession of Faith as containing the system of doctrine taught in the Holy Scriptures. I do also, in like manner, approve of the Presbyterian Form of Government; and I do solemnly promise that I will not teach or inculcate anything which shall appear to me to be subversive of said system of doctrines, or of the principles of said Form of Government, so long as I shall continue to be a Professor in the Seminary."[7] This form was used until 1905.

The decision to plant a seminary in a large city was a controversial step, for many believed that "the quiet of the country was more favorable to study and high scholarship," and Union's move was later cited as a "sorry example."[8] Seminaries at that time were often deliberately located in towns or small cities, away from the "temptations" of the expanding cities of the time. The determination of the founders to have an urban seminary was an important part of their vision for their new institution.)

2. This institution (while it will receive others to the advantages it may furnish) is principally designed for such young men in the cities of New York and Brooklyn as are, or may be, desirous of pursuing a course of theological study, and whose circumstances render it inconvenient for them to go from home for this purpose.

3. It is the design of the Founders to furnish the means of a full and thorough education, in all the subjects taught in the best Theological Seminaries in the United States, and also to embrace therewith a thorough knowledge of the standards of Faith and Discipline of the Presbyterian church.

(All four of the ordained ministers in the October preliminary meetings, who were on the committee of five to draw up the outlines of a plan for instruction, had studied at Princeton Theological Seminary. They drew on that experience in designing a curriculum. As the leader of a voluntary society which was especially concerned with ministerial education, the energetic William Patton was much aware of trends in the field.)

4. Being fully persuaded, that vital godliness well proved, a thorough education, and a wholesome practical training in works of benevolence, and pastoral labours, are all essentially necessary to meet the wants, and promote the best interests of the Kingdom of Christ, the Founders of this Seminary design, that its students, living and acting under pastoral influence, and performing the important duties of church members, in the several churches to which they belong, or with which they worship, in prayer meetings, in the instruction of Sabbath schools and Bible classes, and being conversant with all the social benevolent efforts of this important location, shall have the opportunity of adding to solid learning and true piety, enlightened experience.

5. By the foregoing advantages, the Founders hope and expect, with the blessing of God, to call forth from these two flourishing cities, and to enlist in the service of Christ and in the work of the ministry, genius, talent, enlightened piety, and missionary zeal, and to qualify many for the

labours, and management of various institutions, Seminaries of learning, and enterprises of benevolence, which characterize the present times.

(Here the founders stated in classical form the threefold emphasis of theological education for the new seminary: on solid learning, true piety, and enlightened experience. The first two points were familiar, but the third was their distinctive contribution and an important part of their vision for the institution. It was later widely copied, for their aim was to draw on the rich educational and religious resources of what by then was America's largest metropolitan area for preparing ministers. They also supported a broad view of ministry as certainly including but going beyond the pastorate to embrace service to the voluntary societies—to "various religious institutions, Seminaries of learning, and enterprises of benevolence." Much of the seminary's history provides a commentary on the advantages and difficulties of these views.)

6. Finally, It is the design of the Founders to provide a Theological Seminary in the midst of the greatest, and most growing community in America, around which all men, of moderate views and feelings, who desire to live free from party strife, and to stand aloof from all the extremes of doctrinal speculation, practical radicalism, and ecclesiastical domination, may cordially and affectionately rally.[9]

(In this final article, the dislike of the New School Presbyterians for what they regarded as an over-rigid subscription to the Westminster Confession on the part of the Old School is clearly demonstrated, and to that end they wanted no domination of their school by any judicatory of the church—it was to be an independent institution under its own self-perpetuating Board of Directors. Their appeal to moderate views and feelings extended to the major crisis of their time regarding slavery. While in general they espoused the antislavery position, some conspicuously, few then went along with what they regarded as the extremism, the "ultraism," of abolitionism as they perceived it at that time. Though they were believers in temperance, they resisted its extreme, ultraistic form, which they included under the heading of "practical radicalism.")

The Preamble was the decisive document; the actual constitution, really a section of the bylaws they drew up, was to be

Union's first faculty member of international renown, biblical scholar Edward Robinson.

frequently amended, often with respect to some detail, but occasionally in a more thorough fashion. It provided for a board of 28 members, half lay and half clergy, arranged for the details of its operation, and listed the duties of the faculty and rules for the students. Significantly, it provided that the seminary "shall be equally open to every denomination of evangelical Christians for the admission of students of requisite qualifications," defined broadly in academic, moral, and church membership terms.

At its February 1836 meeting the board set to work to choose a faculty—it was not an easy business, for some they would like to have secured declined the invitation. They named the president, Thomas McAuley, as professor of pastoral theology and church government, and another founder and board member, Henry White, as professor of systematic theology. After graduation from Union College in 1824, White studied two years at Princeton Seminary, served the American Bible Society in the South, and in 1828 was installed as pastor of New York's Allen Street Presbyterian Church. Anxious to get the seminary open, the board also elected two of its own members to undertake part-time teaching as Professors Extraordinary (a term that went out of use in a few years; its modern equivalents are lecturer or visiting professor). Erskine Mason taught ecclesiastical history, while Ichabod Spencer, a Brooklyn pastor, dealt with biblical history. On this basis, late in November, the opening of the seminary was announced, and on December 5, 1836, thirteen students came to the home of President McAuley at 112 Leonard St., for there was no building as yet, and there they were duly enrolled and instruction began. For several years, classes were held in professors' homes or in church or society buildings.

A big boost for the infant school came early in 1837, when the board was successful in attracting a rising star, Edward Robinson, as the professor of biblical literature. A graduate of Hamilton College in 1816, he later served as instructor in Hebrew at Andover Theological Seminary (1823–1826), where he was closely associated with the distinguished biblical scholar, Moses Stuart. He then studied abroad for four years, chiefly at Halle and Berlin, becoming acquainted with such world-famous scholars as Tholuck, Gesenius, Neander, and Ritter. As professor extraordinary of sacred literature he returned to Andover, where he founded and edited the

Biblical Repository, writing nearly half of the articles in the first four volumes. He resigned his position because of poor health, but continued his literary labors as his health improved. On January 20, 1837, he accepted the call to the chair of biblical literature at the newly opened seminary in New York. In his letter, he explained that it was a matter of high gratification that the seminary was "the nursling of the churches in the city," and he gave his full and cordial assent to its "great principles of faith and practice." He then offered a few suggestions which laid the basis of what to this day has been one of the great departments in the history of the school and indeed in the history of theological education:

> The constitution properly requires every Professor to declare that he believes "the Scriptures of the Old and New Testaments to be the Word of God, the only infallible rule of faith and practice." This is placing the Bible in its true position, as the only foundation of Christian theology. It follows as a necessary consequence, that the study of the Bible, as taught in the department of Biblical Literature, must lie at the foundation of all right theological education. To understand the Bible, the student must know all about the Bible. It is not a mere smattering of Greek and Hebrew, not the mere ability to consult a text in the original Scriptures, that can qualify him to be a correct interpreter of the word of life. He must be thoroughly furnished for his work, if he be expected to do his work well. A bare enumeration of the particulars that fall within the department of Biblical Literature will show that it covers a wider field than is generally supposed. To it properly belong full courses of instruction in the Hebrew, Greek, and Chaldee languages, and also, as auxiliaries, in the Syriac, Arabic, and other minor dialects, in Biblical Introduction, or the History of the Bible as a whole, and its various parts, its writers, its manuscripts, editions, versions, etc.; in Biblical Criticism, or the history and condition of the text; in Biblical Hermeneutics, or the theory and principles of interpretation; in Biblical Exegesis, or the practical application of those principles to the study and interpretation of the sacred books; in Biblical Antiquities; and, further, a separate consideration of the version of the Seventy, as a chief source of illustration for both the Old and New Testament.

He knew well it would take time and increased resources to achieve such ends. In a statement curiously prophetic of the new seminary's course for well over a decade, he observed that "there must be in every great undertaking a day of small things, there must be months and even years of weakness, though yet of growth," to prepare the way for further action. He indicated his great concern for the development of the library. [10]

In closing, he called attention to his long-laid plans for travel in Europe and Palestine to prepare a Biblical Geography, and arranged for an academic year's leave of absence. So, after teaching during the first half of 1837, he sailed in July, settled his family in Berlin, and early in 1838 spent two and a half months traveling and working in the Holy Land, making many illuminating discoveries. Back in Berlin, he prepared the manuscript for the three-volume *Biblical Researches*, published simultaneously in Germany, England, and the United States in 1841. It was a classic, epoch-making work that set the geography of the Holy Land on a more fixed basis than it ever had been before. [11] He did not get back to the seminary until the fall of 1840, and it was a tribute to his eminence that the seminary waited. During his absence, Isaac Nordheimer, a devout Jew, served as instructor in the elements of Hebrew and cognate languages. Another board member, Samuel H. Cox, a former faculty member at Auburn Seminary and then pastor of the First Presbyterian Church of Brooklyn, was called to teach both biblical and ecclesiastical history as a professor extraordinary.

When Robinson returned, he brought new distinction to the young and struggling school. He had been a part of the group of New England scholars led by Moses Stuart of Andover who had begun to assimilate the critical study of the Bible, which Robinson mastered in his years of scholarly study and work in Germany. His reputation increased and various honors were heaped on him as the reviews of his great work came in. A modern writer finds that he was "the one American scholar to achieve an international reputation in biblical studies before the Civil War." [12] It was further augmented when a second sabbatical granted by the board in 1851–52 led to an additional volume of the *Researches*.

Union students found their famous mentor to be a physically large, industrious, modest, and irenic man, a prodigious scholar and writer. Years later, one of his students of the 1840s reported how high his standard of ministerial scholarship was, and how "he strove to hold those whom he taught to honest and faithful work in study." Hence he had "a look and tone of severity which chafed some. But it proceeded from the kindest intent, and there was a warm side to his heart, and a personal interest for every earnest student." [13]

Robinson was also conversant with the growing technical specialization of the disciplines of theology as centered in the German universities, and as Union's librarian in the 1840s laid solid foundations for a great collection. His work was highly influential in bringing the new seminary into the forefront of developments in theological education. He was active in teaching until very near the end of his fruitful life, which came in 1863 when he was in his sixty-ninth year.

It took nearly two years for the seminary to get a building to house its students and activities. One of the earliest acts of the board was to acquire property, a 200 foot square between University Place and Greene streets, between 6th and 8th streets. The area was then well uptown on the outskirts of the city, above the University of the City of New York (later New York University). A building fronting on University Place, No. 9, was started in March of 1837, but financial difficulties in that year of panic stalled the effort for a time, so that the building was not available for use until the fall of 1838. Dedicated on December 12, the three-story building had rooms for only thirty students, and was quickly outgrown. Students did not have to pay for their rooms, but it was estimated that fuel for fireplaces (there was no central heating) cost about $5.00 for a year, and laundry $4.00 per term. Two rooms in the basement were set aside for a refectory, student managed, with board at $1.50 per week. A chapel was part of the building, with prayers conducted on week days by the faculty at 5:00 P.M. The attendance of students was required and (as at lectures and recitations), monitored. As the building soon overflowed, additional space was obtained in various rented apartments for student occupancy.

The board may have had some difficulties in gathering a faculty and erecting a building, but they had none in attracting students. During the first, short academic year of 1836–37, 10 additional students had joined the original 13. By the close of the second year this had more than doubled to 56, but by the fall of 1838 there were 92, making the seminary already the third largest in the land, following Andover and Princeton. To the great surprise of the directors, few students came from the cities of New York and Brooklyn, but they came from many states. The first commencement in 1837 saw only one graduate, who hailed from Massachusetts. The second,

The original seminary building, 9 University Place, erected 1838, upper two floors added in 1852.

a year later, had nine graduates, only one "'local," while three others came from upstate New York, and the rest from other states. By 1839 the graduating class numbered 30, which included only six from the two home cities.

The board quickly enlarged its vision of service to welcome students from other geographical areas, and it altered its rule that directors should be residents of New York and Brooklyn by adding (and interpreting broadly) the words "and vicinity." Before the 1840s were out, students had begun to come from other countries; the records cite Canada, Scotland, Bohemia, and the Sandwich Islands. From the early years, in addition to regular theological students there were those, most of whom had completed their work at other seminaries, who were registered as "resident licentiates"; later they would be identified as graduate students. Though the curriculum was fixed in those days and there were no electives, presumably they were drawn by the growing reputation of the faculty and the opportunities of the urban location. There was no charge for tuition at the seminary until the twentieth century, but in 1841 an "annual tax" of $10 was levied on all students, while other expenses remained the same. Examinations in those days were oral, conducted by the faculty and sometimes by directors, with the whole class present. They came at the end of an academic year over a period of several days.

The cause of missions, both home and foreign, was of great concern in the seminary from the beginning, as it was in other evangelical institutions. The first (1837) student organization was a Society of Inquiry Respecting Missions, which requested and received meeting space and a reading room when the building was opened. The first Monday of each month was set apart for consideration of the missionary cause. A member of the class of 1838, Samuel Robbins Brown, was one of the early missionaries to China, and as women were not then admitted there, his wife was listed as "freight." Henry Martyn Scudder graduated five years later and departed for India and later founded the Arcot Mission; he was a member of a famous missionary family. By 1846 sixteen students were candidates for the foreign field. A story of missionary dedication well known in the Union of the nineteenth century was that of George Bowen, the author of the comment on Robinson quoted above. A self-educated man who had been an unbeliever, he came to the seminary because of a spiritual experience following the death of his fiancée. As had many students before and since, he threw himself into Christian work in the city, while as a devout student leader he aroused enthusiasm for the missionary cause. On graduating in 1847 he at once sailed to India, where he labored for forty years without furlough and with few visible results. He gave up salary to live the life of the natives; his impact was primarily in the way he inspired other missionaries and through his literary gifts.[14] The emphasis that Union and other schools put on missions was a clear indication of their determination to serve the churches.

Though faculty and students agreed on the missionary emphasis, there was sharp disagreement at another point. Members of the board and faculty were opposed to slavery, a position strengthened, for example, by the coming to both bodies of Samuel H. Cox, whose advocacy of the cause of black people in 1834 had exposed him to the anger and violence of a proslavery mob. But at the outset the directors believed that abolitionism was on the edge of fanaticism; it did not suit their more moderate style, and they did not want the seminary involved. Hence on January 31, 1839 the faulty forbade the students to use seminary rooms for meetings of any type without faculty permission, explaining their views in a long sentence:

The faculty considers, in reference to subjects so exciting & peculiar, & at present connected with the secular law and politics of the country, as those of colonization and abolition, that no action of the students such as sending delegates to conventions, or otherwise, which may be adapted to commit this institution in reference to these or any similar subjects, ought at anytime to be admitted or performed in the institution; while the faculty disclaim all purpose or desire to influence the private views of the students on these subjects, they wish them to understand that the interests of the institution are of their own sort, their own sacredness, and their own importance; & that no man or set of men, have a right or a reason to commit its character or peril its influence by their private views or feelings, in any way, or on any occasion, in the premises; & this opinion, the faculty view as only a proper application of a provision in the Constitution, which must not be violated.[15]

Three students demurred, but the faculty did not change the position that had been taken.

An educational institution requires books, and although

the seminary was still reeling from the financial difficulties caused by the fire of 1835 and the panic of 1837, an opportunity to get a remarkable nucleus for a great theological library arose. At the dawn of the nineteenth century political conditions rendered it advisable for the Benedictines of the monastery of St. Mary at Paderborn in Germany to divide their possessions and move to places less threatened by secularization. Brother Leander Van Ess had been in charge of the collection of prohibited books, and was able to move some 6000 volumes, including some very rare works, with him to Marburg, where he served as professor in the Catholic faculty. He became deeply interested in the translation of the Bible into vernacular languages, cooperating with Protestant scholars in the effort. When he retired he put the collection up for sale. Edward Robinson heard about the opportunity from another biblical scholar, Calvin E. Stowe of Cincinnati's Lane Seminary, and was instructed by the board to have it inspected and, if advisable, to obtain it. The bargain was struck, and Union purchased a library of 13,000 items including manuscripts and incunabula valued at 50,000 florins for a fifth of that. In American dollars, when it arrived in October 1838, it amounted to $5070.08. It was an act of faith—the seminary was in debt, so President McAuley advanced the funds, which had to be secured by a mortgage. As librarian, Robinson wisely and vigorously built up the collection through purchase and gifts, often of the personal libraries of ministers and professors as they retired or died. The foundations were solidly laid for what was to become a great theological library with immense resources.

When the seminary became legally incorporated on March 26, 1839, there came a surprise, for the name of the institution was changed during the legislative process to "The Union Theological Seminary in the City of New York." Perhaps the directors knew a change was in the offing, for just before that, on March 15, they had passed a resolution: "That the committee on the charter be requested to solicit an act of incorporation for the Seminary under such name as they may find acceptable to the Legislature."

Two explanations as to the reason for the change have been perpetuated. One of the prominent early historians of Union, Edwin F. Hatfield, believed it was done because there was already a seminary in the city—the General Theological Seminary, an Episcopal institution which in 1827 located permanently on Tenth Avenue between 20th and 21st Streets. To avoid confusion, Hatfield said, a distinctive name was given to the newer school.

The other explanation was emphasized by Roswell D. Hitchcock, who joined the faculty in 1855 and served as president in the 1880s. He reported that Richard T. Haines, one of the original founders and directors of the seminary who served as board president from 1840 to 1870, had said that the name was proposed by the directors in protest against the division of the Presbyterian Church. In 1837 the Old School got control of the General Assembly, and not only abrogated the Plan of Union but made it retroactive, thus exscinding the four synods formed under the plan, three in New York and one in Ohio. The New School was unable to reverse the decision the next year, and regrouped in a separate church, nearly half the size of the previously undivided body. All of this caused great anguish and bitterness, and was deeply resented at the seminary. True to their moderate and irenic ways, they did not oust two persons who continued in the Old School church but were willing to work with what was in fact though not formally a New School institution. The two were Ichabod Spencer, a director and professor extraordinary, and Henry White, the first full-time professor and also (until 1840) a member of the board. Hitchcock was convinced that the Union designation for the seminary had been sent up from New York to the Legislature, and "was meant to be a monumental protest against the unhappy rending of the Presbyterian Church in 1837, as also both a prayer and a prophecy against it."[16]

Hatfield, however, who joined the board in 1846 and was a member for 37 years, firmly adhered to the other account, declaring that the new name was not desired, much less chosen by the board, though he admitted that it was "prophetic of the position that the Institution has ever since maintained."[17] It is doubtful now that the question can be resolved unless hitherto unknown documents turn up. .

By the end of the decade of its founding, the seminary thus had its board, faculty, students, name, books, and building—but it still had debts, no endowment, and insufficient funds. The New York fire of 1835 followed by the financial panic of 1837 meant that certain pledges could not be fulfilled. The very life of the institution was threatened, but the board held on, resolving late in 1839 "that it is the opinion of this meeting that it is of incalculable importance to the cause of our Redeemer that this Seminary be sustained."[18] Early the following year, when McAuley resigned as president of both board and faculty, it was decided that the new president should serve also as "financial agent." An attempt to raise money by subscription produced just enough so that by May the board saw the way clear to continue the seminary for another year.

Joel Parker was then elected president and professor of sacred rhetoric. After graduating from Hamilton College in 1824, he had studied at Auburn Seminary, served pastorates in Rochester, New York, New Orleans, and again in New York at Broadway Tabernacle. He was a forceful preacher, and a leader in the revivals of the early 1830s. Though his resignation in less than two years was apparently sincerely regretted by students and directors, for he was made honorary director and in later years a regular member of the board, he had not turned the financial tide. Indeed, his own salary was $1400 in arrears at the time he returned to the pastorate. No president was then appointed for 31 years. Seminary presidents did not then play the central administrative roles that they later filled. The faculty was small and close-knit, and the board's president kept watch over seminary affairs, calling special meetings when necessary.

By early 1843 the salaries of both Professors Robinson and White were seriously in arrears. Dr. White raised some money for his own salary, took a part-time job, and borrowed, while Mrs. White turned her home into a boarding house to help support the family of five. In 1843 he received an invitation to teach at Auburn but said if he could have some evidence of permanent support he would stay at Union. A public meeting then raised $25,000 to endow the chair of theology—the first permanent fund. The directors also wrote to alumni, requesting them to raise at least $50 each for the seminary, and by 1845–46 some congregations were contributing. For a time, the situation of Dr. Robinson was a little easier because of the special gifts given over three years by James Boorman, an English-born member of the Mercer Street Presbyterian Church who was prominent in commerce, banking, and railroading. But when payments on his salary became irregular again, the famous biblical scholar submitted his resignation as of early 1846, demanding his back pay in full. Happily, a compromise was worked out, and he remained at the struggling institution.

The seminary was still short-handed; a third regular faculty member was much needed, and the generosity of Boorman and other members at Mercer Street helped to provide for the transition of their eminent pastor, Thomas H. Skinner, to Union in 1848 as professor of sacred rhetoric, pastoral theology, and church government. A graduate of the College of New Jersey at Princeton, he soon forsook the study of law for that of theology, both through further study at his alma mater and as an apprentice with a leading pastor of the day. After various pastorates, he taught sacred rhetoric at Andover for three years before accepting the Mercer Street pulpit in 1835. He was a Union founder and director, resigning from the board to take up his new duties with great enthusiasm. He had long been prominent as pastor and preacher. Nearly 60 when he accepted the professorship, he continued his pastoral ways with great effectiveness. Students and colleagues alike spoke of his deep spirituality and his sincere personal concern for them.

Originally the directors had hoped to appoint a professor of sacred music, but funds were insufficient, so the subject was taught intermittently by instructors. In the first period of the seminary's life, Abner Jones and Edward Howe, the latter a graduate of 1845, gave instruction in music. In 1839 the students were given permission to form a "Haydn Society for the purpose of improving themselves in Sacred Music," which apparently lasted for about a dozen years.[19]

The appointment of Skinner, who eventually contributed a great deal to the life of the seminary, was not enough by itself to halt a decline in student enrollment. There had been 115 regular students in 1846–47, but by 1850–51 the number was down to 73. The original hopes of the founders had hardly been fulfilled; the building was inadequate, and the faculty remained very small. Only Robinson was widely known. In 1850 the directors decided to increase the faculty to four by adding a chair in church history, again stretching their resources, for the new incumbent, Henry Boynton Smith, soon discovered that his pay was frequently in arrears. When they invited the young, promising professor of philosophy at Amherst to come, he investigated carefully, discussing the call with the professor of theology. As he summarized the conversation in a letter:

Last evening I spent wholly, till eleven o'clock and after, with Dr. White, talking over the whole Seminary and matters thereto belonging. He was rather curious about some of my theological opinions, and we got into a regular discussion of two hours on the person of Christ, in which he claimed that I advocated something inconsistent with the Catechism, and I claimed that he taught what was against the Catechism, which was rather a hard saying against an old-established professor of theology. However, it was all very well and kind on both sides, and did not prevent his urging my coming here.[20]

Just before coming, Smith wrote to his friend George L. Prentiss his understanding of the seminary's lack of standing:

I go to New York in full view of all the uncertainties and difficulties of the position, . . .

The literary character of the Seminary is slight, its zeal in theological science is little, the need of a comprehensive range of theological studies and of books thereto has got to be created. The theological position is not defined. It stands somewhere between Andover and Princeton, just as New School Presbyterianism stands between Congregationalism and the consistent domineering Presbyterianism, and it will be pressed on all sides. Whether it is to be resolved into these two, or to be consolidated on its own ground, is still a problem.

These things will make one's position a little more free, but at the same time they will make it more ardous. I am going there to work,— to work, I trust, for my Master.[21]

Smith's coming to Union marked the beginning of a new period in the life of the young seminary; he was to be instrumental in giving it definition and direction that put it on the theological map. The vision of the founders had not yet been fully embodied; the new professor was to help bring that about.

Change came not only with the coming of the new but also with the passing of the old, for unexpectedly death came to Union's first professor in late August of 1850 when Henry White was in his 50th year. He had sacrificed much for the young seminary, and his solid work had earned the respect of his students. We know about his theological teaching primarily through their class notes, for he published little. A convinced Calvinist, he had followed the New England theology rooted in the teachings of Jonathan Edwards and refracted through the philosophy of Scottish common sense realism.

But his emphasis on two kinds of faith shifted his constructive focus away from overemphasizing faith as intellectual assent to truth. "General" faith in God's promises could move in that direction, but his attention to "specific" faith in the acknowledgement that Christ was a believer's personal savior allowed him to stress faith in terms of relationship between persons. [22]

At the time of his death, the graduates of Union adopted this statement: "Resolved, that as alumni we remember with the most grateful interest Dr. White's faithful instructions, the deep and earnest piety which characterized all his duties as connected with the Seminary, and the earnest and active concern he always manifested for his pupils, not only while under his care but also in their subsequent life and labors." [23] When George Bowen of Bombay reflected on his teacher from the perspective of some thirty years, he remembered that White had not been "eminent for brilliant genius or profound learning, or commanding eloquence, or polished manner," yet was "a most excellent teacher of the science of God," for "he had a clear head, discriminating judgment, sound common-sense, wise tact, and a warm heart—all pervaded with a child-like faith in Christ and his salvation." [24] He taught in such a way as to encourage each student's own individuality and way of working. His faithful, self-effacing industry helped the seminary to survive its first difficult decade and a half. But now he was gone, and new voices took up the rhythm of theological instruction for a new day.

CHAPTER TWO

Strengthening the Seminary's Identity (1850–1870)

When a former student of Henry Boynton Smith wrote that "the true life and power of the seminary began with the advent of Professor Smith himself"[1] he undoubtedly exaggerated somewhat, for as can be seen from the records and remarks of alumni, a lot of thorough teaching and learning had gone into the early years of struggle. Yet Smith's coming to Union in 1850 was a very important event for the young seminary. In the judgment of a twentieth-century scholar, "Within the next two decades . . . Smith's influence was decisive in transforming the institution into an important center for theological study."[2] Keen of mind, small of size, frail of body, gifted as lecturer and writer, able as translator and editor, this industrious man dominated the theological life of Union and of New School Presbyterianism for a quarter-century.

He was born in Maine, reared in Unitarianism, and graduated from Bowdoin College in 1834. In his last spring there he had an intense religious experience, which convinced him of the innate sinfulness of humans and of his need for an infinite savior, and led him to the confession that "Christ is my Redeemer and has atoned for my sin."[3] The experience gave his life new direction, and provided the Christocentric basis of the theology he was to preach and teach. He entered Andover Theological Seminary, and plunged into his studies with such intensity that he overworked and had to drop out, but not before he had been decisively influenced by the New England theology as shaped in the eighteenth century by Jonathan Edwards and taught in the nineteenth by Leonard Woods. The next autumn he tried again, this time at another Congregational seminary, Bangor in his native state, and again was instructed by a teacher of the New England theology, Enoch Pond. After a year he accepted the opportunity to tutor at his alma mater, teaching Greek and studying German.

Confronted again with problems of health, Smith passed the winter of 1837–38 in Paris, resting, reading, and observing. Then came two eventful years in Germany, where he was drawn to the mediating theology, a broad movement between orthodox confessionalism and extreme theological liberalism and rationalism. Its leaders undertook to mediate between traditional Christianity and the modern spirit of scientific and philosophical inquiry by combining biblical faith with the idea of a religion's inner principle (for Christianity, the incarnation) expressing itself in organic historical development. This was brought home to the young American in Halle especially by Friedrich A. G. Tholuck, leading theologian of the resurgent evangelical pietist movement, one of the strands in the mediating theology, which also included former students of Schleiermacher and some philosophical theologians. Smith, whose religious life had been shaped by the Second Great Awakening, found his teacher's piety congenial and inspiring, and the two became friends.

The following year he spent in Berlin, where Smith heard some of the famous scholars give lectures. He was especially impressed by August Neander, a church historian who formulated a synthesis of Christocentric piety and idealistic historical understanding, interpreting evangelical faith in the forms of modern thought. He combined a probing of primary sources with the idea of organic historical development. For him, church history was the story of the divine life incarnated, pervading and transforming humanity.[4] In this heady atmosphere, Smith grew in faith, scholarship, and reputation.

It took him a while, however, to get established again in his own country, where German theological thought, though little

Henry Boynton Smith, systematic theologian who put Union on the theological map.

known, was much mistrusted by religious leaders. Few had the ability to make the distinctions that he had learned between the evangelical and rationalistic tendencies in German theology. He taught a year at Bowdoin as "temporary additional instructor," and finally, late in 1842, was called to the pastorate of the Congregational church in West Amesbury, Massachusetts, where he ministered for five years, and where he was soon married to Elizabeth L. Allen, daughter of the president of Bowdoin during his student years there. He did enjoy the experience as pastor, and also the opportunity to teach Hebrew on the side at Andover.

Then at last in 1847 he won a full-time academic post as professor of mental and moral philosophy at Amherst College. His growing reputation was greatly enhanced when he delivered the annual address before the Porter Rhetorical Society at Andover in 1849 on "The Relations of Faith and Philosophy." It was a response to Horace Bushnell, controversial Hartford pastor-theologian, who had delivered the address the previous year on the theme "Dogma and Spirit," in which he stressed the role of spirit but was critical of the hold of dogma.[5] Smith countered by defining terms: evangelical faith is trust in God, embracing doctrines of faith drawn out into a definite system, denoting a full reliance on Christ that leads to salvation, and resting on the divine authority of "the very word of God recorded in the Scriptures." Philosophy, on the other hand, is the product of human thought, starting with facts, seeking for law, demanding truth, searching to account for all things. They are often seen as opposites, Smith explained, but with his characteristic emphasis on mediation, he stressed that they are complementary, for both deal with the facts of reality from different perspectives. Faith needs philosophy for clarification and precision, for the avoidance of mysticism and fanaticism, for undertaking the important tasks of theological reflection and correction, including the systematic ordering of doctrines. Philosophy as a mode of knowledge must face facts; Christian faith is based on a revelation historically attested and presents as "another series of facts" the experience of believers across the centuries.

Much aware of the existence of philosophic unbelief, the young scholar held that such views are unsound on philosophical grounds, for it is unphilosophical "for philosophy to be dogmatic in the face of a recognized reality." Skepticism, therefore, can and must be met by sound reason, not by name-calling. Then, insisting that "in Jesus Christ is to be found the real centre of the Christian economy," and after commending Schleiermacher and German evangelical theology, Smith concluded that Christianity gives "what man most needs, and, unaided, never could attain."[6]

All this and much more was presented lucidly and reasonably, made a strong impression, and won him an invitation to come to New York. In the audience was one of the founding directors of Union, William Adams, who would later become its president. Originally a Congregationalist who had graduated from Andover, he had changed denominations when he was called to pastor the Broome Street (later Central) Presbyterian Church in New York. Years later he wrote of Smith's 1849 address, "None who were present on that occasion will forget the glow of enthusiasm with which that address was delivered and received."[7] Adams knew that Smith could fit into almost any department, but nominated him for the chair of church history, where Union's need was.

The call presented a difficult decision for the young professor, for he was very popular at Amherst and it was relatively the stronger institution. To come to New York meant a transfer to New School Presbyterianism from Congregationalism, where he held a prominent place in the New England theology of Edwards and Hopkins, the stricter Calvinistic party which was opposed to the modified Calvinism of New Haven theology in which Yale's Nathaniel W. Taylor was central. A mediator by temperament, conviction, and education, Smith was seeking to draw the best from Edwardsean theology, Old School Calvinism, and the German theology of mediation. He believed that neither the New Haven nor Princeton theologies would quite do, for the one overemphasized philosophy without faith, the other faith without philosophy.[8] After much reflection and investigation, he finally accepted, taking up his new duties late in 1850.

The new professor introduced the historical spirit and method into the curriculum, bringing the perspectives and skills he had gained from his work in Germany. His inaugural address, "Nature and Worth of the Science of Church History," was typical of his mediatorial style of combining classical Christian theological positions of the Reformed tradition with new scientific approaches. He explained that the history of the church or kingdom (the words were used interchangeably) "is an account of the rise, the changes, and the growth of the most wonderful economy the world has known, embracing the most comprehensive purposes which human thought can grasp." Church history provides the key to understanding all history: "He who would know the principles which have really controlled human thought and action, will, if he be wise, explore the records of that kingdom which has had the longest duration and the strongest influence." Divine in origin, the church is placed "in an apostate world, centering in the incarnation of the Son of God, and having for its object the redemption of the race, through the might of the Holy Spirit." As such it lives "in a theatre of strife, where the strongest energies of good and ill, and all the forces of a supernatural, and all the forces of a natural kingdom wage perpetual warfare."

Smith knew that church history had often been presented without any lively conviction of its inherent worth,—that is, had been regarded as the driest of studies,—and with a rare touch of humor he observed that "its sources are buried in the dust of alcoves, and when exhumed, it is seldom with the insignia of a resurrection." But in his bold view, church history is "the record of the progress of the kingdom of God, intermingling with and acting upon all the other interests of the human race, and shaping its destiny." Such history ought to be studied by use of a scientific method, he insisted, as facts are brought under their legitimate laws or principles, and viewed in their connections with causes which have produced them and the ends to be accomplished by them, for when "so presented, it is one of the noblest objects to which human thought can be directed." The historical progress of the church is not mere development but is movement toward a predetermined end. The test of progress, "to the believer in a divine revelation," is given in the Scriptures, for by its truths and doctrines all history, and especially the history of the church, is to be judged.[9] For Henry Boynton Smith, church history was understood as historical theology, as one of the four main branches of theology, the others being exegetical, doctrinal, and practical. The fourfold pattern of curricular organization that had been established in German theological education quickly became standard at Union as at other seminaries.[10]

In the force of his personality and his abilities as teacher, researcher, and writer, the new professor brought a new historical dimension into Union's life that quickly became a permanent feature of its theological educational approach. His sweeping and dynamic vision of Christian history as a key to understanding both world history and the progress of redemption excited the interest of students and colleagues, not only at Union but in the larger world of church and seminary life. He set to work to prepare a *History of the Church of Christ in Chronological Tables* (1859), and to translate from the German certain historical works, especially those of Gieseler and Hagenbach.

Though he was a very able historian, his deepest interests were philosophical and theological. Henry White had died late in the summer as the plans for bringing Smith as church historian were maturing, and it was too late to consider him for that post. It was filled the next year by James Patriot Wilson, a graduate of the University of Pennsylvania, who had studied theology privately with his father, and served in several pastorates and a college presidency. But he remained at Union only two years before returning to the pastorate, leaving the systematics chair open again.

Meanwhile, the financial picture at Union slowly began to improve—unfortunately, not in time to spare Smith from the difficulties of facing arrears in salary payments and forcing him to overload with outside responsibilities. But prospects for the future looked brighter. An unexpected legacy from the estate of a friend of the seminary, prominent New York merchant James Roosevelt, helped. His grandson, James R. Bayley, was one of the Episcopal priests who was caught up in the High Church trend following the Oxford movement, and in 1844 was ordained to the Roman Catholic priesthood. Though it was not known until Roosevelt's death, because of Bayley's change the inheritance originally intended for him was redirected to Union. That was contested, but the matter was settled in Union's favor in 1850; Bayley went on to become Bishop of Newark and eventually Archbishop of Baltimore. Union's first endowed chair, the Roosevelt professorship in systematic theology, was the major outcome of the legacy.

The next step toward financial integrity was initiated by Dr. Skinner's successor at the Mercer Street Church, George Lewis Prentiss. By 1850, about $11,000, most of which went for professors' salaries, had to be raised annually to keep the seminary open. About

$4000 of the total came from Prentiss' congregation. As he studied the situation, he came to the conclusion that the founders, for all their good intentions, had made a "radical error" in not providing for adequate endowments:

> an error rendered more serious by their not considering that the proper function of a theological seminary is not only to train young men for the ministry by giving them thorough instruction in all branches of divinity, but also to be itself a living, perennial centre of theological learning, science, and power; and that, in order to fulfil this last all-important function, it must depend not merely upon popular sympathy and annual contributions, but upon sources of supply unaffected by fluctuations of business and the changing moods of the hour; in other words, upon solid, permanent endowments.

Prentiss decided to do something about it. Late in 1851, he preached a strongly worded sermon in his church, repeated it before the Synod of New York and New Jersey, and was requested to publish it. In his sermon he called attention to what would later be called the ecumenical character of the institution (though the definition was to be broadened considerably):

> The character of Union Seminary is eminently catholic, in the true sense of the word; it is at once liberal and conservative. . . . It stands in special connection with our own branch of the great Presbyterian family; but it numbers on its Board of Directors, and among its warmest friends, influential members of the other branch; while it seeks its professors and attracts its students as readily from the old Puritan body of New England, as if its predelictions were all Congregational.

In so saying he pointed to the way the New School founders wanted their school to serve not only their needs but those of evangelical Protantism generally:

> I do not know how you can well come nearer to such a plan than have the founders of the Union Seminary. Its main advantages are as accessible and useful to a Baptist, a Methodist, an Episcopalian, or a Congregationalist, as to a Presbyterian; and students of all these and of other denominations have availed themselves of them.

He emphasized that the city—especially New York—is to be preferred to the country as a place for training ministers. "Let a wise, tolerant Christian theology flourish here," he preached, "and it would diffuse a beneficent radiance over the land, and even among pagan nations. The position, then, of the Union Seminary is unsurpassed, both for the training of ministers and the cultivation of sacred learning."[11] He concluded with a powerful appeal for endowments, restating and enlarging on the vision of the founders.

The response was promising. The directors were impressed and early in 1852 called for a special meeting of friends of the seminary at the home of Charles Butler, a founder who served on the board for 61 years, the last 27 as its president. A lawyer who had become wealthy through real estate and railroad interests, he became well known for his philanthropic activity, from which the seminary frequently benefited. At the meeting, it was decided to send out copies of a circular about the seminary, the Prentiss sermon, and an appeal (which Smith penned). Prentiss soon found himself elected to the board on which he was to serve for 21 years—then becoming a faculty member for 26, and the first major historian of the seminary.

A new financial agent, who got some immediate results, was appointed. Through the century and a half of its life, Union has been served by able, often insufficiently noticed persons in positions now referred to as "support staff." Only a few such persons can be mentioned in a one-volume history; Joseph S. Gallagher well illustrates the service rendered by many faithful workers. He had been an army officer who, after his conversion while on active duty, regularly conducted services of worship wherever he was stationed. When based in Maine, he seized the opportunity to study Hebrew at Bangor Seminary. Resigning after 15 years of military service, he took further studies at Andover and Princeton, and entered the pastorate. In his new role at Union, he rather quickly secured subscriptions for more than $100,000, and late in the 1850s he raised an even larger sum for the endowment. From 1863 to 1874 he was a director and treasurer of the seminary with the title of General Secretary.

Thanks to the help of Prentiss, Gallagher, and many other workers and contributors, the seminary was at last out of financial danger. Some of the funds were designated for special purposes. James Boorman in 1853 increased his regular subscription to found the Davenport professorship of sacred rhetoric (later designated for Hebrew and the cognate languages) for his former pastor, Dr. Skinner, who had served on the faculty since 1848. The chair was named for the Reverend John Davenport, the first minister of New Haven, of whom Mrs. Boorman was a direct descendant. Two years later Mrs. Jacob Bell endowed the Washburn professorship of church history in memory of her brother, a Baltimore pastor. In 1865, the Baldwin professorship of sacred literature was founded by a board member, John Center Baldwin. What later became the Brown professorship of homiletics was founded by the Brown Brothers, James and John A., founders of a famous banking firm and generous patrons of the seminary. These and later named chairs have played an important role in the history of Union and of theological education to the present time; their descriptions sometimes have been changed in accordance with new needs. They have had to be enlarged and supplemented as time has gone on, for what could endow a professorship in 1865 would fall short of providing a month's salary and benefits in 1986.

The improved situation immediately permitted some refurbishing and expansion of the building at 9 University Place; two floors were added in 1852 so that a total of 80 students could be accommodated. By that date, the vision of the founders was more fully embodied, a full-time faculty of four was in place, and the seminary's reputation was growing. A passage on Union in the *New York Evangelist* of February 19, 1852 concluded that the advantages of a seminary in a great metropolis "has been abundantly proved by this experiment," and noted that "the Seminary has always had a full proportion of the theological students of the country; and these, as they have left its walls and mingled with the churches, have proved themselves to be among the best furnished and most useful ministers of the day, or have commended themselves on the foreign field as devoted and well adapted ministers."[12] The flow of students increased; by the end of the decade—in part as a result of the Great Revival of 1858—a new high of 146 was recorded. For Presbyterian students who were attracted to the New School position, Union was offering an increasingly viable alternative to Princeton seminary, with its strong Old School orientation.

When Henry Boynton Smith was deciding on the invitation to come to Union, he had noted that its theological position was not defined. As church historian, his attention had to be given primarily to other than theological matters. With Wilson's resignation in 1853, the way was clear for him to be transferred to theology the following year. In his 1849 address he had said that "systematic theology is the combined result of philosophy and faith; and it is its high office to present the two in their most intimate conjunction and inherent harmony." The responsibilities on his new chair increased the overload of work for the frail professor, for he took them very seriously. Among his duties for all the years he was at Union was that of librarian—a sizable additional task, for the library was steadily growing. For example, in 1854 Professor Robinson donated 900 volumes, some of them rare and valuable. By 1860 the library was getting overcrowded—a complaint that was to emerge again and again in the seminary's history. The overworked professor much appreciated the strength of the library, but was convinced that none was worse situated or more limited in space.

His interrelated problems of overwork and health in part accounted for the fact that Smith never completed his long-planned work on systematic theology. Nevertheless, through his articles, editorials, reviews, sermons, and lectures (posthumously published), he became one of the leading theologians of his time, clearly the outstanding theological voice of New School Presbyterianism. He has been ranked by historian James Hastings Nichols as "among the first half-dozen American theologians" of his generation, along with Charles Hodge, Edwards A. Park, Horace Bushnell, John W. Nevin, and Philip Schaff.[13] Under his theological leadership, Union became a force to be reckoned with, especially within the Reformed or Calvinistic tradition.

There was a freshness and power in his theological work. He was among those of his time seeking to move away from a one-sidedly objective, largely static approach to scriptural and confessional statements to a more dynamic and subjective theological position. The developmental approach that he used so effectively in teaching history also informed the way he did theology. He probed the strengths and weaknesses of the conflicting theological parties of his time, seeking to reconcile them not by glossing over basic principles but by pulling them toward a common center of unity, drawing them away from diversionary extremes. As a scholar thoroughly conversant with the developing specialized disciplines of theological study, he was one of the early "professional" systematic theologians, up to date on the technical aspects of his steadily expanding subject.

In his "second inaugural" at Union as systematic theologian early in 1855, he spoke on "The Idea of Christian Theology as a System." Smith explained that "In reaction from a too exclusive theory of divine sovereignty, others begin their systems in the reverse order, with man rather than God, sometimes making God to be but an indefinite extension of man, and theology a mere adaptation to human wants." He began with Christology, with the mediatorial principle of the Christian religion as its center of unity: "In the fact of the incarnation of the Son of God for our Redemption, may be said to be the grand principle of the Christian faith, its centre of unity." In Christ's mediation is to be found the central principle of the divine economy; it may be called either the Mediatorial or the Christological principle. From this position was derived his mediating theology: "To mediate between our extremes is our vital need, and such a mediation can be found only in Christ, and not in an ethical system. As the central idea of the whole Christian system is in mediation, so should this be the spirit of our theology, the spirit of our lives."[14]

As a mediating theologian working from a clear central principle he had no fear of conflict and controversy. He welcomed it, for out of sharp exchanges could come theological progress. Stearns remarked that "he had an innate love of controversy,—which, however, he knew how to keep within due bounds,—and never appears to better advantage than when defending the truth that was dear to him, or attacking views that he believed inimical to the best interests of orthodox Christianity."[15] He could keep controversy within bounds because his first principle of historical development was education, while conflict was the second, to be invoked in the interest of a higher unity. His aim was to bring the churches closer together under principles that he stoutly believed were moderate and correct. He was comfortable in the New School, but longed to overcome the division in his new denomination. He sincerely believed that one of the glories of the Reformed tradition was its emphasis on the sovereignty of God, but when carried too far, he argued, it produces error on the other side. So he plunged into the fray, taking on too many invitations and assignments, writing, editing, translating, arguing, lecturing, preaching.

His theological approach was dynamic and mediating, but his own system remained orthodox, following closely the New England school of Jonathan Edwards. He found this to be the better way between the Princeton theology of Charles Hodge and Old School Presbyterianism with its conformity to the stricter interpretation of the Westminster Confession, and the New Haven theology of Nathaniel W. Taylor with its innovations, especially its modifications of the doctrine of original sin. It was certain that humans would sin, said Taylor, yet they had power to the contrary; Smith saw this as a dangerous "ethical theory" based on Scottish philosophy, not on sound theology. Like Edwards, he held to the doctrine of predestination. He also remained an orthodox Calvinist in his confidence in the historical veracity of the biblical records. He believed in the infallibility and the plenary inspiration of the Bible, which, he said in an 1855 sermon on "The Inspiration of the Holy Scriptures" before his synod, not only contains, but is the Word of God. The external evidence for this was the testimony of witnesses in Scripture to its own authority, the internal was the witness of the Spirit in human hearts. The witnesses in Scripture—the apostles of Christ—are eminently worthy of credit, so their claims to inspiration may be accepted. He handled the topics of the canonicity, genuineness, and authenticity of the Bible in quite traditional fashion.

Henry Boynton Smith was in many ways the voice of the future at Union, especially in his mediating style, his longing for bringing divided Christians closer together, his Christocentric approach, and his knowledge of the continental theological scene. His rather strict adherence to the older New England theology and his views of biblical infallibility were later to be sharply challenged, so that rather quickly he seemed to be a figure from the past. But for several decades he dominated the Union scene and exerted wide theological influence, especially within Presbyterianism. Union became considerably more conspicuous on the theological map of the time.

His transfer to the teaching of theology left a vacancy in history, and Roswell D. Hitchcock moved into the position in 1855. He too was from Maine, a graduate of Amherst and later a tutor there, briefly a student and then resident licentiate at Andover. An ordained Congregationalist, he served a church in New Hampshire for seven years, during which time he took more than a year off to study in Germany, at the universities of Halle and Berlin. After three years as professor at Bowdoin, he became Union's professor of church history, to serve for 33 years, the last seven also as president. He was a polished orator, much in demand in pulpit and platform, a popular and influential man. He wrote little; his colleagues later apologized for him gently. George L. Prentiss said that "it is to be regretted that he gave to the world so few fruits of his study in permanent form; but he seemed to have little ambition for literary distinction; his ideal was high and exacting, while his intellectual modesty caused him to shrink from the responsibility of authorship." Prentiss quoted his prolific colleague, Philip Schaff, who put it more concisely still: "He always spoke like a book, and could spare himself the trouble of writing books."[16]

   In 1857 the board placed three of its faculty of four into the chairs that had been endowed. Smith became the Roosevelt professor of systematic theology. Skinner, who had made an important place for himself at the seminary and among the churches, was named the Davenport professor of sacred rhetoric. Students and faculty members both spoke of his personal concern for them, and remembered him as a saintly man of great spiritual force. His younger colleague Hitchcock once characterized him as "a courtly, gallant man, of Southern birth and blood, but of Northern training, a man of most positive, intense, and resolute theology, wrapped in the mantle of a flaming evangelism."[17] Skinner was an industrious scholar who labored over his lectures, sermons, and essays, many of which were published in periodicals, pamphlets, or collections. His most carefully prepared book, *Discussions in Theology*, appeared three years before his death in 1871. The newest addition to the faculty, Hitchcock, became the first Washburn professor of church history. These three were all still active when the seminary entered a new period in 1870, and, with their distinguished senior colleague, Smith, were largely responsible for one of the great times of flowering in the seminary's history, and brought the vision of the founders closer to fulfillment. Unfortunately, a named chair for the teacher of Bible had not been sufficiently endowed by that time to inaugurate it.

In 1863 Edward Robinson, the immensely learned and productive biblical scholar without whom the seminary might well not have survived its years of struggle, died in his 69th year. He was followed by another New Englander, William G. T. Shedd, a graduate of the University of Vermont and Andover Seminary. He was ordained as a Congregationalist, but after a year in the pastorate taught English literature at his alma mater for seven years. His versatility was displayed in the range of his next four appointments: two years as professor of sacred rhetoric and pastoral theology at Auburn, eight years in church history at Andover, another year in the pastorate at Brick Presbyterian in New York, and then to Union in Bible, soon becoming the first Baldwin professor of sacred literature (1865). He continued the generally accepted historico-philological method of biblical interpretation that he had learned at Andover under Moses Stuart, who had taught there from 1810 to 1848. The precise meaning of the text was sought by viewing it in its historical setting and making use of new materials from philology and textual criticism. The developmental point of view that had already become part of the teaching in history and theology at Union was to come for biblical instruction in the next period of Union's life, but by then Shedd (a member of the Old School) was teaching systematic theology.

Among the students, preparation for the pastoral ministry was the main concern, but enthusiasm for foreign missions remained high. Henry H. Jessup of the class of 1855, for example, decided early on a missionary career, and would serve for 53 years in what was then called the Near East. While a student he was quite typically involved in Christian witness and good works in the city. "Just before sailing," Coffin wrote, "he returned to the Seminary for a missionary-prayer meeting where he knelt with Harding, later of India, White of Asia Minor, Byington of Bulgaria and Kalopothakes of Athens." In preaching at Newark the next day he anticipated the approach of the Student Volunteer Movement that developed thirty years later, suggesting to young people that after careful thought they write "Resolved, that if the Lord will give me grace, I will become a missionary."[18]

As always, however, student interests were diversified. The political struggles of the time were a concern, sometimes to the annoyance of the board who represented the churches of their time in trying not to get involved in partisan politics. Some measure of the difference in atmosphere then and now can be glimpsed when a group of students visited Col. John C. Frémont, a candidate for President in 1856. The directors disclaimed any desire to influence the political action of any student, yet stated that they felt it was "a duty as decisively to express their regret at the proceedings in question, and to declare their opinion that any action of the students in party politics in the character of members of this institution, is inconsistent with their relations to it, and to the principles on which it has been commended to the support and confidence of the Christian community."[19]

At the "internal" political level, dissatisfaction with the refectory was manifest from time to time. It was student-operated until 1853, when poor management made it advisable for outsiders to be employed for food service. That was not always satisfactory: in 1866 the students served notice that the refectory would cease to operate as of a given date, forcing a change in management.

The religious life of the seminary was quite intense, though it was necessary for the board to remind students that their attendance at chapel (which for a long time was at 5:00 P.M. daily) was "expected to be specially uniform and constant," and was monitored, just as was attendance at classes. A common feature of seminary devotional life that long persisted at Union began in 1852 as the "Faculty Monthly Conference," which met one Monday a month at 4:00 P.M. with faculty members speaking and leading discussions on the spiritual life.

The academic year was then not divided into terms, and typically extended from early September to mid-May. The curriculum remained entirely prescribed, with every regular student taking every course. Faculty debates over the distribution of hours of instruction go on in every generation; in 1856, for example, Professor Robinson protested against devoting four hours a week to church history. Three would be enough, he affirmed, and would not interfere with his plans to devote two hours a week to the exegetical study of the scriptures with middle and senior classes. The lecture hours were set at 3:00 and 4:00 P.M. daily, with language, vocal culture, and sacred music courses meeting at other times. Some of the leading church musicians of the time were invited to share their talents with the student body; for example, Lowell Mason, remembered as "the father of American church music," was an instructor in 1854–55. As the seminary's reputation grew, auditors were attracted. With the permission of the instructor, audit privileges were granted, especially to ministers.

The student body diminished in size with the coming of the Civil War as some got involved in the struggle and some potential students were diverted by it. In the academic year 1863–64 the enrollment dropped to 85. The seminary's antislavery stand had become more pronounced through the 1850s; Henry Boynton Smith, for example, drafted a strong statement which was endorsed by his presbytery, and on the eve of the conflict Roswell Hitchcock spoke forcefully for the Northern cause. They were leaders in the New School's commitment to the Union; Marsden has observed that "in theological terms the New School's response to the war may be described as an identification of the doctrines of the Church's mission to prepare the world for the millennium and to call the nation to its covenantal obligations with the patriotic dogmas that the Union must be preserved and slavery abolished."[20] In the student body in those days was Union's first black student, John Bunyan Reeve of the class of 1861. He later became an outstanding pastor and the first dean of what is now Howard University Divinity School.

When the war came, at least a dozen students were given permission to work with the United States Christian Commission, an agency of the churches for ministry among soldiers. Several senior students were allowed to seek ordination early so they could serve as military chaplains. George Fredrick Root, who had given instruction in sacred music in the early 1850s, wrote some of the memorable Civil War songs that were effective weapons in the struggle for the Union. During the strife, a number of graduates or former students served in the army, and a few lost their lives. One faculty member, Henry H. Hadley, died at James River, Virginia in 1864 while serving with the United States Sanitary Commission. He had studied at Yale and Andover, and was assistant professor of Hebrew at the time of his death. Some of those who entered the seminary in war years were veterans of the conflict. As early in 1861, for example, Charles A. Briggs, who had cut short his course at the University of Virginia to march with the Seventh Regiment of the New York State Volunteers in defense of Washington, returned to his native city to begin his preparation for the ministry at Union. Union's life, however, was not seriously disrupted by the war. In looking back from the year that the nation entered World War I, Arthur C. McGiffert said, "In the Civil War, deep as it cut into the nation's life, the Seminary, like most of our other educational institutions, kept open during the entire time, while its Faculty remained intact and its student body was reduced by less than one-third."[21]

Union bounced back quickly after the war; the student body had increased to 123 in the academic year 1865–66. The seminary both contributed to and shared in the enhanced strength and prestige of New School Presbyterianism. Its crusading spirit of national revival and moral reform had fitted in with the cause of the North; its virtual identification of Christian and American objectives during the struggle seemed to be justified by its outcome. The future looked bright, for the nation had been saved and slavery ended. Many anticipated that progress toward the kingdom of God would continue, bringing great blessing and benefit to church and state. At the ecclesiastical level, the New School emerged from the war in a changed relationship to the Old. The former lost its relatively small Southern branch in 1857, the latter its much larger judicatories in the South in 1861. (The two separated bodies merged in 1864, soon taking the name Presbyterian Church in the United States.) The Old School Assembly in the North was thus free to support the preservation of the Union, and the issues of slavery and sectionalism that had stood between it and the New School were largely resolved. As early as 1862 it unexpectedly proposed an exchange of fraternal delegates with the New School church, the continuators of the synods it had exscinded a quarter-century before.

New School leaders were interested in the possibility of the reunion of Northern Presbyterianism. That appealed strongly to Henry Boynton Smith, who as a mediating theologian saw it as an illustration of his belief in progress through conflict. He was elected as moderator of his church in 1863, and seized the opportunity as he retired from that office the next May to deliver an eloquent discourse on "Christian Union and Ecclesiastical Reunion." He pointed to ongoing contests against infidelity and Romanism as arguments for union, but characteristically insisted that its real source and center is in Christ:

"When our theology, our preaching, and our very lives, say that Christ is our all in all, then we shall meet and flow together." He defined three conditions for Northern Presbyterian reunion: a spirit of mutual concession, commitment to the Presbyterian system of church order, and acceptance of the Westminster Confession interpreted in its "legitimate grammatical and historical sense, in the spirit of the original Adopting Act [of 1729], and as 'containing the system of doctrine taught in the Holy Scriptures.' " He believed his branch of the church was closer to its standards than it had been, and hoped the other had abated what was thought to be its exclusiveness. Admitting and spelling out the continuing differences between the two bodies, he insisted that "the questions between us are about shades of orthodoxy, and do not reach the dilemma, orthodoxy or heterodoxy." In his forceful peroration, he proclaimed that the consummation of union might be delayed, but would surely come.[22]

It was not delayed for long, in part because of Smith's own role in what followed. The major problem of reunion was to find a way to bring together parties that had different views on the way subscription to the Westminster Confession should be affirmed: in a strict, quite literal sense in accordance with Old School emphases, or as containing the system of doctrine taught in Holy Scriptures in the fair, historical sense as it had been accepted by both sides. A minority in the Old School feared that that "fair, historical sense" allowed too much latitude of interpretation, tolerating such views as those of the New Haven theology. Opposition to the union centered in that minority; its most effective voice was that of Charles Hodge, the able systematic theologian at Princeton Theological Seminary, and defender of the scholastic Princeton theology, which "seemed to offer an almost mathematical demonstration of an unchanged and unchangeable religious outlook."[23]

When a joint committee of the two Assemblies set to work in 1866, the opposition succeeded in slowing full acceptance of its proposals by the Old School. There was a spate of articles pro and con in Presbyterian publications; Smith was the most prominent writer on the side of union. A turning point in the debate came in November 1867 at an unofficial but well-attended Presbyterian National Union Convention in Philadelphia. Obviously responding to Hodge's criticism that New School views on subscription were too broad, the me-

diating theologian suggested that it be stated in the reunion agreements that the Westminster Confession be received in its proper
historical, that is, in its Calvinistic or Reformed, sense. That was a
little too limiting for some on his side, and the joint committee worked
out a statement providing that various methods of interpreting the
confession which would not impair the integrity of the Reformed or
Calvinistic system be allowed in the reunited church. Hodge was
never quite won over, but he appreciated Smith's approach, and the
minority in opposition grew smaller.

There was also a trend toward orthodoxy, broadly interpreted, in the New School, and the presence at Union of William
G. T. Shedd of the Old School along with Smith's moderation helped
to convince many that the seminary was "sound." The basis of union
as finally presented to the presbyteries of the two churches simply
required subscription to the Westminster standards without any qual-
ifying or interpretive clauses. The New School's 113 presbyteries were
unanimous in acceptance, the Old School had an affirmative vote of
126 of its 144 presbyteries, 3 being opposed and 15 not replying.
Special meetings of the two assemblies late in 1869 recognized that
reunion was an accomplished fact.

Henry Boynton Smith was later called "the hero of Reunion" by Professor Francis L. Patton of Princeton Seminary, and
more recently "the chief architect of Presbyterian reunion" by another Princeton professor, Lefferts A. Loetscher.[24] But when the moment of triumph came with the final ratification of the Plan of Reunion by both Assemblies at Pittsburgh in November 1869, Smith's
health had declined, and he was in Europe to rest and recover. Another strong proponent of reunion, a close friend of Union as founder,
director, and occasional teacher, was William Adams, who chaired
the New School's delegation on the Joint Committee on Reunion,
and then the joint committee itself. He became a leading actor in
the adjustment of Union to what had transpired.

When the Assemblies in 1869 adopted the Plan of Reunion, they also made a series of concurrent declarations, the ninth
of which read as follows: "In order to a uniform system of ecclesiastical supervision, those Theological Seminaries that are now under
Assembly control may, if their Boards of Direction so elect, be trans-

ferred to the watch and care of one or more of the adjacent Synods; and the other Seminaries are advised to introduce, as far as may be, into their Constitutions, the principle of Synodical or Assembly supervision; in which case they shall be entitled to an official recognition and approbation on the part of the General Assembly."[25] But before the time of the first meeting of the reunited General Assembly in Philadelphia in May 1870, it had become clear that Princeton Seminary could not be released from control of the assembly without imperiling its endowments.

The problem then became how to relate the General Assembly equally to its various seminaries, for such a former New School seminary as Auburn was responsible to its Synod, and Union of course was not responsible to any ecclesiastical jurisdiction. Princeton's board of directors therefore requested that control by the assembly be redefined so that seminaries could appoint professors subject only to veto by the Assembly. Knowing of this in advance, in the interests of harmony Union's directors on May 16, 1870, three days before the first reunited General Assembly met, sent a memorial agreeing with the idea of a veto over professorial appointments by majority vote of the assembly. Believing that it was in the interests of the larger unity of the church, Adams favored this. Opposition to it, however, was expressed by one lay director, D. Willis James, who could not bring himself to vote for it. Later events would show how farsighted he was in this matter. James did succeed in getting the board not to allow any veto power over the appointment of seminary *directors*.

So Union, along with Lane and Auburn, other former New School seminaries, accepted the veto by the General Assembly over the appointment of professors in the interests of peace and harmony, while Princeton was freed of the requirement of election of its theological professors by the assembly. Union's action at the time was widely regarded as an act of generosity and courtesy, a contribution to the well-being of newly reunited northern Presbyterianism. For two decades Union reported its actions to the assembly along with others; in all that time the veto was not used at all.

Union entered the new period in a healthy state; the original vision of the founders at last was largely fulfilled. As Hitchcock was later to put it, referring back to the early 1870s, "It was proved that a great Theological Seminary, of the highest grade, both scholarly and practical, may be made to flourish in a great commercial centre."[26] The prospects for Union, related now officially to the reunited northern Presbyterian church as one of its major seminaries, looked bright indeed.

CHAPTER THREE

Union as a
Denominational
Seminary (1870–1890)

From its inception, Union was in fact though not formally a
Presbyterian seminary with close ties to the New School Assembly. When the directors voted in 1870 that it become an institution
of the reunited Presbyterian Church in the United States of America
by allowing its General Assembly a veto over appointments to professorships, it was a generous act of goodwill in the interests of denominational cooperation. Despite the difficulties of its early years, Union
had done well as an independent Presbyterian seminary open to students of other denominations. In a sincere effort on behalf of Presbyterian unity, it now accepted the formal link with the General Assembly.

For several decades, the change seemed to make little
difference in the internal operation of the seminary. Enrollment in
the regular three-year theological course increased somewhat; from
1861 to 1871 (which included the Civil War years of low attendance)
it averaged 111.4, while in the period 1871–91 it averaged 126.8.
Though he was not a wholly unbiased interpreter, Prentiss concluded
that it was doubtful that the tie with the church "added a dozen
names to the roll of students in Union Seminary."[1] Presbyterians did

continue to be the largest single denominational group in the student body, but those from other churches, especially Congregational, enrolled as before.

A task of the 1870s was the expansion and reconstruction of the faculty as new instructional needs arose and older members departed. The decade began with the appointment of a mature theological scholar of the first rank. Born in Chur, Switzerland in 1819, Philip Schaff had studied at the universities of Tübingen, Halle, and Berlin in the late 1830s, becoming acquainted with some of the leading theological giants of the time. He was much influenced by Ferdinand Christian Baur and Isaac Dorner at Tübingen, Julius Mueller and especially Tholuck at Halle, and Frederick W. Hengstenberg and Neander in Berlin. After several years as a private tutor, during which time he had the opportunity for extensive travel and, as was his custom, for interviewing leading scholarly and ecclesiastical figures, including Pope Gregory XVI, he became *privatdocent* in exegesis and church history at Berlin. Then, in response to a call from America, in 1844 he was ordained in the German Reformed tradition and journeyed to Mercersburg, Pennsylvania, where he was inaugurated as professor in the Theological Seminary of the Reformed Church in the United States. He and his colleague John W. Nevin were the leaders of an important theological and liturgical movement in their denomination, and his impressive record of publication of articles and books as author and editor increased, attracting attention far beyond his small denomination.

His inaugural address at the outset of his American career, published the next year as *The Principle of Protestantism*, expressed ecumenical concerns unusual for that time and place as he argued for movement toward an "evangelical Catholicism," offering a more favorable interpretation of the Roman Catholicism of past and present than was customary, even as he opposed "Romanism." He was subjected to trial for heresy by his church's Synod of York, but was completely exonerated.[2] The young professor published his views on the nature of church history in 1846 in book form, *What Is Church History? A Vindication of the Idea of Historical Development*. His general view of church history was much like that of Henry Boynton Smith, for the two had studied with some of the same masters at about the same time.[3] What was to become a multi-volume series on

Philip Schaff, ecumenical prophet.

the history of the Christian church began with the publication of his *History of the Apostolic Church; With a General Introduction to Church History* in German in 1851 and English two years later. His deepening understanding of his adopted land was presented in lectures given in Germany in 1854, quickly translated and published in the United States the next year as *America: A Sketch of the Political, Social, and Religious Character of the United States of North America*.[4] Again, contrasting Catholic authority and Protestant freedom, he saw the forces of history moving toward an enriched evangelical Catholicism, a noble harmony arising out of the most thoroughly developed Protestantism and the freest Catholicism. Though much of his writing was historical, he lectured on all branches of theology, and became known for his great breadth of theological and historical knowledge.[5]

During the Civil War, when the invasion of Confederate troops led to the suspension of activities at Mercersburg, Schaff moved to New York. Here he served for six years as secretary of the New York Sabbath Committee, for he had come to have a great appreciation of the Anglo-American Sabbath with its distinction between the religious and the civil observance of the day. In those years he traveled extensively at home and abroad, widening his circle of friends and his knowledge of church life. After having declined an earlier invitation, he resumed his teaching career as professor at Union in 1870, becoming a Presbyterian. As a moderate Calvinist, he honestly stated certain objections he had to the Westminster Confession and was assured that there was ample room for his dissenting views.[6]

His versatility as a scholar was immediately displayed as he took up his new duties. He taught for a year as professor of theological encyclopedia and Christian symbolism, a title soon changed to professor of apologetics, symbolics, and polemics. One of the outcomes of his scholarship at that period was the useful three-volume *The Creeds of Christendom*, first published in 1877, but revised and republished many times. He switched to the teaching of Bible in 1873, serving for two years in the Davenport chair of Hebrew, and then for thirteen years as Baldwin professor of sacred literature. In this period he chaired for a time the American Bible Revision Committee, which was preparing the American Standard Version. The climax of the teaching career of this versatile scholar came in the years 1887–93 when he was named to the Washburn chair of church history, and it is as a church historian that he is primarily remembered.

Throughout his long life he was an inveterate traveler, speaker, and organizer. Prentiss, who first met him at Tholuck's home in 1839 and was later his colleague at Union, tried to summarize the many aspects of his career in a sentence: "One is fairly staggered in reading over a list of the books he wrote, the journeys he made, the societies he founded, the plans he formed, the addresses he delivered, the funds he raised, and the solid, lasting effects he produced in furtherance of good learning, Christian union and fellowship, and other vital interests of the cause and kingdom of Jesus Christ."[7] He had perhaps less theological originality than Henry Boynton Smith, for he was more eclectic, but, blessed with sturdy health, he was more productive and became more widely known, the most conspicuous scholar at Union during the period of Union's life as an official denominational seminary. He was a colleague of Smith's for only a few years, for though the latter recovered somewhat after his time abroad in 1869–70, he had to resign for reasons of health early in 1874, and died three years later. This left open the Roosevelt chair in systematics for Shedd and, as has been noted, at the same time allowed Schaff to take the Baldwin professorship in sacred literature.

Meanwhile, two other appointments had been made. When the beloved Thomas H. Skinner, who had long taught sacred rhetoric and pastoral theology, died in 1871, his major duties were divided between two new professors, both New Englanders who had originally been ordained as Congregationalists, and both with many previous connections with Union. William Adams, graduate of Yale and Andover, had come to New York as a Presbyterian pastor in 1834. He was a founder, director, and occasional part-time teacher at the seminary, well-known preacher and author, and a key figure in Presbyterian reunion. For twenty years he had served as pastor of the Madison Square Presbyterian Church, enlisting the support of some of its members and friends for Union. Though no president had been named for 31 years, the board now wished to fill that office, so in 1873 Adams became Union's third president and Brown professor of sacred rhetoric (at the age of 66). Something of his wisdom and power can be discerned in the tributes his students and colleagues paid to him. He touched the lives of students most directly in their senior year, when he met the class daily for work in homiletics. His successor in the presidency was to say of his seven years at Union, "The whole institution was toned up. Professors and Students, equally and all, felt the magnetism of his courtly and stimulating presence. On all public occasions, he was our ornament and pride."[8]

With his many connections, Adams was effective in the raising of funds. He was a close friend of James Brown, Union's largest contributor of the period. Long after Brown had established the famous banking firm of Brown Brothers & Co. (later Brown Brothers Harriman & Co.), a terrible tragedy had touched his family: lost at sea were a son, two daughters, a daughter-in-law, and two grandchildren, with two nurses. His religious life was deepened by the experience, and his interest in Union, which was near his home, increased. His many gifts to the institution were crowned in 1873 with $300,000 for enlarging the endowments for the professorships so that they could produce sums adequate for the times. His growing confidence in Union and his closeness to Adams were important factors in his generous gift. The new president won the confidence of a number of prominent New York business leaders who were also persons of deep piety and who had a strong sense of Christian stewardship in relation to their growing wealth. In 1875 he procured the means to renovate the seminary's buildings, and a few months before his death received a letter from former Governor Edwin D. Morgan of New York offering a gift of $100,000 for a new fireproof library building. Since Adams, Union without a president has simply been inconceivable; when he died in 1880, Professor Hitchcock was promptly chosen to succeed him as president, while continuing to teach church history.

The other new professor named in 1873 likewise had been related to Union for a long time, and has already been conspicuous in these pages. George Lewis Prentiss had graduated from Bowdoin College in 1835, taught for several years, and then studied in Germany at Halle and Berlin at the same time that Smith and Schaff were there. After serving a Congregational church in New Bedford, he became a Presbyterian and was pastor of the Mercer Street church when he delivered the eloquent 1851 sermon on behalf of Union which was so important in its financial strengthening and which won him a place on the board. At the time of Skinner's death Prentiss had been serving New York's Covenant Presbyterian Church for more than a decade, but added the responsibilities as instructor in pastoral theology at Union for two years until he was called to the newly endowed Skinner and McAlpin professorship of pastoral theology, church polity, and mission work. It was the first of a number of chairs to honor former Union professors. The principal contributor to this tribute to Thomas H. Skinner was David Hunter McAlpin, a manufacturer with many charitable interests, and a Union director for nearly thirty years. His name has been perpetuated not only through his share in the endowment of this chair and the library's famous McAlpin Collection, but also through the long continuing interest in Union of his descendants. The addition to the curriculum of some teaching on missions as part of the new professorship was a pioneering venture in American theological education at the time.

Early in the following year, 1874, a teaching career that was to last for almost forty years at Union and was to mark a major turning point in the seminary's life began when a former student, Charles A. Briggs, was named "provisional professor" of Hebrew and the cognate languages. Briggs had had to drop out of school in the fall of 1863, assuming the management of the family's barrel works when his father became seriously ill. In this period he married, and when he was free to resume his studies went to Berlin for three years. He took no degree but studied with Dorner, Hengstenberg, Emil Roediger, and Heinrich Georg Augustus Ewald, focusing on the study of the Bible. Though his conversion while a student at the University of Virginia had brought him into the Old School, he found the mediating theology he had learned at Union under Smith and encountered again in Germany attractive. He also came to have great respect for the historical critical method of studying the Bible, which richly illumined its pages for him in a fresh way. "I cannot doubt but what I have been blessed with a new—divine light," he wrote in a letter. "I feel a different man from what I was five months ago. The Bible is lit up with a new light."[9] His interest in developing a biblical theology based on an exegetical approach to the scriptures in their original tongues became a lifetime passion. After returning home, he finally received a call to the Presbyterian Church in Roselle, New

Jersey, serving there until beginning his duties at Union. The "pro-visional" period soon passed, and in 1876 the slight, blue-eyed, blond-haired professor was inaugurated as Davenport professor of Hebrew, joining Schaff in the teaching of Bible.

Some other changes in the faculty occurred later in the decades covered by this chapter, but two are best mentioned here. Adams' replacement as Brown professor of sacred rhetoric in 1881 was Thomas S. Hastings, who served in that position for a quarter century. A graduate of Hamilton College and Union, where he had also studied as a "resident licentiate," he served in the pastorate for thirty years before joining the faculty. The career pattern of Francis Brown was quite different: he anticipated what was to become a very familiar, increasingly standard, vocational pattern in theological ed-ucation. A graduate of Dartmouth and Union (1877), he studied for two years in Germany, immediately joined the faculty as instructor in biblical philology for two years, was ordained but did not serve in the pastorate, and in 1881 was promoted to associate professor. He was granted a Ph.D. by Hamilton College in 1884, the first member of the faculty to hold that degree, and six years later was named Davenport professor of Hebrew. His coming made what would later be called the biblical field the first real department of Union, with three members.

These, then, were the main figures in the reconstruction of the Union faculty in the 1870s: Schaff, Prentiss, Briggs, Adams (followed by Hastings), and Brown, who, along with Hitchcock and Shedd, brought full-time faculty strength to seven. Small by twen-tieth-century standards, in its time this was not only a sizable faculty for a theological seminary but an outstanding one. Its members were in close touch with European centers of theological education, and were conspicuous in public address and/or publication. Within Pres-byterianism, Princeton now had to share the limelight with Union. Union's maturity was further signaled by the fact that three of the teaching staff had themselves been students at the seminary. Early in the 1850s, when the Congregationalists were debating whether to lo-cate Chicago Theological Seminary in a country or city setting, some pointed to Union as a bad example of the latter for it had as yet trained not one professor for its own chairs.[10] It took another quarter century for that criticism to be decisively answered; by that time Chicago had long since followed Union's example in settling in an urban location.

Union was also prominent in the formation of scholarly societies in the disciplines of theological learning. The preliminary meeting that led to the formation of the Society of Biblical Literature was held in Schaff's study in 1880; Briggs was present and was on the committee to plan the first meeting and draft a constitution, and became the first treasurer. Francis Brown was the third president, Briggs the fourth.[11] When Schaff became professor of church history after Hitchcock's death in 1887, he soon founded (1888) the American Society of Church History, and served as its president until his death five years later. The vacancy thus created in the Baldwin chair of sacred literature was filled by Marvin R. Vincent, a graduate of Columbia, a former professor of Latin who then had served for 24 years as a Presbyterian pastor before joining the faculty.

Union's conspicuousness in church life was further increased by the part played by members of the board, faculty, and alumni in the affairs of the Evangelical Alliance. The international body had been founded in London in 1846 as an effort to bring Protestant churches of many nations into conversation and cooperation. An attempt to form an American branch the next year quickly foundered on the issue of slavery. Efforts to reconstitute it began as soon as the war was over at the New York home of Philip Schaff, who had attended the Berlin Conference of the World Evangelical Alliance in 1857 while he was still at Mercersburg. Henry Boynton Smith, leading advocate of Christian union as well as of Presbyterian reunion, chaired the executive committee of the revived American Alliance for four years from the time of its reorganization in 1866. The president was William E. Dodge, a Presbyterian layman active in supply preaching at local revivals and in the affairs of many of the evangelical voluntary societies of the time, a prominent business man (in the extensive Phelps-Dodge mining and metal importing corporation), and a member of Union's board for nearly thirty years. When the American Alliance hosted the Sixth General Conference of the World Evangelical Alliance in New York in October 1873, it "captured American attention as the major media event since the Civil War itself." William Adams, Union's new president, welcomed the participants from around the world, declaring that the conference was not to be concerned with the forms of church organization, for "we meet to manifest and express our Christian unity." Schaff and William E. Dodge Jr., like his father a long-time Union director, continued to be conspicuous figures in the Alliance throughout this period.[12]

The growth of faculty, student body, and library made the seminary building at 9 University Place (plus some satellite structures) look less and less adequate. When the seminary offered its first formal report to the General Assembly in 1871 in its new status as a denominational seminary, there was an indication that nearly $350,000 had been subscribed for a new campus on St. Nicholas Avenue, between 130th and 134th Streets, where ground had been purchased. D. Willis James, a prominent board member, at first favored the site on the east slope of Harlem Hill, but on reflection the rocky, hilly location (later a park) did not look so suitable. The financial panic of 1873 also interfered with the payment of pledges. James shifted his attention to Lenox Hill, near the Lenox Library. Then in 1880 came Governor Morgan's offer of $100,000 for a new library, along with his willingness to sell ten lots on the west wide of Park Avenue between 69th and 70th Streets accompanied by a second gift equalling the first. The offer was accepted, additional funds were soon raised, and four new interconnected buildings, surrounding a hollow square, were ready for occupation in September 1884.

When Philip Schaff returned from Europe and saw the new campus for the first time, he was much impressed and excited. He penned in his diary, "What a change between this literary palace & the old building in University Place!" Then at age 65, the professor reflected, "A new departure, new zeal & devotion. Would like to teach now for 20 or 30 years longer."[13] The chapel, the library, and the lecture hall fronted on Park Avenue, while the dormitory for 160 students, paid for by James, ran from 69th Street to 70th to the east of the other buildings. The attractive and well designed structures received very favorable notice in the press; when one compares the artist's rendering of the new campus of 1884 with that of the stark, unadorned structure of 1838, one can better understand some of President Hitchcock's enthusiasm at the formal dedication of the Park Avenue buildings on December 9, 1884:

Union at 700 Park Avenue, 1884–1910.

The present location is apparently for many decades, if not for all time. This commanding site, so near the centre of the island, is in little danger of losing its advantages. Right behind us is the grand Central Park; close around us are hospitals, schools, and galleries of art—the trophies and adornments of an advancing Christian civilization.

Then, expressing the deeper purposes of the institution in a rhetoric familiar among Protestant evangelicals as they crusaded for a Christian America, he continued:

But this institution of sacred learning, which we dedicate today—interpreter of God's word, herald of God's grace, outranks them all. Our work lies along far-reaching lines. The spiritual and eternal must dominate the material and temporal. We must steer, not our commerce only, but our whole civilization, by the stars. Religion is the supreme arbiter and architect.[14]

The sense of elation, confidence, and determination of the moment was obvious. Beneath the surface, however, currents were flowing that were to reshape the seminary once again, and change its patterns of education so that the impressive new buildings were to be quickly outmoded.

For the time being, however, Union seemed secure as a

denominational seminary carrying out its design to furnish "a full and thorough education, in all the subjects taught in the best theological seminaries in the United States" in its chosen urban context, and doing conspicuously well at it. All through this period the school benefited from the leadership on its board of a group of devoted, moneyed Presbyterian laymen who served on through the years of growth and transition into the twentieth century. Some of the names are still familiar at Union because they are associated with endowed chairs or campus locations: John Crosby Brown (son of James), D. Willis James, David H. McAlpin, William E. Dodge Jr., Morris K. Jesup. Their sincere piety, loyalty to Union, and generosity as they gave of their time and means was a major factor in the stability and enlargement of the seminary in a time of religious and educational change.

Union's academic strength was improved in 1884, when it moved to its new location by the new quarters for the library; in its old location it had become hopelessly overcrowded. Following Henry Boynton Smith as librarian was Charles A. Briggs, who threw himself into the new task (in addition to his other duties) with characteristic energy, competence, and assurance. He extended the hours that the library was open, and replaced the four-volume manuscript catalogue with the card system. He also instituted a historical and missionary museum, with exhibits from biblical and Christian antiquities, the Holy Land, and missionary fields. The book collections continued to grow significantly; in addition to his specialized knowledge of scholarly work in the biblical area he had a deep interest in Presbyterian history, with particular emphasis on the work of the Puritan and Westminster divines.

Briggs' attention to those historic writings was stimulated by the resurgence of premillennialism—a teaching, based on literalistic interpretations of such biblical books as Daniel and Revelation, that Christ would soon return to usher in the millennium. Such millenarian views were promoted with a great deal of public notice at a Bible and Prophetic Conference in New York in 1878 in which many conservative Presbyterians participated. Convinced that such teachings were not those of the Westminster divines or of the Confession, which was the main confessional standard of his church, Briggs industriously collected the relevant materials on which a thoroughly scholarly interpretation of the Westminster documents could be based. The basis for a particularly important collection in British theological history in the late sixteenth and early seventeenth centuries had already been laid through the informed labors of Ezra H. Gillett of the class of 1844, aided financially by David H. McAlpin, one of his parishioners. Under Briggs the collection grew to some 12,000 volumes, including many rare first editions of major writings related to its subject.

In 1883 Charles R. Gillett, son of Ezra, took over the librarianship as his main responsibility at Union. He would hold the position, along with various other duties, for a quarter of a century. When he superintended the transfer to Park Avenue the library had about 60,000 volumes, with almost as many pamphlets. At that point McAlpin endowed the collection of British theology and history which bears his name. Gillett continued his father's interest in British history and theology, 1500–1701, purchasing thousands of books during summers abroad. Many others contributed in various ways to the continued growth of the McAlpin Collection, one of the great, permanent treasures of the library.

Throughout this period the curriculum remained largely a prescribed one, including courses in Hebrew and Greek. Under the influence of President Adams it was reviewed and adjustments made in view of the enlarging faculty and an increasing number of course options. Schaff combined carefully prepared lectures so typical of European education with the recitation method of questioning classes, more familiar in America. While he found the latter irksome he discovered it did get results, yet preferred the other approach. "It was his habit to keep constantly revising and re-copying his lectures to the end of his life," his son wrote of him. "Students well remember him hurrying through the streets with his lecture book under his arm and reaching at the last sound of the bell the lecture room, all out of breath."[15] A daily morning lecture hour for regular classes at 11:00 was added to the afternoon lecture hours at 3:00 and 4:00, while various voluntary classes in "cognate oriental languages" (including at various times Arabic, Assyrian, Biblical Aramaic, Chaldee, and Syriac) were usually held once a week at 2:00. In the 1880s much theological interest focused in Old Testament study. Classes in vocal culture and sacred music were also arranged when part-time teachers could be secured; in 1884 an instructorship in vocal culture and elocution was created, and two years later an orderly succession of music instructors began.

The custom of requiring students to sit in alphabetical order in classroom and chapel—the better to take attendance—was continued. The student body remained all male; a laconic faculty minute in 1874 read, "Two young women having applied for admission to the Seminary, it was voted to say in reply that no provision has been made for the education of young women in this institution."[16] One of the achievements of the Adams administration was the origination of what later came to be called "the travelling fellowship" for outstanding graduates, often used for further study abroad. Francis Brown was the first recipient in 1877.

In 1881, early in the period of Hitchcock's presidency, the academic year was divided into two semesters. Until that time final examinations had been conducted in a two-week period at the end of the year; for many years they were apparently oral, by class, conducted by the faculty with the cooperation of committees from the directors, the alumni, the presbytery, and the synod. With the division of the year, they filled a week at the end of each semester. The move to Park Avenue understandably contributed to an increased enrollment; by 1889–90 it passed 150 for the first time. There was no refectory in the new buildings; actually food service had been suspended in 1872, and was not restored until more than half a century later. Students continued their services to churches, Sunday schools, and missions; the perennial problem of keeping the work within reasonable limits was often felt. By the late 1880s Dr. Adolphus F. Schauffler of the New York City Mission Society superintended such work, and also taught early courses in religious education. Faculty members continued to be wary of student involvement in anything that sounded political; in 1887 they voted that it would be inexpedient to allow the formation of a prohibition society, as students had requested, for that was, in their judgment, largely a political question. Two years later they were authorized the publication of "The Seminary Student," with Briggs as faculty adviser. It was apparently the first such student-edited paper, and like many that were to follow was short-lived, for it was discontinued after several years.

A major change in the seminary schedule came early in the presidency of Thomas S. Hastings, who took over the office following Hitchcock's death in 1887. In 1890 arrangements were made with both New York University and Columbia College by which properly qualified students were admitted without fee to a wide range of courses. Many students took advantage of the opportunity. Columbia was then at Madison Avenue at 50th Street, relatively near Union at Park and 69th. Students then petitioned that the major Union classes, which had met since the beginning in the afternoon, be shifted to the morning so they would have a wider selection at the other institutions. The change was made, with classes at 9:00, 10:00, 11:00, and chapel at noon. Later on further adjustments in hours occurred, and a 12:00 class hour was added.

Union was increasingly conspicuous in the life of the city, at a time when religious news was a prominent feature of the daily papers, and when Sunday sermons were regularly reported on Monday. When a Union Alumni Club was formed in 1890 and began to hold public meetings, often at lunch time in a well-known Manhattan restaurant, they were not only well-attended but were fully covered by the press. The first such meeting at Martinelli's featured three speakers: President Hastings, board member Charles H. Parkhurst, the minister of Madison Square Presbyterian Church (who was then becoming conspicuous as an urban reformer), and William S. Rainsford, an Episcopal rector remembered as an early advocate of the social gospel. A scrapbook of newspaper clippings from the period that has been preserved in the Union archives provides vivid reminders of the public prominence of church and religious affairs in the latter part of the nineteenth century.

In the early 1890s Union became front-page news across the country. A series of events familiarly known as "the Briggs trial" brought the seminary into conflict with the Presbyterian General Assembly and led to the disruption of their relationship. But as the first extended historical interpretation of that complex affair put it, "Dr. Briggs was the occasion, though not the cause, of the struggle between the Assembly and Union Seminary."[17] Though the explosion came in the years 1891–93, the tensions that produced it were deepening in the 1880s. They will be discussed in this chapter, and the crisis itself in the next. A closer look at Briggs and his activities in

Charles A. Briggs in 1886.

the 1880s is essential for a full understanding of the trials, which were not only a major turning point in the story of Union but also an important event in the history of Presbyterianism and of American Protestantism.

"Briggs knew early what it was that God had called him to do and never seemed for a moment to have entertained any doubt as to his calling or his capacity to perform it," Channing Jeschke concluded after a careful reading of the sources. "He was totally dedicated to his work; wholly consumed in his preparation for it and in his performance of it." [18] In a curiously prophetic letter written from Germany in 1867, Briggs declared:

The Christian Church ever contains the *body* of truth. At times, when God wishes to lead them into higher truth, he *reveals* the truth to certain men chosen of him. . . . I now stand *firm* on all the *received doctrines* of the Church, & I defy any man to show that I do not. . . . I shall remain in & with the Church until it takes the sin upon itself of *casting* me out, which God grant many never happen. I feel assured that the world needs this light. [19]

His feeling of assurance did not diminish with the passing of the years. One of his students of the late 1880s, William Adams Brown, later to become a colleague, found that "as an interpreter of the Bible Doctor Briggs had no superior," and characterized him as "a kind of walking encyclopedia" who "combined an essentially conservative theology with a critical scholarship—at once exact, ingenious and pedantic." Briggs' own concern for competence is reflected in an anecdote from Brown's pages:

I recall the scorn with which he dismissed the familiar rendering of the thirty-first chapter of Proverbs, "A virtuous woman who can find?" "Nonsense," he exclaimed, "the woods are full of them. *Competent*, the word should read. A competent woman—oh! that one might find, for far above rubies is her price." [20]

There was no doubting Briggs' own competence, nor the single-minded devotion with which he pursued his vocation. Though he could be witty in class and in public address, he had that certain humorlessness that can plague those who take themselves with such seriousness. "As a result," Jeschke observes, "there was a grim quality to his personality that was reflected in his relations with others," especially to those with whom he disagreed, but even among close colleagues he had little time for informal conversation.[21]

In controversy he could be relentless, especially when he knew he was right on matters under discussion, as he so often was. Very revealing is a remark in a letter to him from a friend, an alumnus of Princeton Seminary, who wrote in 1889,

. . . your weakest point as a controversialist is, that you do not allow your enemy to run away when he wants to. You so corner him and becudgel him that he must fight back. Before the plain statement of the true doctrine, as you put it, the Princeton theories must wane, but the Hodgeolators are backed against the wall, and will scratch and bite as long as nails and teeth last.[22]

As a great scholar and teacher guided by a vision of what he confidently believed God willed for the church in his time, Briggs won the respect and loyalty of most the students, colleagues, and board members at the seminary, and of many of his fellow Presbyterian ministers, especially those of his own presbytery who knew him well. Great scholar he was, but hardly a disinterested one, for he used his formidable expertise in what he understood to be the service of God and the church. He had a passion for action, rooted in his doctrine of sanctification to be perfect even as Christ was perfect, by pressing after that goal, expecting to attain it. "Briggs was never happier than when he was able to combine the life of scholarship with the role of the man of action," Jeschke aptly observes.[23] Hence he faced his educational task in seminary, church, and world with a characteristic combination of great self-confidence and remarkable energy.

It was in this spirit that Briggs took the lead in 1880 of a new publishing venture, *the Presbyterian Review*, a joint project of Union and Princeton theological seminaries, with representation from the other Presbyterian seminaries. The two managing editors were Briggs and Archibald A. Hodge of Princeton, the successor to his father, Charles Hodge, and likewise devoted to the continuation of the Princeton theological tradition. The *Review* quickly became a thorough and comprehensive publication. It was designed both to promote theological unity in the reunited church and to resist the premillenarianism that some Presbyterians, especially in the Midwest, were espousing. The two eastern seminaries could agree on that, though for different theological reasons. Attention soon focused, however, on the question of biblical interpretation, and the new *Review* ran a series of eight articles on the subject, which revealed marked differences between Union and Princeton. The first article by A. A. Hodge, assisted by Benjamin B. Warfield, then of Western (now Pittsburgh) Seminary but later of Princeton, argued that the inspiration of the Bible meant that the original autographs of the Bible were inerrant and infallible, though copying errors have crept into translated texts through the centuries. This was the basic postulate of the Princeton theologians, who believed that their views were rooted in the teaching of historic Calvinism and the Westminster Confession.

Charles Hodge had been convinced that the Princeton theology was unflinchingly faithful to the view universally held by the church through the centuries and to the original Presbyterian position of the sixteenth and seventeenth centuries. It was this that led him to assert what to him was a very positive claim about the founders of that theology in the early nineteenth century:

They were not given to new methods or new theories. They were content with the faith once delivered to the saints. I am not afraid to say that a new idea never originated in this Seminary. Their theological method was very simple. The Bible is the word of God. That is to be assumed or proved. If granted; then it follows, that what the Bible says, God says. That ends the matter.[24]

But it did not for people like Briggs, who were steeped in the historical understanding of the Bible and history; they saw it as an adaptation of the scholastic Calvinist theological teaching of the seventeenth century, especially as taught by Francis Turretin. Briggs hoped to convince his denomination that through the "rationalistic" biblical criticism emanating from certain German scholars must be rejected, a moderate position was consistent with sound evangelical theology, contributed to a fuller understanding of the Bible, was a positive contribution to theological truth, and need not be feared.

Briggs so argued in the second article of the series, rejecting the dogma of verbal inspiration and the theory of the original autographs, but, as he sought common ground with his fellow-editors, endorsing "the view of plenary inspiration, which acknowledged the presence of errors and inconsistencies in the Bible yet accepted it as the infallible rule of faith and practice."[25] But he directly challenged "scholastic theology" as the deluded foe of moderate, evangelical biblical criticism. The first two articles had clearly marked out a cleavage within Presbyterianism, roughly following the familiar Old/New School dichotomy; the remaining articles continued the debate, deepening the tension between the two positions. The final article in the series was by Francis L. Patton, who succeeded the younger Hodge as Princeton's managing editor. Formerly at the Presbyterian Seminary of the Northwest in Chicago (now McCormick), Patton was aware that Princeton had to be careful not to alienate its supporters more conservative than it was, for some were openly premillenarian and suspicious of anything that sounded like the so-called "higher" criticism—i.e., beyond the merely textual level. He concluded his long, scholarly article by affirming the Mosaic authorship of the Pentateuch. Despite continuing difficulties, Briggs and Patton continued their editorial partnership, but in 1888 Warfield replaced Patton, who had been appointed president of the nearby College of New Jersey (later Princeton University) of which the seminary was not formally a part. It soon became clear that Warfield and Briggs simply could not work together. Both offered their resignations and the *Review*—and the partnership between the two seminaries—came to an end.

Meanwhile, various other events involving Briggs also gave evidence of a widening difference of opinion within the Presbyterian Church in the United States of America and indirectly reflected a growing cleavage in evangelical Protestantism. An 1883 book by Briggs, *Biblical Study: Its Principles, Methods and History* was a collection of previously published writings which provided a convenient handbook for the evangelical biblical criticism of the mediating type. Provoking no general controversy at the time, it filled a need and was reprinted nine times in the next decade. Two years later came his work on *American Presbyterianism: Its Origin and Early History*, which challenged Old School assumptions, then widely accepted, as it argued that colonial Presbyterianism was not the pure orthodoxy it had been interpreted to be but had been corrupted by increasing admixtures of scholasticism. That same year, when the American Revised Version of the Old Testament appeared, Briggs focused a review on its weaknesses, which even his friends thought was overly sharp. It was particularly resented by the chairman of the revision committee that had prepared it, William H. Green, a noted Princeton Seminary professor, who counterattacked in a long article.

As the decade of deepening tension drew to a close, a movement to revise the Westminster Confession was gathering strength. At first, with his often conservative theological instincts, Briggs remained neutral, but by late 1889 he entered into the fray on the side of revision along with most of his colleagues, and represented that view in a sharp debate with Patton, which, as he later put it in his own brief statement relating to the whole "Briggs trial," "drew the fire of the entire anti-revision party on me."[26] That year had also been marked by the publication of a book which certainly drew on his massive scholarship but was also a tract for the times as it sought to show that the Princeton theologians, as well as his own colleague Shedd and other conservatives, had actually departed from the Westminster Confession under the influence of Calvinistic scholasticism. Again, some of his friends regretted the sharpness and polemical style of *Whither? A Theological Question for the Times*. All this made Briggs a suspect and feared figure among this growing number of theological opponents, and tended to push them further to the theological right. The battle lines for a decisive showdown were forming, and it was not long in coming.

CHAPTER FOUR

The Trials
of Charles Briggs
(1891–1893)

For several years, much public attention across the nation and beyond was focused on Union as Charles Briggs was vetoed as a professor by the General Assembly of the Presbyterian Church of the United States of America, and then subjected to a presbytery trial for heresy. He was cleared, but on appeal to the assembly by the presbytery's prosecuting committee was ordered to be tried again; he was then cleared a second time, but on further appeal was suspended from the ministry by the assembly. All this was accompanied by much publicity, controversy, and bitterness. The Briggs affair proved to be a major event in American church and theological history, and became well known in other lands. Union emerged from the struggle as a champion of freedom for scholarship in matters of faith and religion.

Some inkling into the complexity and turmoil which those crowded years brought to the seminary can be seen by contrasting the two volumes on Union's history produced by George L. Prentiss. The earlier effort, covering the first fifty years of the seminary's life, was published in 1889 as an expansion of an address given when the seminary celebrated its semicentennial, along with many biographical sketches and other supporting material to make a work of nearly 300 pages. The second, published ten years later, dealt only with "another decade," with heavy emphasis on its opening years, but it was such a stormy and controversial decade for Union that the book was almost twice as long as its predecessor.[1]

When the academic year 1890–91 opened, Briggs had already been teaching at Union for sixteen and a half years, first as a "provisional professor" and then since 1876 as Davenport professor of Hebrew and cognate languages, and librarian, and in those roles he has already appeared in these pages. Because of his editorial, publication, and ecclesiastical activities in the 1880s, discussed briefly in the last chapter, he had attracted much opposition. In the fall of 1890 an entering student at Union, John McComb, deeply disagreeing with Brigg's teaching, wrote an article on his reactions which was published in an ultraconservative church paper, for which he agreed to supply lecture notes taken while attending the controversial professor's classes. The *Mail and Express* used the information for editorial attacks on Union and Briggs, who found them to be based on false reports of what he actually said. (McComb's role was later discovered by chance, and he was dismissed.) Though the attacks were bitter and were repeated by others, in the interests of the peace of the church little response came from the seminary. While this was going on, the president of Union's board and the surviving founder, the venerable Charles Butler, prominent lawyer and financier, presented a gift of $100,000 to establish the Edward Robinson professorship of biblical theology, with Briggs as his first choice to fill the new chair. Briggs was delighted to accept, and was elected by the board to the new position late in the year.

At first Briggs planned to devote his inaugural to biblical geography, the field in which Robinson had so distinguished himself and the seminary. But for decades Butler had been deeply interested in the scholarly study of the Bible; to him Robinson in 1856 had dedicated the third volume of his *Biblical Researches* in appreciation of Butler's encouragement and support. The elderly lay leader was well aware of what was at stake in the controversy over biblical criticism, and urged Briggs to face the burning question of the day to vindicate the seminary and himself, and so he chose as a theme "The Authority of Holy Scripture," which he delivered at Adams Chapel on January 20, 1891, speaking for an hour and three quarters. Though much that was in the address he had said before at greater length and in a more qualified way, the sharp and polemical side of Briggs was much in evidence. He felt himself to be on the defensive; as he put it in a later statement, "The limits of the discourse required the condensation of a very great many points of difference, which in the nature of the case were exceedingly disagreeable to the ultra conservative section of the Church, and the situation exacted of the speaker that his rhetoric should be fired to some degree of passion in view of the defense of himself and the cause that he represented, after more than a year of unjust attack."[2]

At the outset, he magnified the divine authority, for though humans in their finitude cannot ascend the heights to seek and know the transcendent, God has revealed the divine presence and authority. Historically, he declared, there have been three great fountains of divine authority—the Bible, the Church, and the Reason, each a means of God's grace. John Henry Newman, the noted Anglican convert to Roman Catholicism, for example, found God in the Church; James Martineau, a prominent English Unitarian, in the Reason; Charles H. Spurgeon, a famous British Baptist preacher, in the Bible. Human folly has often thrown up obstructions in each of these avenues, Briggs asserted, and the duty of God's servants is to remove these stumbling blocks, for "it is a sin against the divine majesty to prop up divine authority by human authority." The heart of the address was the discussion of six barriers to the operation of divine authority in the Bible. When Protestants think of *superstition* they often attach it to "Roman Catholic Mariolatry, Hagiolatry, and the use of images and pictures" in worship, but it is also to be found in Bibliolatry, in using the Bible as having external magical power; it is no better than witchcraft to "seek for divine guidance by the chance opening of the Book." In touching on *verbal inspiration* as the second barrier Briggs was on familiar ground as he highlighted the fact that the English Bible is a translated book, and that there is no claim in it or in the historic creeds that the originals were verbally inspired. "The divine authority is not in the style of the words, but in the concept, and so the divine power of the Bible may be transferred into any human language."

In discussing the *authenticity of the Scriptures* as the third barrier he was not only attacking again the concept of canonicity of the Princeton theologians but was also departing from the position of his own revered teacher, Henry Boynton Smith. Authenticity is not dependent on the superintendence or sanction of the prophets and apostles, or human authors, but on the divine testimony. "It is just here that the Higher Criticism has proved such a terror in our times," he declared, and provided a check-list of the "certain result of the science of the Higher Criticism" beginning with the position that Moses did not write the Pentateuch and that Isaiah did not write half of the book that bears his name. Actually, he affirmed, we know little about those who wrote much of the Old Testament. In his view, however, the higher criticism had rendered an inestimable service for it "brought us face to face with the holy contents, so that we may see and know whether they are divine or not."

Briggs was again on ground well known to him in dealing with *inerrancy* as the fourth barrier as he declared sharply that the Scriptures contain errors that cannot be explained away, and the theory that they were not in the original text is sheer assumption. Characteristically he observed that the errors were all in the *form* of Scripture, in *circumstantials* and not essentials, and did not conflict with the claim that the Bible is the infallible rule of faith and practice. He did declare, however, that the claim of inerrancy is not to be found in the Bible.

Briggs touched briefly on one of the great controversies of his time in pointing to the fifth barrier, the conception of miracles as a *violation of the laws of nature*. Such theories of miracles that have been taught in the churches are human inventions for which the scriptures and the Church have no responsibility; biblical miracles are those of redemption and remain "the most wonderful exhibition of loving purpose and redemptive acts of God and of the tenderness and grace of the Messiah's heart." The final barrier, *minute prediction*, is a misunderstanding of prophecy as "a sort of history before the time," and leads to anxious searching for fulfillment of details. Then, in an illustration that later caused him much difficulty, he said "Kuenen has shown that if we insist upon the fulfillment of the details of the predictive prophecy of the Old Testament, many of these predictions have been reversed by history; and the great body of the Messianic predictions has not only never been fulfilled, but cannot now be fulfilled, for the reason that its own time has passed forever." He found that the Book of Jonah offered a valuable suggestion here, for God did not fulfill a prediction but recalled it, making it part of the divine redemptive purpose.

In a "constructive" section on the theology of the Bible, Briggs stressed that God is there portrayed as a loving, merciful God of equity and judgment, transcending human powers of conception. He criticized the tendency of theology to overemphasize the doctrine of original sin. He also called attention to a distinctive view of sanctification which he had developed when he had come under the influence of Dorner years before in Berlin. Briggs declared that "progressive sanctification after death, is the doctrine of the Bible and the Church," and not the view that the Christian at death was immediately made perfect. Though he explicitly repudiated universalism, he did believe that salvation was extended to the majority of humanity. In discussing biblical ethics he offered a progressive view of moral advancement. A Christological passage called for greater emphasis on the "wondrous doctrine of the Incarnation," and praised his beloved teacher, Henry B. Smith, who "made *Incarnation in order to Redemption* the structural principle of his theology." In conclusion, he returned to the Scriptures, the Church, and the Reason as sources of divine authority in complete harmony; to him it was clear that "the Bible needs the Church and the Reason ere it can exert its full power upon the life of men."[3]

When he had dealt with these themes before, he had set them more carefully in the context of his own evangelical views, and with greater clarification and qualification. This time some of his points were not carefully stated; for example, one could interpret his remarks about the three sources of divine authority to mean that they were coordinate or even mutually independent. His choice of the Unitarian Martineau as an illustration was disturbing to many of his fellow Presbyterians. Even friends who believed in him and his position had trouble with the bluntness and one-sidedness of some of his remarks, for they obscured his love for the Bible and the conservative aspects of his own theology. The frontal attack on positions held by his theological opponents of various shades only united them against him and against Union. Perhaps, as Loetscher has suggested, he thought that a good hard blow "would hearten wavering progressives and stop reactionary forces in their tracks."[4] But he was not prepared for the tremendous hue and cry that was raised as both the religious and the secular press devoted much attention to the address and to the storm that followed. Most of the religious papers condemned his inaugural; some conspicuous defenders of his views spoke out as the controversy went on, only to be answered in sermon, editorial, article, and pamphlet.

The General Assembly was scheduled to meet in May in Detroit. It was known in advance that overtures from presbyteries asking that appropriate action be taken were coming in (69 were received by the time of meeting). Briggs' own Presbytery of New York in April named a committee to examine the address to see if action should be taken against him. In one of the many unfortunate incidents that marked the long struggle, Briggs was then confined to bed with the grippe and was not present when the committee was appointed, contrary to regular practice. When the presbytery met on May 12, with Briggs present, it accepted by a vote of 44 to 30 its committee's majority report, which cited three areas in which the inaugural conflicted with the Westminster Confession. The presbytery then adjourned to meet a few days later to name a prosecuting committee of five to arrange for a trial before it in the fall.

There had long been some internal criticism of Briggs at Union. With his Old School sympathies, Shedd did not share his colleague's views, while some who did felt he was pressing a good cause too hard. As the meeting of the General Assembly was set for the third week in May, the seminary had to make its stance clear. Pressures on members of the board not to endorse Briggs became intense. A second edition of the inaugural with an appendix that put some of the disputed matters in a more adequate context helped his cause, but the board was not fully satisfied, and presented him with eight categorical questions requiring a yes or no answer. He denied that he considered the Bible, the Church, and the Reason as coordinate sources of authority, or that he believed in a second probation or Purgatory. He answered all the other questions affirmatively (for example, that the scriptures are the only infallible rule of faith and practice, that reason includes the conscience and religious feelings, that the Bible is inerrant on all matters concerning faith and practice, and that the miracles recorded in Scripture are due to an extraordi-

nary exercise of divine energy either directly or mediately through
holy men).

The directors thereupon unanimously passed a resolution
on May 19, 1891 indicating their satisfaction with his replies, and
affirming that "They will stand by him heartily on the ground of this
report, and affectionately commend him to the leading of our common Master, having perfect confidence in his honesty of purpose."
Just three days before that the faculty had produced its own statement, which did "recognize and deprecate the dogmatic and irritat-
ing character of certain of Dr. Briggs' utterances," but found that his

The Faculty at the time of the Briggs trials: l. to r: Thomas S. Hastings,
Francis Brown, Philip Schaff, Charles A. Briggs, W. G. T. Shedd, Marvin
R. Vincent, George L. Prentiss.

address propounded no views that he had not already advanced, contained nothing that could fairly be construed as heresy or departure from the Westminster Confession, and interpreted some of his statements helpfully against misrepresentations of them. Toward the end of their long statement they declared:

> We know Dr. Briggs to be an earnest Christian, a devout student of the Bible, an indefatigable teacher and worker, and one who holds the standards of the church with an intelligence based on an exhaustive study of their history and literature. The numerous testimonies of his students during seventeen years prove that he inspired them with a deep reverence and enthusiasm for the Bible.
>
> In like manner we protest against the manner and temper of assaults upon Union Seminary. By its history of over half a century, by the character, standing and services of its graduates, and by the account and value of its contributions to Christian Literature, this Institution should be insured against such assaults. . . .
>
> We assert and must insist upon the liberty exercised by the Reformers and by the early Church, to discuss the Scriptures freely and reverently and to avail ourselves of the light which may be thrown on them from any source. [5]

The statement was signed by Hastings, Schaff, Prentiss, and Vincent. Shedd, who had entered emeritus status the year before but was still teaching, as his successor in theology had not arrived, was opposed to Briggs' views and did not sign. Francis Brown—Briggs' closest friend on the faculty—was in Oxford superintending the publication of his Hebrew Lexicon, and could not sign it directly; but he indicated his assent.

The signature of the gracious, mild-mannered president, was especially significant, for Hastings had apparently not previously accepted critical views of the Bible, and some felt that he was not a strong enough leader for the crisis. But he proved to be firm as well as gentle and held the confidence of Union's friends in the struggle. He worked closely with strong lay members of the board to formulate policy during the long period of turmoil. Thus the seminary closed ranks in support of its controversial professor, and Briggs wrote happily to Brown that the directors, students, alumni, and faculty rallied about him, "each body in its own way." [6]

Just two days later, on May 21, 1891, the General Assembly met in Detroit. Its conservative cast was evident in the election of William H. Green, senior professor at Princeton Seminary, as moderator, and of Francis L. Patton, formerly of that seminary but now president of the college in the same town, as chair of the Standing Committee on Theological Seminaries. Both had had previous sharp encounters with Briggs. The committee did not agree with Union's assumption that the transfer of a professor from one chair to another was not the same as an election and hence that a veto was not in order, but Union's board had decided in advance that it would not be good strategy to press that matter at that time. Hence when the committee on seminaries reported on May 27, it recommended two actions to the assembly: that it disapprove of the appointment of Briggs to the Robinson chair by transfer, and that a committee of fifteen be named to consult with the directors of the seminary regarding its relations to the assembly.

The standing committee, however, had consulted with nobody outside of its own membership, to the surprise of three Union directors who were present and who expected to be invited to appear before it. Then, as was highlighted during two days of debate, no reasons were given by the committee for asking the assembly for the veto! Patton indicated that many might be given, but actually none were, on the ground that the Presbytery of New York was taking steps to prosecute Briggs on the charge of heresy, and that therefore to provide reasons would prejudge the case. But when some then pled for delay, Patton and John J. McCook, a lawyer and a member of the prosecuting committee appointed by New York presbytery, argued that action had to be taken then or the right to disapprove would be lost forever. All of these matters were hotly debated then and for months after. The final vote late in the afternoon of May 29 was overwhelmingly for the resolutions offered by the committee and against Briggs, 447 to 60. Alternate ways of conceiving the Bible and theology had come into conflict, and the familiar old patterns won decisively in a conservative assembly. Without a hearing, without Briggs (who was not at the Detroit assembly) or representatives of Union having a chance for explanation or defense, without a reason being given, the veto power concerning a seminary professor had been exercised by the assembly for the first time.

The Union board met on June 5, and voted 20–2 not to

DR. BRIGGS CONDEMNED AS HETERODOX.

Full Text of the Majority Report of the Presbytery Committee Declaring His Views To Be Contradictory of the Confession of Faith.

HIS TRIAL DEMANDED.

Radical Opinions on the Authority of the Church, the Inerrancy of the Bible and Sanctification After Death the Principal Reasons.

HOW THE COMMITTEE STOOD.

Drs. Birch, Lamke and Forbes and Professor Stevenson Against Dr. Briggs; Dr. McIlvaine and Mr. Edwards in His Favor.

VIEWS OF THE MINORITY

To Try Dr. Briggs Would Very Likely Disrupt the Church Irrevocably and, Besides, His Views Are Conformable to Church Tenets.

DR. BRIGGS AT BAY

TURNS ON HIS CRITICS AND SHOWS HIS TEETH—TECHNICALLY.

It Was a Drawn Battle Yesterday, but a Hard Wrangle.

THERE WERE SOME SHARP WORDS BROTHERLY, PERHAPS.

HIS COLLEAGUES DEFEND DR. BRIGGS.

The Faculty of the Union Theological Seminary Out in a Strong Statement in Favor of the Alleged Heretic.

DEPRECATING BITTER ONSLAUGHTS

His Position, They Say, Is That of the Protestant and Presbyterian Position, and His Utterances Are Not New.

CLERGYMEN AND ALUMNI UNITED.

PRIMING THEIR GUNS FOR THE BRIGGS FIGHT.

Gigantic Wirepulling Deftly Performed by Worldly Brethren at the Presbyterian General Assembly.

AND THERE WAS LOBBYING, TOO.

Possibility That the Contest Over Briggs and Brown Will Lead to a Separation of the Seminary from the Presbytery.

A QUESTION OF SNAKES.

Newspaper headlines on the Briggs trial, May 1891.

heed the disapproval of the transfer by the General Assembly. Then, in October—at the joint gathering of the board with the conference committee that had been named by the assembly—Union stuck to its position that a transfer was not an election, that it had not been considered as such and that the seminary's by-laws for an election had not been followed, so the meeting ended inconclusively. A few days later, on November 4, the presbytery trial of Briggs was held at the Scotch Presbyterian Church on West 14th Street in New York. It was so crowded that by the time set for opening, seats for the prosecuting committee and the defendant could be found only with difficulty. Prominent on the Committee on Prosecution were two ministers—the chairman, George W. F. Birch, and Joseph J. Lampe— and an elder, John J. McCook. Briggs served as his own counsel, aided by several legal advisors.

The first charge was that he taught doctrines in conflict with the Scriptures and Presbyterian standards. Seven specifications were drawn from the inaugural address. The second charge found his doctrine of sanctification erroneous, and the single specification again pointed to the inaugural. In response, with a carefully prepared text, Briggs relied on his vast knowledge of Presbyterian history and polity to criticize sharply the form of the charges and specifications against him. He objected to point after point, citing the law of the church, quoting eminent authorities, and drawing on various precedents with telling effect. He showed that the prosecution read meanings that were not there into his words. When he was done, there was much debate, in which Shedd spoke against his colleague. A resolution was finally framed; it did not approve of the positions taken by Briggs in his inaugural, but concluded that in view of his presentation, declarations of loyalty to the Scriptures, and disclaimers of interpretations put on his words, the case was deemed dismissed. The resolution passed by a vote of 94 to 39.[7] Though Briggs had won a round, he did not get what he really wanted—full clearance. The prosecution gave notice that it would appeal.

The Committee on Prosecution decided to appeal directly to the General Assembly when it met next in Portland, Oregon in May 1892, for the Synod of New York, which would normally have been the next step in an appeal process, was not scheduled to meet until the following October. The committee's members sensed that the coming assembly would again be dominantly conservative in tone. The appeal accused the New York presbytery of irregularity in procedure, receiving improper testimony but declining to hear that which was important, manifesting prejudice, hastening to a decision before the testimony was fully taken, and making a mistake or an injustice in the decision.

Meanwhile, every step in the continuing battle combined complex procedural and difficult theological problems in a crucible of contention. An adjourned meeting of the board with the assembly's conference committee in January 1892 ended in stalemate; the directors still insisted that the assembly had no right to legislate on what had been a transfer, and suggested that the agreement of 1870, in which Union had accepted the veto in the interests of peace and harmony, be mutually abrogated; but that was not acceptable to the committee. When the question of arbitration came up, both sides agreed that it was not appropriate in this case, to the great relief of the Union directors who knew that Briggs and perhaps others would resign if the matter went to arbitration. The directors felt that they could not yield on other matters so vital to the seminary.[8]

As attention then focused on the next meeting of the assembly, the trend toward conservatism in the church seemed to be continuing, to the point that even the fourteen commissioners elected from the Presbytery of New York were, with one exception, on that side. The war of editorials, articles, pamphlets, and books went on unabated. Many were highly critical of Briggs, others supportive. His colleague Schaff, for example, who had himself been through a trial nearly half a century before, defended him in an article that put the matter in a wider perspective, for "in Germany Dr. Briggs would be classed with the conservative and orthodox rather than with radicals and rationalists. He is, in fact, a Calvinist in everything except the questions of higher criticism, where he adopts the opinions of the school of Ewald and Wellhausen, though not without some modifications, and with a distinct disavowal of rationalism."[9] But because Briggs did advocate the higher criticism, in America his opponents viewed him as a radical and a heretic, and their strength in the Presbyterian church was growing as the General Assembly of 1892 in Portland approached.

The new moderator elected when the assembly met on May 19, Dr. William C. Young, showed himself to be a fair-minded man who named representatives of the minority on the important judicial and theological seminaries committees. Clearly, however, his sympathies were not with Union and Briggs, who was present and addressed the assembly twice, defending the presbytery against the appeal. As he wrote a few days later, the commissioners "heard me patiently, but would not hear any further discussion," and added that "no heat or passion was manifested in my case, only cool determination."[10] The conference committee which had been negotiating with Union's board offered several options, one of which was to send the disputed question of the transfer to arbitration. That was in violation of the January agreement with the board not to go that way, and it angered the Union representatives. On the surface it seemed fair, but it put the seminary in a difficult position. The secretary of the seminary, Ezra M. Kingsley, presented two papers, a report and a memorial which had been prepared by the board. The report insisted again that the transfer under Union's laws was not an election and that the inauguration had been technically unnecessary. The memorial indicated that this first test of the veto power of the assembly showed it was not working for the peace of the church but could be "hasty, arbitrary, unjust and even cruel," and indicated that while either party could abrogate the 1870 agreement, yet it was the board's "earnest hope that your reverend body may cordially concur with us in annulling the arrangement of 1870, thus restoring Union Seminary to its former relations with the General Assembly."[11]

What to do with the appeal in the Briggs case was settled before the matter of abrogation came up. The Judicial Committee's majority report recommended that the appeal be heard directly by the assembly, but there was also a minority report that no exception should be made in this case and that it should go before the Synod of New York. The chair of the prosecuting committee, Birch, and McCook, the lawyer member, spoke for the majority report; Briggs again defended himself. Debate began on the late afternoon of the 25th and was concluded late on the 28th; much time was devoted to parliamentary matters and at times there was considerable confusion. It was finally voted to entertain the appeal, but the moderator had ruled that if it were sustained the case would not be tried by the

Assembly but would returned to the presbytery for a full formal trial. The final vote was decisive: 431 to sustain the appeal in whole or in part, 87 opposed.

All this was followed with avid interest by the press as the story of the maneuverings was reported daily across the country. Briggs had devoted his attention primarily to procedural matters, as the situation required, but in the fall in the retrial biblical and theological matters would be at the center of attention once again. The trend in the church at large was clear from a pronouncement by the assembly on its last day that included the sentence "Our Church holds that the inspired Word, as it came from God, is without error."[12] This "Portland Deliverance" was an ambiguously worded effort to make the rigid Hodge-Warfield doctrine of inspiration official.

Another important matter remained, however, for Union had memorialized the assembly that the agreement of 1870 be annulled by mutual consent. On May 30, however, the assembly voted a series of resolutions proposed by its committee on theological seminaries which refused to break the compact with Union, appointed a committee of fifteen to confer with all the seminaries in the interest of a still closer relation to them, and referred the differences over transfers to a committee on arbitration. When a special meeting of Union's Board of Directors was called on October 13, 1892, official notification of the assembly's action on its memorial had come from the stated clerk. The board adopted a paper summarizing its views by an almost unanimous vote: 19–1. Noting that the assembly had not given any official attention to the reasons it had given for mutual annullment of the arrangement of 1870, the board reported that by charter the seminary could not rightfully give the veto power to anyone else. Had the constitution been amended at that time things might have been different, but that had not been done. Legal advice confirmed the board's belief that the agreement of 1870 was clearly illegal in light of the charter.

Therefore, the board rescinded its action of May 16, 1870, and Union became again an independent seminary, still pledging its undiminished loyalty to the doctrine and government of the Presbyterian Church in the United States of America.[13] "The feeling of satisfaction and gratitude caused by the action of the board was very profound, both in the seminary and among its friends throughout the country," wrote Prentiss later. At the time, Director D. Willis James, calling the event a "wonderful triumph," sent a note of congratulations and thanks to President Hastings, saying "Had it not been for your marvelous tract, good temper and great ability, the results which have been accomplished could never have been reached." At the next meeting of the board on November 8, James and three other directors, John Crosby Brown, William E. Dodge, and Morris K. Jesup, expressed "our hearty approval of the principle of its management by its own Board of Directors, and also our confidence that its affairs will be so administered as best to promote the spiritual life and growth of its students and of the Presbyterian Church, of which we are members," and backed up their position by presenting to Charles Butler an unconditional gift of $175,000 to place the seminary on a sound financial basis.[14]

The very next day the New York presbytery met and presented Briggs with a revised list of eight charges, and arranged for the trial to begin on November 28 at the Scotch Presbyterian Church. Floor and galleries were quickly filled, and national attention was focused on the trial, which continued for five weeks, meeting three or four afternoons a week. In his opening reply to the charges, Briggs demanded that two of them be withdrawn because they accused him of teaching doctrines he had expressly disclaimed. Though he had quoted Kuenen in the inaugural, the context indicated that he had rejected Kuenen's position; the prosecution had missed the force of his conditional "if." In his answers to the categorical questions of the Union board he had denied any belief in the doctrine of a future probation. After long debate, the presbytery dismissed the two charges relating to those matters, despite the protests of the prosecuting committee. To the six charges that were then left, Briggs pleaded not guilty.

The case for the prosecution was made by those whom Briggs had faced several times before—Birch and McCook, who developed the points of the charges and specifications from the point of view of traditional Presbyterian orthodoxy. Procedural wrangles were frequent throughout the trial. As had happened before, when Briggs' turn came he criticized the form of the charges and the way they had been presented by the prosecution, and prefaced his point for point response by explaining that where the Confession of Faith has not given a position, a believer could hold a private doctrinal opinion as long as that is supported by Scripture or human experience. To the charge that he taught the reason is a fountain of divine authority which may and does savingly enlighten men, even those who reject the scriptures, contrary to the scriptures and standards, he responded that he never exalted the reason, which for him combined both conscience and religious feeling, above the Bible. The reason for him was a fountain of divine authority but not a rule of faith and practice; it gave humans the capacity to understand the Holy Spirit speaking through scripture.

To the charge that he taught the church is a fountain of divine authority which savingly enlightens apart from Holy Scripture, he repeated that the church does possess divine authority through Christ, and that if the Presbyterian Church has no divine authority, he must renounce its jurisdiction. The church, however, is not an infallible rule of faith and practice, only the Bible is that. To the charge that he taught that errors have existed in the original text of the Holy Scriptures—a charge clearly based on the Princeton doctrine of inspiration—the defendant argued, as he had done so often, that the plenary doctrine of inspiration, which he held, did not include verbal inspiration and textual inerrancy, nor did the presence of long-acknowledged errors in scripture (which were not of deceit or falsehood but of inadvertance and lack of knowledge) impair its infallibility in matters of faith and practice. That of course did not satisfy the opposition, which could not accept the distinction between the substance and the form of scripture. As Birch put it, "the jot and the tittle are as divine as the concepts." [15]

Another pair of charges found that Briggs taught that Moses was not the author of the Pentateuch nor Isaiah the author of half of the book that bears his name, contrary to Holy Scripture and the standards. The prosecution had based those two charges primarily on several clauses of the Westminster Confession; according to Briggs' interpretation of those clauses, they forced the conclusion that Moses did not write the Pentateuch. He had prepared for presbytery a pamphlet, "Who Wrote the Pentateuch?" published that year as *The Higher Criticism of the Hexateuch*; revised editions appeared the next year. Referring to many authorities through the centuries, he explained that the church had not taught Moses wrote the first five books of the

Bible, and that a simple literary approach showed Isaiah as a book had emerged over several centuries. He criticized the view that an infallible rule of faith and practice could come only from well-known prophets and apostles. A position such as the one held by the Princeton theologians, he declared, was based on neither Bible nor confession. He asked rhetorically, "Will you follow Calvin or Dr. Shedd, the Reformers or the Hodges, Westminster theology or Princeton theology?"[16]

The last charge was that he had taught sanctification was not complete at death, and in answering he interpreted the confession as teaching that it involved rising to a higher grade of Christian life and experience, which required time. He did not claim this doctrine of progressive sanctification as essential but as a valid interpretation of the Bible and the confessional standards in the field of eschatology.

It took Briggs four sessions for his defense; there were frequent interruptions and protests. Then when a third prosecutor, the Reverend Joseph J. Lampe, took three afternoons for rebuttal, Briggs objected several times that large amounts of new evidence were being introduced, and was given an opportunity to reply. He pointed out errors in Lampe's testimony, and became sarcastic as he declared that the prosecution "live in the cavern of a dogmatic faith" and are "as blind as owls and bats to the truth of history and the facts of the world of reality."[17] Briggs was aware that except for the last charge he was in fact affirming the very doctrines that the prosecution insisted he had denied through his alleged errors in the inaugural. He knew that he was being tested against a particular view of the infallibility and inerrancy of the original autographs and that there was no real communication. "From first to last the prosecution and defense were at cross purposes," a younger colleague wrote. "Their minds never met."[18] When final voting occurred on December 29 and 30, once again Briggs was cleared. None of the charges were sustained. The closest vote was on the third charge about errors in the original text, 61–67, but by the margin of 6 the charge was not sustained. The fifth charge, on Isaiah, showed the widest spread, 49–73. The majority of the ministers sided with Briggs, but the lay elders sustained three of the six charges and split evenly on a fourth.[19]

When the presbytery met on January 9, 1893, the formal

report of the trial was before it and was adopted. Again, in fully acquitting Briggs of offences alleged against him, the words "without expressing approval of the critical or theological views embodied in the Inaugural Address, or the manner in which they have been expressed and illustrated" were used. The decision went on to relieve the Committee on Prosecution "to the extent of its Constitutional power" from further responsibility, intending by the action "to express an earnest conviction that the grave issues involved in this case will be more wisely and justly determined by calm investigation and fraternal discussion than by judicial arraignment and process."[20] It was time, the decision concluded, to turn from the paths of controversy to the great and urgent work of the church.

In his study of theological issues in the Presbyterian Church since 1869, Loetscher observed that the decision had been drafted by Henry van Dyke and George Alexander, who with four others circulated among the ministers early in 1893 A *Plea for Peace and Work*, privately printed, with 235 signatures, calling for harmony and united devotion to practical church work. In the twentieth century the motif of subordinating unresolved issues to the necessities of cooperation for the successful prosecution of the church's program emerged more clearly; it was a trend to a more pragmatic doctrine of the church, just at the time that the philosophy of pragmatism was spreading. Presbyterians did not formally hold such views, Loetscher adds, but the same forces in American life were at work in both developments. At the time the trend indicated that a third party was emerging within Presbyterianism (as in other denominations) between the parties demanding theological innovation and those resisting it, a party "who were resolved to transcend ideological differences in united action."[21] The trend was to dominate the church's life through much of the twentieth century—but not in time to help Briggs. Its early manifestation was sharply attacked as "broad churchism," and it was not a strong force in presbyterianism for some years. After its second defeat before presbytery, the Committee on Prosecution appealed again to General Assembly, scheduled to meet at the New York Avenue Presbyterian Church in Washington, D.C. in May 1893.

At this point in the long struggle personality issues had become so mixed up with theological, ecclesiastical, and institutional ones that the church had become sharply polarized in an often ugly way. William Adams Brown, who was at the 1893 assembly, later observed that "in the days of controversy over Doctor Briggs, I had seen party spirit carried to such lengths that there was not a single trick known in the political game that I did not see churchmen using in their struggle with one another."[22] Opponents of A *Plea for Peace and Work*, for example, published an apparently fabricated letter to weaken its credibility.

By the time the General Assembly met in Washington, the leadership in the attack on Briggs had passed from the Princeton group to the ultraconservatives, strong in Pennsylvania and the Ohio Valley. The conservative views of the new moderator, Willis Green Craig of McCormick Seminary, was evident in the appointments to important committees. The majority report of the Judicial Committee that the appeal be entertained by the assembly before the parties had been heard was prejudicial and contrary to the Book of Discipline (as the minority report pointed out), but nevertheless it was adopted, and the question came before the assembly as a supreme court with all seating and standing room fully occupied. Once again, Birch and McCook presented the prosecution's case. Briggs appeared against entertaining the appeal, being given five hours over two days.

He again showed his mastery of Presbyterian history and governance as he focused on matters of procedure, but to no avail, for after the prosecution concluded and a lengthy discussion took place, the assembly voted on May 26 to try the case on appeal by a decisive 410–145 vote. At that point Briggs saw what the result would be, and wanted to withdraw from the Presbyterian ministry, but close friends among the Union directors urged him to stick it out. "You are not on trial so much as the Presbyterian Church," said John Crosby Brown in a telegram, while Charles Butler in a letter affirmed that "The interests of the Seminary and the Presbyterian Church and the cause of truth require you to to remain in the Church & stand fast—unless like Luther, you are driven out."[23]

The climax of the series of trials and appeals began on the following Monday, May 29, 1893, at the New York Avenue church. Although it was a rainy day, even standing room in the galleries was quickly filled; three sessions a day were scheduled. The scene was by now familiar to those who had been following the matter. The appellant's case was presented by Birch, McCook, and Lampe, while Briggs again defended himself, with his colleague Francis Brown seated beside him. The appellants were given four and a half hours, Briggs seven, with four hours given to limited discussion. Much of the ground that had been gone over several times before was covered again, but out of the many particulars, one especially reveals how far apart appellants and appellee—prosecutors and defendant—had been from the beginning. This time Lampe was the first main speaker, and in the course of his address (83 pages long in the official printed version) he said:

According to Section 58 of the Book of Discipline, if the specifications of fact on which a charge is based have been shown to be true, then the charge is to be considered as sustained. Dr. Briggs offered no proof to show that he had not made the statements [in his 1891 inaugural] which are cited in the specifications. On the contrary, he admitted and authenticated them all. The charges were based on these statements and sustained by them. Under such circumstances, a verdict of acquittal could be justified only on the ground that the charges themselves were not relevant or that they contained no valid offences. But when the Presbytery declared the charges and specifications to be sufficient in form and legal effect, it thereby decided that the charges severally alleged an offence. Otherwise, the charges and specifications would not have been sufficient in form and legal effect. And therefore, since the charges were sustained by the facts stated in the specifications, it must be that the verdict of acquittal was not reached in accordance with the law and evidence in the case.[24]

From this point of view, Briggs' words in the inaugural had only the one meaning which the prosecution placed on them, and therefore his only way out would have been to show he had never said them. All his efforts to explain what he did mean and to support his views by appeal to the Bible and the confessional standards were thus not regarded by his opponents as significant. He reaffirmed his faith in the scriptures as the only infallible rule of faith and life, but because he denied that they were the rule of science, geography, or chronology, his words fell on deaf ears.

     The same point emerged again in McCook's closing argument in reply to Briggs. Referring back to the presbytery trial the previous December when the presbytery had found the amended charges and specifications in order and sufficient to require the accused to defend himself, he exclaimed:

What then remained for the Prosecuting Committee to prove? Simply that the accused had spoken and published the words from the Inaugural quoted in the specifications. The merits of the case involved simply the question of fact. But the fact was openly admitted by the accused that he had spoken and published the words quoted in the specifications. The proof was complete. The verdict should have been guilty, and each of the charges and specifications should have been sustained.[25]

He soon got what he had long been seeking. The vote was by roll call on May 31; more than a hundred commissioners availed themselves of the privilege of taking no more than three minutes to explain their vote, so it was late in the evening when the count was complete: 295 voted to sustain the appeal as a whole, 84 in part, and 116 not to sustain it—379 to 116. The next day the assembly adopted a report which suspended Briggs from the office of Presbyterian minister "until such time as he shall give satisfactory evidence of repentance to the General Assembly of the Presbyterian Church in the United States of America."[26] On that same June 1 the assembly accepted the report of its committee on theological seminaries disavowing all responsibility for the teaching at Union Seminary, declining to receive a report from its board, and recommending that the church's educational board give aid only to students attending approved seminaries. The body also reaffirmed the Portland Deliverance on biblical inerrancy of the year before, unanimously resolving "that the Bible as we now have it, in its various translations and versions, when freed from all errors and mistakes of translators, copyists, and printers, is the very word of God, and consequently wholly without error," declaring that this had always been the belief of the church.[27]

  Thus the Hodge-Warfield position was unambiguously declared to be the official teaching of the church. Though there were protests concerning the actions against Briggs and for the deliverance, they did not have enough backing to stand against the conservative tide. So the trials finally came to an end. Though rumors had circulated that Briggs and others might seek to divide the church, there was no movement in that direction—for five years Briggs remained in the church as a suspended minister, preaching now and then as a layman. This time there was no schism as in 1837–38—only a few suspensions and withdrawals from the ministry.

There was some doubt at first as to what action the Union directors would take, but once again they rallied around the Robinson professor. "The action of the General Assembly is what I anticipated, but done in a spirit worse than the Dark Ages ever exhibited and by comparison the action of the Inquisition in the dark ages seems gentle," wrote D. Willis James to Charles Butler on June 3. "The Seminary must of course stand by Dr. Briggs and retain him as Professor."[28] Ten days later the board met and passed a strongly worded statement: "Resolved that the unanimous desire of this Board that Dr. Briggs should continue his valuable service in the department of Biblical Theology be communicated to him with the assurance of our unabated confidence, affection and sympathy; and that a copy of this Resolution be sent to Dr. Briggs by the President of the Faculty."[29]

At the seminary the patterns of educational life went on little changed through all the excitement of the events of 1891–93, though some claims that there was little discussion of the trials at 700 Park Avenue were somewhat exaggerated. For example, in reviewing the 1890s Charles R. Gillett said, "Irrespective of storm and tumult without, and unwounded by the shafts leveled at it, Union is a place of studious calm, where there is that union with God and man wherein is strength."[30] William Adams Brown said more than once,

The work of the Seminary proceeded as quietly as if nothing were happening without. We used to say, half in jest, and yet I think it was literally true, that the only place where you could go without hearing the Briggs case discussed was Union Seminary.[31]

It was not quite that simple. Students were often present at those crowded presbytery trials in New York. The biographer of Henry Winters Luce, then a student at Union, wrote that at the trial in 1892 "Luce and his seminary mates often listened to learned theological debates and watch ecclesiastical history in the making. Meantime, their studies were badly disrupted by the controversy."[32] From another student's letter we know that the opening of seminary was delayed a day in the fall of 1892 because of the trial, and that Vincent took over Briggs' classes when he became deeply involved in defending himself. "We all think he is right in his higher criticism ideas but as a teacher & prof. we don't like him very well," Henry Ranck wrote about Briggs at the end of October. "In fact he is no teacher. You must ask questions and even when you do that he seems to antagonize you."[33]

Briggs also antagonized colleagues and board members from time to time, but in the crises the seminary swung to support their professor, who was notorious in some circles, but of growing fame in others. For some he was a heretic; for others he was a champion of liberty and unfettered scholarship against stubborn traditionalism. As Schaff wrote to Butler, "The General Assembly has made him a hero & martyr of world wide reputation," and from abroad S. D. F. Salmond of Aberdeen, Briggs' coeditor in the International Theological Library series, said in a letter to the deposed minister, "It has been scarcely possible for us on this side of the Atlantic to imagine that a great Church like yours could not only override its own established order of procedure, but commit itself to a definition of the inerrancy of Scripture which must make it a gazing stock and object of wonder to intelligent Christians everywhere."[34]

Despite the bitterness of the time and the often biased coverage in the religious and secular press, the controversy did focus attention on religious matters; Prentiss believed that it taught people "more than in all their lives they had know before about theological seminaries, Biblical study and learning, 'higher criticism,' and the close connection of all these with human life and progress."[35] A historian going over the evidence more than half a century later concluded that from the point of view of the biblical theologian's opponents "the net result of the Briggs case was undoubtedly opposite of that desired—it publicized and disseminated the new critical views within the Church and far beyond."[36] By then the seminaries related to the General Assembly were teaching as a matter of course positions similar to and often more extreme than those for which Briggs had been repudiated, for his peers were soon going beyond his rather conservative positions in both theology and criticism.

Following the trials, twenty more years of a very active career at Union were left to Briggs. One of his many interests, that of church union, soon surfaced both in his own life and in that of the seminary. In his own way, he carried on the ecumenical work of

Philip Schaff. The last appearance of that colleague who had publicly so firmly backed Briggs came in the early autumn of 1893 at the Parliament of Religions and the National Conference of the Evangelical Alliance in Chicago. Against the advice of his physicians he traveled there to deliver an address on "The Reunion of Christendom" which anticipated many of the emphases that were to become familiar in the twentieth-century ecumenical movement with its national and world councils of churches. "Our theological systems are but dim rays of the sun of truth which illuminates the universe," he declared, "Truth first, doctrine next, dogma last." He advocated the forward look: "The Church must keep pace with civilization, adjust herself to the modern conditions of religious and political freedom, and accept the established results of biblical and historical criticism, and natural science," and displayed the optimism so characteristic of his time in hoping that the progress of science and international law would in due time make an end of war, linking "all the civilized nations into one vast brotherhood."[37] A few weeks later the distinguished scholar was gone, but Briggs and others—including students, graduates, faculty, and directors—continued his pioneering work.

Present at the famous trial in Washington was a boy of sixteen—Henry Sloane Coffin, who had accompanied his father, an adviser to the board, to the assembly and "had witnessed the scene which left an indelible impression on his mind." His biographer, Morgan Phelps Noyes, observed that after college and study abroad, "Coffin entered the Seminary fully convinced that Union Seminary had an important mission to perform in promoting Christian unity, honest fearless scholarship and enlightened, loyal churchmanship."[38] Many years later Coffin was to remember the occasion as the time when the seminary accepted "a mission under God to champion the freedom of Christian scholars."[39]

The storms of the early 1890s had confirmed and reinforced some of the original purposes of the directors, but it also dramatized important changes in theological thought and education. The event was of significance for many other theological schools. Even before it was over, the Briggs affair did not halt but if anything encouraged the acceptance of the historical-critical approach to the Bible in a number of conspicuous seminaries in the Northeast, for example, at Andover and Yale among the Congregational institutions, at the Episcopal seminaries in Cambridge and Philadelphia, at Colgate and Newton among the Baptist schools, and at Lancaster, the inheritor of the German Reformed tradition of Mercersburg. The movement spread in the late nineteenth and early twentieth centuries to other traditions and sections, and some seminaries pressed toward a nondenominational status as Union was doing. In keeping with its historic tradition of moderation, however, it took some time for the New York seminary to redefine itself after the controversies of the early 1890s.

CHAPTER FIVE

Liberal Evangelicalism Faces Twentieth-Century Realities (1894–1908)

S oon after the suspension of Professor Briggs from the Presbyter- ian ministry in 1893, Robert W. Patterson, remembered by Prentiss as "the patriarch of American Presbyterianism in the great Northwest," wrote to President Hastings the comforting words that "Union Seminary will live and be a great power in this struggle for liberty."[1] The survival of the seminary was never in doubt, but it had to redefine its role as an independent institution at a time when some striking changes were going on in American theological education. Though the major directions of redefinition took shape after Hastings left the presidency in 1897 to resume full-time teaching, several im- portant steps were taken under the leadership of the man who had seen the seminary through the storm of 1891–93.

A revised course of study was introduced at the beginning of the academic year 1894–95. The catalog for that year detailed two permanent changes in the way theological education was being con- ceived. First, the curriculum up to that point had been almost en- tirely prescribed, with a few optional courses and seminars for those who could manage an increased load. Now for the first time the course offerings were organized not under the junior, middle, and senior years but under departments: Propaeductics (Introduction), Biblical Philology and Exegesis (with divisions of Old and New Testament), Biblical Theology, Church History, Systematic Theology, Apologetics and Ethics, Vocal Culture, and Sacred Music. The "departments" were largely curriculum divisions and were not formalized; at that point only two had more than one instructor and four were handled by part-time instructors or by faculty members whose primary assignments were in another department. Second, a number of elective courses were listed, both at the seminary and at Columbia College and New York University. The latter could be taken by "students of superior scholarship" without charge provided that such courses "shall not interfere with the regular work appointed by the Seminary." The bulk of the three-year theological curriculum was still prescribed, largely by class, but some of the requirements were "variable as to class"—they could be done when convenient.

These two significant modifications of the traditional theological curriculum reflected changes then underway in American higher education as major universities had increasingly developed and expanded their departmental and elective systems. For a relatively small[2] professional school enrolling primarily college graduates (though one could still enter by examination), to add electives meant that increased human and material resources would be needed. It immediately created some administrative burdens; the office of registrar was created in 1894, and for a number of years the post was filled by members of the teaching staff, in addition to their other duties.

These changes were accompanied by efforts to raise academic standards. One sign of this was increased attention to written examinations at the end of the terms. Originally examinations had been oral and public, by class. This apparently continued through much of the nineteenth century, with decreasing emphasis on the "public" aspects. The last time that visiting committees of the directors, alumni, and synod at examinations were listed on the published examination programs was in 1882. In 1895 Francis Brown reported the use of written examinations to the directors, and by the end of the decade the faculty was recommending the use of blue books for examinations at the end of term. As a given class was no longer studying all the same things at the same time, the older system was being outmoded. It had been predicated to some extent on the long-familiar recitation method of instruction, while the lecture method was now in the ascendancy, along with an increase in special seminars for advanced instruction.[3]

Another indication of a greater emphasis on scholarly standards appeared in the catalog for 1896–97—the last year of Hastings' presidency. In addition to the regular diploma course, an honors course for the degree of Bachelor of Divinity (B.D.) was offered, through the cooperation of the Regents of the University of the State of New York. The standards were formidable; candidates had to be college graduates of high rank, had to take 180 hours of elective work beyond the regular course of 1260 hours, maintain a standing of at least 80 percent in their seminary work, attend a seminar, and write a thesis. Through the period of this chapter, only a slowly increasing minority of theological students worked for and received the B.D. Those who were graduates of other theological seminaries could receive the Union B.D. for a full year's work of high quality.

Another important development occurred toward the end of the Hastings period: the admission of women students. In the fall of 1895 some women requested and received permission to attend some courses, apparently as "guests" at the recommendation of their pastors and with the consent of the instructors concerned. Then on December 4, Emilie Grace Briggs, daughter of the professor, was admitted as a "special student and a candidate for a certificate," and allowed to take courses for credit.[4] At first she was required to sit at the rear of the classroom, entering last and leaving first, but that rule soon disappeared. She did so well that, on presentation of a thesis in the spring of 1897, she received a B.D. *summa cum laude* in the first group to receive the degree, and as the degrees were awarded alphabetically, she received the first B.D. diploma Union issued. She taught New Testament at the New York Training School for Deaconesses from 1896 to 1915, assisted her father in some of his scholarly projects, wrote articles, and later returned to the seminary for graduate study.

Hastings was very pleased with this development, exclaiming that "her achievement marked an epoch in the history of the Presbyterian Church in the United States, and also in the history of the advancement of women." Several other women were admitted in the fall of 1897, one to the junior class, the other as a special student, while a larger group came to the seminary for a course or two. Hastings wrote:

> Our experience with these young women has been so satisfactory that we are firmly persuaded that in opening our doors to women we have done a wise thing, and hereafter women will have all the privileges of our seminary. . . . Our Board of Directors have become really enthusiastic upon the question of the higher education of women.[5]

In all, from the time Grace Briggs entered to the commencement of 1910, some 18 women were admitted as full-time students, the majority of them as special students who stayed usually for a year or two, but four of them did graduate. Yet they remained a small minority of the student body; only toward the very end of this period, when total seminary enrollment reached 182, were there as many as five in residence at any given time. But that Union among some other seminaries admitted women into degree and special programs was then a significant step.

The attempt of the seminary to keep up with trends in American higher education, especially by the introduction of a range of elective courses and seminars, pointed to the need for maintaining and if possible increasing faculty strength. A glance back briefly into the early part of the decade shows that efforts to do this were carried on during the storm of the Briggs trials. Finding a replacement in systematic theology for Shedd proved to be difficult. He became an emeritus professor in 1890, but continued to do some teaching as certain unusual problems emerged in the naming of his successor. The call was extended in 1890 to a rising young theologian at the Congregational Seminary of Bangor, Maine—Lewis French Stearns, who was then writing a book on Henry Boynton Smith. Aware of the difficulties he might have in transferring to Presbyterianism, he declined the call. The invitation was then extended to Henry Jackson Van Dyke, who had been educated at Yale, the University of Pennsylvania, and Princeton Seminary. Long a prominent pastor in Brooklyn, former moderator of the General Assembly, and father of the Henry Van Dyke who later became a noted author, he received a call to fill the Roosevelt chair in his sixty-ninth year. With some misgivings he accepted in April 1891. But it was not to be; he died of a heart attack a month later.

Union then turned to one of its graduates, John H. Worcester Jr. of the class of 1871, who had also been influenced by Henry Boynton Smith. A graduate of the University of Vermont, he interrupted his seminary course to travel and study at Berlin and Leipzig. He served in several pastorates, in which he was recognized for his scholarly preaching. At the Detroit General Assembly in 1891, when the veto of Briggs was being debated, this man of rather conservative temper made a long-remembered speech criticizing the proposed action sharply, stressing that no reason for the veto had been given. In that same month he had agonized over a call to teach systematic theology at Hartford Seminary, but refused it—only to receive a call for the same task at Union two months later. This time he accepted and began his work that autumn, but was failing in strength and died early in 1893 in his 48th year.

After that series of unhappy events, Union tried another approach, asking a promising young instructor to change fields. William Adams Brown, grandson of William Adams and James Brown and son of John Crosby Brown, was a graduate of Yale and Union who won the traveling fellowship in 1890 and studied in Berlin. He focused his attention primarily in church history, working with the great Adolf Harnack but also hearing such lecturers as Julius Kaftan in systematics and Otto Pfleiderer in ethics. He returned to the seminary as instructor in church history in the fall of 1892, but was drafted to help in systematics during Worcester's illness, was shifted to that department the next year, and in 1895 was made a "provisional professor." As his teaching thoroughness and theological productivity were demonstrated, he settled into the Roosevelt chair three years later, and would hold it for 32 years.

Another instructor destined for a long career at Union was also appointed in 1892. Charles P. Fagnani was the son of a famous portrait painter. Born in New York, he had received much of his early education in Paris. After graduation from the College of the City of New York, several years of study at Columbia Law School, and six years of public school teaching, he came to Union, graduating in 1882. After two brief pastorates, he went abroad for reasons of health. Ten years after he had left Union he returned as instructor in Hebrew, proving to be an effective and popular teacher. "No class he taught could be dull, although much that he brought in might be remotely related to the subject at hand," Coffin wrote. "Generations of Seminary students remember him with affection as a unique and refreshing character."[6]

Another major appointment was made in the fall of 1893, for the aging Schaff had had to lay down the burdens of his chair. Again Union turned to one of its own. Arthur Cushman McGiffert had come to Union from Western Reserve in 1882, and after graduating from Union three years later studied abroad at Berlin, Marburg, Paris, and Rome. At Marburg he was close to Harnack, and received his Ph.D. from the university there in 1888. Ordained in that same year, he taught for five years at Lane Seminary until he was called to Union as Washburn professor of church history in 1893, soon becoming known as the best lecturer on the faculty. Like Fagnani, he was to serve the seminary well for 34 years.

To sum up, the faculty that was reshaping Union's educational patterns during the middle 1890s combined older and younger colleagues: Hastings, Prentiss, Briggs, Francis Brown, and Vincent from the 1870s and 1880s, with William Adams Brown, Fagnani, and McGiffert added in that century's last decade. One more full-time appointment was made just at the conclusion of Hastings' presidency—James E. Frame as instructor in New Testament in 1897. A graduate of Harvard and Union (1895), he studied at Berlin and Göttingen before returning to the seminary as a meticulous and thorough scholar and teacher. His was to be a long, rich career of 41 years on the faculty. Possibly it was a reflection of the influence of European academic customs to which so many of the faculty had been exposed that led to the adoption of a rule in 1895 that faculty members were to wear gowns (made by wives of the directors) at chapel and whenever they met students in a body—a custom that persisted among some members of the faculty for half a century.

A development that was to influence the education of Union students for many years was not organically part of the seminary but was closely related to it. The settlement house movement, dedicated to the lowering of barriers between classes and helping recent immigrants and those struggling with poverty to improve their situation, was then rapidly burgeoning. Stanton Coit, one of the early residents of the pioneer (1884) Toynbee Hall in London, founded the first American settlement house in New York a year or two later; Jane Addams' famous Hull House in Chicago was organized in 1889. From a meeting of the Union Alumni Club came the suggestion that a new settlement, New York's fourth, be founded. Named Union Settlement, it opened its doors on East 96th street in 1895, soon moving to a location at 237 East 104th street on land owned by the seminary, which was represented on its board. Other seminaries were also involved in establishing settlements, notably Robert A. Woods' Andover House in Boston in 1892 and Graham Taylor's Chicago Commons two years later. Students who worked at Union settlement often found it a challenging and informative part of their preparation for ministry.

A small but intense group of students devoted themselves to the cause of foreign missions. In the years 1892–94 three Yale graduates at Union—Sherwood Eddy, Henry W. Luce, and Horace T. Pitkin—shared rooms in the dormitory and devoted much of their weekends to serving the Student Volunteer Movement for Foreign Missions (SVM), which had grown out of the Northfield conferences conducted by the famous lay evangelist, Dwight L. Moody. They then spent a year as traveling secretaries for the movement, arousing enthusiasm as they appealed to students on many college campuses to accept the SVM's declaration: "It is my purpose if God permit to become a foreign missionary." Eddy and Luce completed their studies at Princeton, the former to serve the YMCA in India for fifteen years and then to travel the world in the missionary cause, the latter to become a missionary educator in China. In 1927 Luce returned to Union and Columbia for a year of study and refreshment. He is remembered at the seminary through the establishment in 1945 of the Henry W. Luce visiting professorship of world Christianity. Pitkin returned to Union to complete his theological studies, graduated in 1896 and went off to serve in China, where he would become a martyr on July 1, 1900, during the Boxer Rebellion, while trying to shield two woman missionaries.[7]

1897 was a year of leadership changes. Hastings left his administrative tasks to resume his full-time teaching service as Brown professor of sacred rhetoric, and Prentiss retired at the age of 81. And the last living link with the founders was severed late in the year, when Charles Butler died at the age of 95, to be succeeded in the presidency of the Board of Directors by John Crosby Brown.[8] A graduate of Columbia College, Brown climaxed his career in banking by heading the firm founded by his father, Brown Bros. & Co.

The faculty felt keenly the pressures of a growing elective system and the demands of new teaching areas. In the 1896–97 catalog there appeared a rather unusual item for an academic catalog— one more to be expected in a promotional brochure: "There are various lines of progress, both scholarly and practical, along which the seminary must move if it is to keep abreast of the times, and meet the demands now made upon an institution for the training of ministers. It cannot do so without a substantial increase of its funds." Union was seeking appropriate ways of keeping pace with the progressive spirit of the times.

To take the lead in responding to the challenging opportunities the board chose one of its own members from the pastorate, Charles Cuthbert Hall. Born in New York City in 1852, he graduated from Williams College, studied at Union for two years, and then spent a year at the Presbyterian College in London.

On his return Hall served briefly as pastor of the Presbyterian Church in Newburgh, New York, and then for twenty years achieved eminence in the pulpit of First Presbyterian in Brooklyn. Early in this period he became a member of Union's board. An able preacher and writer, Hall was an outgoing person who communicated to others his personal interest in them. As an aftermath of the Briggs case, there was some effort in presbytery to launch a move against him on the basis of alleged heresies in several of his books, but the matter was quickly tabled and did not again arise, for in him a liberal spirit and an evangelical theology were well matched.

In May of 1897 Hall began his new work at Union, taking over the presidential duties from Hastings and the teaching responsibilities of Prentiss as Skinner and McAlpin professor of pastoral theology, church polity, and mission work. At his formal inauguration as president of the faculty on February 8, 1898, the charge was given by his predecessor in the presidency, who congratulated him on the unanimity of his selection ("No other name than yours was considered in the Board or mentioned in the Faculty"), and pointed

Charles Cuthbert Hall, who guided the seminary into the twentieth century.

to the desirability of the further enlargement and expansion of Union's work:

The beautiful catholicity, which has characterized this institution from the beginning up to this sixty-second year of its life, is demanding a fuller expression than that of open doors as toward students of all denominations of Christians. We look and long for a Theological University, broad and comprehensive, which shall be the natural evolution of the spirit and aim of our honored Founders.

The idea of a seminary becoming a "theological university" was being widely discussed at the time, but Union was in a stronger position than many others to work toward that end. His reference to what would later be called the ecumenical character of the seminary was closer than he knew. While affirming that the seminary's doctrinal basis in the Westminster Confession "must and will be maintained inviolate," Hastings found no inconsistency between that and making all students "better in and for their respective denominations." In ways he could not quite anticipate, the fuller expression of the "beautiful catholicity" was only six years away. His prophecy was nearer to realization that he had imagined.

In response to his predecessor's challenge, as Hall delivered the inaugural address he spoke on "The Expansion of the Seminary." His remarks at once summarized major themes in Union's history to that point and laid out the lines that the seminary was to follow in the twentieth century. In a notable way, his address provided an interpretation of the past and offered formative projections for the future. Gathering up and giving shape to many suggestions that had been made, he described four lines of expansion for Union "which would be at once concurrent with the ideals of the Founders and adapted to some great needs and great opportunities of the times into which we are moving." Very much aware of the pressing social problems of that time, he affirmed that the "Quadrilateral Expansion" he was projecting "would indeed bring the seminary into warm and practical touch with some of those most broad and most earnest sociological movements which are seeking to purge and uplift and bless with gladness the lives of the poor, but it would not confuse nor obscure in any way the chief end of the founders which was, to use their own language, 'to furnish a competent supply of well-educated and pious ministers of the Gospel.' "

The academic line was the first of the four he articulated, insisting that by providing resources "for the most advanced study of Christian Ethics, Canon Law, Symbolics and Comparative Religion, the Seminary can meet and answer comprehensively, irenically, and on the highest grade of Academic discipline, that fundamental need of a clearer faith, a more intelligent ethics, a more catholic and Christlike churchmanship, of which all over the land many of our finest and ablest men are conscious."

What he called *the university extension line* was his second, meaning by it to share with lay workers the resources of the seminary, with particular attention to the practical application of Christianity to the religious and social problems of the time. Believing that the distinction between the ministry and laity was fading from view, he argued that what was taught in seminary should also be presented in appropriate ways to lay workers in the church.

The line of social service was Hall's third emphasis as he pointed to the way a new population of more than one hundred thousand primarily working class persons had pressed into the upper East Side in the past ten or fifteen years. He saw Union Settlement, "an emanation from this Seminary; an expression of the spirit of social love which prevails within this institution," growing to the point where it would provide "a sublime opportunity for the students of this seminary to learn all the new, loving, generous methods of helping mankind to a better life."

The line of spiritual power was the fourth point in his plan for expansion, and he pressed its ecumenical aspects in picturing the chapel as "a place where those of all branches of the Church who desire to worship in the Spirit and to ponder the principles and objects of the life which is hid with Christ in God may come together, free from the saddening influences of controversy and far from the dark shadows of doubt, to sit together in heavenly places in Jesus Christ and commune in the Unity of the Spirit and under the bond of peace."[9]

In the nearly eleven years of Hall's presidency the seminary did expand in many ways, some not mentioned in the inaugural, while the record of advance along the four lines he stressed was uneven. The ideas and labors of many persons—directors, faculty members, students, alumni/ae, donors, friends—contributed to the achievements of those years, but his ability to lead and to inspire others was central. He carried heavy burdens, for in addition to his administrative and teaching loads, he was frequently in great demand as preacher and speaker.

The academic life of Union was broadened by the addition of new teaching areas, evoked by new trends in theological education and by the ideal of a seminary as a theological university. A very important appointment was made in 1899 when George William Knox was named Professor of the Philosophy and History of Religion (five years later the professorship was endowed as the Marcellus Hartley chair). A graduate of Hamilton College and Auburn Seminary, Knox had served as a missionary in Japan for some sixteen years, most of that time as professor of homiletics at Union Theological Seminary in Tokyo, but in 1886 he held the chair of philosophy and ethics in the Imperial University. Returning to a pastorate in Rye, he taught courses in apologetics at Union until called to the professorship. A brilliant thinker, he was a remarkable speaker who never appeared to have any notes before him but who was clear and well-organized. "He was a potent factor in shaping the thinking of students," wrote Coffin.

His independence of current trends may be judged from the Taylor Lectures, delivered at Yale in 1903, on *The Direct and Fundamental Proofs of the Christian Religion*. His thinking was a refreshing break from the current immanentism which believed it could go "through nature to God."[10]

For Knox, the Christian starts with being found by God in Christ, and then interprets nature in that light. He made a deep impression on colleagues and students, and was sorely missed when he died abroad in Seoul in 1912 in his 59th year.

Knox was remembered as a quiet man, but another appointment of 1899 which also opened an important new area of study in the curriculum was famous for his forceful eloquence. Thomas C. Hall was a tall, commanding figure; "the torrent of his speech was impressive."[11] A graduate of the college at Princeton and Union (1882), he studied for a year in Berlin and Göttingen, and served three pastorates in Omaha and Chicago. He identified himself with the mush-rooming social movements of his time, and courageously spoke for those he deemed to have been unjustly denied fair economic opportunity. Beginning with courses on the history and principles of Christian ethics, he soon added new ones on Christian social thinking, social ethics, and morality and the economic factor—introducing themes to be much debated in twentieth-century theological education at Union and elsewhere.

Though new disciplines attracted considerable attention in this period of educational innovation, the older ones were not neglected. The Old Testament department soon acquired a third member. Julius A. Bewer, born and educated in Germany, earned his B.D. from Union in 1898 and his Ph.D. from Columbia two years later, and after further study in Basel, Halle, and Berlin taught Old Testament for two years at Oberlin. Called back to Union in 1904 as assistant and soon associate professor of biblical philology, he was to serve on the faculty for 41 years. Eloquent as a lecturer, he was at his best when making the prophets come alive for his students, one of whom remembered that "he so identified himself with the prophet of whom he happened to be speaking that for us he seemed to be Ezekiel, and we felt the prophet speaking to us."[12]

Church history also received an additional faculty member to help the overburdened McGiffert when William Walker Rockwell, a graduate of Harvard and Andover with further study abroad in Germany (he received Göttingen's Ph.D. in 1914), joined the faculty as assistant professor in 1905. Teaching courses in the medieval and modern periods, he also introduced the study of American church history to Union. Alternating between service as historian and librarian, he continued at the seminary for 37 years.

The resources in practical theology and especially homiletics were also significantly increased. Though Hastings continued to do some teaching in pastoral theology after his retirement in 1904, President Hall was named Brown Professor of Homiletics, and Henry Sloane Coffin (1900), then pastor at Bedford Park but soon to fill the pulpit at Madison Avenue Presbyterian Church, was called in 1904 as assistant professor of homiletics on a part-time basis; his role on the faculty was to continue for 41 years. The complement of homileticians was filled out when a famous Scottish preacher, Hugh Black, was called in 1906 to a new chair as Jesup graduate professor of practical theology—a post he was to hold for 33 years. He was much in demand as a preacher across the land, and helped to heal old wounds, as he appeared in pulpits that would not normally at that point have welcomed a Union professor. A conspicuous prince of the pulpit, he was at his very best in expository preaching. Assisting the work of these prominent preachers was a man who served as instructor of public speaking and vocal interpretation for a quarter-century: Francis Carmody, a Roman Catholic layman who was also a lawyer and teacher of law at Brooklyn and then Fordham law schools. Instruction in the importance of music in worship was given for 22 years by a founder of the American Guild of Organists, Gerrit Smith. Under Cuthbert Hall's leadership, the faculty resources were thus significantly expanded, and most of those added were to have notable lifetime careers at Union. Less conspicuous outside the seminary but highly regarded within was a person appointed in Hall's last year, Harold H. Tryon (1905). A graduate of the University of Pennsylvania, Columbia, and Union, who then studied abroad at Berlin, Heidelberg, and Jerusalem, he taught Greek, New Testament, and church history, and served for twenty years as registrar.

One of the expansionist developments of the time proved not to be permanent: the establishment of a graduate department and faculty, a particular interest of Briggs, who had been actively promoting the idea of Union as a "theological university." The number of graduate students had increased to about forty in the middle years of the first decade of the new century. As a consequence of the acceptance by the faculty of a "university plan" in 1903, during the following year Briggs was transferred once again, this time becoming graduate professor of theological encyclopedia and symbolics. In the 1905–6 catalog the new department was rather elaborately outlined. Intended primarily for graduate students, the plan detailed three curricular sections for encyclopedia, symbolics, and Christian institutions, though only a few courses were actually given.

The following year a number of other departments listed some courses under the graduate rubric, along with some of the Columbia and New York University offerings. Black, formally the other graduate professor, taught one of the courses in this new department, which was also given responsibility for guiding qualified students through a program leading to an earned Doctor of Divinity, though normally that is an honorary degree. The creation of the new department was resisted by some of the faculty and board members, and caused considerable tension, but Briggs got his way. Later a "graduate faculty" was created, and though it was unanimously approved by the faculty in 1909, six indicated some reservations to the plan because it seemed pretentious for a small faculty. There were no more designations as graduate professor. The plan was rescinded a few years after Briggs' death in 1913, though the offering of earned doctorates was continued. But even though the idea of a graduate faculty did not finally mature, Hall's plans for expansion along the academic line bore rich fruit in introducing new disciplines and enlarging the faculty; the full-time faculty increased from nine to fourteen during his years in office.

Cuthbert Hall's hopes for extension work among the laity were not significantly fulfilled, however, despite considerable effort. In 1901 Richard Morse Hodge, a graduate of both the college and seminary at Princeton, was appointed as instructor in biblical literature and methods of teaching for lay workers. He was assisted for two years by William D. Street, a graduate of Columbia and Union who served as instructor in English Bible for lay workers. A fairly ambitious schedule of courses of study in evening and Saturday hours was laid out, and some good work was done, but the program failed to grow. Hodge was reacting against his own very conservative background, and lacked the ability to present the findings of biblical scholarship to unprepared lay persons in a tactful way. The rigors of the president's schedule left him little time for the venture, and in 1907 it was given up. A new, more focused and effective effort launched in that same year was an annual conference for social workers, often billed as the "Lincoln's Birthday Conference" or "A Quiet Day for Social Workers." It lasted for some years under faculty leadership, often with distinguished outside speakers participating.

Hall's "line of social service" fared much better. What was then called "Christian Work" was reorganized as a department under a faculty committee: Hall, W. A. Brown, and Fagnani. Work for students was available in various settings: in churches and chapels, as pastors' assistants, with the City Mission Society, in settlements (especially Union Settlement), in public institutions, in regular and occasional preaching, and with choirs. Almost the entire student body became involved in this program. It was given strong leadership in 1901 when Gaylord S. White was named director of Student Christian Work, a position he was to hold for many years. After study at New York University, the College of New Jersey, and Union (1890), he served in several pastorates, and then was named head worker at Union Settlement, becoming its "most potent figure" as he held that post concurrently with his role at Union. "Under him the Union Settlement had become widely known for the excellence of its ministry to its neighborhood and for the delightful fellowship of its residents," Coffin wrote. "Mr. White was trusted and beloved by the social workers of New York City and served effectively as a connecting link between this rapidly developing profession and the Seminary."[13] His role was much appreciated by students as he supervised their work in various field settings.

That there was advance along the line of spiritual power—Hall's fourth objective—was in great measure because of his personal influence. In 1898 religious services at the seminary were made voluntary, including daily chapel at 8:30 A.M., four or five days a week. Hall's own leadership was important in the effectiveness of the transition. Harry Emerson Fosdick (1904), a student at Union in Hall's day, later spoke of "the impressive quality of his spiritual life, particularly when he was engaged in worship." When he conducted a service of worship, "he became translucent and the whole Chapel glowed with the radiance that shone through him."[14] Coffin, both student and faculty member during the Hall years, declared that "his love for worship was contagious and changed the climate of the Seminary."[15] "Cuthbertian" was a word students and colleagues applied to his high standards of excellence in worship.

The 8:30 hour for chapel continued for some seventy years in the life of the seminary, with members of the faculty heavily involved in conducting the services. Through those decades Dr. Briggs was only one of many to be troubled when chapel ran late. Starting a nine o'clock lecture promptly to a group of students who had skipped chapel, he was soon interrupted by those coming from a poorly timed service. When order was restored, he observed that he often had to protest against such excesses of devotion.[16] On the practical side, one of the first things Hall had done was to have the chapel refurbished and new chancel furniture installed.

As he sought to carry out his vision for the seminary along those four lines, Cuthbert Hall endeared himself to the student body. A four-story brick and brownstone house on East 70th Street adjoining the dormitory was fitted up for the president and his family, and a door was cut through so that there was ready access to the place where students lived and worked—and it was used as the president sought out students, or as they were invited into the home. He had the ability to give his whole attention to a person with whom he was talking. Fosdick remarked that he had never seen in any other the power of attention to individuals and care for them so amazingly developed. But Hall was also concerned about the quality of student life; in accepting the call to Union he had arranged for the renovation of the dormitory, the equipment of a social room, a rearrangement of parts of the library, and provision for evening hours. He wanted a refectory for the students, but location and resources were lacking; when the seminary finally got one twenty years after his death it was fitting that it should be named after him, and that his portrait—a good likeness, those who knew him have told us—hangs over the fireplace. Hall became the intimate friend of many students and was generally held in warm affection. It was hard for him to assess a person objectively, as Coffin observed, and he permitted some students to go on into the ministry when other avenues might have been better. Much in demand as a college preacher, where he attracted students to the seminary, he also instituted, in cooperation with other seminaries, an annual Conference for College Men on the Work of the Ministry. Usually held in the early spring, the conference circulated among the participating schools: Union, Andover, Yale, Hartford, and Episcopal Theological Seminary.

One of Hall's policies, however, tended to reduce sharply the enrollment of students in the three-year diploma and B.D. programs, which dropped from 137 in his first year of office to a low of 74 six years later. In his effort to raise academic standards and improve the quality of the ministry he instituted a policy of awarding scholarships on the basis of merit only, regardless of need. Total enrollment was kept up because the number of graduate students greatly increased, from 9 to 41 in those first six years. Toward the end of his years of service, however, he had the satisfaction of seeing the number of students in the three-year regular theological curriculum steadily rise again, to 123 in 1907–8, when total enrollment was 182, 25 more than it had ever been before.

The seminary moved in an increasingly liberal and nondenominational direction during the period of Cuthbert Hall's presidency. His own liberalism was more a matter of spirit and temper than of theology, which was evangelically centered. At a time when certain tendencies in American Protestantism were pressing toward polarization between liberal and conservative forces and obscuring the middle ground, he stood firm for freedom for scholarship and expression of variant opinions. Union increasingly became a model for the liberal way in theological education. His son called him "both a conservative and a liberal. His orthodoxy was strong but never intolerant." He was an irenic, reconciling figure, attached to many traditional forms of belief and worship, yet clearly devoted to personal freedom. Charles H. Brent, the Episcopal bishop who was the founder of the Faith and Order Movement, once said of him, "Like a bridge over a mountain torrent, he joined two precipices, and the stream of controversy passed beneath him."[17]

A significant broadening of denominational patterns occurred in those years. The student body, which had been interdenominational from the start, became more diversified until about twenty denominations were represented. In 1899 a Unitarian was accepted in the graduate class, the first time that a person not a member of an evangelical church was admitted, and seven years later the faculty voted that an "accredited" person might be admitted though not a member of any Christian church.[18] There were also some changes in the denominational affiliation of faculty members. Up to 1898, all the regular members of the faculty had been Presbyterians. In that year, after remaining for five years in the Presbyterian Church as a suspended minister, Briggs withdrew and was ordained a deacon, and in May of the following year a priest, of the Episcopal Church. There was uneasiness in the Board of Directors over this departure from tradition, but in a strongly worded letter to its president, John Crosby Brown, Hall urged that no action be taken:

I hope you can still agree with me that *nothing* must be done by our Board. I hope and pray that Dr. Briggs may now be allowed to rest in peace, . . . To haggle over this old question now, after all the strong men of the Episcopal Church have shown such splendid spirit would be to throw our Seminary into chaos, and I for one would have little heart to remain in connection with it.[19]

Another denominational change quickly followed. In 1897 McGiffert's *A History of Christianity in the Apostolic Age* was published. In the book critical historical methods were utilized in the study of New Testament passages. The next year the Presbytery of Pittsburgh made overtures to the General Assembly to take action against the author of the book, calling it a daring and thoroughgoing attack on the New Testament. The assembly replied that the church needed peace and brotherliness, and took no action, hoping that McGiffert could satisfactorily explain his position or withdraw. Characteristically, Hall stood firmly behind McGiffert, writing to one critic's charge that "I am in a position to know that no more devout believer in the Deity of Christ can be found than is Dr. McGiffert."[20] Agitation continued, however, and the 1899 assembly was faced with ten overtures on the matter. Applause greeted a letter from McGiffert to the assembly in which he stated that he believed his views "were in accord with the faith of the Presbyterian Church and evangelical Christendom in all vital and essential matters, and I, therefore, cannot feel that it is my duty, or even my right . . . to withdraw from the ministry of the Presbyterian Church."[21]

The assembly, however, referred the matter to the Presbytery of New York without instructions. A special committee met with McGiffert and reported to the presbytery, which proceeded to condemn parts of the book, but in view of his positive affirmations of faith found that a trial for heresy would do more harm than good. But the stated clerk of the presbytery—George W. F. Birch who had chaired the prosecution in the Briggs trial—filed heresy charges as a private prosecutor, and when the presbytery refused to act on them, he appealed to the General Assembly scheduled to meet in May 1900. It was fairly clear what the outcome would have been, and McGiffert in consultation with the directors decided he should withdraw from the Presbytery, and he promptly became a Congregationalist. Briggs was pleased with this decision, for he no longer stood alone on the faculty as a non-Presbyterian.

In 1904 the board took a decisive action, altering the vow professors and directors took when they entered office. Up to that point, they had to state that they had received and adopted the Westminster Confession of Faith in all its essential and necessary articles as containing the system of doctrine taught in Holy Scripture, and approved of the Presbyterian form of government. A much simpler form of affirmation was prepared, in which those taking office promised to maintain the principles and purposes of the institution as stated in the preamble to the constitution adopted by the founders. This was a logical result of the action of 1892 that removed any semblance of denominational control; it put the seminary on a clearly nondenominational, "ecumenical" basis. D. Willis James and other directors were very pleased with this move. It was then that, in memory of her late husband, Mrs. William E. Dodge endowed a chair in Applied Christianity to prepare students to render practical service to the world, especially to the poor and alienated, and Morris K. Jesup endowed the graduate professorship of preaching that Hugh Black was soon to fill. By this time Union had two professors who were not Presbyterians, though they had been when they had come to the school, but now the seminary was free to reach out across the denominational spectrum in calling professors, as was done when William W. Rockwell, a Congregationalist, came in 1905.

The action of 1904 also brought about a change in the way courses in denominational polity were taught. In 1903–4 Cuthbert Hall taught for the last time a polity course aimed at preparing Presbyterian, Congregational, Methodist, and Baptist students in the practical requirements for entering upon their ministries. By 1906–7 the transition had been made to polity courses focused on single denominations well represented in the student body and taught by someone of that communion, a professor or a part-time lecturer. Thus Knox took over Presbyterian polity, Briggs Episcopal, McGiffert Congregational, and Dr. Edward Judson, pastor of Memorial Church, Baptist.

This did not mean that Union lost its interest in Presbyterianism, however. In his irenic way, throughout his presidency Hall worked at improving relations with Presbyterian congregations and judicatories, as far as that was possible in view of all that had happened. Active in the affairs of his communion, he was able to foster more accurate and favorable attitudes toward Union than many had held after the years of controversy. In May 1900, for example, he attended the General Assembly at St. Louis as chair of the Standing Committee on Foreign Missions, where his address was received with hearty applause. On the next day he preached at the First Congregational Church on "The Person of Christ" with many commissioners in attendance. Such occasions—he traveled widely, speaking and preaching often during his busy years at the seminary—helped significantly to improve Union's public image, not only within Presbyterianism, but across the Protestant world. He also became a Christian ambassador in addressing missionaries and interpreting the faith to those of other religions, especially through the Barrows Lectures in Asia on two occasions.

Taking a leave of absence from his duties at Union in the early spring of 1902, as Francis Brown became acting president, Hall carried out his final preparations for the demanding Barrows series at the Bodleian Library in Oxford, where he widened his acquaintance with the philosophy of Hinduism and Buddhism and with the mood of the Orient, and deepened his knowledge of the Christian missionary enterprise. The lectures, delivered in what was then Ceylon, at five university cities in India, and in four cities in Japan, with selections from the series along with various addresses at other locations, were published in 1903 as *Christian Belief Interpreted as Christian Experience*. Though leaving no doubt as to his own quite conservative Christian position, he did give serious and respectful attention to other views, and while some thought he conceded too much to Hinduism, others believed that he did more than any before him to bridge the gulf between East and West. He arrived back in North America in April of 1903, but the experience was not really over until he had reported on the lectures in various ways, especially in seven addresses at the University of Chicago, the sponsoring institution, in October.

Union's president created such an impression that Chicago sought him again for a second set of lectures. At first there was considerable resistance to this at the seminary, but the board's president, John Crosby Brown, was won over, asking Hall, "Is not God leading the Seminary and yourself in ways not of our own but of His wise guidance?" D. Willis James, board vice president, regretted that the president of the faculty would be away again, but concluded, "The opportunity and the Call are so unique, the marvellous openings and changes in the Orient for the extension of Christ's Kingdom so providential, the leading of Providence pointing you as the man fitted for the work so marked, that I for one cannot do otherwise than vote most heartily to have you accept and discharge again this Duty, as best you can, God using you as His instrument to do, as I believe, the largest work to be given to anyone to do in the opening of the Twentieth Century." So, as George Knox assumed the acting presidency this time, in the early spring of 1906 Hall was back again at the Bodleian, preparing the lectures that were to be published in final form in 1909 as *Christ and the Eastern Soul: The Witness of the Oriental Consciousness to Jesus Christ.* Again he lectured at many places in Ceylon and India and drew huge crowds; once more, some felt that he was too irenic in his effort to understand non-Christian religions. On the whole his work was much appreciated; the principal of a college wrote,

I have been nineteen years in Calcutta and never in that time has Christianity been so winningly set forth for educated Hindus. You preached Christ and Him crucified with all courage and faithfulness. At the same time you praised in generous terms all that is greatest in Eastern thought.

Unfortunately, Hall contracted some obscure infection that was never fully identified, and it began to undermine his health. On the way home he lectured during a short stay in Manila and then more extensively again in Japan, where introductions from President Theodore Roosevelt, with whom he was well acquainted, opened doors to conferences with the prime minister and other leading officials. He preached in the pulpits of young Japanese ministers who had been educated at Union, and delivered some of the lectures he had so carefully prepared, with suitable changes for the different situation. But his work was brought to a halt by the serious illness, diagnosed as a form of influenza, and it was a weary man who got back to the seminary in time to take part in the commencement activities of 1907.[22]

In the fall he plunged into his seminary duties again, but by the turn of the year had to stop, and died in March in his 56th year.

By the time of his death, Hall had already played an important part in preparing for the move of the seminary from Lenox Hill to Morningside Heights. Though at the dedication of the fine new buildings on Park Avenue in 1884 Roswell Hitchcock had exclaimed that "the present location is apparently for many decades if not for all time," in fact within a decade the change in educational patterns from a prescribed curriculum to one with electives and with a larger body of graduate students rendered a plant with four classrooms inadequate. Space for the many new courses and seminars became urgently needed. The library grew overcrowded once again as many more books were needed for the broadened curriculum and the new research interests evoked by the introduction of degrees, theses, and graduate work. The dormitory was overflowing, and the growing faculty needed more suitable working and meeting space. From Oxford in June 1898 McGiffert wrote to Hall stating his conviction that the theological work Union was doing was superior to what was going on there, but regretting the lack of a social life at Union "which can be had only if the professors reside near together in the neighborhood of the Seminary and have a 'common room' where the life of the institution can centre. I hope sometime this ideal may be realized either where we now are or in some better location."[23] The expansion of the seminary that had marked the 1890s was by the turn of the century already being checked because of limitations of space. The board discussed ways the seminary could expand "along university lines," and Morningside Heights, to which Columbia had moved in 1897 as it became a university, and where courses were open to qualified seminary students, was found to be the most desirable place. The new subway line would soon link it with the rest of the city.

When Hall asked a potential donor for a large gift for new seminary buildings, he did not know that the person was ready to give generously once all denominational ties had been severed, but had not wanted to condition his gift on that action. Once that step had been taken, early in 1905, the donor—who requested that his name be kept confidential—offered a gift of $1 million for the new site and buildings. At the same time the giver, later known to

be board vice president D. Willis James, an English-born philan-
thropist who had grown wealthy as a metal importer and manufacturer, quietly procured options on thirty-six lots forming the two city
blocks from 120th to 122d Streets between Broadway and Claremont
Avenue, adjacent to Columbia. He offered to sell the site to the seminary. That purchase absorbed 85 percent of his original donation,
but other gifts for buildings were received; James himself added an
additional $300,000, and it was agreed that the proceeds from the
sale of the Park Avenue buildings would go to increase endowments
of established chairs and to found new ones.

Board president John Crosby Brown headed the building
committee, which set resolutely to work, utilizing many concrete
suggestions provided by Hall and the faculty. The new buildings were
to have at least six seminar rooms, adequate offices for faculty and
administration, a dormitory suitable for two hundred students, a president's house, a much larger library with a reading room twice as
large as the one being left, and a chapel also doubled in size. The
architectural firm of Allen and Collens was selected to draw up plans.
James did not live to see the results of his generosity, as he died in
1907, having served on the board for forty years. Mrs. James offered
$300,000 for the chapel in her husband's memory, and then added
$200,000 for an apartment house for the faculty, later named Knox
Hall in memory of the departed professor.[24] When the cornerstone
for what became the seminary quadrangle was laid on November 17,
1908, Charles Cuthbert Hall had also died, and as it turned out the
auspicious occasion of setting the cornerstone was to be the last day
John Crosby Brown appeared in public. As the stone was put in place,
he said, "Sharing with the Founders the belief that for all enduring
religious work 'other foundations can no man lay than that is laid,
which is Jesus Christ,' the Directors set apart this Stone as the symbol
of the spiritual foundation upon which this Seminary rests."[25]

That night at the Madison Avenue Presbyterian Church
in the context of a service of inauguration, the board's president made
the formal statement of the unanimous election of Francis Brown as
the new president of the faculty to succeed Charles Cuthbert Hall.
Within a few months John Crosby Brown too was gone from earth;
thus none of the three leaders who had been so instrumental in ar-
ranging for the spacious new buildings for the expanded educational

The new buildings arise on Morningside Heights.

program of the seminary lived to see the fulfillment of that for which they had hoped and worked. But other competent hands took up the responsibilities, anticipating a promising but challenging future for the school as it moved across town from Park and 70th to Broadway and 120th Street. Board member Charles H. Parkhurst stressed the intellectual challenges in his charge to the president-elect:

> The era is a critical one and not easily dealt with. The church is having to recede from certain positions which it had previously treated and advertised as essential; the natural result is a disturbance of the confidence of those whose concurrence the pulpit is anxious to secure and to hold. The church has known too many things that were not so.[26]

As it prepared for its move to a new location under new leadership, Union shared in the predominantly optimistic spirit of its time, confident it could deal with the intellectual and other challenges it would soon be facing from Morningside Heights. The years since 1893 had seen a significant transition and expansion in the seminary's life and outreach, thrusting it on a larger stage immediately adjacent to the campus of a growing university.

CHAPTER SIX

A Shift of Emphasis:
The Scholarly Dimensions
of Theological Education
(1908–1926)

With the laying of the cornerstone on November 17, 1908, affairs at the seminary were directed toward preparing for the future in a new setting next to Columbia University on Morningside Heights. Ever since the somewhat grandiose idea of a seminary serving as a theological university had become current in the latter part of the nineteenth century, it had attracted attention at Union. Briggs especially believed that the time had come to develop that idea more fully. An important component in the concept was attention to high scholarly standards, strongly emphasized by the two presidents of the seminary in the nearly two decades covered by this chapter, Francis Brown and Arthur Cushman McGiffert. Both had been students and colleagues of Briggs, had undertaken graduate study abroad, and had earned doctorates. Both had devoted their lives to theological education and had not had pastoral experience though they were ordained church leaders. Both were renowned for their teaching skills and their scholarly productivity. They were deeply rooted in the traditions of the seminary and were concerned with the preparation of ministers, but they also were devoted to the molding of theological scholars. Under their leadership the seminary did not significantly change direction as it moved to its spacious new buildings, but there was a shift of emphasis toward the scholarly aspects of theological education.

On the very evening that the cornerstone was laid Francis Brown was inaugurated as the new president of the faculty. His life had been devoted to biblical scholarship; indeed, he was serving as director of the American School for Oriental Research in Jerusalem when he was elected, and his colleague Knox had once again been pressed into service in the interim. Brown was a large and impressive man of great dignity, a shy and reserved person not comfortable with small talk. Coffin observed that "he carried an atmosphere with him which suggested the majesty of the Divine Presence"; small wonder that his nickname among the students was "Yahweh." Another colleague who knew him well wrote critically of the portrait of him that hangs over the fireplace in the social hall that is named after him, a painting that portrays him wearing a red Oxford gown. Gillett complained that he never wore that gown in public, and that in the portrait its expanse dwarfs his massive head, and its blaze of color causes his face to lose its true look.[1] Though Brown wrote various articles and books on Old Testament subjects, his crowning scholarly achievement was the preparation of A *Hebrew and English Lexicon of the Old Testament* in cooperation with Briggs and S. R. Driver of Oxford. Published originally between 1891 and 1906, it has gone through a number of editions and remains a standard work.

Brown was a scholar through and through, and his ideal for theological education was celebrated in his inaugural address, "Theology as the Servant of Religion." He emphasized the priority of religion, and the seminary as an institution of religion, "founded by religious men, with a religious purpose," drawing its standard and inspiration from Jesus Christ. But the seminary is more than that—it is "an institution of theological knowledge and our specific function is the application of theology to religion." For Brown, that function involved high and exacting academic standards:

We contemplate, not something less than a full, scientific study of theology but something more. All the mass of scientific detail, all the rigour of scientific method, all the thoroughness of scientific induction, all the insis-

Francis Brown, biblical scholar, Union's seventh president.

tence upon facts and the unwearying search for all the facts, and the refusal
to go beyond the facts, with which the laboratory has made us familiar,
belong in our study of theological truth. There is no easy road to that truth.
. . . It is an exacting pursuit. All who engage in it, seriously, must share
in its processes, as well as its results. . . . It is only through this earnest
rigour of the process that theology can fulfil its service to religion.

The emphasis on the laboratory provides a clear illustration on the
way the prestige of the scientific approach was then influencing theological education.

Brown's scholarly ideal for Union was indeed a demanding one which pointed to departmentalization in academic life; he
was prepared to go "to the verge of the permissible in encouraging
specialization," both in preparation for specific lines of religious and
theological work and for the ministry at large, insofar as the latter "is
consistent with the design of preparing broadly for the ministry, with
its demands on knowledge and on capacity."[2] Thus on that same
November day in 1908 that a cornerstone for spacious new buildings
was laid, a plan for an academic program emphasizing the scholarly
dimensions of theological education had been unveiled by the new
president.

The remaining year and a half at Lenox Hill was a time
of preparation. The annual seminary catalog for the academic year
1909–10, for example, was revised and lengthened. Though many
further changes were to be made through the years, the basic format
which was then chosen remained influential in catalog style for some
six decades and more. Far more formidable was the task of preparing
the rapidly growing library for its new location. Existing classification
systems were not fully adequate for the increasing volume of both
general and specialized theological books, pamphlets, and periodicals, and a new scheme needed to be developed. The library then
contained about 97,000 volumes, 55,000 pamphlets, and received
some 125 periodicals. Professor William Rockwell was named acting
librarian in 1908, a position he would hold for five years. Julia Pettee
was brought to Union the next year to reclassify the library. She had
previously been involved in the reorganization of the library of the
Rochester Theological Seminary, and was to remain at Union for
fifteen years as chief cataloguer, developing and testing the classification plan for Union's collection. It was widely adopted for use in

other seminaries as well; her labors also were influential in the development of the Library of Congress subject headings for religious and theological works.[3] Her creative work marked a significant advance in theological librarianship.

A major appointment made in 1909 proved to be a preparatory step for an important innovation in Union's educational program as soon as it moved into its new location. Theological educators in the early twentieth century, especially those influenced by liberal theological currents, were taking a new interest in the study and practice of religious education. Influenced by fresh understandings of the learning process stemming from the work of psychologists and such progressive educational leaders as John Dewey, new departments of religious education were being formed in seminaries, usually located within the field of practical theology. In the optimistic opening years of the new century, religious education promised a way of democratizing congregational and denominational practices. It was hoped that the reform might begin with the Sunday school and then be extended to other aspects of church life. This liberal, tolerant, crusading approach to reform was advanced by the formation in 1903 of the Religious Education Association. The vision and determination of William Rainey Harper, president of the University of Chicago, precipitated this organization of persons involved in various aspects of church education, especially within Protestantism. The call to the founding meeting of the R.E.A. was signed by some two hundred educational leaders, including Francis Brown, Charles C. Hall, and Thomas C. Hall of Union.

When the seminary made its first full-time appointment in this increasingly popular area of theological studies in 1909, it chose the leading figure in the field, George A. Coe. Elected president of the Religious Education Association in that same year, he has been called by the association's historian its "most significant intellectual mentor" in its early decades.[4] A graduate of the School of Theology of Boston University and a holder of its Ph.D., Coe had taught at Northwestern for more than fifteen years before coming to Union. Author of such books as *Religious Experience and the Scientific Movement* (1897) and *The Religion of A Mature Mind* (1902), Coe was in the forefront of a movement which was to play an important role in twentieth-century theological education. At Union he was to build a conspicuous department of Religious Education and Psychology, offering a broad array of courses in the psychology of religion as well as in education. The first faculty representative of the Methodist tradition, he also taught what was then a quarter (one hour) course on "Methodist Principles and Polity."

Union moved to its new campus soon after the 1910 commencement. The buildings were an excellent expression of Collegiate or English Perpendicular Gothic, one of the earliest American campuses designed in this style. Constructed of native random ashlar flatrock taken directly from the site, with window tracery and finish trim of Indiana ashlar limestone, the buildings—administration, library, president's house, dormitory, and apartment house for faculty families (the latter were later named Hastings and Knox halls)—formed an open quadrangle covering two city blocks. The apartment house made it possible for the majority of the faculty to live on campus. At the faculty's urging, the apartment floor plans were reversed so that the living rooms faced the quadrangle rather than 122d Street, and it was rumored that Mrs. Briggs' refusal to live in a "flat" was responsible for the three two-level apartments at the west end of the dwelling. Photographs taken in 1910 display the present buildings when they were brand new and unweathered, without the tower at Broadway and 120th Street. James Chapel (twice the size of the previous one) was separated from the president's house to the south and the apartment house to the north, for the refectory and Dickinson Hall were not added until later. Compared with the Park Avenue campus, the buildings, five to seven stories high, were massive.

The seminary once again had space for expansion for its growing faculty and student body, for the great library, and for the elective system with its hunger for class and seminar rooms. The stimulus of the Columbia University and Teachers College was now just across Broadway. The new facilities were completed by a small gymnasium across Claremont Avenue from the president's house on rented land. Like so much of the new campus, it was a gift of D. Willis James.

A spirit of celebration was in the air at the time of the formal dedication of the new buildings on November 28–29, 1910— a time also chosen to recognize the seminary's 75th anniversary, which normally would have come the following May. In an address to the

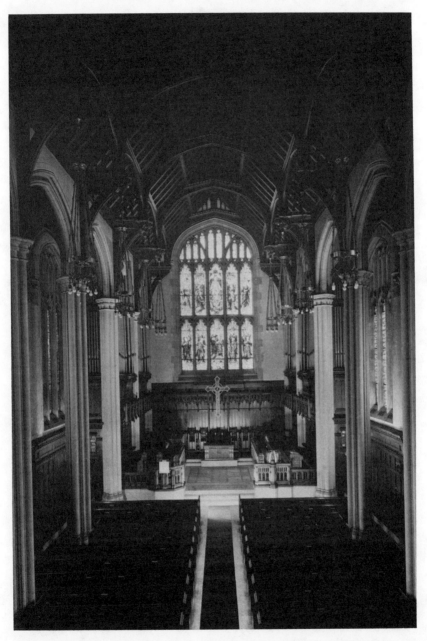

The new quadrangle's place of worship: James Memorial Chapel.

student body, William Adams Brown paid special tribute to the late President Hall, saying that "as we survey these spacious buildings and study their refined decoration and graceful form, they seem to be the incarnation in stone of that exquisite personality, himself the expression in human life of the spirit of religion pure and undefiled." When Francis Brown addressed the alumni on "The Seminary's New Era," he reflected the optimism of the time: "It is an era for the imagination. Great pictures of the future take shape." The Address of Presentation was given by Robert Curtis Ogden, a prominent merchant, retired member of the firm of John Wanamaker, generous supporter of causes important to black people, and successor of John Crosby Brown as president of the board. He observed that "now the entire personnel of the Seminary, Students, Professors, President of the Faculty, and Executive Staff are comfortably installed in commodious, elegant and practically completed quarters and have fully entered upon the practical work of the seventy-fifth academic year of the Seminary."

The major address was appropriately given by the senior professor, Charles A. Briggs. He had been a student in the original building, had taught in all three, and had known personally several of the founders and "most of its directors, professors and benefactors." He rejoiced that the original ideals of the founders, including freedom from ecclesiastical domination, had been vindicated as the seminary "fought a hard but victorious fight against it." Referring very compactly to some painful events of the institution's history, he declared:

> The Seminary has not escaped from conflict. It has been obliged to defend itself against wanton attacks, and its professors have been forced into ecclesiastical conflicts of more or less severity, from the foundation of the Seminary to the present time. But such conflicts have not in the least turned the Seminary from its great ideals of moderation, peace and unity.

He praised the directors for standing by the faculty "for the rights of Christian scholarship and for the free untrammeled search for the Truth." He stressed once again that the university and the seminary needed each other, and rejoiced in their proximity.

Briggs also highlighted the importance of Union's independence in order to fulfill one of its aims, the development of vital piety, because "the study of theology in the university tends to become merely intellectual and scholastic." The seminary, however, could adopt university standards and approaches, for "in Union Seminary at least, the field of theology is as completely covered as in any university of Europe; and every method of instruction used whether in Germany, France, Great Britain or America, is employed by one or more of our professors." His was another effort to state the importance for the seminary of the close relationship of piety and knowledge at a time when there was growing attention to the latter, but tension between them was to increase in the early years at the new location. At the conclusion of his lengthy address (during which a representative of an ancient Scottish university dozed off and slipped from his seat in the chancel), he stressed Union's irenic role, for it "claims to be something better than undenominational or interdenominational, namely as the late statesman Bishop, Henry Codman Potter, delighted in saying, 'superdenominational.' "

The festivities were closed with a banquet at the Waldorf Astoria, and the note of celebration reached a high note (which perhaps included some understandable overstatement) with such comments as those by Bishop David H. Greer of the Diocese of New York and President James G. McClure of McCormick Seminary. The former said, "If I interpret aright Union Seminary, it is a great theological university and not simply another theological school," and the latter observed that the material plant was "the most stately and dignified of any institution of the kind in the world."[5]

Expectations that the student body would increase were quickly met, as the first year on the new campus saw the numbers grow from 164 to 193, most of them in the regular three-year theological program. The next year there were 260 students, the increase resulting from a few more regular students, a dozen more graduate students (to 45), and 41 in a new category of "students on recommendation from other institutions"—especially Columbia University and Teachers College, but also including some from New York University and General Theological Seminary. These folk were taking the bulk of their work at Union and often lived in the dormitory. In addition there were many part-time special students taking a course or two, so that in 1915 it was reported to the board that some 1100 persons were under Union's influence—nearly four times the formal enrollment.[6] While the number of full-time women theological students remained small, many more women were part of that larger number of students from other institutions.

Some seminary students also found it convenient to enroll in Columbia courses, many of which continued to be listed in Union's catalog until 1917. Union also cooperated in various ways with Columbia's summer course program—an arrangement which continued for nearly sixty years. In President Brown's last year (1915–16) the enrollment reached a new total of 273. Because of the increased number of students, the post of dean of students was created in 1913, and Charles Gillett filled it for some fifteen years, in addition to his continuing work as registrar and as secretary of the faculty and of the alumni. Students were not yet charged for tuition or room, but a fee of $40 was assessed for heat, light, and the care of a dormitory room.

The change of location to Morningside Heights did not diminish the appeal of the social gospel among students and their mentors. Coffin observed that the publication of Rauschenbusch's *Christianity and the Social Crisis* (1907) came "like a gust of fresh air blowing into a stuffy room," sweeping much student interest from comparative religion and "the minutiae of Biblical criticism" to the "salvation of society." This concern continued as a dominant interest for the next three decades. The coming of George Coe, a popular teacher, served to advance this interest further, for "his psychological teaching further stressed the social interpretation of the Christian message."[7] Many students continued to work in social settlements and institutional churches, where they saw first hand the human effects of low wages and of crowded slum tenements. Abraham J. Muste, for example, who graduated in 1913 and later became prominent in labor and pacifist movements, found that the Old Testament prophets "really [came] alive for me at Union" as he began to see them as "fellows who preached politics, got into the actual struggle and cursed those who were grinding the faces of the poor." He also found that William Adams Brown was helping to make the prophetic tradition relevant to contemporary times as he oversaw the work of two pioneering efforts to address the needs of people living in slum poverty, the American Parish in East Harlem and the Labor Temple at Second Avenue and East 14th Street.[8]

There were no extensive changes in the faculty in this period; many of those appointed in earlier administrations had been at the beginning of long and fruitful careers, and carried on their work in the new surroundings. But not all—when the beloved George William Knox died while abroad in Seoul in 1912, Robert Ernest Hume was named to succeed him as Marcellus Hartley professor of the philosophy and history of religion, and missions. A graduate of Yale who earned his Ph.D. there in 1901, Hume then took a B.D. at Union (1904), was ordained a Congregationalist minister, and served as a missionary teacher and editor for seven years. After four years in the Hartley chair he was transferred to the Charles Butler chair of the history of religions, the field in which he made his reputation, and in which he was to serve until his retirement in 1944.

Charles Briggs died on June 8, 1913, still active in his 72d year. Since becoming graduate professor in 1904, his teaching had been primarily in the areas of theological encyclopedia, symbolics, and irenics. His interests had focused heavily in the latter area; in 1909 he produced a major volume in the field, *Church Unity: Studies of Its Most Important Problems*. He cherished hopes for closer ties between Protestants and Catholics, and had even discussed the matter in an audience with Pope Pius X in 1905. In a letter to a Catholic prelate, he wrote "I had consecrated the remainder of my life to the Reunion of Christendom." He was disappointed when the suppression of Catholic Modernism closed doors instead of opening them.[9] His labors contributed to the heightening of ecumenical enthusiasm at Union; a number of Union students of those early years at Morningside Heights went on to distinguished careers in cooperative and conciliar Christianity, among them Hermann N. Morse (1911), F. Ernest Johnson (1912), Samuel McCrea Cavert (1915), Hugh Chamberlain Burr (1915), and Henry Smith Leiper (1917). Union's commitment to the cause of Christian unity grew steadily stronger in this and later periods as the seminary identified itself with many ecumenical causes.

Briggs' own basic theological conservatism had kept him from moving toward some of the conclusions of the advancing liberal theology of that period. His high Christology was reflected in his acceptance of the historicity of the infancy stories of Matthew and Luke and of the historical reliability of the passages about the virgin birth. It took all of President Brown's tact to restrain Briggs when some of his younger colleagues began to draw theological conclusions he did not find congenial. Briggs and McGiffert disagreed on many questions of New Testament interpretation, and some hostility developed between them. The senior professor was about to complain to the Board of Directors about his colleague's teaching when the president pointed out that it would be unfortunate if the one whom the seminary had supported when he was under attack should now become an attacker of a colleague and former student. Happily, Brown prevailed, and Briggs' brilliant, productive, controversial career was not marred by what might have been an unpleasant incident.

William Adams Brown's comment on the famous biblical scholar in his historical address at the seminary's 100th anniversary provides an informative summary of the scholar's later years at Union:

How well we remember the insatiable zeal with which when he had mastered one field of learning he turned to others—symbolics, irenics, canon law. To his imperialistic mind the Seminary was more than a training school for the ministry. It was to be a Christian university in which all branches of theological learning should find a place and scholars from every part of Christendom flock to study under its graduate faculty. Even the Pope of Rome was not exempt from Dr. Briggs' paternal care, and some of us can remember his mingled sense of surprise and disappointment when after an interview in which he had explained to the Holy Father the proper way to secure the reunion of Christendom he found that well-meaning but misguided man still unconvinced. We may smile at his faith in the power of scholarship to bring healing to the world; but something he gave us that we would not willingly let go.[10]

Though Briggs' hopes for a discrete graduate faculty never fully matured and the plan was later dropped, many graduate students had been drawn to the seminary. The Charles A. Briggs professorship in Christian institutions was founded in part to carry on the increased graduate program. It was filled in 1916 by a distinguished English scholar of the New Testament and early church history, Frederick John Foakes Jackson, formerly dean of Jesus College, Cambridge. A prolific author, this prominent Anglican, who was 61 at his coming, taught at Union for seventeen years. His courses were in such areas as worship, sacraments, creeds, councils, and the English prayer book.

Most of the additions to the faculty in the Brown years were in practical theology, where a strong emphasis was placed on raising the scholarly standards of the courses. The teaching of homiletics became widely recognized as unrivaled anywhere when the work already being done by Hugh Black and Henry Coffin was furthered by two notable appointments. Born in Scotland and educated in Edinburgh, George Alexander Johnston Ross had served pulpits in his native country, in England, and in the United States. He was teaching at the Presbyterian theological college in Montreal when he accepted the call as Brown professor of homiletics in 1912. A man with an original mind and great skill in coining apt and memorable phrases, he was described by one of his students as "the most thrilling lecturer and the one through whom we came closest to the heart of the Gospel."[11]

Three years after Ross' coming another preacher of growing fame was installed in the newly created Morris K. Jesup professorship of practical theology, with responsibilities in homiletics and English Bible. Harry Emerson Fosdick was already a familiar figure at Union, for after Colgate and a year at Hamilton Theological Seminary he had graduated from Union in 1904, had taught the course in Baptist principles and polity, and in 1911 also became instructor and then associate professor of homiletics, in addition to his main post as pastor of the First Baptist Church of Montclair, New Jersey. In 1915 he assumed the new chair and moved to the quadrangle. He was already well known through his preaching on the college circuit and the publication of such widely read books as *The Manhood of the Master* and *The Meaning of Prayer*. Soon to become the foremost preacher in America, he was known at the seminary as an inspiring teacher of preaching who exemplified the art in his Friday chapel services. His lectures on the modern use of the Bible were so popular that eventually tickets had to be issued as the largest classroom was filled to overflowing. He was a highly disciplined, industrious man, much in demand as speaker and writer; students and colleagues came to know his warmth of personality as they worked with him. As his biographer has made clear, his remarkable career had many facets, a number of which were especially significant for Union's life during his long association with the school.[12] His main role at Union, however, was the teaching of homiletics. He and Coffin often taught courses on sermon outlines, sometimes jointly. Students used to report that Fosdick had a tendency to remake outlines that pointed toward his style of preaching, while Coffin was good at getting the students to shape their own ideas in a better way. Not only the professional homileticians but some other members of the faculty were also fine preachers, and when the seminary moved to Morningside Heights the Sunday chapel services, rescheduled from the afternoon to 11:00 A.M., drew a considerable following.

The new department of religious education and psychology grew rapidly in its new setting. At the turn of the century there was no Protestant church on Morningside Heights, although Sunday School at Teachers College operated from 1903 to 1910. With Union's coming, it was replaced by the Union School of Religion (USR), a graded Sunday program designed as a demonstration and experimental school under the new department. While Sunday school teachers were normally not paid, in the new USR they were; through its nearly twenty years of existence many seminary students were involved in its work, and some earned academic credit for their laboratory experience. Riding the wave of the growing popularity of the religious education movement—one especially favored by theological liberals with their experimental and empirical methods and their emphasis on the nurturing of religious experience—the department soon added an additional faculty member to work with Coe. Hugh Hartshorne, an Amherst graduate who had earned his M.A. and B.D. degrees at Yale, became the principal of the Union School of Religion in 1912 while he was a resident graduate student at Union working toward a Ph.D. at Teachers College. Completing the degree the next year, he was named an instructor in religious education at the seminary, and was soon promoted to assistant professor. The USR flourished under his leadership; by 1915 there were 195 pupils, and 22 officers and teachers. With such trained specialists in education as Coe and Hartshorne guiding the department, the scholarly side of practical theology was much emphasized.[13] As vocational opportunities for women in the field of religious education increased in the churches, growing numbers of them took advantage of Union's course offerings and teaching opportunities in the USR to prepare themselves for future service.

Another major addition to the curriculum began in 1914 with the formation of a department of foreign service. Looking back to the period before World War I, Gaius Glenn Atkins once remarked,

> The first fifteen years of the twentieth century may sometime be remembered in America as the Age of Crusades. There were a superabundance of zeal, a sufficiency of good causes, unusual moral idealism, excessive confidence in mass movements and leaders with rare gifts of popular appeal. . . . The air was full of banners, and the trumpets called from every camp.[14]

One of the crusades that was especially attractive to American Protestants in those years was that of foreign missions. It is difficult now for many to recapture the excitement, the intense dedication, and the romantic overtones that accompanied the missionary movement in the nineteenth and early twentieth centuries. There was genuine hope that Christianity would peacefully conquer the world. One scholar who studied missions in China has written that "missionary fervor reached a high water mark during the imperial years after 1890 and the first two decades of the twentieth century."[15] The cause was one which could be supported by both conservative and liberal evangelicals, the one stressing more the salvation of souls and the other the Christianization of civilizations, but both affirming the importance of missions. The crusading spirit of the Student Volunteer Movement (1888) and the Layman's Missionary Movement (1906) were influential in guiding the footsteps of numerous young persons into seminary life. Many Union graduates through the years had become missionaries, and one, Horace Pitkin, had become a martyr for the cause. In 1913 another young alumnus was lost in missionary service abroad: Charles H. Holbrook (1910) was killed in Turkey, the victim of a case of mistaken identification in a troubled land.

Though Prentiss, C. C. Hall, Knox, and Hume had done some teaching in the field of missions, there had not been much curricular emphasis on this aspect of ministry. This all changed with the appointment of Daniel J. Fleming as organizing director of the Department of Foreign Service in 1914. He had studied at Union while earning a Columbia M.A. in 1903, served as a missionary teacher in India for eight years, and completed a doctorate at the University of Chicago the same year he joined the Union faculty. Soon the catalog reflected the rapid growth of the new department, as Fleming, Hume, White, McGiffert, and various lecturers offered relevant courses, and as many Columbia courses germane to an understanding of "mission fields" were listed in Union's catalog. An intense, outgoing man, Fleming was a prolific author on themes related to missions, with a great interest in the aesthetic side of Christian faith. Four years after his arrival at Union he became the first professor to focus wholly on missions, serving in this position until his retirement in 1944.

One of the trials of Francis Brown's presidency was a renewal of the attack on the seminary by ultra-conservative Presbyterian leaders. The spirit of what later came to be called Fundamentalism was evident in the adoption by the General Assembly (U.S.A.) of a five-point doctrinal deliverance in 1910, which declared that five doctrines are "essential" for the preservation of faith: the inerrancy of Scripture, the virgin birth, the substitutionary atonement, the physical resurrection, and the miracles as a demonstration of Christ's power and love. The growing strength of the ultra-conservative spirit across Protestantism was further evident in the publication and wide circulation of twelve little books, *The Fundamentals*, between 1910 and 1915. It was in this atmosphere that a well-intentioned effort on the part of certain ministers and lay members of Presbyterian churches was successful in securing the adoption of a loosely and somewhat inaccurately drawn resolution by the General Assembly in 1911. It declared that in the faculty and directorate of Union there were those in accord with evangelical Christianity as expressed in Presbyterian standards and authorized the appointment of a committee to seek the reestablishment of relations between seminary and assembly.

The effort backfired as conservatives determined that no such thing would happen. The atmosphere at the 1913 meeting of the assembly in Atlanta recalled that of the years of the Briggs trials. William Adams Brown came under bitter attack. He was called a "Hindu Pantheist" who denied the personality of God—and then a parliamentary move by the leader of the opposition to Union, Mark A. Matthews, deprived him of a chance to say a single word in his own defense. The next day Francis Brown addressed the assembly on behalf of the seminary and his colleague. As the latter remembered it,

we were spectators of the most remarkable triumph of character and ability over a hostile audience which it has ever been my privilege to witness. By the sheer weight of his arguments, his fairness and consideration for his opponents—the evidence, all the more impressive because indirect, of a deep religious faith—he won over may who had come to condemn and laid the foundation for the ultimate solution of what, at that time, seemed an insoluble problem.[16]

But that solution was delayed, for that afternoon Mark Matthews took the offensive. A very tall, formidable man, often called "the lone pine of the Sierras," he had been educated in the law and entered the ministry from service as a lay evangelist in the South, later rising to great prominence as the minister of the First Presbyterian Church of Seattle, which during his long pastorate grew from approximately 400 to 9000 members.[17] He was successful in moving that the committee on conference be dismissed and be replaced by one to make a thorough investigation of all the legal, ecclesiastical, and doctrinal questions involved in the relations between the assembly and Union. In accordance with custom he chaired the new committee.

The committee of seven visited the seminary. Its subcommittee on legal questions, composed of three elders who were distinguished corporation lawyers, was able to have the committee include in its final report a statement—not very palatable to its chairman—that "the compact of 1870 is legally unenforceable, and the action of the Directors of the Union Theological Seminary in returning to the Charter method of selection of the professors, was, in the opinion of Committee, in conformity with their legal duty."[18] Thus the General Assembly finally accepted the seminary's position on that controversial matter. It was further stated that by its subsequent actions Union had ceased to be theologically a Presbyterian institution. Hence it was not possible for it to return to the situation before 1892, especially since the 1904 statement to be made by incoming directors and professors had been greatly simplified with no reference to the Westminster Confession.

Matthews made one more effort, however, at the 1915 assembly in Rochester, New York. He undertook to show, despite his committee's action, that the funds for the seminary had come from the Presbyterian Church and that the action of the directors was a violation of trust. The usually shy President Brown, who found public speaking an ordeal, was thoroughly aroused. Taking the podium, he said bluntly that what Matthews had said was not true, and that he knew that it was not, for he had been shown the sources of Union's funds, and knew that their donors were thoroughly in accord with Union's charter and approved the institution's independence. Matthews, for once, ventured no reply to this cogent and forceful speech. The assembly was satisfied that Union students who were Presbyterian were properly prepared in Presbyterian doctrine and polity. Students of the seminary could still be harassed by opponents as they went through the presbytery processes of licensing and ordination, but with the air thus cleared, Union graduates continued to pour into Presbyterian congregations and institutions.

After the excitement of the Rochester assembly, the directors issued a clarifying statement of the principles followed in chosing professors. First, they sought those "of simple and humble faith" who "take Christ as their master and seek to know and to do God's will as revealed in him." Then, they wanted "men of scholarship and love of truth, who employ scientific methods of study, because they are the methods of truth, and have no fear that truth will vindicate itself to the sincere mind." Finally, their quest was for those "of personal power, who can teach with enthusiasm, and whose influence will be felt on students and community."[19] This emphasized their belief that excellence in scholarship could be conjoined with sincere Christian piety.

The many responsibilities that fell on Brown as president of the faculty took their toll. He proved to be a good fund raiser, but his colleague Gillett suspected it had shortened his life. A plan to raise the sum of $2,160,000—then an astronomical amount for a seminary—was developed during his administration, and much of the burden fell on him. In 1912, John D. Rockefeller Jr. offered a gift of $500,000 toward that goal, provided it was soon reached. That deadline had to be extended, however, and the total was not obtained until after Brown's death in 1917.[20]

Late in the fall of 1915 Brown reported to the board that he was seriously ill with a heart ailment. A confidential letter from his physician to the board indicated that he was not fully aware of the seriousness of his condition. McGiffert and W. A. Brown were jointly entrusted with the administration, but when it was recognized that an acting president would be needed, the former was named to the post. The president died on October 15, 1916. At the memorial service McGiffert emphasized that "Francis Brown was first and foremost a scholar, and it is as a scholar that we, his colleagues, chiefly think of him."[21]

The reputation of the seminary he had entered 42 years before was at a high point as his life came to an end, and though many persons were responsible for that, his long years of leadership in theological scholarship and education, and his firm hand at the helm as the seminary moved to its new location and seized new opportunities, was especially significant in what had happened. His administration was crowned by what was then the largest student body in the seminary's history—students not only from the United States but also in increasing numbers from Canada, and a few from overseas. As one of the Canadians, James Mutchmoor, put it in 1913, "Union is by all odds the leader in the theological college and seminary field." He reported an experience that many before and since have reported in various ways, "I believe that at Union Seminary, with all its liberalism, I found God. Or, I was found by my Heavenly Father. Henceforth, I can truthfully report, I had only one desire and purpose."[22] Francis Brown would have rejoiced in that.

When the board met soon after Brown's passing, McGiffert was continued as acting president of the faculty at the request of his colleagues, but the directors concluded that an experienced pastor should be sought for the post. Three such persons were approached but did not accept. As the months passed the faculty felt the need to settle the matter, especially in view of the changes caused by America's entry into World War I on Good Friday, April 6, 1917, and unanimously requested that McGiffert be permanently appointed, which was finally done on November 13. Because of the wartime situation, it was decided to postpone the inauguration until the 1918 commencement and keep it as a very simple ceremony.[23]

Meanwhile, once war was declared the majority of students and faculty rallied behind the government. Battered copies have survived of a petition to the faculty signed by many students asking that classes be suspended at noon April 19, 1917, so that they could take their place with other student delegations in the citywide celebration of Wake Up America Day. A sharp exchange occurred when a representative of the pacifist Fellowship of Reconciliation was announced as a speaker. One set of students signed a petition protesting his coming, noting that calls were coming in asking "if Union Seminary stands for him and his views" and observing that "our reputation for patriotism is already none too secure." A larger group signed a counter petition which said that "though approving of America's part in the war," a better way of expressing loyalty to the government could be found than barring a speaker who was not scheduled to "speak on pacificism, but on problems of democracy in which supporters of the war and pacifists share a common interest."[24]

Faculty opinion was divided, too. The war brought deep anguish to German-born Julius Bewer, who favored the side of his native land and adopted a pacifist position. As the majority of the faculty swung strongly toward the allied cause, especially after the American entry into the war when some became deeply involved in war service, there were some tense moments. One was when Bewer refused to take the hand of a colleague (Ross) who had lost a son in battle. Ever the scholar, however, Bewer did not let the international crisis influence his Old Testament teaching.

The ugliest illustration of tension over the war was the firing of a tenured professor in his absence shortly after the country declared war. Thomas C. Hall, tall, eloquent, forceful, and popular with students, had been on the faculty since 1899. He had studied in Berlin and Göttingen, and as many others did (Francis Brown, for example), he had married a German woman, and was anxious that American neutrality continue. In a letter to the press and in a public address immediately after the sinking of the S. S. *Lusitania* by a German submarine on May 7, 1915, he defended such action as a necessity of war, deeply offending those who were mourning lost relatives and friends as well as many others who deplored military actions that involved the killing of noncombatants. A board member, L. Mason Clarke, pastor of the First Presbyterian Church of Brooklyn, submitted his letter of resignation in protest, and urged the board to take strong action against Hall. Clarke's resignation was not accepted, but he did not withdraw it and continued to press the matter, arguing in the fall that academic freedom was really not relevant in this matter, for "some matters of morals cannot be always arguable."

During the academic year 1915–16 Hall had been granted leave to work among prisoners of war in Switzerland and Germany. The absence was extended for another year by the president of the board, and Professors Arthur Prince Hunt of General Theological Seminary and Harry F. Ward of Boston University were invited to teach courses in ethics for the first and second semesters respectively of 1916–17. At the Board of Directors' meeting of May 15, 1917, after the nation had declared war on Germany, the finance committee recommended that another year's leave without pay be granted to Hall. A substitute motion, however, was unanimously adopted. It declared "That because in the judgment of the Directors Dr. Hall's attitude towards, and his public expressions upon, the moral issues involved in the war disqualified him for the occupancy of the Chair of Christian Ethics in the Seminary," the relationship of Hall with the seminary was terminated. It was done in his absence, without a hearing or exchange of correspondence on the matter.[25]

Union did not stand against the tide of public opinion in this case any better than did its neighbor on Morningside Heights. As William Summerscales has written, "The standard set in the war years by [Nicholas Murray] Butler and the University was conditioned by a headlong patriotism that abrogated democratic principles and denied scientists and scholars not only security and dignity but also basic civil rights."[26] At Columbia the struggle centered around a controversial professor of psychology, J. McKeen Cattell, dismissed from the University without pension rights on October 1, 1917, at the beginning of his twenty-seventh year as professor.

The president of Union's board at this time was William M. Kingsley, who had succeeded Ogden when the latter died in 1913. Kingsley, then first vice president of the New York Trust Co. and later its president, was sincerely devoted to Union, and was well known as a very able, polished, witty public speaker. Following the board action he wrote to Hall, but in the confused conditions of wartime the letter did not reach the rejected professor, nor did a second missive. In the wave of patriotism that swept over the nation, there was little protest over the dismissal. An inquiry to the board came from the Department of State, asking if the relations between Hall and the seminary were determined by the latter because of the professor's pro-German sentiments or activities. In reply, Kingsley simply cited the board's action which severed the relationship because his attitude to and remarks upon the moral issues of the war disqualified him for the occupancy of the chair of Christian ethics in the seminary.

Hall did not learn until several months after the event that he had been fired. A long, poignant letter, to Kingsley, written in New York on October 3, 1919, came at last from Hall, and was bound with the board minutes dated November 11. He declared that he had been wronged and the best traditions of Union had been betrayed—the former, he said, was of little consequence, but the latter was "a most terrible tragedy." He explained that when he went to Europe on sabbatical leave in the summer of 1915, the United States and Germany were at peace, and President Wilson was urging kindness and neutrality. He accepted an invitation from John R. Mott to serve prisoners of war in German camps, supervising the work of the YMCA. He was caught by the war in Germany, and could not return because of lack of papers, poor health, and his obligations to the Y. Not until the revolution in Germany did he receive the proper papers, only to find on his return home that his apartment had been vacated, property sequestered, contract violated, and salary stopped. Some of the remarks alleged to have been made by him in a speech in Newark he denied, and he berated Kingsley and the board for being misled by malicious gossip. He insisted he had kept quiet on the war issue once America had entered the struggle, and concluded by saying he had been stabbed in the back, with no way to defend himself. The board received the fourteen-page document and ordered it recorded in the minutes. Cattell at Columbia eventually had his pension rights restored, but no evidence has come to light that Hall was ever compensated by the seminary.[27]

The emotions released by the war had led Union's board to override its own standards. Hall returned to Germany and made his home in Göttingen, becoming professor extraordinary of history and civilization in the English and American world at the university, serving from 1921 to 31, and continuing as lecturer there until his death in 1936. In 1930 his widely read book, *The Religious Background of American Culture*, was published in Boston.

The dismissal of Hall occurred at the end of an academic year, and when the fall semester opened in September 1917, nation, city, and seminary were deeply involved in the war. In an opening address, McGiffert reported that forty or more students were in active service in connection with the war, but declared that the exemption from military service of theological students as well as ministers suggested that there were many important things for them to do in preparing for and providing religious leadership both at home and abroad.[28] In the academic year 1917–18 the four traveling fellows all took leaves of absence for war-connected service: William Menzies Whitelaw served as a YMCA secretary in England; Samuel McCrea Cavert as assistant secretary of the War-Time Commission of the Churches, and then briefly as a chaplain in the army; Sterling Power Lamprecht as a soldier in France; and Arthur Cushman McGiffert Jr. as an army chaplain. Whitelaw was a Canadian; others from north of the border also left for military service, as did James Mutchmoor. Five students lost their lives in the war, and are commemorated by a memorial window in the chapel. Those who returned to complete their work, as many did, were given two and a half years to complete their seminary studies.

Faculty members also became involved in various ways in the war effort. The preaching and writing of many of them illustrated their commitment. Fosdick, for example, described in his autobiography the thrill of moving large audiences to support the war effort—a role he later deplored in his disillusionment with war and his espousal of pacifism. He also regretted having written a wartime book, *The Challenge of the Present Crisis* (1917), which he later withdrew from circulation. In February 1918, however, he had sailed in a troopship, serving under the auspices of the YMCA and the British Ministry of Information in England, Scotland, and France, where he saw the horrors of modern warfare at close range. Coffin also experienced the war in two strenuous months of speaking to troops in France during the summer of 1918. William Adams Brown and Gaylord White both took leaves of absence on behalf of the War-Time Commission of the Churches. They were both associate secretaries of the commission, while Harold Tryon was one of the assistant secretaries.[29]

Though enrollment did not decline sharply, the seminary shared its available space; according to one report to the board, for example, from November 24, 1917 to July 31, 1918, individual lodgings were provided at low cost for 11,736 soldiers. Late in the war the gym and unused dormitory space were made available for the Air Service Radio School.[30]

It was in this context that McGiffert, noting that he was completing twenty-five years of service to the seminary, finally gave his inaugural address at commencement on May 14, 1918. The omnipresent reality of war and the crusading spirit of the nation was reflected at several points in his remarks. "More than ever it is necessary now to enlist all our resources, not material alone and not alone of flesh and blood, but moral and religious and intellectual as well, if a righteous victory is to be won and a lasting peace secured," he exclaimed. "No form of endeavor dare be overlooked; no line of service neglected." But "if there was ever reason for a school of theology, there is double reason for it today," for not malice but ignorance is the deadliest foe of human progress, and "if the present war was conceived in iniquity, at any rate it was born and has been nourished in ignorance." Therefore, "Enlightenment is the world's chief need now as always," and there is no more sacred duty than to keep alive the fires of education, both secular and religious." He went on to center his inaugural around a confession of educational faith, emphasizing that there was to be no lessening of the emphasis on scholarship as the seminary pursued its twofold function "to train Christian ministers and to promote theological science." As for the first, "no consecration of purpose or fervor of spirit can atone for the lack of rigid intellectual discipline and of a careful theological education; and we are determined here to do our utmost to maintain, and if possible, to heighten, our scholarly standards."

Calling attention to the great expansion of knowledge in the disciplines of theology, to the way law and medicine had lengthened their courses of study, to the increasing specialization within the ministry, and to the importance of field work to give the student the opportunity of putting principles into practice, McGiffert pointed to the importance of a period of study of "at least four years" for a profession "never so exacting as now." "It is nothing short of a scandal," he exclaimed, "that the professional training of a Roman priest

Arthur C. McGiffert, left, church historian and eighth president. Harry Emerson Fosdick, right, preacher and teacher of preachers.

should take longer than the professional training of a Protestant minister."

The newly installed president rejoiced that five communions were represented on board and faculty, claimed as "one of our chief distinctions" that "no such interdenominational group exists anywhere else in the world," but observed that the contact with those of other polities and the growth of movements toward Christian unity and cooperation further complicated the task of theological education. While hoping for no diminution in the number of regular students, McGiffert stressed that "we are eager that the numbers should steadily grow of advanced students coming to us from other theological institutions for a fourth and fifth year," for they could contribute "to theological scholarship and to an efficient ministry in all the churches."

In discussing the seminary's second function, the eminent historian was aware that the phrase "theological science" had a pretentious sound, but insisted that "theology embraces many subjects of a strictly scientific character": the study of sacred books, of the history of religions, of the religious nature and beliefs of the race. With the revolution in the conception of authority in religion—"the profoundest and most far-reaching revolution in the church has witnessed since the second century"—the spirit of scientific investigation could govern theological study as never before. Asking only "what the facts teach, . . . we are able to move in the field of theology with the same freedom that the scientist enjoys in any other field." But the theologian goes farther in dealing not only with facts but with ideals, and passes "from the realm of science into the realm of creative art." Theology involves not only exact scholarship but constructive thinking; it exists for practical purposes. In view of the war, the president said, Germany's preeminence had come to an end, and America is in a strategic position to assume leadership—with Union in a peculiarly fortunate position to do great things for theology.

In conclusion, McGiffert stressed that the seminary remained profoundly Christian in character: "To serve the cause of Christ through the discovery and interpretation of Christian truth and through the teaching and training of those who are called to Christian leadership, this it makes its chief concern." But it is always hospitable to new truth, and confident in the possibilities of the future. McGiffert resolutely held both to Union's history as a Christian institution and to the new emphases on scientific scholarship.[31] In retrospect, the rhetoric of the address sounds inflated and triumphalistic, but at the time it echoed much of the national mood. It also reflected Union's self-confidence in the form of liberalism it had adopted and in its prominent role in theological education.

The changes in the faculty during McGiffert's term as acting and regular president of the faculty were not extensive. They were made primarily to maintain faculty strength as members left. Francis Brown had long held the Davenport chair of Hebrew and cognate languages; after he died Henry Preserved Smith was appointed to the post in addition to his duties as librarian. A graduate of Lane Theological Seminary who had studied at Berlin and Leipzig, Smith returned to Lane to teach Hebrew and Old Testament. In 1892, when the excitement over the Briggs case was at its height, he was charged before presbytery with not adhering to the doctrine of biblical inerrancy, and was suspended from the Presbyterian ministry. Appeals to synod and assembly were not sustained. He then taught at Amherst and Meadville until he was called to Union as librarian in 1913, serving in that post until his retirement in 1925. As Davenport professor he taught courses in Old Testament history. Emil Kraeling, a Lutheran minister who had earned a doctorate at Columbia, taught biblical languages from 1919 to 1944.

What proved in later years to be another highly controversial appointment was made when the successor of the dismissed Thomas C. Hall was chosen. Harry F. Ward of the Boston University School of Theology had twice taught a semester course in ethics during Hall's absence. He was named as professor of ethics in 1918. The English-born Methodist had been educated at the University of Southern California, Northwestern, and Harvard. After experience in settlement house work and as pastor in the Chicago area, Ward had gone to Boston in 1913. He was the principal author in 1907 of what was originally known as the Social Creed of Methodism. It was officially adopted by each of the three bodies that later became the Methodist Episcopal Church (1939), and also by the Federal Council of Churches as the Social Creed of the Churches. In 1907 he was also a founder of the Methodist Federation for Social Service. Five years later he became its part-time but very active secretary. A tireless traveler and platform speaker, he was conspicuous in those years as an ardent proponent of the social gospel. According to Coffin, "The wretched plight of the underprivileged in this land of plenty had entered into his soul."[32] Beginning his full-time responsibilities at Union in 1918, he plunged into the teaching of a cycle of courses on such topics as the development of social ideals, modern social movements, social Christianity, industrial conditions and relations, social reconstruction, social teaching of the Bible, ethics of the state, and ethics of economic organization. Ward had much in common with George Coe, for they both stressed the authority of experience and the importance of social justice. As a forceful crusader for the social gospel, Ward was an influential figure in promoting that movement in the 1920s.

A field of growing importance in theological education at that time was the philosophy of religion. Pioneered by a number of prominent European scholars, its leading American figures had been Josiah Royce and William James. The discipline was of deepening concern to liberals, especially those with a particular interest in empirical approaches to the understanding of religion, some of whom tended to view it as a more important discipline than systematic theology. Both Knox and Hume had combined the history and philosophy of religion, but as both fields grew in importance it was decided to divide them in 1918. Hume devoted his attention to the history of religions, while Eugene W. Lyman was called to teach the philosophy of religion in the Marcellus Hartley chair.

Educated at Amherst and Yale Divinity School, Lyman had studied abroad at the universities of Halle, Berlin, Marburg, Heidelberg, Jena, and Paris, and taught at Carleton College in Minnesota, the Congregational College in Montreal, Bangor Theological Seminary, and the Graduate School of Theology at Oberlin. He devoted a great deal of personal attention to students, striving to understand their points of view and guiding them to develop their own mature positions. He lectured infrequently, preferring to teach by the discussion method, but provided carefully prepared reading lists and mimeographed materials, urging his students to examine all sides of every question. As a convinced liberal in theology and politics, an enthusiast for the social gospel, and an opponent of militarism, he championed causes dear to many seminarians in the 1920s. But as a devout and convinced theist, in such courses as Theism, Religion and Ethics, the Religious Aspects of Contemporary Philosophy, and the Truth of the Christian Religion, he opposed the trend toward a nontheistic humanism which had attracted a number of students in the postwar years. His *magnum opus* was *The Meaning and Truth of Religion* (1933).

The retirement of Marvin Vincent created an opening in the New Testament department. The replacement, installed as Edward Robinson professor of biblical theology in 1919, was in many respects almost the opposite of Lyman, and indeed differed with a number of his colleagues in one point or another. English-born Ernest F. Scott had been educated at Glasgow, Oxford, and Edinburgh. After a short Presbyterian pastorate, he taught for eleven years at the Theological College of Queen's University in Kingston, Ontario. He was a masterful, polished, witty lecturer. One of his students found him to be "one of those brilliant geniuses whose lectures were nearly always exciting events." Skilled in critical judgment and synthesis, Scott's generalizations, the student remembered, "were so convincing in form and unity as to make us feel that the problem was settled. Thus he gave us answers, while Frame [his colleague in New Testament] gave us questions. The two formed a marvellous team."

The short, peppery Scott has a way of using humor in passing to criticize some of the seminary's enthusiasms and heroes: psychology he labeled "pseudo-science," methods in religious education as a "bag of tricks," the social gospel as an "intellectually disreputable creed," and Mahatma Gandhi as a "half-wit, naked fanatic"—at a time when pacifism had a deep hold on many Union folk in the disillusionment following World War I.[33] An extremely competent, industrious scholar, Scott was the prolific author of many widely read books, a number of which were selected by the Religious Book Club, and his publication record continued after his retirement in 1938.

A major change in the popular department of religious education and psychology came in 1922. The forceful and outspoken Coe drew a sharp line between merely "transmissive" and genuinely "creative" education, putting much that was traditional in the former category. His tendency to move away from Christological and biblical emphases in religious education brought him into deepening tension with McGiffert and other colleagues. When his partner in the department, Hugh Hartshorne, was not given tenure in 1922 and took a professorship at the University of Southern California, Coe resigned in protest and took a part-time post at Teachers College. "The series of letters between President McGiffert and Coe, though laden with human misunderstanding and personal bias," wrote Stephen Schmidt, "clearly reveal that Coe moved to Teachers College simply because he felt that his colleague, Hartshorne, had not received justice at Union." (Ironically, McGiffert had been president of the Religious Education Association in 1921.) The matter was apparently not widely known; the minutes of the Board of Directors simply noted that because of Hartshorne's resignation in order to take his new position Coe had not felt up to reorganizing the department and wanted more time for study and writing, which his new post offered.[34] Hartshorne later taught at Yale for a quarter century.

Harrison S. Elliott, like Coe a Methodist layman, was quickly secured to staff the vacated department. He had attended Antioch and Ohio Wesleyan, earned a B.D. at Drew in 1911 and an M.A. at Teachers College eleven years later. He had served as a YMCA secretary for a dozen years, and been an instructor at Drew. Appointed as assistant professor, he was promoted the next year to the associate level and two years later to the Skinner and McAlpin chair of practical theology. Even for such an able and experienced man, that was a uniquely swift move up the promotional ladder. A student of Coe, he carried on that tradition, especially as outlined in his mentor's influential A Social Theory of Religious Education (1917), with particular emphasis on group process and the discussion method in his teaching. He also played an important role in the Religious Education Association.

In 1917, burdened by the demands of the presidency but anxious to continue research and teaching, McGiffert asked Gaylord White to move up to the seminary from Union Settlement to carry some of the administrative load. White performed this task with great efficiency. Union played a prominent role in shaping a new emphasis in theological education. The older model of the minister as pastoral theologian was now matched by increased attention to the religious professional model with its emphasis on preparation for a specific church vocation. In the academic year 1919–20 an additional vocational diploma was made available to either B.D. or diploma students for special preparation in the areas of the pastorate, religious education, foreign missions, or home service. White was made director of the new department of home service, which focused on preparing students for home, industrial, and immigrant missions and for social, institutional, and interdenominational ministries. The resources of Union Settlement, where White still served as headworker, were utilized.

White's new duties at Union gave him less time for guiding field work at a time when the professional model of ministry directed fresh attention to it, and the president had emphasized it in his inaugural. Thus in 1918 Arthur L. Swift was named director of field work—a position he was to hold for thirty-eight years, becoming a recognized leader in that aspect of theological education. A graduate of Williams College who earned a Union B.D. (1916) and served in the Congregational pastorate, the new director became associate professor of applied Christianity in 1926 after earning a Columbia M.A. (and later a Ph.D.). Beginning in 1919, at least one year of *supervised* field work carrying academic credit became a requirement of the theological curriculum.

In a pioneering study of theological education published in 1924 and based on a survey of 161 institutions, Robert L. Kelly underlined Union's development in the direction of "applied Christianity":

Practical theology is now approximately coordinate with exegetical theology in number of hours offered. Great expansion has taken place in all departments but the greatest development has been from the theoretical disciplines of former years to an entirely new group of studies having to do particularly with the present world order. Many of these courses seek to acquaint the student not only with present-day thinking but also with the means of making the church a living force—a vital servant of and in the community.[35]

The general intention of the faculty was to keep these professional courses at the highest academic level, so that rigorous intellectual standards would be maintained. The home service department did not last long; by 1924–25 it had been replaced by separate departments of church and community, and field work, with White in the leading role in the first, Swift in the second.

Under McGiffert's leadership, some changes affecting the work of the faculty and requirements for degrees were made. The provision for a somewhat separate graduate faculty had never been effectively developed. It was quietly dropped in 1918. This did not mean, however, less attention to study for advanced degrees. In the academic year 1917–18 an M.Th. (later S.T.M.) was offered for students who had completed a year of graduate study after the B.D. or its equivalent from Union or another recognized school. The D.D. degree (only one had been earned) was changed to a Th.D. degree, which had rigorous language requirements, a residency of not less than three years, and the publication of a substantial book. The first recipient was E. C. Vanderlaan in 1924. McGiffert believed that the seminary should fulfill some of the functions of a university theological faculty, and be open to qualified persons who wanted to study religion. Hence in addition to the classified graduate students, the number of students from other institutions doing substantial work at Union (now called special students) almost doubled in the first year after the war, and in 1924–25 numbered over two hundred. The increased load necessitated provision for clerical assistance to help the faculty with their seminary and university responsibilities.

One consequence of the emphasis on the scholarly and professional aspects of theological education was the levying of tuition charges—then a radical step for seminaries. The divinity schools of the University of Chicago and Harvard had already taken the step, but generally seminaries resisted the change. As recommended by the faculty and then by a special committee, the Board of Directors approved the measure early in 1918, prefacing its action with two clauses:

WHEREAS
It has long been deemed wise by educational and other authorities that theological schools should be placed upon a financial basis, closely corresponding to that of other professional schools, and in harmony with the immemorial policy of theological seminaries of Great Britain and other countries, and heretofore accepted by several prominent institutions of our country
and
WHEREAS
It is believed a reasonable tuition charge will increase the dignity of the sacred profession, and permit of the more liberal recognition of individual

scholarship, and remove certain embarrassments in the exchange relations with other schools of learning . . .[36]

A consultation with representatives of other seminaries was arranged. (The issue of tuition disclosed a need for the exchange of views on many matters by seminary leaders, and later that year at Harvard was organized the Conference of Theological Seminaries and Colleges in the United States and Canada, which eventually became the Association of Theological Schools.) Beginning in September 1919, the charge at Union of $150 per year was made for all regular students; for special students or any taking less than a full load the cost was $6 per curriculum point. Though a number of seminaries did not change their policies then, the trend toward charging tuition slowly spread through the theological educational scene.

A second consequence of the policies stressed by McGiffert was the introduction in 1920–21 of a four-year B.D. program, requiring 112 curriculum points. There were sufficient provisions for transferring credit from affiliated institutions and recognized summer schools, and for securing credit by examination, so that anyone who had transferred as few as six points could complete the degree in the customary three years. In effect the four-year curriculum was largely optional, though at first a number of students chose it. In the long run, however, it did not prove to be a popular move at Union or beyond, and was soon dropped as a requirement.

During the academic year 1920–21 seminary enrollment topped 300 for the first time. Pleased with this increase, McGiffert signed on behalf of the faculty a confidential statement, "Plans for Expansion," which called attention to the actual and prospective changes, and noted the increase in the number of graduate students, including more from abroad. "The presence of so many advanced students of high grade," it was said, "undoubtedly helps to broaden the horizon and raise the scholarly standards of our student body as a whole." The increasing needs of the library, on which ever greater demands were being made, were highlighted, as was the value of the foreign service department and its fellowships for missionaries on furlough. Space for the latter, for professors (rent was being paid for six who could not be accommodated on the quadrangle), for more offices and seminar rooms, and for an adequate social hall and a refectory—students signed petitions for the latter—was needed. The statement concluded by detailing these and other needs, including taking care of the annual deficit, which was then running in the vicinity of $800,000, and requesting a financial drive to raise nearly three million dollars.[37] The enrollment continued to increase: in 1923–24 it climbed to 424, of which 192 were special students. The report of the faculty to the board in 1924 noted that 145 of that number were women. There were then only seven women in the regular student body, but even that was a new high, and long-range provisions for more housing for them was an emerging concern.

The financial basis of the institution was sound, and its devoted board was committed to raising what funds as were shown to be necessary. In his 1924 study, Kelly found that Union's productive endowment of about $5.5 million headed the list of the 161 North American theological seminaries he examined.[38] But it was not enough to erect new buildings, or pay all the bills—annual deficits were piling up. When the board finally decided to undertake a major campaign for funds, it concluded that $4 rather than $3 million were needed. This view was supported by John D. Rockefeller Jr., who offered what would later be called a "challenge" gift of $750,000 if the seminary could raise the balance to make $3 million, and $333,000 more if it could raise $4 million. When the seminary launched its campaign for $4 million in the fall of 1924 at the Hotel Astor, it called upon some of its most gifted speakers. With Board President Kingsley as toastmaster, major addresses were given by Coffin, Fosdick, and a rising young Methodist pastor, Ralph W. Sockman (1916). The large gifts of such donors as Rockefeller, Edward S. Harkness, Arthur C. James, and Emily O. Butler, combined with the contributions of some 1500 more of Union's friends and graduates, insured the success of the drive.

The benefits became visible in the spring of 1926 when the purchase of an apartment house at 99 Claremont Avenue, renamed "Missionary House," provided space for missionaries on furlough, faculty, and women students. Plans were prepared for a tower at 120th Street and Broadway, and a building north of the chapel on Claremont Avenue for the social hall and refectory. These additions fully enclosed the quadrangle, and when finished in 1928 brought to completion the original design for the buildings on Morningside

Heights. Early plans for what was named the Brown Tower, in memory of John Crosby Brown, show a massive square structure going up some 25 feet higher than what was finally built. The cost factor led to a shorter, more graceful design, although the elevator from the rotunda could not ascend into the tower. Those wishing to ride up to the new offices had to change elevators on the fourth floor.

Even as the funds were being raised and the building plans detailed, however, there was some uneasiness among various members of the board, faculty, and student body about the direction the seminary was taking. In his inaugural, President McGiffert had insisted that "the spirit of independent scientific investigation can govern theological study as it never could before," and encouraged students who wished to study religion regardless of their vocational direction to come to Union. The great increase in the number of special students brought into the classrooms and life of Union many who were not headed for the ministry. While McGiffert himself was a deeply sincere Christian, he was not a prominent leader in church life and was not characterized by an outward piety that had been characteristic of many of his predecessors. More importantly, the general spiritual and intellectual climate of the 1920s was not a very congenial one for religion, for the churches and seminaries. The crusading spirit of the war years soon gave way to a deepening mood of disillusionment and a negative reaction to idealism and reformism. An ambitious Interchurch World Movement for a united drive for world evangelism and cooperative Protestant advance involving many of the major denominations took shape soon after the armistice in 1918 in a mood of great enthusiasm. "No one who was present in the upper room on that momentous December day when the Interchurch World Movement was born can forget the thrill of expectation which stirred those who had gathered there," wrote William Adams Brown.[39] By May of 1920 a paid staff of more than 2600 was at work—but the movement ran out of funds and collapsed during the summer as the idealistic, crusading spirit noticeably ebbed.

The changing atmosphere of the times was disquieting for theological student bodies across the continent, and especially at a nondenominational seminary where a number of students could be found who were not seriously committed to church or ministry. Many were, of course, and they felt encouraged by the growing number of missionaries on furlough who resided at or near the seminary. But the combined effects of fading idealism and differences of attitude among students meant that what had long been the central core disciplines in theological education—Bible, church history, systematic theology—no longer seemed as exciting as religious education, the philosophy of religion, and social ethics became dominant interests. Chapel attendance declined in this difficult period.

The tensions caused by such changes added to the president's burden. His health had suffered because of the demands placed on him by the campaign to raise funds. Early in January 1925 the board asked the faculty members present, including the president, to withdraw, and after "mature deliberation" passed the following resolution:

that the Board of Directors wish to express to President McGiffert their appreciation of his devoted and successful efforts in the campaign to secure the Seminary funds. They realize the unusual strain to which he has been subjected for a long while and they feel compelled to insist with all possible urgency that he accept a leave of absence for the remainder of the academic year.[40]

William Adams Brown again served as acting president. When McGiffert returned in the fall, he had the satisfaction of knowing that the fund for $4 million was all pledged, some $840,000 of it going to wipe out the cumulative deficit. The problems were not over, however, for the regular, normal income for 1924–25 amounted to about $350,000 while expenses were just over $500,000—the two-pronged academic emphases of the seminary, to foundational and graduate theological education, were expensive to maintain. McGiffert worked through the following winter, but in April tendered his resignation as both president and professor.

The board accepted the first part with deepest regret, but did not act on his resignation as professor, instead voting him leave for a year, hoping he would be able to return to continue teaching. But health did not permit: a year later he had to resign the Washburn chair. In his retirement he produced the work based on a lecture course he had given many times, now much expanded and enriched, the two-volume *The History of Christian Thought* (1932–33). The second volume, carrying the story to Erasmus, appeared in the year of his death, which interrupted plans to write a third volume carrying the story into the Reformation and modern periods.

Despite the difficulties of those years, the reputation of the seminary continued to grow. The annual report of the faculty to the board in 1921 was not recording an idle boast in stating that "from the beginning Union has held a high place among American theological institutions, but it was only within the last few years that it was attained what may fairly and without vain glory be called a unique position."[41] In his survey of theological education, Robert L. Kelly was properly cautious in his estimate of Union: "Perhaps it is wielding in the liberal school of thought the strongest influence, as is Princeton in the conservative school, of the institutions [161] here considered."[42]

It was just at the close of the Brown-McGiffert period that a young theologian-to-be, fresh from two years at Oxford, chose Union as the place to study for two degrees. When asked in retirement why he had decided to take that step in 1926, John Bennett replied laconically that it was "the top seminary then."[43] Another assessment of the seminary was offered by a rising young Detroit pastor who had not attended Union, Reinhold Niebuhr. He wrote of "the ripe scholarship and moral earnestness of Union with its fine sense for the social mission of our faith."[44] Under Brown and McGiffert the seminary had clearly made its mark in the world of theological scholarship, and was using its new buildings and its nearness to a major university effectively. But had something central in its history been minimized in its climb to the scholarly heights?

CHAPTER SEVEN

Advance Through Storm: The Coffin Years (1926–1945)

TRANSITION (1926–1933)

Henry Sloane Coffin (1900) had served as a part-time faculty member for more than twenty years when he agreed to become president—a position which had been offered to him once before, at the time McGiffert had been selected. He took the helm at a difficult time; at the inaugural dinner on November 4, 1926, the representative of the Alumni Council, prominent Chicago pastor Charles W. Gilkey (1908) pointed out that "in these days the cause of religion is facing contrary winds."[1] Soon the economic storm of the Great Depression would sweep over the nation, bringing widespread suffering, and fueling intense debate and controversial political action relating to the social and economic order. The rise of totalitarian dictators caused much anxiety, focused attention of many persons on the issues of war and peace, and finally triggered World War II. Despite various controversies and periods of declining enrollments and income during the Coffin years, the seminary not only

Henry Sloane Coffin: 41 years on the Faculty, 19 as president.

maintained but actually increased its conspicuous role in theological education; it continued to advance in the face of stormy times.[2]

In his remarks on inauguration day, Dr. Gilkey invoked a metaphor from sailing to indicate the significance of the selection of Henry Sloane Coffin at a difficult time in Union's history. "Those of us who spend our vacation down by the salt water and get our best recreation from sailing boats in the good old-fashioned way, are very familiar with the only principle of possible progress when the winds are contrary: the willingness, namely, to get ahead by tacking zigzag, first in one direction and then in the other." Under Charles Cuthbert Hall, he remembered, the seminary sailed on the tack of spirituality, while under his two successors, Francis Brown and Arthur C. McGiffert, the emphasis was on scholarship, for they "have stood forth, not only in reputation before the whole Christian world but in person before us who have been their students, as veritable incarnations of that attitude of sound and fearless scholarship, of sympathetic and constructive interpretation of the Bible and of our Christian heritage, that has been one of the great glories of Union Seminary." Both emphases were necessary, but to remain too long on one tack might be to veer off course. Affirming that both spirituality and scholarship were needed in the face of adverse winds, as the seminary "has grown great because it has had such leadership in both directions," Gilkey declared "it is not only natural but right that the emphasis of this new administration should swing the ship over in the direction of training for active Christian service as its urgent present task."

Coffin, who knew the seminary intimately and had a profound understanding of his native city, was well prepared for his task. He had lived there all of his life except for college years at Yale and two of his seminary years in Scotland. He was aware of the changing currents of thought in university life, and was a popular and widely recognized preacher in college chapels in a day when they played a quite visible role in campus life. From study, but especially from practice, he knew the problems, the opportunities, and the challenges of the ministry. He had started the hard way. After graduating from Union in 1900 he launched a mission church at Bedford Park, in the Bronx. His early sermons there were delivered in a hall over a meat market with a chopping-block for a pulpit, but within five years a congregation was gathered and a building erected. When he left the Bronx for Madison Avenue Presbyterian Church, the prospects for that congregation's survival were clouded, but he built it into a great institution. He was able to minister to many types of people, those who resided in depressed areas near Third Avenue as well as those who enjoyed the comfort of homes on or close to Fifth and Madison Avenues. He was a great believer in pastoral calling, logging an average of one hundred calls a month—all this in addition to teaching classes at Union, filling an increasingly larger role in the life of his denomination, and writing a number of books, such as *The Creed of Jesus* (1907), *Social Aspects of the Cross* (1911), *Some Christian Convictions* (1915), *In a Day of Social Rebuilding* (1918), *A More Christian Industrial Order* (1920), and *What to Preach* (1926).[3]

Though he chose to call his own theological position "liberal evangelical," in the days of the controversy between fundamentalism and modernism in the 1920s he was a force for liberalism, defining it as the spirit which reveres truth and claims freedom to pursue and publish it. In 1924 he took a leading part in the preparation of a significant document in Presbyterian history, widely known as the Auburn Affirmation. *An Affirmation designed to safeguard the unity and liberty of the Presbyterian Church in the United States of America* was a plea for theological tolerance, for holding to the great facts and doctrines of faith but allowing for a variety of theories in an effort to explain them. Thus even as he retained a strong evangelical emphasis, he became a recognized leader of the liberals.

That the seminary was indeed on a new tack was evident from the very beginning of the new presidency. Because of the sudden illness of a colleague, Coffin delivered the opening address of the academic year on the theme "Evangelistic Preaching." Dealing directly with four "defects that have deservedly brought evangelism into disrepute," he declared that "evangelism is the supreme duty of the Christian preacher," who should select great and moving themes for the sermons, seek "a haunting or a wooing text," try to use a language which makes the hearers *see*, and finally press them to decision. Many examples and suggestions were provided in that effort which pointed to some of the emphases of the new administration. Though the address signaled a return to certain emphases which had been somewhat neglected in the life of the seminary, the service itself opened with an innovation which demonstrated that the new administration was willing to break fresh ground. As the *Alumni Bulletin* reported it,

When the academic procession entered the chapel at the opening service on Sept. 22, it must have been something of a shock to some of the older generation to see it led by women students. For there was a mixed choir! But the novelty soon wore off and now the girls in mortar boards and gowns not only present a pleasing picture but add much to the quality of the chapel music.[4]

Commenting on that event at the time of Coffin's retirement, Henry P. Van Dusen said:

Union had been one of the first theological schools to admit women to its classes and to grant them its degrees. In the new residence building acquired in this same year, a dormitory for women was provided. Now, they were accorded full equality with men in all privileges and activities. From this time forward the training of women for a varied Christian ministry, as teachers in colleges and schools, as directors of religious education and pastors assistants, as choir-masters and organists, even as ordained clergy, was to hold an ever larger place in the Seminary's work.[5]

At that September opening in 1926 there were also new hymn books in the chapel—an indication of the new president's interest in church music. The books were the latest edition of *Hymns of the Kingdom*, which Coffin and Ambrose W. Vernon (1894) had originally compiled and edited in 1910.

The dormitory mentioned by Van Dusen was the apartment house at 99 Claremont Avenue, used also to house missionaries on furlough. A tunnel under the street connected it to the seminary; in lieu of taxes a lump sum was paid annually to the city. Through the years, the board spent an unconscionable amount of time on the details of that tunnel, which later had to be altered because of new construction on the western side of Claremont.

At the formal inauguration on November 4, the president's address, "The Ideals of the Seminary," focused on the three main historic strands of the seminary's life, minimizing none but clearly articulating their relative importance as he saw it.

First, it is a training school for Christian ministers, recognizing the varied ministries for which our time calls, in the churches at home and abroad, in allied Christian organizations, in the teaching of Christian ideals and convictions in schools and colleges.

Second, it is a school of graduate study whither those who have already received their ministerial training may come for further education, and where scholars may prosecute special research in some branch of Christian learning.

Third, it carries on what may be termed (in clumsy phrase) extension education in theology, offering training for workers in churches and kindred institutions, opening many of its courses to special students, conducting conferences for ministers and missionaries, and supplying through its faculty and occasional lecturers information and inspiration for the public.

Coffin noted that Union had been called a theological university, a name which it should merit by seeking to furnish education in every department of Christian theology, but stressed as most important that "it is always a vocational school, preparing its students for careers as ministers and teachers of the Christian faith." He rejoiced in the connection with the great university across the street, but explained that "our debt to Columbia and her schools lays on us an obligation to supply any of her students who desire it opportunity for study in our distinctive province of the Christian faith and life; and sharply to delimit our province, expecting the University to enroll in one of her many departments students whose main interest is not preparation for some form of the Christian ministry." In matters of curriculum, he stressed the importance of the "classical" disciplines of Bible, church history, and systematic theology, with a "modest number of hours" in practical training.

He discussed the seminary's ideals as disclosed by its character and history under four headings: scholarship, churchmanship, worshipfulness, and a passion for the world-wide kingdom of Christ. He celebrated Union's eminence in scholarship, mentioning by name his two distinguished scholarly predecessors in office, but insisting that every professional school is committed to foster some point of view. As for Union, it "is committed to the cause of Jesus Christ, to His faith and His purpose and His redeeming power, to training men and women to spread His Gospel. That is our *raison d'être*." Coffin also insisted that the faculty were responsible for giving a fair and honest presentation of all views, hostile or favorable to what they themselves hold, for the seminary has been a protagonist for the freedom of the Christian mind—a never-ending struggle.

In church life, Coffin interpreted the seminary's stance not as nondenominational but interdenominational, as standing for a more inclusive Christian church to be reached by leading existing denominations into a more comprehensive church. He stressed worship as a principal bond of unity in the seminary, explaining that "doubtless we of the directors and faculty all share the great convictions commonly subsumed under the caption 'evangelical Christianity'; but no one of us would venture to phrase them and expect to satisfy all his colleagues." In order to maintain at Union "a glowing fellowship of Christians who explore together the life of Christ in God, we exalt our corporate worship." The minister "must acquire the art, a most difficult and complex art which embraces imagination, language, architecture, music—the art of expressing the longings and gratitudes and penitences of a group of folk feeling after a Wiser and Better than themselves, the art of affirming and making real the sufficiency of God."

Finally, Coffin articulated in the familiar idiom of that period a passion for the world-wide kingdom of God: "we have taught here the gospel of Christ as the power of God not only for the salvation of individuals, but for the redemption of society—for the christianization of industry and commerce, of education and statemanship, of the relations of races and of nations." He closed by stressing Union's "no small trust to discharge" in making possible religious rebirth and advance. Union did advance under his nearly two decades of leadership, but in the face of storms unanticipated on that November day in 1926.[6]

He immediately began to put these emphases to work. He would ask members of the student body and faculty directly, "Do you pray?" and remind some that their attendance at morning chapel left something to be desired. Of greater importance was his own regular attendance at and enthusiasm for the brief service at 8:30 A.M., and chapel attendance noticeably picked up and became more central in the life of the seminary. Some students who resisted the renewed attention to preparation for some form of church ministry soon encountered a firm president. A group of five who disliked some of his early statements complained to him, only to be informed that those who were not purposing any ministry connected with the church could no longer occupy dormitory rooms. But seminary enrollments were not negatively affected by such changes; for the first time during the academic year 1929–30 the total number of students (including just over 200 from other institutions, among whom were many women) topped 600.

With Coffin at the helm, interesting changes could be expected. In an academic procession in the fall of 1927 two women, newly appointed lecturers, walked with the faculty for the first time— Sophia Lyon Fahs and Mary Ely Lyman. Fahs, who had received an M.A. from Columbia in 1904 and earned a Union B.D. in 1926, became lecturer on religious education and psychology and principal of the Union School of Religion.[7] As Mary Redington Ely, Lyman had earned the B.D. in 1919, winning the traveling fellowship and then going on to teach at Vassar for six years, earning her Ph.D. at the University of Chicago in 1924. She married the widowed Eugene Lyman in 1926, and soon became a lecturer on English Bible.

Plans for completing the quadrangle with the tower at Broadway and 120th Street and the building for the refectory and social hall just north of the chapel tower had been largely developed before Coffin's appointment, and funds had been raised under his predecessor. But it was during his administration that the bids were received, contracts signed, construction done, and the new facilities dedicated in May 1928. As the refectory took shape, it was evident that it was a floor lower than had been originally intended. Oral tradition forwards several explanations: one that the residents of upper floors of Knox Hall did not wish their view westward to the Hudson obscured, the other that the new president, a careful budget-balancer, wanted to keep the cost down. Probably the latter was decisive.

Much of the detailed supervision in connection with the construction was carried out by the seminary's business manager, Charles T. White, son of Gaylord White, who as Bursar (later Comptroller) brought new efficiency into the seminary's financial affairs. The dedications of the new structures as the Charles Cuthbert Hall Refectory, the Francis Brown Social Hall, and the John Crosby Brown Memorial Tower took place on May 28–29, 1928. These much-needed facilities were soon put to good use, and opened the way for some important additions to the seminary's program. The Alumni

Club, for example, no longer had to hold its luncheon meetings away from the seminary. At its meeting on November 5, 1928, for example, a new portrait of McGiffert, to be placed in the refectory, was received by his successor. The 39th annual dinner of the club could be held at the seminary for the first time on May 27, 1929, when the topic was "The Church and Our Industrial Order." Attention was focused on William Adams Brown, who had officiated that day at the wedding of famed aviator Charles Lindbergh and Anne Morrow, daughter of Dwight L. Morrow, Ambassador to Mexico and a director of the seminary.[8]

The new social hall quickly came to be a favorite place of meeting for the seminary community; many informal presentations and some more formal lectures were given there. Various social occasions and seminary parties were held in the room, which replaced the smaller gate room over the main street entrance to the quad as the main place for such events. The faculty turned down student requests for dances there or in the refectory late in 1928 "on grounds of propriety"—it was not an accepted practice in many churches. One more major building project remained: a large dormitory to replace the apartment house at 99 Claremont Avenue but located directly beside the new Riverside Church at the corner of Claremont and 122d Street. It was designed to include apartments for a growing faculty, missionaries on furlough, married students, and single women students. The board voted late in 1930 to call it McGiffert Hall, at the same time that what was then known as the men's dormitory was named Hastings Hall and the adjoining apartment house for faculty Knox Hall. Generous donations from John D. Rockefeller Jr., Arthur Curtiss James, and Edward S. Harkness helped to finance the new structure, which was not opened until 1932 because of construction delays.

The new president was more concerned with educational then with building development. While arrangements had been made earlier in the decade for properly qualified Union students to work for advanced degrees at Columbia and Teachers College, under Coffin's leadership a new agreement with the university was adopted in 1928. In effect, while retaining its full independence, the Union faculty became one of the constituent faculties of the university, and on its recommendation, M.A. degrees were granted by Columbia in the literature and religion of the Bible, the comparative study of Christianity and other religions, and (by 1930) Christian education. Coffin saw that this relationship left Union free to go its own way, yet provided advantages to both institutions. Modified in certain details through the years, this basic agreement was still in force as Union entered its sesquicentennial year. Not so long in duration, though continued for more than forty years beginning in 1929, was Union's six-week summer academic program in July and early August as part of Columbia's summer session. Union professors and those visiting from other institutions taught the equivalent of full-semester courses on a concentrated schedule. Many students from other seminaries got a taste of Union and New York in this way.

When Coffin thought the time was ripe for a new development, he could move quickly. Early in January of 1928, when Clarence and Helen Dickinson asked to talk with him, he set the time for that very night. Clarence Dickinson received his M.A. (1909) and Mus.D. (1917) from Northwestern, studied in Berlin and Paris, served a number of churches and temples as organist and choirmaster, especially at New York's Brick Presbyterian Church (1909–1959), and taught at Union as Harkness instructor of sacred music since 1912. Mrs. Dickinson had earned a M.A. (1895) from Queen's University in Ontario and a Ph.D. (1901) from Heidelberg, where she had specialized in historic liturgies and religious art. Together they conducted an annual series of historical organ lecture-recitals which drew large audiences from both the students and the larger public. They told Coffin that they hoped that a place could be made at Union for church musicians to receive the best possible professional training and also undertake some study in church history and theology, in order to understand in some depth the worship of the churches they served. At that time, theological seminaries did not have degree programs for persons preparing for a career in church music, nor did graduate schools in music have courses in religion.

Coffin had long been deeply interested in church music, and responded enthusiastically. He took the proposal to the directors on January 10; they accepted the idea but expressed misgivings as to the costs of such an endeavor, and were concerned about the possible drain on seminary funds. The president then secured pledges from board members Edward S. Harkness and Arthur Curtiss James suffi-

Helen and Clarence Dickinson, central figures in the history of the School of Sacred Music.

cient to pay the expenses for the new School of Sacred Music for one year. Application for the awarding of the degrees of S.M.M. and S.M.D. (Master and Doctor of Sacred Music) was made to the New York Board of Regents, and in due course permission was given. Candidates for the S.M.M. were to be college graduates, enrolled as seminary students, and required to take some of the courses designed for theological students. The Dickinsons had already developed plans for curriculum and instructors, and had little difficulty in lining up highly qualified persons to give instruction. The first listing of the faculty of the School of Sacred Music in the 1928–29 catalog carried seventeen names, including Helen and Clarence Dickinson, the latter as director and Harkness associate professor of sacred music, and Coffin himself, who taught hymnology. This was a new venture in theological education, and it brought an immediate response. Eighteen degree candidates, half of them women, and ten part-time students were officially enrolled for the school's first year. The presence of the school was quickly felt throughout the seminary. The chapel choir was reinforced, musical talent was readily available for various seminary events, and many theological students became more aware of the importance of music in the church. It soon became apparent that little difficulty was faced in placing the school's graduates.[9]

The School of Sacred Music contributed to Coffin's concern for deepening and enriching the spiritual life of the seminary, as did the opening of a small chapel across from the social hall in the new building. Dedicated on November 11, 1929, it was provided by the son of Lewis Lampman, a graduate of the seminary in 1870 and later a director for 25 years. Lampman daily chapel services were planned and conducted by students at various hours across the years, often in early or late evening. They supplemented morning chapel, and gave students a chance to lead in such devotional exercises more frequently and to learn more about worship in various traditions.

It was not long before the seminary's impressive new Brown Tower was put to use. A number of offices for faculty and staff were located there, but there were still considerable space available, especially in the upper reaches of the tower above the eighth floor. The Missionary Research Library had been founded by the foreign missionary boards of a number of denominations soon after the historic World Missionary Conference at Edinburgh in 1910. By 1929 the library contained more than 70,000 books and pamphlets, including scarce and informative materials on what were then familiarly known as missionary lands. It needed new quarters, and while maintained for many years under its own board, an agreement was worked out for it to be housed in the tower. With the assistance of such large donors as the three who had already given much for McGiffert Hall, a reading room, offices, and stacks were equipped, and Union's own collection of 12,000 volumes of similar materials honoring Charles Cuthbert Hall was also placed in the new library. Scholars and students soon found new resources in this prominent missionary collection. Charles H. Fahs, its director and curator, was given faculty standing as director of missionary research. Another development involving books had been launched in 1927—a circulating Lending Library for seminary alumni/ae. In 1929 what had been the student-operated Book Shop in Hastings Hall was found to be inadequate for the increased pressures put on it, and was taken over by the administration as the Seminary Book Service and located to the right of the rotunda as one entered the seminary. The management of the lending library was also entrusted to it.

The coming of The Riverside Church immediately to the west across Claremont Avenue influenced Union's history in direct and indirect ways. In addition to his duties as Jesup Professor of Practical Theology, Harry Fosdick had become pastor of Park Avenue Baptist Church in 1925 with the understanding that a larger church, with membership open to all disciples of Jesus Christ, would be built in the vicinity of Columbia. John D. Rockefeller Jr. secured the land. The cornerstone of what became a beautiful Gothic structure, with its architectural principle taken from Chartres Cathedral, was laid in November of 1927. Thirteen months later a disastrous fire, fanned by a stiff wind and fed by the wooden scaffold, swept through the partially completed structure. Parts of the building were ready for use in 1929, but the new sanctuary was not ready for worship until October 5, 1930. At the beginning of the week of dedication events, February 8, 1931, Fosdick's famous hymn, "God of grace and God of glory," written for the occasion, was sung for the first time.[10]

Questions concerning the continuation of the Union School of Religion because of Riverside Church's coming to Morningside Heights was raised as early as 1926. The problem was intensified by the growing difference of opinion between Coffin and the board and the department of religious education in its conduct of the Union School of Religion. Mrs. Fahs, a recent seminary graduate, had just become principal. The strong liberalism and experimentalism of the department came into tension with Coffin's liberal evangelicalism. He believed that a Sunday school should be related to a church. Several events increased the tension. A fundamentalist layman got hold of some tests reflecting a very strong modernist position and complained to the board late in 1926. Coffin was later present at an Easter service at the school conducted by a seminary student whose interpretations seemed to the president to be very naturalistic and lacking in a Christian emphasis. All this, coupled with the financial problems that the school was facing and the intention of Riverside Church to launch an educational program in its more adequate facilities, brought the Union School of Religion to an end by faculty vote. Sophia Fahs later became an influential figure in religious education at Riverside, and continued to be a lecturer at Union until 1944.[11]

Some of the changes in faculty that took place in the early years of Coffin's presidency have already been mentioned, but there were a number of others, as retirements and deaths left vacancies to be filled. George A. Johnston Ross retired from his post in homiletics in 1926, but continued as lecturer until 1930. Francis Carmody, instructor in speech, died in 1928. Charles R. Gillett (1880), retired in 1929 after having served the seminary for forty-six years in many capacities: teacher, librarian, registrar, secretary of the faculty, dean of students, and alumni secretary. In the following year, at his own request, William Adams Brown laid down the burdens of the Roosevelt chair of systematic theology, which he had filled so ably for thirty-two years, to become research professor. Gaylord White, long an influential figure at Union, who had just reduced his teaching load to become dean of students, died in harness in 1931. F. J. Foakes Jackson, graduate professor of Christian institutions, retired in 1933.

To offset these losses, eight appointments were made from 1926 to 1933; some served relatively short terms but others were destined to play long and significant roles in Union's history. In 1927 three experienced teachers joined the faculty. One was James Moffatt, a native of Glasgow, who had been educated at the university and Free Church College there, and had been minister of several Presbyterian churches, former professor of Greek at Mansfield College, Oxford (from which universities he won an M.A. at the same time), and professor of church history in the city of his birth. He was widely known through the translation of the Bible that bears his name. Moffatt succeeded McGiffert in the Washburn chair of church history. An industrious man of immense erudition, he rarely covered the ground laid out for a course. His lively sense of humor was often evident, and in the proper season he was glad to leave his office to watch a baseball game. He was such a devotee of the sport that the management of the Polo Grounds (of happy memory) furnished him with a season ticket. He was greatly missed when he retired in 1938.

Another professor known for his Bible expertise came the same year as Moffatt: A. Bruce Curry Jr. Skilled in teaching the Bible by discussion method, he had taught many years at Biblical Seminary while he earned a Ph.D. at New York University. After doing some lecturing at Union, he became associate professor of practical theology, and was elevated to the Jesup chair in 1934, but ill health forced him to resign two years later. John W. Wetzel, a gifted teacher of speech who had taught at various seminaries and law schools, also began work at Union in 1927, quickly moving into the Harkness instructorship following the death of Carmody, and holding that post until his retirement in 1942. In 1928, Canadian-born Erdman Harris, graduate of Princeton and holder of a Columbia M.A. who had taught in Egypt, began nine years of teaching at Union in the field of religious education and psychology. He earned his B.D. and Th.D. degrees before focusing his energies in preparatory school teaching and administration.

John Baillie was chosen to replace William Adams Brown in the Roosevelt chair of systematic theology. Born in Scotland and educated at the university and theological college at Edinburgh followed by graduate study in Germany, he served in serveral educational posts in Europe and taught theology at Auburn Seminary and at Emmanuel College, Toronto before coming to Union in 1930. Baillie was a skilled preacher, lecturer, and writer who understood the contemporary scene but took seriously the historic patterns of Christian theology, stressing their relevance to a generation that had minimized them. His influence was increasing at Union when he was called back to his alma mater in 1934 as professor of divinity. Coffin, who found him immensely helpful in clarifying Union's tasks in theological education, later observed that "his departure was a great gain for Scotland and a sore impoverishment to the Seminary."[12] The Scottish presence at Union was strong when Moffatt and Baillie joined Hugh Black and Ernest Scott. Although Scott was English born, his university and seminary education had been in Scotland, and he was ordained and served a church there for some thirteen years.

Three of the appointments made in the early years of the Coffin presidency later emerged as very visible figures in the Union story. One of Coffin's first acts was to name Henry P. Van Dusen (1924) as an instructor in systematic theology and the philosophy of religion. A graduate of Princeton who had studied a year at Edinburgh before coming to Union, he had served as a student assistant at Madison Avenue Presbyterian Church, and was elected president of the student body. When Van Dusen and one other student were ordained by the presbytery of New York in 1924 even though they were unwilling to affirm or deny the virgin birth of Jesus, it was partly because of the effective leadership of Coffin that the presbytery was not censured and the liberals did not walk out of the denomination. After several years of service with the student department of the YMCA, the tall, able, self-confident Van Dusen took up his new post at Union, at first continuing some of his work with college students. He was quickly promoted to assistant and then (in 1931) associate professor, and also assumed the duties of the dean of students when Gaylord White died. He took sabbatical leave to complete his Ph.D. at Edinburgh in 1932. Deeply influenced by William Adams Brown, with whom he worked for a time as a student assistant, he was theologically a Christocentric liberal with wide ecumenical interests. His reputation was increasing through the publication of books aimed primarily at lay readers, especially *In Quest of Life's Meaning* (1925) and *The Plain Man Seeks for God* (1933).[13]

In 1928 an unusual opportunity came Union's way—how extraordinary it was would quickly unfold. Reinhold Niebuhr, who had studied at Elmhurst College and Eden Seminary and then earned B.D. and M.A. degrees at Yale, had taken the pastorate of Bethel

Evangelical Church in Detroit in 1915. The church flourished under his ministry even as he became sharply critical of the paternalism of Henry Ford and championed the rights of working people. He wrote frequently, especially for the liberal weekly *The Christian Century*, and was especially popular with student groups. The Fellowship of Reconciliation wanted to bring this convinced pacifist to New York to edit the periodical it backed, *The World Tomorrow*. Sherwood Eddy, who had studied at Union in the early 1890s, approached Coffin to ask if the seminary would give Niebuhr an appointment so that he could both teach and do the editorial work. The vote in the faculty was close, for Niebuhr's lack of an earned doctorate and his polemical style troubled some. But Coffin thought that the Midwestern pastor would be a good influence on the students, and the appointment was initially without expense to the seminary, for, as Eddy recalled with understandable pride in his autobiography, "I had the privilege of paying Reinhold Niebuhr's salary during his first years at Union."[14] Niebuhr's brilliance and virtuosity as a teacher, preacher, and writer quickly flowered as he became a conspicuous world leader of Christian thought and life.

Originally appointed as Associate Professor of Christian Ethics, Niebuhr was soon promoted to the Dodge professorship of applied Christianity. This was precipitated partly by Yale's plan to bring Niebuhr back there as professor of Christian ethics. Coffin responded by promising to take the matter to the board, noting to his colleague in a letter: "Meanwhile let me say, what you certainly must know, that we all here consider your work a brilliant contribution to the Seminary and, what is more, that we know that you have added to the spiritual quality of the institution." [15] As the depression deepened, Niebuhr moved past reformism to espouse socialism and make discriminating use of Marxist social analysis. At the same time, his increasing dissatisfaction with the naïveté, sentimentality, and intellectual flabbiness that plagued theological liberalism—especially its optimism about human nature—led him to become the central theological writer and speaker of the developing realistic, neo-orthodox theological movement in America, which despite his criticism of "liberal illusions" was more flexible and pragmatic than European Barthian neo-orthodoxy. His famous *Moral Man and Immoral Society* of 1932 quickly became one of the major theological writings of the century. While some students resisted his probing and disturbing analyses and were not attracted by his immense personal magnetism, many more found him highly stimulating intellectually and spiritually and were greatly influenced by him. As a prolific author of articles and books and a highly popular preacher and lecturer on the college and university circuit, Niebuhr was frequently on the road on weekends, often gathering large audiences and making Union more widely known as he traveled.[16]

Though his name was later to be often closely linked with those of Niebuhr and Van Dusen, John C. Bennett (1927) was away from Union during much of the Coffin administration. While serving as a graduate assistant he completed an S.T.M. in 1929 and was named instructor of systematic theology and the philosophy of religion. The following year he took a post at Auburn Theological Seminary, and moved half a dozen years later to the Pacific School of Religion. Then he actively re-entered the Union scene late in the Coffin years (1943) as professor of Christian theology and ethics.

The seminary was shielded at first from the impact of the stock market crash of October 1929 by its endowment, listed late the following year at just over $8.5 million. The plant assets were then valued at slightly over $4.5 million, while the income for the academic year 1929–30, approximately $775,000, exceeded expenditures by more than $3000.[17] Despite this sound financial base, as the depression deepened its effects were more strongly felt. Student enrollment declined. Precise comparable figures are not easy to ascertain, for students who were part time and/or from affiliated institutions were counted differently from year to year, and estimates varied depending on the time of year they were taken. A report late in 1931 reported a total of 431, while in the following academic year it dropped below 400. To keep the budget balanced, the faculty, noting that living costs had gone down more than 10 percent, unanimously recommended that faculty and educational staff salaries be reduced by that proportion and that the salaries of other employess be cut 5 percent. The board gratefully accepted the 10 percent figure for all employees, in some cases modifying the reduction for employees in the lower income brackets, and the budget remained in balance. The problems of deferred maintenance caused some anxieties, and Coffin had great difficulty in raising the budget of the School of Sacred Music.[18]

A number of students had to struggle to remain in seminary; some could not afford the refectory prices and ate too little. Students characteristically showed their concern for those out of work; by late 1930 they were caring for ten to twenty-five unemployed young men in the gym and raising money to support them until they found jobs. The goal for their budget in 1930–31, to be raised by the seminary community, was $6500, of which $5400 was designated for the unemployed. When all of the graduates of 1932 who were studying for the ministry were placed, it was duly noted as a considerable achievement.[19]

The great majority of the student body during the entire Coffin period lived in the dormitories, under rules carefully regulating the times and conditions for an exchange of visits between areas set aside for men and women students—a familiar pattern in American education at the time. Students were urged to defer marriage until after graduation, but the president somewhat reluctantly allowed exceptions. It was difficult for married applicants to receive scholarships. Though the student body was considerably more homogeneous than it was later to become, as it was drawn largely from representatives of the "mainline" Protestant communions who were recent college graduates, there was some increase in the number of endowed fellowships open to graduates in theology of high standing from England, Scotland, France, Switzerland, and Germany, which enriched the international flavor of an interdenominational mix. Since the beginning of Union's history, the great majority of graduates played useful, sometimes conspicuous, roles in the life of religious, educational, and reform institutions. Some became very prominent in later years.

Dietrich Bonhoeffer, for example, came from Germany to study at Union in the academic year 1930–31. In view of his Licentiate in Theology from Berlin, it was not deemed necessary for him to take a degree. He was quite critical of much that he saw in American life and in its patterns of theological education; as one of his closest friends, Paul Lehmann (1930, 1936), later remarked, "his aristocracy was unmistakable yet not obtrusive." His close friend and biographer, Eberhard Bethge, speaks of Bonhoeffer as "an artist in offering unqualified friendship." At Union he extended that gift to A. Franklin Fisher (1936), who opened doors to his German friend in Harlem as they worshipped and worked together at Abyssinian Baptist Church, and who later made important contributions to black theological education. Bonhoeffer's other two close friends were students from overseas, Erwin Sutz from Switzerland and Jean Lasserre from France, both of whom received S.T.M. degrees in 1931, and whose paths were later to cross in Europe. Bonhoeffer returned to Union only once, staying for a few weeks in the Prophets' chamber in 1939. Here he made his fateful decision not to take a post in America but to return to Germany. He became famous only after his martyrdom in 1945; as Bethge writes:

A man suffered shipwreck in, with, and because of his country. He saw his church and its claims collapse in ruins. The theological writings he left consisted of barely accessible fragments. In 1945 only a handful of friends and enemies knew who this young man had been. In Christian Germany other names were in the limelight. When his name began to emerge from the anonymity of his death, theological faculties and churches felt uncertain and did little.

Only later did his true stature as Christian and theologian become widely known.[20]

The presence of Frank Fisher in the student body in Bonhoeffer's day highlights another aspect of Coffin's presidency. As his colleague and successor Van Dusen expressed it,

From his earliest ministry, Dr. Coffin has been a fearless advocate of racial equality. The opportunities of the Seminary have always been open equally not only to students of every denomination of Christians, but to men and women of all races. Not a few of the foremost Negro Christian leaders of the country have had their education there.[21]

Though occasional black students had attended the seminary since the mid-nineteenth century, the number significantly increased during Coffin's presidency. In the years 1926–33, for example, those who came to the seminary in addition to Fisher included William H. King, Leroy J. Montgomery, J. Neal Hughley, Shelby A. Rooks, William E. Carrington, Claude L. Franklin, Colbert H. Pearson, M.

Moran Weston, Charles E. Byrd, Porter W. Phillips, and Seth C. Edwards—and the succession has continued to the present.

The number of women graduating from the seminary also increased in the Coffin years, in part because of the founding of the School of Sacred Music. Coffin, however, was not particularly keen on women as theological students; a number of the denominations served by Union had not yet taken the step of ordaining them. Many of those who received theological degrees in those years had careers in education. To illustrate, Virginia Corwin (1929) later earned her Ph.D. at Yale and became well known as a professor of biblical literature at Smith College, and Mary Frances Thelen (1934) completed her studies in the joint program with Columbia (Ph.D., 1945) while teaching at Hollins College, later rising to full professor at Randolph-Macon Woman's College. Coffin had several encounters with a breezy westerner, Doris Webster Havice, who entered the seminary in the same year that Niebuhr joined the faculty. As she described one of the encounters,

Reinie smoked a pipe, and one evening when we were sitting in the lounge he asked me if I had ever smoked a pipe. I said I had not, so he offered to let me try his. Just as I was getting the hang of it, the president . . . walked by and nearly fainted. I did not know it until years later, but the question of women smoking came up at the next faculty meeting. Someone proposed that there be a rule that no women could smoke in the seminary. The rule never passed because the two women on the faculty (Mary Ely Lyman and Sophia Fahs) filibustered for five hours against it. Neither of these women smoked nor believed in smoking, but they were clear that there could not be a rule that applied to one sex and not to the other.

When Havice sought Coffin's permission to complete the last year of her degree abroad (at New College, Edinburgh), she remembered that his response was "I will do everything in my power to get rid of you," stating that he did not believe that men in the seminary should marry while in school, and that the presence of young women was "hazardous." [22] In later years she earned a doctorate at Columbia and served various educational institutions.

The transition to a Union that was faithful to both piety and scholarship was clearly completed by the early 1930s. But as the effects of the depression deepened and war clouds began to gather on the horizon, new problems emerged. Were the liberal theological and social patterns with which Union had become identified the right ones for a threatening time? Could an expensive plant and a distinguished faculty be maintained in the face of financial limitations? Various tensions in the life of the seminary, in part reflecting troubling concerns in the nation and its religious institutions, became noticeably more acute by the academic year 1933–34.

TENSIONS (1934–40)

The continuing effects of the depression adversely affected the financial situation of the seminary into the middle and late 1930s. Some of those who had long been donors had to reduce or forgo their usual contributions. Early in 1935, after the faculty and staff had already taken cuts in salaries, it was thought necessary to reduce the amount paid to pensioners, which then came directly out of seminary funds. In addition, the first steps were taken toward a contributory faculty/staff retirement plan, with the seminary putting in 7.5 percent of annual salary, the individual 5 percent. It was a difficult time financially for many persons associated with the seminary. Among the students were those who had to work hard at part-time low paying jobs to get through, sometimes not eating enough. The dean of students, Van Dusen, reported to the board on the way various resources were marshaled for student aid.[23] The president himself had to live through a stringent period for the first time in his life as personal income from outside sources rapidly disappeared. Maintaining the five-story president's house at the corner of 120th and Claremont, at which guests were regularly entertained, became a burden, and certain of the Coffins' personal belongings had to be sold.[24]

  To maintain faculty strength in the face of financial austerity was difficult, but it was done, sometimes by calling promising younger persons to take heavy assignments in lower faculty ranks. Two such persons, destined for long service at the seminary, were secured in 1934. Frank W. Herriott, who had earned a B.D. at Union in 1926 and a Ph.D. at Teachers College seven years later, an ordained Baptist minister, was called as instructor in religious education and psychology, devoting particular attention to the field of youth work in which he had much experience. A much younger man, Cyril Charles Richardson, was made instructor of church history. Born in England, educated in Canada, where he had received the licentiate in theology at Emmanuel College, Saskatoon in 1931, he came to Union for graduate study, earning the Th.D. in 1934, and was ordained an Episcopal priest soon after. A specialist in patristics and early church history, his versatility across the entire field was soon displayed in his writing and teaching, and he later (1949) was named Washburn professor of church history. His lectures were much appreciated both for their broad erudition and salty witticisms.

Budget limitations made it very difficult for Union to respond easily to opportunities to take in refugee professors from Germany as they began to flee from their posts following Hitler's rise to power in 1933. There was one major exception in this period. When Coffin attended a meeting at Columbia of a committee to help such refugees, he spotted the name of Paul Tillich, who was on the first list (April 13, 1933) of those suspended from university teaching. He had been driven from his post as professor of philosophy at Frankfurt-am-Main for warning his country that the Nazis would crush all liberty of investigation and teaching. Reinhold Niebuhr heartily backed the president's offer to find a post for Tillich, and the faculty voted that each professor would contribute 5 percent of salary toward a stipend for the first year.

Tillich was born in Prussia in 1886, and educated at the universities of Tübingen, Halle, Berlin, and Breslau, where he received his Ph.D. 1911. Ordained a Lutheran minister the next year, he served as an army chaplain during World War I, and then taught at a number of universities in the fields of philosophy and theology, becoming well-known for his writings and for his leadership in the movement of radical religious socialism.[25] Named lecturer in philosophical theology, he arrived in New York with his family late in 1933, moved into a Union apartment, and began to work at improving his scanty knowledge of English. At first his English was not very intelligible to his American hearers, and a German accent was unmistakable to the end of his brilliant American career. Students immediately took to him, and the stories that circulated about his linguistic gaffes were told with affection. His efforts to say "all faiths have gnosis" was parodied by students as "all faces have noses," and he was reported to speak of persons as having been "salvated." To make room for such a person in a time of austerity was not easy; a foundation and an emergency committee on displaced German scholars contributed to his support. In 1937 he was named an associate professor (in part because of a student petition) and three years later a full professor. Soon a stream of articles and books made him one of the best-known theologians in America.

The seminary was still struggling with financial problems; in 1936, anticipating a continuing decline in income, the faculty and board had to wrestle with a retrenchment plan that called for certain reductions in departments that had two or more professors.[26] In 1936, William Adams Brown retired and was not replaced as research professor. It was decided that when Eugene Lyman retired, a full professor of the philosophy of religion would not be called to his position. In preparation, a brilliant young instructor was appointed in 1936. David E. Roberts had won the traveling fellowship in 1934 and two years later completed his Ph.D. at Edinburgh. According to plan, when Lyman retired in 1940, Roberts, by then ordained as a Presbyterian minister, was named associate professor on the Hartley Foundation.

The meaning of retrenchment became very clear in 1938, however, when there were four major retirements: Moffatt in church history, Frame and Scott in New Testament, and Black in practical theology. The full professorship in church history was not filled for five years, and Richardson ably took over the introductory courses. Only one appointment was made at that time to replace the two vacancies in New Testament, as Frederick C. Grant became Robinson professor of biblical theology. A graduate of General (B.D.) and Western (Th.D.) theological seminaries, Grant had served in a number of Episcopal parishes and filled several teaching and administrative posts, most recently as president of Seabury-Western. His impressive learning was better demonstrated in the seminar room than the lecture hall, and in later years the great breadth of his theological knowledge was displayed not only in his many books but as he became the director of graduate studies. The retirement of Hugh Black left the practical field further understaffed, for the Jesup chair had

Two famous figures, brought to Union by Coffin's alertness: Reinhold Niebuhr right, and Paul Tillich.

been vacant since 1936. Hence a new appointment in the field was pressing, but not until 1939 was Walter Russell Bowie (a graduate of Episcopal Theological Seminary in Alexandria who had also studied for part of a year at Union) named as professor of practical theology. He knew the seminary well, having been a director and a lecturer in homiletics, and in his new role was much respected.

The long-lasting effect of the depression on American society increased the desire for social and political reform and, in some cases, radical reconstruction. A number of church groups favored various social movements of both the moderate and the more revolutionary types. A number of faculty members, graduates, and students participated in one or another of them, and in some cases assumed major leadership responsibilities.

During the winter and spring of 1934 a small group of students decided that what was needed was radical reconstruction, going far beyond the reforms of the New Deal in the direction of a socialist cooperative commonwealth. Some of them pointed to the Soviet Union as an example. Wanting to act on their principles, they participated in various protests in the city and turned part of their zeal on the seminary itself, becoming quite critical of the administration. Several such students were members of what was then called the Agenda Club, a social-action arm of the student cabinet. As Coffin reported to the Board of Directors early in 1934, a committee of students was appointed by the Agenda Club to investigate the wages and working conditions at Union, but he told its members that they would not be able to make any general study, although they could request information on specific questions, except that detailed information on wages was deemed personal and confidential. The committee prepared an extensive report, adopted by the student cabinet, which criticized the seminary for its low wages, especially for the maids who made beds and cleaned offices and dormitory rooms, and for workers in the refectory. The report called for an increase of 15 percent in the pay of the latter because they were laid off for 13 weeks each year. Coffin thought the students were going too far into matters that were not their responsibility, while some of them believed that the administration was being defensive and evasive.

The growing tension was heightened by several incidents. Some students joined in the picketing during the Waldorf-Astoria Hotel strike carrying a sign identifying themselves as from the seminary, which the Hearst papers duly exploited in implicit criticism of Union. Then, when the rector of the Church of the Heavenly Rest sent a telegram of congratulations to the Governor of California, who was reported to have approved the lynching of two kidnappers, a group of students, sensitive to the terrible evil of lynching in American life, picketed the church the following Sunday, again placarding their affiliation with the seminary. In a resulting scuffle with parishioners a student was jailed. Coffin reprimanded the student for the way the seminary's name had been used, but when a committee from the church demanded the expulsion of the picketers, he refused. In response to a question of his, the committee members indignantly indicated that they had no intention of asking the rector to resign. Thereupon the president declared that if they were not going to ask their mature rector to leave because he had done a foolish thing, he was not going to expel the youthful students for doing something foolish.

Such episodes triggered an internal debate about the use of the seminary's name. The chair of an "Authorized Committee of the Agenda Club" wrote an open letter to the president saying that a conference between him and students had agreed that no individual or minority group had the right to participate in public activity of a controversial nature—but that Coffin had done it and therefore so could they. On April 7 Coffin replied that as president and member of the board he was "expected to represent the Seminary before the public," but that students "are admitted to the Seminary to prepare themselves for the Christian ministry, but are not chosen to represent the Seminary, unless for some specific purpose to which they have been duly appointed by it."

On the night of May 1 the most remembered of the series of events occurred. Someone ran up a red flag, symbolic of the revolutionary stance, on the seminary's flagpole above the gate at Broadway and 121st Street. The police demanded its removal; the president was greatly annoyed because the incident brought discredit to the seminary. The student cabinet posted a notice requesting the responsible person or group to acknowledge it, but no one did so. To some students Coffin was a "fascist despot," but he retained the loyalty of the majority of the student body, which accorded him a spontaneous expression of appreciation at their spring meeting.

To a group of graduates at commencement time later in May, Coffin reviewed the events of the year, discussing the "extreme social radicalism" of some of the students and noting that they would be asked to go elsewhere if they could not subscribe to the purposes of the seminary. In a letter addressed to the student body dated May 23, 1934, the president, speaking with the approval of the faculty and board, called attention to the purposes of the seminary as set forth in the preamble to the charter, and observed that "the discussions of the past year, although well meant, have, by the way which they were pressed, menaced the cordial relations among us and seriously interfered with the scholastic work of some students and members of the faculty, besides consuming much of the time of the administration." He concluded that "all who re-enroll next autumn will be assumed heartily to accept the purpose and organization of the seminary." [27]

That did not close the matter. The press reported what was going on; the *Times* headlined a story "Union Seminary to Curb Radicals." The whole series of events was reviewed in a national magazine by an alumnus. Hubert C. Herring (1913), secretary of the department of social relations of the Congregational education society, had been present when Coffin had addressed the alumni/ae, and in June his sensational article, "Union Seminary Routs Its Reds," in *The Christian Century* attracted great attention. He interpreted the academic year that had just closed as one "in which presidential misery reached a high pitch, and in which a substantial number of students have become troubled and rebellious." In his review of events he admitted some excesses on the part of students, but decisively took their side, declaring that their concern for doing something about social evils had been met with resistance on the part of the administration. He feared that the seminary would lose its eminence: "Today, there is no finer theological faculty in the world. Never was the quality of the student body finer." But he added, "It would be a calamity if this school of the prophets shall degenerate into another training camp for priests. That is the clear danger in the present situation." Referring to Coffin's letter to students, he declared that the latter "are writing the president of Union seminary their sober judgment that if there is no place in the church for a revolutionary, the time will soon come when there will be no place in the world for the church." Believing that he spoke for many graduates, he called on them to write to Coffin against his "purification" of the seminary. Many did write to the *Century*, which published a number of the responses. Most of those selected were critical of Herring, called attention to various errors and misrepresentations in the article, and challenged his claim to speak for its graduates.[28]

The trouble smoldered on into the next academic year. A group of students wanted the preacher at an Armistice Day service to be Dr. Julius F. Hecker, a Russian-born Methodist minister and author of pro-Soviet books, who had addressed the regular Forum for discussion of issues. According to these students in "The Undercurrent," one of those duplicated student publications that come and go in seminary life, the administration said no to their request, and they then pressed the issue of free speech: "If the administration wanted to take issue with our economic or tactical views, we could be forgiving. But any time it wants to fight about free speech and student government we lick our chops with glee. On these grounds Union Seminary will never rout its REDS."

Denied the use of the chapel, the students took the service to the social hall on Monday evening, November 12, saying that "it is not the first time that prophets have forsaken the temple." [29] The service was led by Hecker, who emphasized the importance of world peace.

This and other incidents were reviewed at the time of the 1935 commencement in the address of the class president, Ralph Tefferteller, who observed that many members of the class were anxious about the attitude of the administration. The sharp differences of opinion about the tensions of the mid-1930s persist a half-century later; when the author of these lines discussed some of these matters at a fiftieth reunion of the class of 1935, the debate was resumed. Some argued that there had been no sense of hostility between Coffin and the Agenda Club while others declared there had; some felt that the administration had been overly harsh while others believed it had not, and that Coffin's integrity and sense of humor really had saved the day.

In reviewing that stormy time just ten years later, John

Bennett (who in the mid-1930s had been teaching at Auburn), noted the differences between the sociopolitical attitudes of Coffin and some of his colleagues and those of certain students at the time "when the depression was most acute and nerves were on edge." In Bennett's interpretation, Coffin believed that those who were influenced to some degree by Marxist ideas concerning the role of working-class movements as bearers of justice presented them in a far too simple form. "There was a tendency at the Seminary to identify oneself so absolutely with radical political movements that the distinctive Christian criticism of all movements—radical and conservative—was lost," said Bennett, characteristically adding that "much of my criticism of this tendency comes from wisdom after the event and it should not allow us today to forget that underlying it was a sense of solidarity with the underprivileged which has characterized Union at its best." In a tense situation Coffin was pressed by his convictions and responsibilities to make less of his own commitments to social Christianity than he had done before and was to do later. Though Coffin's ways appeared autocratic to some, those who knew him best observed elements of both the patrician and the democrat in his makeup. His sincere interest in others and his concern for the rights of minorities kept his elitism in check. With his clear sense of order, he was a strong leader, often sounding out colleagues' opinions during walks on Riverside Drive while preparing for meetings.[30]

An illustration of that "sense of solidarity with the underprivileged" in the mid-1930s was the founding and staffing by students of a Neighborhood Center on Broadway down the hill toward 125th Street. Though he felt it was too big a project for the small Union constituency to sustain, Coffin agreed that it had done good work and spoke of the testimonies to its effectiveness that he had heard from various sources in the community. The center lasted for a few years, providing avenues by which students could offer concrete help to persons in need during a period of crisis. They did some of their best work with street gangs, primarily from LaSalle Street, focusing their energies toward athletic pursuits. James H. Robinson (1938), for example, troubled and disillusioned by the racism he encountered at Union, found the center an outlet of service. Though working hard at switchboard and refectory jobs to stay in school, he "volunteered to take over two groups of poor boys, one white and one

Negro." But the future famous pastor of the Church of the Master and founder of Crossroads Africa might have left the seminary except for the understanding and encouragement extended by Professor Lyman, whom he went to see just as he was on the point of departure.[31]

The rather dramatic episodes of 1934–35 were outcroppings of brisk, complex, and continuing debates about theology and ethics that marked the life of Union during the depression decade and focused much attention, both favorable and unfavorable, on the seminary. The story of the rise of Protestant neo-orthodox theology in the 1930s has been told in many places.[32] Stimulated in part by the European theology of crisis in which Karl Barth and Emil Brunner (who had studied at Union in 1919–20) were leading figures, American neo-orthodoxy was a somewhat diffuse theological movement that emphasized divine transcendence but resisted a doctrine of God as "wholly other," and stressed human sinfulness but did not neglect human capacities. It challenged sharply what it viewed as liberalism's overemphasis on divine immanence, human perfectibility, and idealistic optimism. Those views were deep-rooted in the major denominations and interdenominational movements that Union served, and a number of faculty members and students were committed to them.

Unquestionably, the most conspicuous figures in the neo-orthodox impact on American culture, religion, theology, and ethics were Reinhold Niebuhr and his younger brother Richard at Yale. The former was the most publicly visible in the 1930s—the forceful, articulate, prolific, polemical Niebuhr who stumped the country crusading for theological and social change and poured out editorials, articles, and books in profusion. He always insisted that he was not a theologian but a social thinker and ethicist, but he believed so strongly that Christian social thought and action must be firmly based on faith in God as revealed in Christ and the Bible that he became a powerful theological influence in his time. A self-confident controversialist ever open to change of mind as he wrestled with changing realities, he drew some colleagues and students to him and repelled others, but the combination of his faith and intellect was educative for many who did not regard themselves as his followers in any direct sense, and decisive for those who did, including growing numbers of his students. He was a compelling center of intellectual and theological renewal in the seminary as well as beyond, a great lecturer, teacher, and preacher. Theological diversity at Union continued, but there was a growing interest in doctrinal issues, a tendency to ask what is unique about Christian faith and then to work out its implications for many aspects of life.

Niebuhr was also a man of prophetic spirit, an ethicist who was also an activist, a leader of various—and changing—social causes. Though a critic of the utopian illusions of Marxism as well as of liberalism, in the thirties he was informed by concepts of class struggle and the social ownership of the means of production, was a member of the Socialist party, and founder of the Fellowship of Socialist Christians (FSC), becoming in 1935 editor of its new journal, *Radical Religion.* The FSC was not a seminary organization, but it often met there, and faculty members and students got involved in its activities. Like many of those who had been part of the social gospel movement in the 1920s, Niebuhr had long been a pacifist, until his growing realism and mounting criticism of ethical perfectionism led to a dramatic break with that movement in 1933 and with the pacifist Fellowship of Reconciliation, of which he had been national chairman. He wrestled with the significance of Marxist ideas in his book of 1934, *Reflections on the End of an Era,* finding insights in some of them but often criticizing the way they were applied, noting, for example, that "the vigor with which the Russian communist subordinates the peasant to the interests of a collectivized industrial society is an interesting example of the unconscious imperialism of a group expressing itself in devotion to what it regards a universal principle." In a discussion of the conflict between Christianity and communism, he contrasted both communism and liberalism (in both its naturalistic and Christian forms) unfavorably with historic Christianity: "The genius of classical religion is that it finds a basis for optimism after it has entertained the most thoroughgoing pessimism." [33] As the 1930s wore on, his critique of Marxism, especially as it was interpreted by Russian communism, grew sharper.

His colleague Harry Ward, however, was moving in a quite different direction. He had often criticized capitalism sharply, stating his views fully in a book which he regarded as his most significant, *Our Economic Morality,* in which he questioned the "myths" of individualism, laissez-faire economics, and competition. After spending a good deal of time in Russia during a 1931–32 sabbatical, he believed he had found the answer to the socioeconomic problem of modern civilization, wrote *In Place of Profit*, and, as his biographer concludes, thereafter "remained a constant observer and defender of the Soviet Union." [34] He later insisted that he was not a member of the Communist or any political party but did what he did as a follower of Jesus and a teacher of ethics. But his largely uncritical support of various radical causes, including Communism, and his participation in "united fronts" with those who represented them meant that he became increasingly isolated from most of his Union colleagues. His long experience in social reform and action agencies of various kinds had sharpened his organizational skills and platform abilities so that he was well prepared for roles in various united front agencies which flourished in the 1930s, and in which reformers and reconstructionists from differing religious and secular backgrounds worked together for common ends.

Ward was especially conspicuous in the American League Against War and Fascism. Keynote speaker at its Chicago congress in 1934, he emphasized its anticapitalist stance. Over 400 organizations, including youth, labor, Socialist, Communist, and church groups were represented among the more than 3000 delegates. Ward devoted considerable time to the League (the second part of the name was changed in 1937 to "for Peace and Democracy") until its collapse in 1940 following the Nazi–Soviet pact of 1939. His activities at the time also involved continuing leadership in the Methodist Federation for Social Service (the change from "Service" to "Action" in the title was not made until 1947), and the American Civil Liberties Union (which he chaired for twenty years until his resignation in 1940). Years later it became known that he had been under the surveillance of the Federal Bureau of Investigation from the early 1920s until his death in 1969. [35]

At Union Ward influenced many students through his regular courses on such topics as ethical issues in the social order, ethics of social change, ethical viewpoints in modern literature, and ethical interpretations. Despite his many involvements outside the seminary, he did not neglect his classes, in which three characteristic questions were regularly pressed: what are the facts, what do they mean, and what should be done? Some students, of course, did not

take to his approach; others who never became his followers nevertheless respected him for his knowledge and serious concern for the
underprivileged. Some were deeply influenced by his teaching and
example. Critics were quick to notice that among them were those
who went into social work, labor organizations, or radical politics
rather than into religious leadership.

It was Niebuhr, however, who became the increasingly
magnetic figure as his realistic, neo-orthodox theological position
matured. His critical mind saw limitations in all political and pro-
grammatic approaches to human problems. The rift between Union's
two prophetic ethicists widened as deep and permanent differences
between them became fixed, sharpening the debates that raged in
classrooms and refectory. Both had an impact on the student body,
both were available to students. The Wards, who lived across the
Hudson, served a weekly tea in Harry's office, and often had groups
to their home. The Niebuhrs held a Thursday night open house at
stated times during a semester to which everyone was invited. The
event was celebrated in a student song to the tune of "When the roll
is called up yonder"; the opening verse was:

> When it's eight o'clock on Thursday night
>   And books become a bore;
> Then we'll leave our desks and climb the golden stair,
> We will gather at the master's feet
>   A-sitting on the floor,
> When the beer is served at Reiny's
>   We'll be there . . . [36]

Students who respected both Ward and Niebuhr, how-
ever, often fell into intense discussions over the different ways they
faced ethical problems. A novel published in 1951 about a thinly
disguised Union in the 1930s featured the differences between the
two as represented by its fictional professors, Ralph Shaw and Raymond ("Raymie") Unwin, and observed that "many a class in Christian ethics dissolved into a debate as to whether modern Communism was reconcilable with either Christian socialism, Christian
communism or anything that could be called remotely Christian." [37]

It took all of Coffin's skill to remain in close touch with
both his nationally known professors of ethics and to keep the wid-

ening gulf from interfering with the seminary's educational task, but he did it with customary grace and humor. Though he sharply disagreed with Ward on many social and theological issues, he respected his concern, his passion for facts, and his wide knowledge. He wrote, "Dr. Ward was a moving preacher and a devout spirit; but as the years passed he became more and more committed to extreme radical social views, and the administration of the Seminary had more protests from various Church groups concerning his utterances than concerning all members of the faculty combined." The protests came not only from church groups but from patriotic organizations; for example, Elizabeth Dilling's *The Red Network* in 1934 listed Union among its suspect groups, noting that its nickname in some circles was "The Red Seminary." [38] But when Ward reached the normal year for retirement, in 1938, under Coffin's leadership faculty and board voted to extend his term for three more years; a grateful Ward thanked Coffin, saying that Union was "the only educational institution in the country that had shown such forbearance and freedom for teaching." [39]

The seminary's Centennial celebration in May 1936 was used as an occasion to reaffirm its history and its commitment to scholarly, ecumenical theological education and to the Christian churches. A positive sign was an increase in enrollment in that academic year. When the *Alumni Bulletin* reported a total of 295 students (88 of them women) in the fall, it noted that it was the first increase in seven years. The financial picture was less promising. Early in 1936 the board put its retrenchment plan into effect. The 100th anniversary did offer an opportunity to improve the seminary's financial standing, yet there was a little disappointment mixed with significant achievement: the Centennial Fund goal of $403,000 fell short by $23,000—the lean years were not quite over. But the sense of crisis had passed, as notes of joy for a rich heritage and of hope for its future were sounded at anniversary celebrations.

The events began on Saturday, May 16 with a music festival at Riverside Church which brought together 62 massed choirs totalling 1500 voices from various institutions, mostly churches, served by students and graduates of the School of Sacred Music. On the following day Coffin preached the Centennial Sermon in James Chapel and referred to certain highlights in Union's history. He observed that one of the main outcomes of the Briggs affair was this: "the Seminary was assisted by hostile brethren to a larger service—a mission under God to champion the freedom of Christian scholars, loyal to Christ, the one Head of the Church, to explore truth unafraid and to teach it frankly. This is the position of liberal evangelicalism—liberty in loyalty to the gospel of Christ."

Coffin was not engaging in special pleading for his own position, for he had already stressed the inclusivism of the seminary and believed that persons of various theological positions could and did come under that banner. Characterizing this period in Union's history from the vantage point of imminent retirement in 1960, even such a polemical theologian as Reinhold Niebuhr could agree: "Religiously it meant the ascendancy of the 'liberal evangelicalism' of our revered chief, the late Henry Sloane Coffin, . . . whom I followed both religiously and politically more than ever before. I think his thought and spirit dominated the whole Seminary." [40] It certainly dominated the Centennial.

More formal attention to Union's history came in an address, "A Century in Retrospect," by William Adams Brown at the Centennial Service on Monday preceded by an academic procession of delegates in colorful gowns from many educational institutions, and during which all the hymns sung had been written by Union graduates. Brown, who had been associated with Union for half of its hundred years, called attention to a number of prominent figures in Union's history, among them William M. Kingsley, who had just presided for the last time over a meeting of the board of directors. He had joined it in 1901 and served as its president for twenty-three years, missing just one meeting in that period.

Approximately 750 people attended the Centennial Dinner that evening and heard a succession of well-known educational figures, including Nicholas Murray Butler, the president of Columbia University, representatives from General, Yale, Harvard, Princeton, and Chicago seminaries, as well as Coffin and Fosdick. They learned that Kingsley's successor was to be Thatcher M. Brown, also a banker, who had served actively on the board since 1908. Since the Centennial marked the retirement of his brother William, his coming to the chair meant that the Brown leadership in seminary affairs continued for another decade. They also learned of the election to the board of its first woman member, Elizabeth Cutter Morrow, author and educator, widow of former director Dwight W. Morrow.

There could have been no better setting than the Centennial for the presentation at a meeting of alumni/ae of a *festschrift* to Williams Adams Brown, *The Church Through Half a Century*. Its chapters were written by former students, among whom were the editors, Samuel McCrea Cavert and Henry Pitney Van Dusen. The volume surveyed the thought and work of the church since the time the person it honored had entered Union.

The celebration concluded with Commencement on Tuesday evening, a feature of which was the inauguration of Van Dusen as Roosevelt professor of systematic theology. He was an "ethical-social" evangelical liberal who stressed the experiential aspects of faith; he had been deeply influenced by Schleiermacher and Ritschl, by his teachers Coffin (though the shift in emphasis from liberal evangelical to evangelical liberal is significant) and Brown, and had served as graduate assistant for the latter. Dean K. Thompson's careful study of him interprets his liberalism as pragmatic and dynamic, with an emphasis on continuity between divine and human and a sincere concern for mediation among Christian theological positions. He held long theological debates with Niebuhr, and saw the values of the latter's positions and emphases even as he criticized his methods. His address, "The Premises of Theology and the Task of Preaching," served the purposes of both an inaugural and a commencement speech. He advanced four premises to guide both theologian and preacher through a troubled time: tentativeness in conclusions, the faith of high expectancy, the sufficiency of Christ, and the necessity of the Church. The first and third of his points demonstrated his adherence to evangelical liberalism. The second, "which commands breadth, tolerance, catholicity in the Christian mind," and the fourth, which "might have been absent from our thinking not many years ago," were indicative of the influence of contemporary and ecumenical theology on him.[41]

Many references to Union's interdenominational and ecumenical stance were made during the various Centennial events; it was widely known that many of its prominent figures were also playing major roles in some aspect of the ecumenical movement.

Coffin's enthusiasm had been aroused when he attended the famous Edinburgh Conference of 1910. Brown had long been involved in various avenues of ecumenism; for example, he was conspicuous at both the great universal Christian conferences of the 1920s, Life and Work at Stockholm, Faith and Order at Lausanne, and had spent 1932–33 in Europe preparing for the then forthcoming (July 1937) Oxford Life and Work Conference on Church, Community, and State. Van Dusen had been deeply engaged in ecumenical youth work, but stepped into international prominence at the Oxford conference of 1937, in which many Union graduates and faculty members (Bennett, Brown, Coffin, Niebuhr, Tillich) were involved. The following year he took a six-month tour of the Pacific basin, which climaxed in a conference called by the International Missionary Council at Madras (Tambaran) in December 1938, and there he was won to a new admiration and support of the modern missionary movement. Van Dusen served on the provisional committee of the World Council of Churches "in process of formation," and chaired its Study Department for about fifteen years.

The Centennial was an occasion not only for reviewing a rich past but also for looking forward. Many of those who were part of it continued faithfully to reflect the seminary's ecumenical history and commitment. At that time, of course, the ecumenical movement involved primarily Protestant and Eastern Orthodox Christians, for it was not until the pontificate of Pope John XXIII and the Second Vatican Council that Roman Catholics became significantly related to it. But almost as a promise of things to come, a letter arrived from the rector of the neighboring Catholic parish just east of the seminary on 121st Street, which had recently moved into its renovated edifice. The Rev. George B. Ford sent to the alumni, faculty,and students "the greetings of the priests and people of Corpus Christi parish as you recall and rejoice in the labors and fruitful accomplishments of a hundred years. We ask God to bless the coming years for Union as it starts on its way to a second Centenary." Years later in his autobiography, Fr. Ford indirectly paid a compliment to Union's ecumenical openness while discussing something else: "If I met a Catholic scholar from across the seas, it was inevitably Union to which he had been invited; rarely would an American Catholic institution have invited him in those days." [42]

The tension between the administration and certain groups of students diminished after 1935, as can be seen in the way a potentially explosive matter was resolved. In the revulsion against World War I that occurred in the 1920s and 1930s, a strong pacifist movement swept across the student world. One manifestation of it was an annual student "Strike Against War" with anti-war demonstrations at various university centers, such as Columbia. The gatherings were held at an hour conflicting with scheduled classes, and Union students regularly requested a holiday for the action, which the faculty, wanting to honor requests for worthy ends, granted. Following such a vote in April 1936, Coffin asked to have his written dissent recorded on faculty minutes and posted. Indicating that he was heartily in favor of peace, and that he was "glad to share with students and professors in a collective demonstration against the iniquity and folly of War at any suitable time," he nevertheless objected to the way the "strike" was being handled, as it introduced "a form of coercion, compelling professors and students to interrupt the discharge of their academic obligations." At the heart of his dissent was a short paragraph:

If this is a "student strike" (as I am informed it is labelled in the literature of its promoters) faculty cooperation should not be asked. A "strike" with the benevolent patronage of those nominally "struck" against is a piece of infantilism unworthy of the intelligence of men considered fit candidates for the Christian ministry.

Arguing that the demonstrations seemed to be planned deliberately to coerce faculties and students, Coffin wondered how students who could not detect and withstand such "vicious use of pressure" ostensibly in the noble cause of peace would stand up under the "fierce pressure of war-inflamed patriotism." A number of faculty members also signed his statement, which led to a change in the way the continuing demonstrations were conducted, so that in Coffin's judgment they became "orderly meetings where the Christian attitude toward War and Peace was discussed from various points of view." [43] The situation changed dramatically after the outbreak of World War II in Europe and registration for the military draft began in 1940.

Much student attention in the later 1930s was focused

on the curriculum, particularly through the activities of a Student Curriculum Committee and the joint Faculty-Student Committee. In particular, students found the requirement of both comprehensive examinations and theses at the end of the three-year B.D. program excessive. Various student petitions argued against the comprehensives, claiming that they often duplicated course examinations, were predicated on a tutorial system which was not part of Union's educational pattern, and did not serve an integrative purpose, while the thesis requirement often did. The latter was retained, but the comprehensives were dropped. Student requests for a somewhat greater degree of freedom in chosing courses were also honored in a revision of the curriculum worked out by the faculty and reported to the board.[44]

A striking example of student vitality and ability was the founding in 1939 of *The Union Review*, published by students. The first issue appeared in December 1939 with Ernest A. Becker and Roger L. Shinn as managing editors. It was a substantial quarterly, with editorials, articles, and reviews by both faculty and students. The first article was by Coffin on "The Basic Spiritual Requirements for a Minister"; a later article in the first issue was by Ward on "The Dies Committee and Civil Liberties." Shinn became the sole managing editor for the second volume, which opened with an article on "Science and Religion" by Albert Einstein.

Significant new institutional, library, faculty, and student resources were brought onto the quadrangle with the migration of Auburn Theological Seminary to New York City in 1939. Founded in Auburn, New York, in 1818 by presbyteries of the Synod of Geneva (later New York), this institution admitted students of any Christian denomination and had been associated with the New School Presbyterian tradition, but retained its ties with the Presbyterian Church in the U.S.A. primarily through the presbyteries of the state which continued to support it and to name the majority of its board members. By the 1930s its location in a small upstate city deprived it of a viable association with increasingly important university and other educational resources, and its student body became very small. When plans to move it to a more favorable location in Rochester had not worked out, the Auburn directors proposed a relationship with Union, which Coffin enthusiastically supported. Legal and other difficulties were soon ironed out. Auburn retained its institutional independence as a Presbyterian seminary under its own board of directors. Once the students who migrated to the new location in the fall of 1939 had graduated, it no longer matriculated students but continued its teaching role, with special concern for Presbyterian history, doctrine, and polity, within the Union academic context.

Only two Auburn faculty members were available for the move to New York. Robert Hastings Nichols had earned both B.A. and Ph.D. degrees at Yale before attending Auburn, from which he graduated in 1901. After serving in several pastorates, he took up his teaching duties in church history at Auburn in 1910. Elected as Auburn professor of church history at Union at the time of the move, he taught courses in modern European and American church history in addition to those in Presbyterian history and polity. Walter S. Davison, a graduate of Princeton and Auburn (1912), had been pastor of several Presbyterian churches and a teacher at overseas colleges in Beirut and Turkey when he was called back to Auburn to teach worship and homiletics in 1930. As Auburn professor of practical theology at Union he taught in the fields of pastoral theology and the church in town and country, but also had responsibilities as the executive director of Auburn. Coffin was named president of Auburn, but much of the administrative burden was carried by Davison. The Union curriculum was enriched by the labors of these two professors who were added to the faculty. Auburn's contribution to Union resources continued for many decades as certain additions to the faculty were named as Auburn professors and were financed partly from Auburn funds.

The gathering of war clouds in the late 1930s intensified the debate over the way Christians should respond to the realities of war. The growing militarization of Germany under Hitler was regarded seriously by both pacifists and nonpacifists, and as awareness of the persecution of the Jews deepened, anxieties increased. Following the terrors of the attacks on Jews at the time of *Kristallnacht* in November 1938, the faculty and students of Jewish Theological Seminary were invited to Union to share in what was to be a moving memorial to the victims of Nazi hatred. As in the country at large, some who had been pacifists came to believe that such an evil force might have to be resisted by force, while others in both the faculty and student body were convinced that as Christians they could not actively participate in the military. The outbreak of war in Europe in September 1939 intensified the discussion as sympathy for the allies opposing Germany increased. The national debate over and final passage of the Selective Service Act in July 1940 brought a crisis of conscience to a group of Union students who felt that they could not register for the draft. Originally some twenty in number, the group carried on lengthy discussions of the issue, held prayer meetings, and actively publicized its views. Union became the focus of national attention, much of it critical and hostile. Across the seminary world, what was going on at Union was intently followed.

Their decision not to register was acutely embarrassing to the administration. Coffin and some of his colleagues—Niebuhr and Van Dusen conspicuously—were not pacificists, and played active roles in opposing isolationism and urging support for Britain.[45] They were in the process of founding a biweekly Christian journal of opinion, *Christianity and Crisis*, which first appeared under Niebuhr's editorship on February 10, 1941. It vigorously advocated more responsible American involvement in the crisis precipitated by the success of Nazi arms and challenged as perfectionistic and utopian many ideas then widely held by American church leaders. Though it was never an official seminary publication, the ties were very close, especially in its early years when the periodical had its office in seminary buildings and a number of persons closely related to Union served on its editorial board. Coffin, an intimate friend of Henry L. Stimson, the Secretary of War, had played a role in the shaping of the Selective Service Act. He had secured hearings for representatives of the pacifist Fellowship of Reconciliation and for his pacifist colleague Fosdick before the committee preparing the legislation that provided exemption for conscientious objectors to war and for candidates for the ministry. He knew the nonregistering students as "sincere Christians and capable young men," but was troubled by the intense publicity their action was bringing to the seminary, and by the disruption the excitement was causing in the school's academic life. Since none of the students who were determined not to register were residents of the city, he requested that they return to their homes for the act of civil disobedience, but they refused, wanting to make a conspicuous public witness.

At a special meeting of the faculty a resolution was passed

with practical unanimity. It was widely circulated by the press. It expressed "appreciation of the earnest attempt of these students to discover the course which they ought to pursue as Christian citizens in this confusing day," and recognized that "there are circumstances when individuals or groups may deem it necessary to refuse to follow the will of the government because to do so would be to deny their religious convictions." But in the faculty's judgment this principle was not involved in refusal to register:

When the elected representatives of the nation enact a law which takes account of the rights of a minority, they conform to the traditions of democratic government. In this Selective Service Act provision is made for conscientious objectors to participation in military training and an opportunity is afforded for such objectors to state their views. To refuse to register and supply the government with factual information is to refuse what any government has a right to ask of its citizens. No member of the faculty has advised any student to follow this course of action.

Reflecting on the impact of these students, Walter Bowie later observed that:

A few members of the faculty agreed with them completely, and there were none who did not respect and defend their courageous earnestness. But to the Seminary constituency in general it seemed that to try to keep aloof from the tragic actual choices which a world at war presented was morally more intolerable than involvement in it, and that therefore America must be increasingly aligned with resistance to the Nazi threat.[46]

When Union board members wondered if nonregistering students should be expelled, Coffin characteristically resisted any such action, noting that they were not breaking any seminary regulations, though he felt that they had taken a disastrous course. When the Auburn board met the suggestion was again made that they be expelled because as jail-birds the students would be unfit for ministry. The president responded by reminding them of a number of prominent New Testament figures who had spent time in jail.

On registration day, October 16, 1940, a group of eight students did finally refuse to register. The next day they appeared before a grand jury, were indicted, and in November were sentenced to jail for a year and a day. At each step, they presented statements explaining why draft registration was not a possibility for them as

Christians, and therefore they could not take the one step that would have brought them immediate release. In due course they were taken to Danbury Federal Correctional Institution in Connecticut, where they participated actively in athletic programs and in opposition to violence and racism in the prison. They were released the following September; five of them continued their preparation for the ministry at Chicago Theological Seminary. One, Don Benedict, later arrested a second time for failure to register, was sent back to Danbury. He read Niebuhr's *The Nature and Destiny of Man*, reflected on the problem of evil, and came to the conclusion that Hitler was demonic and had to be stopped by force. As he later put it, "the extermination of the Jews by Hitler convinced me that I could not stay out of the war."[47] Released on parole, he soon enlisted, and later returned to Union to complete his B.D. Others in the student body had come to a similar decision. Roger Shinn, for example, had decided during the intense debates of 1940 to waive exemption as a theological student, but was not drafted until after he graduated the next spring. He served as a combat officer in Europe and underwent the rigors of becoming a prisoner of war.[48] For a time he was reported as missing in action. There was a rumor that he had been killed, and a memorial service was held for him at the seminary.

WAR YEARS (1941–45)

American entry into the war immediately following the bombing of Pearl Harbor brought widespread changes into the lives of the American people and their institutions. Because ministers and theological students were exempted from the draft, seminaries were less directly affected than most other types of graduate schools. In view of its location in a major port city where at least token air raids were possible, Union prepared for emergencies. Under the direction of Comptroller Charles White, a defense committee met weekly, set up a building control unit with headquarters in the refectory, and organized the community into four teams, with Professors Richardson, Fleming, Herriott, and Roberts as captains, aided by three student assistants. A first aid station was supervised by the seminary's medical director, assisted by several registered nurses and some ten students with Red Cross certificates. Various special squads were readied under faculty leaders: Grant for the bomb squad, Tryon the blackout, Swift the fire fighters, Elliott the telephone and messenger system, Niebuhr the guards in charge of shelters and security, Tillich the gas squad and decontamination center. The facilities developed were at the service of city organizations, for the local sector headquarters was in Knox Hall, while some forty students were quickly involved as air raid wardens. "It is indeed a healthy sign that our faculty and students are learning, along with the profundities of Kierkegaard and Formgeschichte, that a fire hose will kick like a mule and that an incendiary bomb is made of thermite and magnesium and cannot be extinguished with water," wrote Cyril Richardson, with a touch of the humor so well-known to many generations of Union students. "Even a Church History Professor discovers that a knowledge of how to lay sandbags is sometimes of more value than the most accurate information on the Semi-Arians, especially when he is writing a 'Defense Manual' of the Seminary Unit."[49] Richardson became prominent in the city's civilian defense program, and was active in promoting war bond sales; his very overwork was a factor in his illness (tuberculosis) in the spring of 1943 that necessitated his departure for Trudeau Sanitorium.

In 1943, five northeastern seminaries cooperated to provide an accelerated program in theological education so that students could complete a full semester's work in two six-week periods at Union following commencement in May; the second period was the regular summer session. Faculty and students were drawn primarily from the cooperating schools; a number of those who availed themselves of the opportunity were headed for military chaplaincies. Early in 1944, uniformed participants in the Naval Chaplaincy "V–12" Program began to arrive on the campus to take regular courses and participate in the accelerated program, which by then involved about 35 regular students. The *Alumni Bulletin* regularly published lists of graduates who entered military service, many as chaplains. By April of 1945 the list of those known to have entered the services passed the 200 mark.

Overall seminary enrollment declined only slightly in the

early 1940s, from 347 in 1940–41 to a low of 326, and then, after a
slight increase, jumped to 418 in the last year of the war. Dormitory
patterns changed some; Columbia was pressed for space, and arranged for the top two floors of Hastings Hall to be used by their
students. The number of married theological students increased, so
the second floor of Hastings was rearranged for their use.

The war years were trying for many students; debates over
pacifism continued, along with those on the subject of the propriety
of accepting draft deferment in a time of national crisis, but there
was a high degree of mutual respect among those who held variant
positions. A certain bleakness settled over the campus as windows
were covered and lights dimmed for the "brownout," a switch from
oil heat back to coal necessitated a huge coal pile in the quad, and
food shortages affected the quality of meals in the refectory. Such
matters were of course not unique to Union. The problem of inflation was mounting; the board increased the subsidy to the refectory
in an effort to keep prices down. During the war years the annual
budget for the seminary climbed from about $500,000 to $600,000,
but income from fees, gifts, and endowment increased proportion-
ately.

The first half of the 1940s was marked by the retirements
of a number of faculty members, most of whom had given long service to Union. The retirements of Lyman and Ward have already
been mentioned; in 1943 Hume became professor emeritus of the
history of religions after three decades of service. The next year Tryon,
Fleming, and Nichols became emeriti after serving for 36, 30, and
34 years respectively—for Nichols 29 of those years had been at Auburn before the move. In that same year two long-time members of
the teaching force moved on to other fields of service. Emil Kraeling
had taught part time for a quarter century as instructor and assistant
professor of Old Testament, and Sophia Fahs had been lecturer in
religious education and psychology since the year after her graduation
in 1926. The climax to this half-decade of retirements in 1945 seemed
to mark the end of an era as three long-time stalwarts entered emeritus status: Clarence Dickinson, who had taught sacred music and
guided the musical program since 1912 and then served as the first
Director of the School of Sacred Music; Julius Bewer, who had taught
Old Testament since 1904, combining scholarly care with preaching

fervor; and Henry Coffin, who had begun his faculty career in that same year.

To take care of all the vacancies, on top of the several major ones from the late 1930s that had not been filled, was a formidable task. The chair of the history of religions has never been permanently filled, as offerings in that field were left largely to Columbia. From 1937 to 1959 a Columbia professor, Arthur Jeffery, served as an adjunct professor of Semitic languages and lived in Knox Hall. An Australian who had earned his Ph.D. at Edinburgh, Jeffery taught courses in Old Testament and the history of religions. After Hume's retirement, additional courses in the latter area were taught sporadically by visiting professors and lecturers. In 1935 French-born Samuel L. Terrien, who had studied theology and Semitic languages at the University of Paris and archaeology in Jerusalem, had come to Union as a resident fellow, earned his S.T.M. the next year, taught four years at Wooster, completed his Th.D. in 1941, and was named instructor in Old Testament at that time. Moving swiftly up the promotional ladder, this brilliant teacher became Auburn professor in 1953 and Davenport professor of Hebrew and cognate languages eleven years later.

Faculty resources were increased in 1942 as three persons took up their educational tasks at Union. The teaching of the philosophy of religion was strengthened by the coming of Richard Kroner, a famous German scholar (Ph.D., Freiburg, 1908), who was forced by the Nazis to give up teaching at Königsberg in 1934. Finally getting permission to leave Germany but required to leave all possessions behind, he went to Britain, and was invited to deliver the famous Gifford lectures in Scotland, published in 1943 as *The Primacy of Faith*. An invitation to teach at a Canadian university was blocked by the outbreak of war. He was named lecturer at Union in 1942, and six years later became an adjunct professor. The transition to American theological education was difficult for him, but he did it in a gracious way. In part because all his courses were offered as electives during his ten years at Union, he did not have a major impact on the student body, but those who worked with him came to appreciate his keen mind, wide knowledge, and great spirit. John

L. Casteel, holder of M.A. and Ph.D. degrees from Northwestern, was named director of the department of speech. He left after nine years of service, but later returned in a different capacity. When William Rockwell retired in 1942 after serving 37 years at Union, the last 17 as librarian, he was followed in the latter post by Lucy W. Markley. As ordained Universalist minister who had earned her B.D. and Ph.D. degrees at the Divinity School of the University of Chicago and had served as cataloger of religious books at the university, she had already served for three years as assistant librarian at Union.

Two appointments were made in 1943 and two more the following year. Since his coming to Union Frederick Grant had carried the main burden of New Testament teaching alone, with some help from Harold Tryon, who was also registrar and secretary of the faculty. In 1943 John Knox accepted the call as Baldwin professor of sacred literature, a post he was to hold for 23 years. With a B.D. from Candler School of Theology and a Ph.D. from the University of Chicago, Knox came from the latter's Divinity School faculty. In that same year John Bennett was called back to Union as professor of Christian theology and ethics. Dividing his time between the two disciplines, he worked from a Christian realist position that was indebted to Reinhold Niebuhr. One of his courses, "The application of Christian ethical principles," took up a number of the topics with which Ward had been concerned but from a quite different theological perspective.

In 1944 two broadly experienced individuals whose careers had followed quite different lines joined the faculty. In church history, Moffatt had not been replaced, and the retirement of Nichols made an appointment in that field all the more urgent. Union was fortunate to secure the services of a widely known church historian, John T. McNeill. Born in Canada, with degrees from McGill, Westminster Hall in Vancouver, and the University of Chicago, McNeill had taught at three Canadian seminaries before becoming professor of the history of modern European Christianity at Chicago in 1927. A prodigious researcher who had taught and written across the entire field of church history, McNeill, a Presbyterian, was named an Auburn professor, the salary divided between the two institutions. He delivered solid, comprehensive lectures so packed with information that some students missed the subtlety of his dry humor. The appointment of such a senior scholar meant that he was at Union for only nine years before retirement, but his colleague Charles W. Iglehart who was called to Union at the same time served only six. A graduate of Columbia and Drew (1906), Iglehart had served as a Methodist missionary to Japan for many years, taking leave to earn an S.T.M. at Union in 1933 and a Ph.D. at Drew a year later. The war brought him home as a secretary of his mission board until he followed Daniel Fleming as professor of missions. An energetic, knowledgeable, irenic man, Iglehart returned to Japan to teach at International Christian University after his formal retirement.

As his Presbyterian predecessors in the presidency had done, Coffin worked patiently to improve relationships with the communion of which Union had once been formally affiliated. Always an active participant in its life, he gave particularly effective service to its board of home (later national) missions for nearly half a century and was the first person to be named a member emeritus. It was a great moment for Union and for him when he was elected moderator of the General Assembly in 1943—a high honor and a great responsibility. In accepting, Coffin declared that the first task before his denomination was to seek unity with the Southern Presbyterians— but only after forty years, and many turns on the road, did that union finally occur. During his year as moderator he was an ecumenical and reconciling force, and administrative arrangements had to be made during his long absences from Union. In November he made a fraternal visit to the churches in war-torn Great Britain, with many engagements in Edinburgh and London. On his return, at a dinner honoring him and his leadership in a critical time, he described movingly some of the things he had seen, and characteristically looked ahead to the spiritual problems that the nation would face at war's end. Soon he was off again, this time with Mrs. Coffin, on a moderatorial tour around the country of some six weeks duration. His sermon as retiring moderator at the conclusion of his year's term summed up themes he had long advocated and exemplified in his ministry at Union and in the larger circles of Christian life—the responsibility of the Christian church for a ministry of reconciliation in international, interracial, economic, and ecumenical affairs.

As the time approached for Coffin's retirement, there was an understandable reluctance to let him go, and the board invited him to remain another year, but he declined, holding to the age limit (68) then set for professors. Many honors were heaped on him at various farewell occasions. The board had raised a Henry Sloane Coffin Fund in his honor, exceeding the goal of $500,000 by more than $50,000; $175,000 of the total established the Henry Sloane Coffin chair, and $100,000 provided the Clarence and Helen Dickinson Endowment for the School of Sacred Music. The hitherto unnamed Administration Building was named for him.[50]

An especially fitting tribute was presented to Coffin at the Alumni Luncheon, May 16, by Reinhold Niebuhr—a *festschrift*, *This Ministry*, which Niebuhr had edited. In their years as colleagues the two had become very close personal friends. Though they were different in many ways, their deep respect for each other had continued to grow. When he had read the draft of the first two chapters of Niebuhr's Gifford lectures in Scotland, which became the first volume of *The Nature and Destiny of Man*, Coffin wrote from "Coombe-Pine," the summer home he purchased in 1937 in Lakeville, Connecticut, which later became his retirement home, congratulating Niebuhr, saying "This is far and away the most solid thing which you have done, and it is splendidly done." He did have some suggestions on verbal clarifications and sentence structures; even fewer in 1942 when he read the opening lectures of what became the second volume of Niebuhr's *magnum opus*. "They are superbly done," he wrote, "and your second volume is going to eclipse the first in interest and value." The famous professor was then involved in an extensive correspondence with President James B. Conant of Harvard who had offered him a university professorship. Coffin fought back, opening one letter with this short paragraph:

It would be fatal for the Seminary to lose you now. You have an assured place in the leadership of the thought of the Churches and that place is now bound up with the influence which Union exerts. Were you to leave us, we should be immeasurably impoverished.[51]

The decision was not an easy one for Niebuhr, as Harvard kept pursuing him even after he had dictated several letters, in which he declined. Thus there was a lot of history and feeling behind the little book that Union's renowned Niebuhr presented to the man who was retiring after 41 years of active relationship to the Union student body and faculty, 19 of them as president.

The ten contributors to the volume illumined many aspects of Union's history as they paid tribute to this distinguished alumnus of the class of 1900; for example, Van Dusen called attention to his fearless advocacy of racial equality, and to the fact that the first black member of the board had been elected in his administration—William Lloyd Imes (1915), then president of Knoxville College. In his sprightly summary essay, Niebuhr celebrated the consistency in Coffin's long ministry, observing that "he never wavered in his certainty of the uniqueness and profundity of the Christian revelation; and was for that reason not tempted to maintain its authority by obscurantist, legalistic or authoritarian means," and concluding that his career provides "a unique and yet typical chapter in American Church history."[52] Coffin's many-sided career had indeed touched on many strands of American church life in the first half of the twentieth century and had been important in advancing Union's conspicious role in that period. As president, he had led the seminary through a very difficult period; when he laid down his burdens the war in Europe was over and victory in the Pacific was seen as a matter of time. How would Union respond to the challenges of a quite different sort under new leadership at a time when there had been a great deal of turnover in the faculty and when a larger student body with many veterans in it was expected?

CHAPTER EIGHT

Ecumenicity and Expansion in the Van Dusen Era (1945–1963)

When the time came to select a successor to Coffin the choice was not difficult. The board named a small nominating committee from its own members. At its first meeting it discussed various possibilities and came to the conclusion that Van Dusen was the right nominee, but decided to consult the full professors. At the second meeting the search committee unanimously voted that the Roosevelt professor of systematic theology was the right candidate, and the board accepted the recommendation on May 17, 1944, a year in advance of Coffin's retirement. Van Dusen served as president for just a year less than his predecessor had done, and also guided Union's development with a strong, firm hand, but in his own distinctive way.

In a memorial minute read to the Board of Directors soon after Henry Pitney Van Dusen's death in 1975, David H. C. Read, pastor of the Madison Avenue Presbyterian Church, said:

He was a man to whom the adjectives "big" naturally gravitated—big in physical length and breadth, big in his views and opinions, big in his affections and loyalties, big in his spiritual ambitions, big in his

Henry P. Van Dusen, theologian, ecumenist, and tenth president of Union.

ecclesiastical statesmanship, big in his impact on this Seminary, big in his interpretation of the Christian Gospel and its application to the whole of life—and I am sure he would want me to add that if he ever made a mistake it, too, would be a big one.[1]

He was also a man with a "big" vision for the seminary of which he was a graduate and had already served for nineteen years as teacher and administrator. Soon he was articulating that viewpoint, winning others to it, and working out its implications. Van Dusen envisioned an ecumenical seminary, one expanding in size and services the better to address the needs of the complex and expansive postwar years.

The ecumenical aspect was heavily underlined in his inaugural address as president, delivered at the Riverside Church on Thursday afternoon, November 15, 1945. The stage was set by the president emeritus, who reminded his "dear Son in the Church of God" with a phrase that in one form or another had often come from his lips: "this Seminary is compelled to live by its wits." Characteristically, Van Dusen packed a lot into his address, entitled "The Role of the Theological Seminary." Fresh from a two-year stint as president of the American Association of Theological Schools, he spoke in somewhat general terms, but when he stressed the importance of the ecumenical movement for the churches and their seminaries it was clear that Union was especially on his mind. "You would expect this address to conclude on the note of Christian unity," he exclaimed, "both because of the genius of this Seminary and because of the outlook of the speaker." For, he insisted, in the life of the Christian churches "every problem and every responsibility point to a single inexorable necessity"—Christian unity:

> Unity is laid as an inescapable obligation upon the Protestant Churches because none of their greatest problems can be adequately met, none of their most clamant tasks can be effectively discharged, by individual churches or separate Communions, but only by the total resources of the whole Church of Christ. . . . The halting of secularism, the reclamation of education, the confrontation of Government, the amelioration of social disease and disorder, the reaching of the unchurched—the most flagrant bypassed job of the churches—to each there is only one answer: the massed Christian strength of all churches directed unitedly upon common responsibilities.

The spiritual renewal so greatly needed, the newly inaugurated president concluded, can come only through the united resources of the
whole Church of Christ, which lays an inescapable claim upon the
seminaries, for they "must send forth into the Churches' leadership
men and women alive to the sickness of society and of the Churches,
and deeply impregnated with medicines for the Churches' and society's ills. More than that, the seminaries themselves must in significant measure incarnate and demonstrate the remedies."[2] Perceptive
listeners could hear undertones of a longing for a new version of the
nineteenth-century dream of an American Protestant Christendom in
ecumenical guise.

Van Dusen promptly set to work to translate his guiding
ecumenical vision into reality. To him the seminary was the center
of three overlapping areas of concern: New York, the United States,
and the World. For Union to do its work along the lines of his vision, expansion was the order of the day. In the immediate postwar
years, as veterans flooded into academic institutions, it was not difficult to expand the student body. In his first year the enrollment was
458 (including candidates for degrees in the joint programs with Columbia, but not counting 68 more whose basic registration was in
other institutions), nearly a hundred greater than the previous year.
As the confident president was pleased to do, for the next six years
he could note that the number of students was greater than in the
previous year—647 by 1951–52.

It took Van Dusen several years to develop fully his plans
for expansion, which he presented to the Board of Directors early in
1948. Analyzing the increasing enrollment, he called for holding the
B.D. student body, the large majority of whom were presumably preparing for church ministries, to about 200, but allowing the number
of "graduate" students working for advanced theological degrees to
continue to increase. Their number had already risen markedly, especially in the joint degree programs with Columbia, in part because
veterans could use their "G. I. Bill" educational grants for most forms
of post-secondary education. Van Dusen saw that the need for teachers of religion in seminaries and colleges at home and abroad would
increase—and was not New York the best place to prepare them? As
he enthused to the board, "the same factors which have lifted the
United States to a dominating role in world politics, and are drawing

all eyes to New York City as the world capital, apply in the realm of theological education," and he added that "here should be found, through the next decades, the greatest center of theological learning and teaching in the world." The president also wanted to double the number of foreign students, then running about 25, and to do that he knew that special fellowships and scholarships would have to be provided for them.

More students—therefore more faculty, and increasing pay scales to keep pace with the competition. The student–faculty ratio was formally 19 to 1, and even if one computed candidates for university degrees at half load for the Union teachers, it was still a not very good 15 to 1. Noting that the student body had increased 50 percent while the faculty had decreased 26 percent, Van Dusen pointed to a "dangerous imbalance," and outlined plans for an expanded teaching force. Though the seminary was crowded, the purchase in 1946 of an apartment building, Reed House, across Broadway at 537 West 121st Street, helped considerably to relieve housing pressures, especially for the increasing number of married students. The proposed Auburn Hall, paid for largely from Auburn funds, as an addition to the Coffin Administration building was planned to provide much needed additional office, classroom, and library space when completed in 1950. The actual and projected increases of student body and faculty, however, especially when combined with postwar inflation, did point to a steadily rising budget. The new president had already anticipated that and saw to it that an annual fund to which graduates and friends of the seminary were invited to contribute was started in early 1946. He credited the satisfying response with making a balanced budget possible for that academic year. But he concluded his 1948 report by observing that a larger endowment, then approximately eight million dollars, would be needed along with many other special gifts to finance an ambitious program of expansion.[3] He could then hardly anticipate the inexorable pressure of inflation that would continue throughout his administration; from 1945 to 1963 the budget increased from nearly $619,000 to just over $2.3 million—a combination of expansion costs and inflation. The book value of the endowment just about doubled, from $8.25 to $16.3 million.

Part of the aggressive, energetic new president's style was the use of superlatives in speaking and writing. When informing the board about the selection of professors to fill three major posts in 1950, for example, he declared rather grandiloquently that "In each case, a special committee of the Senior Faculty has searched the world for the best qualified successor, and in each case the nominee of first choice has responded favorably to the Board's call." In speaking informally in 1962 to the Presidential Search Committee that was to nominate his successor, he indicated that Union was the great theological college of the world, with a place of absolute preeminence. His habit of speaking so vehemently did lead to some criticism of him by both friends and opponents, for his claims were sometimes exaggerated. He did have traits of paternalism and perfectionism which sometimes annoyed those most loyal to him. Skilled at locating openings in church and educational institutions for recent graduates, he sometimes resented it when his wishes were not followed. He could not resist editing again documents that required his formal approval. These traits were normally kept in check by his qualities of patience and courtesy. The Union of that era, however, was riding the crest of a wave that had been gathering for some time, and the president usually had command of relevant facts and effective quotations to support his contentions. For example, he loved to repeat comments such as those made by Archbishop William Temple in introducing Coffin at a luncheon in London during the war that Union was "the foremost theological college in the world."[4]

Many others besides the president, however, also recorded their strong favorable impressions of Union during this time. In recalling his days as a student who earned three degrees from 1945 to 1951, William E. Hordern, later a seminary president himself, remembered that while at Union, he "had been exposed to one of the greatest galaxies of theological stars ever gathered into one faculty in this country. My program had exposed me most thoroughly to Niebuhr, Bennett, and Tillich, but the whole spirit of Union had entered into my blood." Another student, Frederick Buechner, like so many had already been following another vocation but found himself drawn to the ministry. He entered Union in the middle 1950s, and later wrote:

> In terms of Union's history, I couldn't have gone there at a more auspicious time. It was in its golden age. Reinhold Niebuhr was there, and Paul Tillich was there, those two great luminaries. . . . Less famous

but no less powerful as teachers there were, supremely, James Muilenburg in the Old Testament department, not to mention Samuel Terrien, and John Knox in the New Testament department. There was Paul Scherer to teach homiletics, Wilhelm Pauck and Cyril Richardson in Church History, and, in the Philosophy of Religion, Robert McAfee Brown.

A faculty corroboration of such a high estimate of the Union of that period came from a professor who was there throughout the period— John Knox. In his autobiography he listed the names of many of his colleagues, and then added,

I feel fortunate to have served mostly under the presidency of Henry Van Dusen, a most vigorous and enterprising leader and an important theologian with rare administrative and pastoral gifts, during whose incumbency the seminary enjoyed the greatest expansion in its history in physical facilities, size of faculty and student body, and range of educational program. . . . I should be surprised if it does not prove to be true that Lois and I had the privilege of being at Union during the most significant period of that great institution's history.

Outsiders were often more guarded in their estimates, and yet reflected the seminary's high reputation. In his biography of Charles H. Dodd, a distinguished British biblical scholar who served as a visiting professor at Union in the spring of 1950, F. W. Dillistone wrote, "It was a peak period in the history of the Seminary—Paul Tillich was at the height of his powers; John Bennett . . . was becoming a key figure within the ecumenical movement as an interpreter of the social and political implications of the Gospel—and the visiting professor, who by this time enjoyed an international reputation amongst New Testament scholars, brought additional distinction to what was then possibly the most famous theological faculty in the world."[5] Van Dusen did use big words when he spoke about Union, but he was not alone, for it was a remarkable period in the seminary's life.

The twin motifs of his administration were humorously caught at a faculty party honoring the Van Dusens after five years in the president's house when Cyril Richardson wrote one of his famous rhymes of many verses for the occasion, two of which were:

> He loves all bishops and clerks in orders
> From India's courts to Scotland's borders;
> His ecumenical arms embrace

Priest and prophet of every race.

In his days the enrollment was biggest of all,
And now he's a-building Auburn Hall.
Of new professors he's made eleven—
Of tutor assistants thirty-seven.

The foundations for these creative years of ecumenicity and expansion had been soundly laid in the past, and a number of Union's world-famous professors were at the height of their powers when the new administration took over. Van Dusen was not only a strong person himself, but one who admired strength in others, and he wanted strong persons in the board, faculty, staff, and student body. The achievements of the Van Dusen period resulted from the efforts of many persons, yet it was the ability of a highly competent president that helped to keep them working together for common ends. He was also president of the School of Sacred Music, of Auburn, and of the Union Settlement Association, though the once close connections with the settlement were generally forgotten in the seminary community.

He worked closely with the Board of Directors, which itself exemplified the motif of expansion as it increased from 34 to 53 members, continuing the pattern of a composition of about equal numbers of clergy and laity. Among the members who joined the board as the new administration was getting under way were such prominent laymen as Charles C. Parlin, soon to be a conspicuous figure in World and National Councils of Churches; John Foster Dulles, then especially noted for his chairmanship of an ecumenical Commission to Study the Bases of a Just and Durable Peace, and who was to remain on the board until he became Secretary of State in 1953; and Henry R. Luce, the famous publisher. When Thatcher Brown stepped down as president of the board in 1947, a man who had been on it since 1933 succeeded him: Benjamin Strong, who in that same year became president of the United States Trust Company. An able leader for a time of expansion, he served until 1961, when the seminary's ability to secure effective leadership for its board was demonstrated again as lawyer John N. Irwin II, a graduate of Princeton who had studied at Oxford and had served on the board since 1954, assumed the chair. To keep pace with the demands of an expanding seminary, the board amended its constitution on a number of occasions. In 1952 the title of the board's presiding officer was changed from president to chair, eliminating what had occasionally been a cause of confusion. In view of the increasing number of decisions is was routinely asked to make, the board depended heavily on the work of Van Dusen and his staff, and on the reports of its committees, especially the executive committee.

The faculty also grew significantly in size in these years: the catalog for the new president's first year listed an active full-time faculty of 25, two of whom were adjuncts, but that of his last year showed a total of 53. Several of these were visiting professors, and six held primarily administrative posts with limited teaching responsibilities. While the policy of calling experienced teachers to full professorships so that each field was properly staffed to guide doctoral candidates was continued, Van Dusen also advocated the appointment of instructors, some 21 of which were named during his administration (half as many as had been appointed in the entire history of the seminary up to that time). Most of them served a year or two, often completing doctoral dissertations and then leaving to teach at some other institution, but some qualified for promotions that happened to become available.

A fuller sense of what faculty expansion meant in the 18 years of the Van Dusen administration emerges when comparisons are made with the 109 previous years, from 1836 to 1945. For those years a quite careful count (though a margin for error must be allowed) shows that there were 123 faculty appointments in all ranks, instructor to full professor, including adjuncts and visiting professors (the six "professors extraordinary" of the seminary's early history are counted in this latter category). For the 18 years of the Van Dusen era, the comparable figure is 107. The largest relative increase, to be sure, was in the number of visiting professors, who by the latter period were appointed for one year only (33, contrasted with 7 previously). Of greater significance, because of their long terms of service those appointed in the Van Dusen era from the outside as full professors or who began at another level but were later promoted to that rank numbered 34, compared with the 64 appointed during the previous 109 years. A somewhat more complex seminary, with a wider variety of curricular options, emerged from this period of rapid expansion, and the student–faculty ratio dropped to a sound 9 to 1.

Faculty morale was generally high during those years, for Union was known as an important theological center for the mainline Protestant churches at a time when they were profiting from the heightened interest in religion of the postwar period. While Union was then able to pull well-known scholars—usually its first choices—into its faculty, few full professors left before reaching the age of retirement. The combination of filling vacancies, adding new positions in a time of expansion, promoting younger persons to professorships, and calling annual visiting professors meant that there were special occasions when a feast of inaugural addresses were given on the same day, climaxed by a convocation when a number of persons were formally inaugurated—for there were six major appointments in 1950, five each in 1954, 1959, and 1960, and four each in 1961 and 1962. The inaugural addresses were usually published in the *Union Seminary Quarterly Review*, the successor to the *Union Review*, which was merged with the *Alumni Bulletin* in 1945.

In such a relatively fluid period in the life of the faculty a sense of solidarity was maintained not only by the monthly faculty meetings, but by weekly faculty lunches in the upper refectory and monthly dinner meetings at which a member presented a paper which was thoroughly discussed. In his report to the board in the fall of 1960, Van Dusen compared the contemporary faculty situation with that of the earlier part of the century, naming some of the great figures in Union's past but noting that they were often "solitary lights," while now the faculty formed a constellation, a fellowship with a strong sense of community.[6] In part, this was the result of the appointment of a senior professor as dean of the faculty; the first was Reinhold Niebuhr (1950–55), who became vice president and was succeeded by John Bennett (1955–63).

An expanding seminary required a larger administrative and support staff. When Charles White resigned from the position of Comptroller, after 27 years of supervising the seminary's business and financial affairs, to represent government interests in what was then called the Near East, Union was fortunate in securing Randolph H. Dyer to replace him. A patient and perceptive man, Dyer fitted well into the heavy responsibilities of the office, which soon included becoming the seminary's treasurer. Of great importance in the administrative sphere was Blanche M. Britton, who had filled various roles at the seminary since 1929, notably as secretary to the president, but who in 1946 was named registrar and later recorder (with rank of associate professor) and administrative assistant to the president before her retirement in 1962. In 1952 a former board member, Edwin O. Kennedy (1924), was named as secretary of the seminary, primarily to direct alumni/ae affairs but also to serve as associate professor of practical theology—"the least theology you can be professor of," he liked to quip.

During the Van Dusen years, some members of the support staff who had served at Union since 1910 retired, notably James Anderson who had been in charge of the General Office for many decades, and George Bayley, who had cared for the grounds before moving to the telephone switchboard. Emmanuel Romero's record went back even further, to the Park Avenue days. He had taken charge of the office of Hastings Hall when it was first opened, and became a close friend and informal adviser to many troubled students through the years. He was an outstanding Catholic layman, and in 1950 was accorded the papal "Pro Ecclesia et Pontifice" award, primarily for his work with the Catholic Interracial Council.

The way the service of the librarian was terminated was the occasion for well-publicized criticism of the administration. There was some dissatisfaction in the faculty with the way Dr. Lucy Markley was running the library, particularly in the handling of book allocations which had been largely under faculty control. The joint board-faculty library committee also learned that the morale of some of the library staff was low. Markley was asked to resign, and was given a year's leave of absence. Then, in response to sharp criticisms of this action, an annual retiring allowance was added for the remaining eight years until her original retirement date.[7] The way was then clear for the appointment of a new librarian, and Robert F. Beach, a graduate of Connecticut Wesleyan and Columbia's School of Library Science, came from Garrett Theological Seminary in Evanston. This genial and respected theological librarian held the rank of associate professor, and industriously worked to maintain and increase the library's rich holdings, continually calling attention to the overcrowding of the stacks.

A former dean of students himself, Van Dusen carefully selected members of the faculty for the role. In 1945 Walter Russell Bowie took the position, serving ably in the period of the rapid growth of the student body until his retirement five years later. He was succeeded by the youthful George W. ("Bill") Webber (1948), a founder of the East Harlem Protestant Parish who also taught practical theology. A magnetic, talented person, Webber was of decisive importance for many students as they prepared for ministry. Another beloved faculty member with multiple assignments was Charles E. Mathews, a graduate of Auburn who served as dean and director of the Auburn program for five years, taught evangelism and rural church studies, became Auburn professor of practical theology, and in 1957 added the responsibilities of being dean of students. Sad to say, he died suddenly early in 1960 in the middle of his fruitful career. In the following year, he was replaced by James M. Ault, a graduate of Colgate and Union (1949) who had served in three Methodist pastorates.

An important innovation in 1950 was the addition of a dean of women students to the list of faculty officers. The person chosen filled several roles well, for she was also the first tenured woman professor—Mary Ely Lyman (1919), a Chicago Ph.D. in Bible who when married to Eugene Lyman had been a lecturer at the seminary. Now widowed, she returned as Jesup professor of English Bible. A capable, kindly, outspoken woman, she stoutly resisted any effort to minimize the place of women at Union, pointing to the important contributions such graduates of Union were making in church and education. When she retired in 1955, she was followed in the deanship first by Rena S. Craig, widow of the former dean at Drew, and later by Helen H. Sherrill, who like Lyman had lived at Union as the wife of a professor. A psychiatric social worker, she held the rank of associate professor. Such competent persons as those who have been mentioned as administrators carried many of the increasingly heavy burdens of managing an expanding seminary, but their responsibilities were quite precisely defined and the center of major decision making and coordination clearly remained in the president's office.

One of Union's strengths throughout its history had been a fine student body, but in part because the flood of applications in this period necessitated careful selection, its strengths became especially evident. Enrollment remained high throughout the period; after a decline in 1952–53, it climbed to a high of 677 in seminary programs (729 when students from other institutions are included) four years later. The student body was drawn largely from well-known educational centers—ivy league schools and others of similar ranking, leading church colleges, and state universities. It was much more homogeneous than student bodies in later periods, for it was drawn to a considerable extent from middle-class backgrounds and mainline churches. Until 1956 an applicant was asked to state "his membership in a Christian church or his connection with some ecclesiastical body." While there were some women in the B.D. classes, most of them—about a quarter of the student body—were in other categories, especially the School of Sacred Music and in the two-year new Master of Religious Education (M.R.E.) program begun in 1954, which averaged about 50 students by the early 1960s.

Forces of diversification were at work in the seminary, however, stimulated in part by the effort to bring more overseas students. Van Dusen reported in the fall of 1950 that there were 64 such students from 27 countries, and those numbers increased later in the decade (especially through the Program of Advanced Religious Studies, discussed below). Another source of diversity was the way the Rockefeller Brothers Theological Fellowship Program operated; it was based in part on Union's experience with "undecided" students, designed with Van Dusen's cooperation and instituted in 1954. Working in cooperation with what was then the American Association of Theological Schools, the program offered one-year fellowships for some 50 persons not already committed to Christian ministry but who were willing to consider it seriously to enter a seminary for a "trial year." In its first year of operation, Union attracted 17 of the 46 granted fellowships; nine of them returned for the middler B.D. year, and two others returned the following year. The number of Rockefeller students, as they were then called (the fellowships were later granted by the Fund for Theological Education), varied from year to year, as did the number who returned to finish a degree, but from among the latter some very promising persons did enter the ministry, and some continued in an advanced degree program. In reporting to the board early in 1961, the secretary of the seminary, Edwin Kennedy, declared that Union probably had admitted more

Rockefeller students than any other seminary, and noted that some leaders of high potential had emerged from their ranks. "On the other hand," he added, "their presence in the Seminary tends to have a somewhat disintegrating effect on the morale of the student body and to establish a norm of vocational indecision, thereby removing some of the pressure on the rest of the students to make up their minds."[8]

The growing numbers of students working for advanced degrees introduced further variety into the student body. In the postwar years, the big influx was in the joint degree programs with Columbia, but by the middle 1950s that markedly declined to less than half of what it had been. Meanwhile, the number of graduate students in Union degree programs increased from the 30s to the 90s by the end of the period.

The increasing diversity of the student body was reflected by the efforts of administrators to gauge the student mind. In 1950 the president, both professionally and personally deeply concerned with moral issues, stated his belief that the student generation was one for whom any accepted *corporate* standard of moral behavior was almost totally dissolved. Five years later in his report to the board he quoted verbatim a long report from the new dean of the faculty, Bennett, who stated that he found it "more difficult each year to generalize about our students." He found no dominant trend of thought or interest among them, but noted that the hold of "neo-orthodoxy" was passing, leaving as its fruit "a great concern for the Gospel—for a Christ-centered Gospel of salvation. The Bible is regarded as a bearer of truth and not primarily as a book of critical problems." He found considerable intellectual passivity among students, which he explained by observing that the confident secular assumptions in which earlier generations had been steeped had lost their power, so that they were less critical of and more readily overcome by the essential Christian faith to which they were being exposed. He did deplore their reduced concern about social issues, a result, he believed, of the high level of prosperity and the very complex character of the problems of the time, especially in international relations.

Another source of diversity that markedly affected the larger seminary community was the increase of married students. Looking back after 15 years in the presidency, Van Dusen remembered that in 1945 it was not thought necessary to tabulate them. Students were encouraged not to marry before graduation, and were expected to consult with the president if they planned to—a statement still in the catalog as his term came to a close. In part the caution was financial; students were told that their scholarship stipends would not increase if they married. But in fact their numbers greatly increased, to nearly 300 by 1960, many with children. To the board Van Dusen dramatized the reality by observing that at a recent meeting of the Wives' Club, he and Eleanor Roosevelt both found that they had never before been "in the presence of so many expectant mothers assembled at one time in one place." The total residential community, including the majority of the faculty and their families, then numbered over 1000 persons.[9]

The costs of seminary education for students increased steadily in this period, but in reviewing figures one must remember also the formidable pressures of inflation. The seminary had charged no tuition until 1919, and then the figure of $150 a year for all degree progams, including the Th.D., lasted until 1946. Then it began to move up, holding at $400 for much of the 1950s, but by the last year of the era reaching $800 for all degree programs at Union, while joint masters and doctors degrees at Columbia reached $1420 by 1963. Rates for rooms and apartments in the dormitories also increased, but more slowly. Simultaneously, the seminary sought to meet financial needs by a liberal scholarship policy. Beginning in 1949, an italicized statement appeared yearly in the catalog: *"It is the intention and policy of the Seminary that every highly qualified candidate for the B.D. degree, who has made and is making his best efforts toward self-support, shall receive sufficient scholarship assistance to undertake and complete his Seminary course."* (The M.R.E. degree was later added to the statement.) The continuing special scholarship funds for music students, for candidates for the doctorate, and resident fellowships to bring students from outside North America to the seminary for a year were appropriately increased. Th.D. and Ph.D. students could also apply for a growing number of tutorships, receiving a stipend for conducting discussion groups in large classes and helping to grade papers and examinations. They played an important part in the life of the seminary, and gained valuable teaching experience.

In the early years of this period, in view of the purchase

of Reed House and especially when Auburn Hall was completed, there was little concern about space. In addition to new offices, including a spacious new one overlooking the quadrangle for the president, Auburn provided a fine large classroom and several attractive smaller ones. The Auburn Library on the fourth floor provided a suitable place for board and faculty meetings. Throughout the later 1940s it was expected that the postwar influx of students, among whom were many veterans, would diminish, and it came somewhat as a surprise when that did not happen. The continued increase in the size of the student body, necessitating a larger faculty and staff, put heavy pressure on available space, and plans were made to raise funds and do some more building. More room was unexpectedly found when the Van Dusens did not find the president's home suited to their needs, and in 1953 moved into an apartment on the fourth floor of Knox Hall. This allowed the faculty lounge and guest rooms to move into the vacated space, and eventually the upper floors were made into offices. The small courtyard between that building and the chapel was filled in as Dickinson Hall was built in 1960, providing new main offices for the School of Sacred Music, additional classrooms, and more faculty offices on the fourth floor.

The major need, however, was for a new, large residence building for both student and faculty apartments. Under the president's aggressive leadership an intensive fund-raising campaign was undertaken. Nearly $4 million of the money raised went for the twelve-story building erected at 527 Riverside Drive, just north of International House. Completed in 1963, it was an impressive monument to an era of expansion in the life of the seminary.

The Van Dusen years are particularly remembered as a time when certain special educational programs were developed, usually based on special grants, while the continuing concern for maintaining high-quality and well-staffed degree programs can too easily be overlooked. Actually, a great deal of the president's attention was given to the central educational tasks of the seminary, especially to the recruitment of suitable persons for the growing faculty. "The ceaseless quest for scholarly talent," he once said, "continues a relentless duty as well as an exciting preoccupation."[10] Though that quest did include the search for those who would direct and teach in the special programs, his concern for overall faculty strength for the seminary's historic educational task never flagged, nor did the attention given to maintaining a strong basic curriculum. To use terminology that has recently become familiar in academic circles, Van Dusen operated both as chief executive and chief academic officer of his institution, or as it was sometimes said at the time, he served as his own academic dean.

To help carry the details of that burden, the offices of director of studies and director of graduate studies were created in 1945 and 1950. Faculty members were chosen for those positions, with some lightening of their teaching roles in view of the responsibilities of supervising degree programs and counseling students. As director of studies for a dozen years, New Testament professor John Knox gave thoughtful attention to the details of the B.D. program and provided helpful advice in guiding students in it. The first director of graduate studies, supervising the students working in the advanced degree programs, was another professor of Bible, Frederick Grant, until he was followed by church historian Cyril Richardson in 1954.

The B.D. curriculum in the Van Dusen years was marked by an effort to provide a sound, basic theological education in the context of a proliferation of interests, subdisciplines, specialties, literature, and courses in the whole field of religious and theological studies. The principal strategy used was the increase in degree requirements. In the last year of the previous administration, no particular courses were required for the B.D. degree; one had to earn 90 curricular points, including a thesis, over the three academic years, including 16 in the biblical field, and 6 each in the historical and theological fields. But in 1945 no less than 6 specific introductory courses were required (a total of 31 points, 8 each in the fields just mentioned plus 7 for the practical), while 8 additional points in each field were to be elected, plus 4 in the area of the thesis, so 67 of the 90 points were needed to fulfill specific field or thesis requirements. In view of a rapid increase in seminary enrollment, this meant that the introductory classes grew very large indeed.

There were various minor modifications through the years. In 1952 the requirements for the practical field were increased to 19 points, with options depending on which vocational field (parish ministry, religious education, missionary service, higher education) a student chose. The next year the student curriculum committee protested the rigidity of the requirements, noting that the entering student was expected to spend 15 hours a week in lectures, with about twice that time needed for adequate preparation, plus 10 hours of field work. The dominance of the lecture system was challenged, and the content of many of the practical field courses was criticized. But the basic curriculum remained intact, and can be interpreted as the result of a general consensus in mainline post-liberal Protestantism that "realistic" or broadly neo-orthodox theology, informed by biblical revelational perspectives and concerned with ecumenical developments, provided a viable road ahead in theological education. The peak of this trend of laying down so many B.D. requirements was reached in 1959, when no fewer than 50 points of specific courses were required (though by passing three placement tests, one could be excused from 5), and 24 other points were consumed in fulfilling field requirements.

The reactions from students did make a difference, however, particularly as a number of faculty members took them seriously in the way they shaped their own courses, and as the small weekly groups related to many of the introductory courses, often led by tutors, allowed for lively exchanges and discussions. When new members of the faculty were selected, the quality of their teaching was a concern, along with their scholarship, productivity, and ability to guide candidates toward doctoral degrees in the departments that offered them. Among the many able persons Union brought to its faculty in those years of expansion were some remarkable teachers. A survey by fields can do little more than list names of persons who meant a very great deal to their many students and colleagues.

From Union's early days, the biblical courses had been taught by some outstanding scholars. That tradition of excellence was powerfully exemplified by James Muilenburg, who came from the Pacific School of Religion in 1945 to teach Old Testament, his years at Union as Davenport professor coinciding with those of Van Dusen's presidency. His dramatic personality and utterly sincere conjunction of profound faith and critical scholarship caught students by surprise as he brought the Bible to life. The famous requirement of a paper on the Pentateuch was often a significant point in a student's career. As he worked on the Jacob narratives in Genesis for the as-

signment, Frederick Buechner—one of the students who had entered
the seminary on a Rockefeller grant—had an experience analogous
to many others when he became convinced that the Bible was not a
"religious" book in a conventional sense but "a great, tattered com-
pendium of writings, the underlying and unifying purpose of all of
which is to show how God works through the Jacobs and Jabboks of
history to make himself known to the world and to draw the world
back to himself."[11] An impressive tribute to Muilenburg was paid
when students coming to his final lecture in a course took off their
shoes before entering the classroom, signifying their sense of standing
on holy ground.

James Muilenburg, left, Old Testament professor, converses with John N.
Irwin, II, chair of the Board of Directors.

In 1956 a young biblical scholar who had just completed
a doctorate at Johns Hopkins came to work with James Muilenburg
and Samuel Terrien. Highly skilled in teaching Hebrew and cognate
languages, George M. Landes soon made a permanent place for himself on the faculty, eventually following both his senior colleagues
into the Davenport chair. In the New Testament department, the
search for a replacement for Frederick Grant led to the selection of
the precise and prolific scholar William David Davies. He had been
educated at the universities of Wales and Cambridge, and had taught
at Duke and Princeton. After seven years in the Robinson chair of
biblical theology (1959–66), he returned to Duke. The person who
was to follow him in that chair had arrived at Union at the same
time as an assistant professor, J. Louis Martyn, who was to become
especially well known for his book *History and Theology in the Fourth
Gospel* (1968).

In the historical field, Cyril Richardson, increasingly
known for a famous course on the history of worship in addition to
his work in the early church, was promoted to the Washburn chair
in 1949. The long search for a successor to John McNeill once again
led to Chicago, and Wilhelm Pauck accepted the invitation in 1953.
It did not take students and colleagues long to discover that they had
secured not only a leading scholar of the Reformation and of the
history of Christian thought, but a master teacher, whose great breadth
of knowledge, keen sense of the dramatic, and inexhaustible fund of
stories contributed to his effectiveness at both the lecture platform
and the seminar table. Pauck had been educated at Göttingen and
Berlin, and had taught at Chicago for more than a quarter century.
In a *festschrift* in his honor published in 1968, the year after he
retired from Union, a former student declared that "it may be that
some future historian will regard it as Wilhelm Pauck's most important scholarly achievement to have continued in the New World and
transmitted to a new generation the interpretation of Luther and the
Reformation that had emerged from the theological work of the first
half of the twentieth century."[12] The decision to add a permanent
member to the field, primarily to teach modern and American church
history, allowed a young instructor appointed in 1950, Robert T.
Handy, who had recently completed a doctorate at the University of

Chicago, to stay on. In 1957 he succeeded John Knox as director of studies, and was named professor in 1959.

The theological field, which John Bennett liked to refer to as the central field—including the philosophy of religion, systematic theology, and Christian ethics—underwent an almost total change in this period, as he was its only professor to teach throughout the period and on into the next. In view of his presidential duties, Van Dusen taught a surprising amount, but had to diminish his load through the years, investing much of his teaching energies on a favorite course, Ecumenical Christianity. Meanwhile, departures hit the field hard, at first among those especially knowledgeable in the philosophy of religion. Much appreciated by those who elected his courses though he never became widely known, adjunct professor Richard Kroner retired in 1952. Then the brilliant young David Roberts, inaugurated in 1950 as the Marcellus Hartley professor of the philosophy of religion, became seriously ill, and died early in 1955, widely mourned and deeply missed.

Later in that same year came the retirement of Paul Tillich, Charles A. Briggs graduate professor of philosophical theology. Since the publication of the first volume of his *Systematic Theology* (1951) and *The Courage To Be* (1952), Tillich had become very famous, and colleagues and students dreaded the day of his departure. "His students sometimes found it hard to follow the intricacies of his thought, but they loved him nevertheless," wrote Lewis Coser. "He was a beloved figure, and, as the years went by and his name became more widely known in the philosophical and theological community, he became an intensely admired exemplar." No one dreaded the thought of his departure more than he, and his friends sought a proper post-retirement position for him. Van Dusen, who was a member of an advisory committee at Harvard Divinity School, had secured arrangements for him to teach as a visiting professor at Union for one semester and at Harvard for the other. But then the president had to put up with what rarely happened to him—he was outmanuvered. President Pusey of Harvard offered Tillich a full-time university professorship at a handsome salary, which he promptly accepted. Tillich's biographers declare that Van Dusen, "who felt that he had been the victim of a double-edged betrayal, was briefly angered that

Tillich had been snatched from him in this way, but quickly reconciled himself to the new situation and arranged instead to have Tillich lecture at Union during several summer sessions in later years."[13] In a farewell address Tillich confessed that Union was his home and that no matter where he went it would always remain so. After seven years at Harvard, he completed his career with three years as Nuveen professor of theology at the University of Chicago.

The retirement of another giant came five years later. For a while it looked as though it might have had to come earlier, for early in 1952 Reinhold Niebuhr suffered a series of strokes which lamed his left side, slightly slurred his speech, gave him two years of enforced leisure, as he once put it, and forced him to live at a reduced schedule thereafter. But he did recover and resumed his classes and his place in seminary life, and it soon appeared that a somewhat more leisurely Niebuhr could still produce an immense amount of work as articles, editorials, and books were drafted on his electric typewriter, notably *The Structure of Nations and Empires* (1959). A Niebuhr sermon in James Chapel was as much of an event as it ever was. Graduate students in his seminars marveled at his spirit and wisdom. The shock of his retirement was mitigated by the fact that he moved from Knox Hall to a nearby apartment and continued to teach a seminar and to advise students on their academic projects. He continued to be listed among the lecturers through the 1968–69 academic year.

Early in his retirement Niebuhr was able to accept visiting professorships at Harvard, Princeton, and Columbia. A former student, Nathan A. Scott (1946), who earned his Ph.D. in the joint program with Columbia in 1949, made many positive and a few critical comments on him in a 1963 essay. He concluded with these words:

> But, though Dr. Niebuhr's rendering of the great themes of the Christian faith is in certain respects unfinished and incomplete, he has yet clarified with a singular power the continuing vitality of Reformation Christianity and the possibilities for cogent interpretation of modern experience that are still resident in its basic message. Perhaps no other native American thinker of the contemporary period has invested a Christian position with such relevance to the political and general intellectual situation of our time;

and, as a consequence, his career is among the most eminent in that forum of thought which gives to the nation today its most creative engagements.[14]

Debates as to the meaning, interpretation, and correctness of Niebuhr's work raged during his lifetime and whoever picks up one of his writings may quickly get involved once again in the continuing discussion stimulated by this dynamic thinker, whose name will always be associated with the seminary where he taught. At his retirement, funds were raised for the Reinhold Niebuhr chair in social ethics, first filled by his close friend and colleague, John Bennett. The Niebuhrs later settled in Stockbridge, Massachusetts, where he died in 1971.

To carry on the work of the field, both younger and older scholars were appointed. Robert McAfee Brown (1946) had served a term as navy chaplain, taught religion at his alma mater, Amherst, returned to Union to earn a Ph.D. in the joint program, and then in 1950–51 was named as an instructor in the theological field while he was completing his dissertation on the British theologian P. T. Forsyth. After two years as professor of religion at Macalester, this impressive lecturer and promising writer was brought back to Union as Auburn assistant professor of systematic theology and philosophy of religion. He was conspicuous both for his great capacities as a teacher and author, and for his role in extracurricular activities, such as tossing off scripts for unforgettable seminary evenings of entertainment. He was appointed full professor in 1959, and when the board's search committee for Van Dusen's successor began its work early in 1962, it was reminded by the president that Brown was perhaps the best known and most highly publicized member of the faculty. But the Auburn professor, a skilled apologist, had decided that his role would be better fulfilled outside seminary walls on a "secular" campus, and resigned that year to teach religion at Stanford University, having helped the seminary greatly during a period of transition in its theological field.

As Tillich's retirement approached, it was recognized that a senior theologian was needed, and the search led once again to Chicago as Daniel Day Williams was chosen. Holding an M.A. from Chicago and a B.D. from Chicago Theological Seminary, Williams was no stranger to Morningside Heights. He had completed his doctorate at Columbia in 1940, working closely with Eugene Lyman, among others, and making extensive use of the library. He had taught theology for 15 years at C.T.S. and the Federated Theological Faculty of the university when the call to Union came; he deferred moving to Union for a year to co-direct with H. Richard Niebuhr and James M. Gustafson of Yale an extensive Study of Theological Education in the United States and Canada sponsored by the American Association of Theological Schools and financed by the Carnegie Corporation. Several important works came out of the study, particularly *The Advancement of Theological Education* (1957), written by the three directors.

Settling in at Union, Williams quickly became much respected and admired, as he taught courses both in systematic theology and in the philosophy of religion. Well known through his books *God's Grace and Man's Hope* (1949) and *What Present Day Theologians Are Thinking* (1952), he was a careful and deliberate thinker, well acquainted with the challenges and stimulation of naturalistic thinking and process philosophy. Because of his wide knowledge of theological education, he was often asked to take part in discussions of the curriculum, which was growing overcrowded as the faculty expanded and new programs and courses were added just as efforts to give the B.D. degree coherence led to more rigid requirements. Once in a community gathering about such matters he exploded, "There's too much of everything around here." He was a very conscientious scholar who gave generously of his time to students as well as carrying large classes.

Another major appointment was made in 1959, in anticipation of Niebuhr's retirement. Roger L. Shinn (1941) had returned to Union right after his separation from military service to complete a Ph.D. in the joint program with Columbia (1949), serving for two years as an instructor of philosophy of religion, then teaching for five years each at his alma mater, Heidelberg College, and Vanderbilt Divinity School before returning to Union as professor of Christian ethics. He taught a wide range of courses, guided many dissertations, was named William E. Dodge professor of applied Christianity, and later followed Bennett in the Niebuhr chair. Author of many books, he became increasingly active in the ecumenical discussion of ethical issues.

Theological field offerings were also enriched by the appointment of younger scholars. As a B.D. student, Robert L. Horn's scholarly abilities and competence in theological and philosophical thought caught the eyes of his instructors. He was permitted to transfer to the Th.D. program, but his studies were interrupted as he taught at Haverford for two years. In 1960 he was called back to Union as assistant professor of philosophy of religion, and taught a wide variety of courses in the field. He left to chair the department of philosophy at his undergraduate college, Earlham, in 1966, and completed the doctorate at Union three years later. Donald G. Dawe served several pastorates after graduating from Union in 1952, and returned to earn his Th.D., also working in the office of the dean of students and teaching as assistant professor of systematic theology before accepting a post at Macalester College.

Toward the end of the period two major appointments brought widely known theologians to the faculty. The tradition of inviting distinguished Scottish scholars to Union had been important in the seminary's history, and was happily renewed with the appointment of John Macquarrie as professor of theology in 1962. A graduate of the University of Glasgow who then completed a Ph.D. there in 1954, Macquarrie had served in the army chaplaincy, filled a Church of Scotland pulpit for five years, and taught as a lecturer at Glasgow for nine. An impressive and knowledgeable teacher, his work was much appreciated by students in various degree programs, while his many writings attracted wide attention. The other major appointment in the field, made that same year, followed another familiar pattern: bringing back a graduate who had earned distinction in a chosen field. Paul L. Lehmann (1930; Th.D., 1936) had taught at Elmhurst and Wellesley colleges, Eden and Princeton seminaries, and was Lamont professor of divinity at Harvard when he became Auburn professor of systematic theology.

Something of the similarities and differences in the approaches of the two theologians to their work was disclosed in their inaugural addresses delivered on the same day in October 1962. Speaking on the question "How is Theology Possible?" Macquarrie's learned answer drew on classical, neo-orthodox, and, in particular, existentialist sources. Coming to his conclusion, he agreed that the theologian could not offer proof for a position taken, but could show that "faith is not just an arbitrary answer"—perhaps not going beyond this, "for it brings us to the point where we see that this discourse about God has to do with the most radical matter in life, the point where, exercising our freedom in finitude, we decide to take either the risk of faith or the risk of unfaith." His new colleague, lecturing on the topic "The Formative Power of Particularity," and taking his point of departure from Pascal, declared that:

The risk of theology is the wager that "Jesus Christ is the end of all, and the centre to which all tends." It is the risk that "Whoever knows Him knows the reason of everything." . . . Pascal, like Paul, and Luther and Calvin before him, and like Kierkegaard after him, understood the doing of theology in terms of the risk of this particularity. Hesitant neither before its embarrassment nor about its expectation—they wagered![15]

Their varying but complementary approaches promised a rich fare for Union's students in the years that lay ahead.

The four academic fields had been more a matter of curriculum conception than departmental organization, but they were moving toward a greater degree of self-consciousness. In this period the practical field became the largest and least clearly defined one, often seen as a collection of specialties loosely related to the practice of ministry rather than to a "subject" or "content" area as the biblical, historical, and theological fields were considered to be. Several of the special programs were located in it. To present a complex situation as clearly as possible, the practical field as it had developed historically will be treated first, and then the special programs, which had a greater impact on it than on the other fields, will be discussed.

Union had long prided itself on the high quality of its instruction in the closely related areas of homiletics and pastoral theology, but as the new administration opened Coffin, who had long taught these subjects, had retired, and several other soon followed. It had been noted that when Harry Emerson Fosdick's responsibilities at Riverside Church grew too heavy he resigned the Jesup chair in 1934, but remained on as adjunct professor, residing in Knox Hall until his retirement from the church and the seminary in 1946, when he moved to Bronxville. He was not only a pulpit giant himself but had been a great teacher of homiletics, and his rare appearances at the seminary during retirement, as at a 75th birthday celebration, were notable events. Decisive action had been taken in the last year of the former administration to maintain strength in these important subjects. Paul Scherer, a graduate of Lutheran Theological Seminary in Philadelphia, had become one of America's best-known preachers during a quarter century as pastor of Holy Trinity Church in New York. A member of Union's board, in 1945 he resigned from it to teach preaching, soon becoming Brown professor of homiletics. The high quality of Scherer's biblically and theologically oriented preaching and teaching made significant contributions to his students and colleagues in his 15 years at Union. His was a hard act to follow, but it was done by another graduate of Lutheran Seminary—Edmund A. Steimle, a famous radio preacher, who after several pastorates taught at his alma mater until he came to the Brown chair in 1961. Renowned for his conversational style and fresh applications of biblical texts to contemporary life situations, Steimle quickly made an impact on the seminary community.

Some teaching in homiletics was also done by Paul W. Hoon (1934), who had earned a Ph.D. at Edinburgh and served a number of Methodist pastorates until he became the Henry Sloane Coffin professor of pastoral theology in 1953, but the bulk of his teaching was in such subjects as pastor and parish, public worship, and the devotional life. A man deeply devoted to the life of the congregation at a time when many students were thinking of teaching and other forms of specialized ministry, Hoon patiently persisted in emphasizing the importance of the parish, worship, and the life of prayer along with the pursuit of scholarly truth in his 22 years on the faculty. Many of the strands of his teaching were woven together in his 1971 book, *The Integrity of Worship: Ecumenical and Pastoral Studies in Liturgical Theology.*

Union's tradition, however, had been to have a several active pastors on the faculty in part-time professorial roles. So in 1945 two such appointments were made as persons who had been on the board and taught as lecturers were named associate professors of practical theology: Morgan P. Noyes (1920), pastor of Central Presbyterian Church of Montclair, New Jersey, and George A. Buttrick of

Madison Avenue Presbyterian Church. They served for six and ten years respectively, but the tradition was continued as others were named associate professors: in 1950 Ralph W. Sockman (1916; Columbia Ph.D., 1917), who served a Methodist congregation in New York (Christ Church) for 46 years; and in 1954 Robert J. McCracken, Fosdick's successor at Riverside. Union's reputation in homiletics and pastoral theology was well maintained by such a core of instructors.

The department of Religious Education and Psychology in this period was classified as part of the practical field, but it had considerable departmental self-consciousness. Candidates for most Union degree programs including the Th.D., and also those in the joint M.A., Ph.D. and Ed.D. programs of Columbia's Teachers College, could major in religious education, and the department developed considerable administrative apparatus of its own as it guided its majors. Its responsibilities grew after the M.R.E. program was launched in 1954, and it made quite extensive use of lecturers in fielding the many courses that were needed. There was considerable turnover of its faculty in this period of expansion. In 1950 Harrison S. Elliott retired after 28 years of vigorous leadership; as president of the Religious Education Association (1939–42) he was a prominent leader in the field.

Elliott was succeeded in the Skinner and McAlpin chair of practical theology by another conspicuous figure in religious and theological education, Lewis J. Sherrill. A graduate of Austin College and Louisville Presbyterian Theological Seminary with a doctorate from Yale, he had taught at his seminary for a quarter century, much of that time also serving as dean. He made an important contribution to the wider enterprise of theological education by serving as the first executive secretary of the American Association of Theological Schools and then its president. A clue to his approach to religious education was given in the title of his inaugural address at Union, "Theological Foundations of Christian Education," also the caption of one of his best-known courses. He saw as characteristic of his time many signs of a spirit of return from the part to the whole, and illustrated that trend in Christian life by pointing to movements away from a fragmented Christianity to an ecumenical church, in Christian thought by the effort to rethink a total theology, and in the theological curriculum by attempts to escape isolated "departments" to find a unity which represents the full stream of Christian life and thought. He also had great expertise in the psychology of religious development, and his experience and wisdom were much appreciated.

After years of faithful service, Frank Herriott was inaugurated full professor simultaneously with Sherrill, and soon a third member was added to the department, Canadian-born Mary Anderson Tully. She had considerable experience in religious education in Canada. After completing an Ed.D. in the joint Union–Teachers College program, she was named instructor, rising to associate professor. She gave much attention to the teaching process, later developing a specialty in fine arts and art education.

To the dismay of the seminary community, Dr. Sherrill died in office early in 1957. It did not take the faculty and board long to name as his successor another Texan and alumnus of Austin College, C. Ellis Nelson. He had graduated from and taught at Austin Presbyterian Theological Seminary for many years, with time off for several other responsibilities and for completing a Ph.D. at Columbia in connection with the Union–Teachers College program in 1955. Taking over such courses as the educational ministry of the church, theological foundations of Christian education, and the curriculum of religious education, Nelson, who was well-known for his keen judgments and dry wit, followed Herriott in the Skinner and McAlpin chair when the latter retired in 1960. Another person already had been brought into the field, Robert W. Lynn. With a B.D. from Yale, Lynn interrupted pastoral service at a Presbyterian church in Denver to undertake graduate study at Union, finally completing the doctorate in 1962. Meanwhile, in 1959 he became a member of the faculty to teach both religious education and church and community, the next year adding responsibilities as dean of the Auburn program. In education, he had particular interests in sociological foundations and in adult education.

The field work office maintained a network of placements so that B.D. and M.R.E. students could get practical experience in congregations or other appropriate settings. In 1956 one of the nation's well-known exponents of field work programs retired after heading Union's department for 38 years—Arthur L. Swift, whose teaching through the years had been primarily in the area of church and community. To replace him as director of field work, Union called back John L. Casteel, while various persons were involved in teaching church and community courses, including Professors Webber, Mathews, Lynn, and in the later 1950s a young sociologist of religion, Robert Lee (1954). He earned a Ph.D. in the joint program with Columbia in 1958 and three years later left to teach on the West Coast.

Also placed in the practical field were courses in missions, under the rubric "Christianity in its World-wide Relations." When Professor Iglehart retired in 1950, his was succeeded by M. Searle Bates, a Rhodes scholar, holder of a Yale Ph.D., and a former missionary to China, where for 30 years he held a professorship in history at the University of Nanking. He had many ecumenical connections, especially with the International Missionary Council and with World and National Councils of Churches. During his 15 years at Union he carried heavy course loads, was deeply involved in working with the growing number of overseas students, and was friend and advisor to the many visiting professors from abroad who taught at Union in this period of enthusiasm for unitive Christianity.

The ecumenical emphasis was intensified by two generous gifts to bring visiting professors to the seminary on a regular basis. As president-elect, Van Dusen had participated in securing from the Luce Foundation an endowment in memory of Henry Winters Luce. It provided income to bring a prominent Christian leader and scholar from another country as the Henry W. Luce Professor of World Christianity each year. The plan worked well through the years, and, with somewhat less frequency, was still operative in the 1980s. The president and the professor of missions worked hard at making arrangements—not an easy task in view of long range negotiations, problems of scheduling (some could only stay a semester), and occasional last-minute disappointments. There were no less than 14 Luce professors during the Van Dusen years:

1945 Francis Cho Min Wei, China
1947 and 1955 Paul D. Devanandan, India
1950 Loofty Levonian, Lebanon
1951 Gonzalo Baez-Camargo, Mexico
1952 Zachariah K. Matthews, South Africa
1953 Tetsutaro Ariga (STM 1924, Th.D. 1936), Japan

1954 David G. Moses (1933), India
1956 Aziz S. Atiya, Egypt
1957 Soichi Saito, Japan
1958 Christian Baeta, Ghana
1959 U Hla Bu, Burma
1960 B. Foster Stockwell, Argentina
1960 A. Michael Hollis, India
1962 Masao Takenaka, Japan

Their courses were often taught in the practical field's "Christianity in its World-wide Relations" section, but sometimes they also had offerings in their own academic fields, and they frequently took part in team-taught efforts. They brought something of the reality of the Christian churches around the world into the quadrangle.

Another endowment for a similar purpose was presented by John D. Rockefeller III to honor Harry Emerson Fosdick. It was provided that the holders of this visiting professorship could come from any part of the world and from any religious affiliation. Normally they were expected to spend a semester teaching at Union and a semester serving other theological institutions and churches in the country. In this period, the Harry Emerson Fosdick Visiting Professorship was held by:

1954 George F. MacLeod (1922), Scotland
1956 Hendrik Kraemer, Netherlands
1956 John Baillie, Scotland
1957 Rajah B. Manikam (1928), India
1959 Daniel T. Niles, India
1960 Johannes E. R. Lilje, West Germany
1960 George A. Buttrick, United States
1961 Douglas V. Steere, United States
1962 Theodore O. Wedel, United States

More often than not, the courses of the Fosdick professors were in the practical field, but some were listed in the theological, strengthening its ecumenical flavor. The Luce and Fosdick professors increased the seminary's awareness of the variety of Christian churches around the world not only through their courses, but also through occasional presentations, chapel addresses, and informal contacts.

Another set of courses in the practical field were taught by the Jesup professors under various headings: "Teaching the Bible" (Walter Bowie), "The Use of the Bible" (Mary Lyman), and "The Bible in the Church" (James D. Smart). Smart, a graduate of the University of Toronto and holder of its doctorate in Old Testament, had pastored a number of Presbyterian churches in Canada, served as editor-in-chief of the Christian Faith and Life curriculum of the Presbyterian Church in the U.S.A., and in 1957 came to Union as Jesup professor. He also taught in the Old Testament field, with particular emphasis on biblical interpretation. When this precise scholar of Calvinist disposition retired in 1971, he returned to the pastorate he had held when he came to Union—Rosedale Presbyterian in Toronto.

Union's speech department had a long record of effective work, which continued even as the numbers of students swelled. When John Casteel left for Colgate Rochester in 1951, a young graduate of Northwestern with a Columbia M.A. who had been a lecturer at Union was made instructor and in a year assistant professor—Robert E. Seaver, who was also experienced in the field of drama. Meanwhile, through gifts of the Davella Mills Foundation and other donors a fully equipped audio-visual center had been constructed on the lower floor of Auburn Hall, with soundproof studios and facilities for recording. There was a growing interest in religious broadcasting, and the person to head up the work in speech with this concern in mind was found in John W. Bachman, a Lutheran minister who had taught in these areas at college and seminary level. He came to direct the speech and audio-visual programs in 1952, resigning after a dozen years of service to become president of Wartburg College. To assist in an area where so much individual instruction was needed, J. Phillip Swander, who earned a degree in speech correction at the University of Michigan and who had taught at Union as a lecturer, was brought on the faculty as assistant professor in 1962.

Thus the major energies and resources of the seminary were invested in the ongoing work of teaching and learning carried out through the regular courses and degree programs under the leadership of the growing faculty. Much attention, however, was also given to the introduction of special programs, financed primarily by grants from foundations. They also brought new faculty members to the seminary—some for stated periods as visiting professors, others as regular additions. The term "program" was chosen to indicate a teaching department within the seminary which was interdisciplinary in approach and made use of other institutions for faculty and other resources in educating Union students.

The seminary's prominence in ecumenical affairs was well established before the Van Dusen years, but it soon increased. In 1945 a special collection of materials on ecumenics and the world church was set up within the main library as the William Adams Brown Ecumenical Library. In connection with the Missionary Research Library, this provided an important center for ecumenical research. Because of available space in Reed House, the seminary was able to provide space to host St. Vladimir's Russian Orthodox Seminary from 1947 until it developed its own campus in Crestwood, New York a decade later. Its dean, a noted Orthodox theologian and ecumenist, George Florovsky, served as an adjunct professor of the history and theology of Eastern Orthodoxy for much of that time; he and his colleagues and students were familiar figures in Union's halls.

Union's role in ecumenical life was markedly increased when one of the most impressive and widely publicized of the special programs was launched in 1955 as the Program of Advanced Religious Studies, familiarly known as PARS. Van Dusen had a part in the conception and formulation of the proposal that led to it, but it formally came to the Rockefeller Foundation from the International Missionary Council and the World Council of Churches. The program brought to Union each year approximately 25 promising younger leaders of the churches of the world, selected by the responsible officers of church bodies and Christian organizations. The purpose was to prepare the participants to discharge their duties more effectively by having them study together the realities of the world's moral and spiritual problems, the beliefs and practices of the principal non-Christian and secular faiths, and the role of Christianity amid the changing world situation. A nearby building at 49 Claremont Avenue was secured and refitted as a residential center with its own small chapel. As an Associated Press editor announced the program, "Union Seminary to inaugurate Staff College for the World Christian Movement." The program was assisted by a Board of Advisors of some 15 members, including such persons as the presidents of Princeton and

Harvard and the general secretaries of the World Council of Churches and the International Missionary Council.

Ralph D. Hyslop was appointed as professor of ecumenical studies and associate director of PARS in 1955; the next year he relieved Professor Bates, the first director. Hyslop, a graduate of Chicago Theological Seminary with a Ph.D. from Edinburgh, had been teaching historical theology and the history of Christianity at the Pacific School of Religion. He was no stranger to Union, having studied there in the late 1940s. Special courses for PARS students were developed; most of them were lodged in the theological field and taught primarily by Hyslop, often with the help of the Luce professors. One was taught in the historical field by Kenneth Scott Latourette, emeritus professor at Yale, throughout the ten years of PARS. His brief reflections on the experience are worth mentioning, not so much for what they say about PARS as they do about one of the problems facing Union in its changing urban context. He was pleased so to arrange his schedule that he did not have to leave New Haven, but could carry his responsibilities as a commuter. "At first I groaned inwardly and outwardly over the burden, partly because I throughly disliked New York City and the physical setting of Union," he wrote in his autobiography. "But as time passed I was profoundly grateful for the experience and for the contacts with the Fellows and colleagues on the Union faculty. But I never ceased to be glad that I did not have to live in New York." [16]

The program heightened an awareness within the seminary community of the churches outside of the United States. In its very first year, the 24 PARS fellows brought the total number of students from other countries to 92, the highest it had ever been. Though the PARS contingent had courses of their own, they also participated in other courses, and some of them who were properly qualified also received a seminary degree at the end of their academic year. American alumni/ae of the period, reflecting later on their experiences, have often spoken of how ecumenical issues became real to them as they came to know PARS and other overseas students. [17]

The program also had its critics. Some felt it isolated the fellows too much by quartering them together and having them spend too much of their time in special courses, away from other students. Others believed that promising church leaders should not be pulled

Overseas students, including participants in the Program of Advanced Religious Studies, 1959–60.

so far away from their own contexts. As an executive of the foundation that gave the grant for PARS wrote in a study of seminary education around the world, "Such students are best trained in their own or nearby countries, and it would appear that the Program of Advanced Religious Studies at Union Theological Seminary in New York City for the rising leaders and graduate students of the younger churches is about as far as it is desirable to proceed along these lines in an organized way."[18] The initial five-year grant was not renewed, but by exercising economies and picking up some other funds the program was stretched out for ten years. At its peak, the experiment attracted much attention and increased Union's reputation around the world. Faculty members and graduates who traveled abroad in the years since have often spoken of the warm welcome they have received, not only from former PARS students but from the many other overseas alumni and alumnae.

The idea of a program in religious drama was first presented to the faculty by the president in 1952, and was approved on the condition that a foundation grant be secured.[19] Robert Seaver was already teaching a course in drama, and his skill as a play director was soon appreciated. The Rockefeller Foundation contributed with a founding grant, and the program got under way in 1956, with Seaver named as director of the program. A prominent British producer and director of plays, E. Martin Browne, was brought in for a number of semesters as Visiting Professor of Religious Drama, and his wife, Henzie Raeburn, actress and author, was named lecturer in religious drama, along with three other practitioners in the field. The program also brought Tom F. Driver (1953), who was completing a doctorate at Columbia, to the faculty as an instructor in drama. The program was designed to assist seminary students in improving their communicative abilities; to develop talent in the areas of writing, acting, and directing; to acquaint the seminary community with the resources and possibilities of religious drama; and to contribute to the elevation of religious drama in the nation through the study and exploration of the relationship of drama to religion. An advisory committee of 15 had prominent figures from the worlds of theater and the church among its members.

For its second year the program developed a "Christianity and the Arts" section in the catalog, with courses taught by Seaver,

Driver, and two of the lecturers for the year, including Kay Baxter, a playwright prominent in the Religious Drama Society of Great Britain. Driver became more closely related to the theological field while continuing to work with drama. The program attracted much attention, and Seaver, by then an associate professor, became a nationally known leader in the field. Room 207 was equipped with stage and proper lighting and interested students gained valuable experience as they got involved in play production, while the larger community had the opportunity to see some remarkable performances.

The special programs had some features in common, but were very distinctive in their subject matters. The program in psychiatry and religion was undertaken in 1956 as a five-year teaching experiment supported by a substantial grant from the Old Dominion Fund, a Mellon interest, assisted by income from the Harkness endowment. For some years there had been a growing awareness of the value psychiatric and psychotherapeutic insights could have for those engaged in theological education. David E. Roberts, for example, had written *Psychotherapy and a Christian View of Man* (1950) in which he had explored the wider field of psychotherapy with a focus on the understanding of human personality by religious workers, and Paul Tillich had so melded theology and depth psychology in *The Courage To Be* and other writings that he was called by some the "therapeutic theologian." The primary goal of the new program was to explore and further the interrelations of psychiatry and theology at every degree level in the training of religious workers and teachers. It was located in the practical field, though some of its courses were taught jointly with members of other departments, especially religious education and systematic theology, for Mary Tully and Daniel Day Williams had a deep interest in this area. An advisory committee of psychiatrists, including professors of psychiatry, was set up to guide the program.

A unique aspect of the program at the outset was that a psychiatrist was appointed as professor and director. Earl A. Loomis Jr., a graduate of the University of Minnesota who earned his M.D. there in 1946, had become a leader in child psychiatry at the University of Pittsburgh by 1952. His talents and vision were instrumental in laying the foundations for a regular place for psychiatry and religion in the seminary curriculum. To work closely with him as associate director and associate professor of pastoral theology Union chose an alumnus, Charles R. Stinnette (1940), who had done further study at Hartford Seminary and Columbia (Ph.D., 1950). Under their leadership the program became very popular; many students wanted to take a course or two in the program, while some took majors in it in connection with their degree programs, including the Th.D. As one of the major emphases of the program was clinical experience, for persistent efforts were made to keep a viable balance between theory and practice, a number of part-time clinical associates, including hospital chaplains, were named to guide students in that part of their work. To reinforce Union's efforts along these lines, a third faculty member joined the program in 1958 as an associate professor. Jack C. Greenawalt, a graduate of Western Theological Seminary with a Ph.D. from the University of Pittsburgh, had also taught at both institutions. The program was so successful that it received a second five-year grant from the Old Dominion Fund.

A crisis in leadership occurred in 1962 when Loomis decided for personal and economic reasons to enter private practice, and Stinnette accepted a call to the Divinity School of the University of Chicago. A graduate student in the program, Robert E. Neale (1954) was named an instructor in the program; two years later he earned the Th.D. and became an assistant professor. Loomis' successor, James Allen Knight, who held a B.D. from Duke and an M.D. from Vanderbilt, had been found after a long search, and when he left to become dean of a medical school after only a year (1963–64), the difficulty of retaining a psychiatrist to direct a program on a theological faculty was evident, and it was decided to have Greenawalt administer the program as part of his responsibilities and to rely on psychiatric advisors, lecturers, and adjuncts to provide the medical imput. By then, however, the program had proved its value and become a regular part of the curriculum.

The adding of special programs enriched the educational life of Union and added to its reputation, but those who made the decisions to add them unconsciously and unwittingly overextended the seminary's resources. As foundation grants ran out, the school often found itself obligated morally if not always legally to faculty and staff members who had been added. Funds given for these special purposes rarely increased the endowment. Though some suspected that seeds of later financial troubles were being planted, it was not until later that the dangers of financing special programs by grants rather than endowments became clear.

Not so much a special program as a curricular emphasis was the area of religion in higher education. It was of particular concern to the president, who had a familiarity with the college and university scene, and knew that many Union graduates found work as chaplains, directors of religious activities, and teachers of religion on college campuses, for he did a great deal of the work of academic placement. Courses to help students prepare for such service were taught through the 1950s by lecturers as part of the offerings in religious education. The Danforth Foundation provided a grant which made it possible to call a full-time faculty member to that area, and in 1960 J. Alfred Martin Jr. was appointed Danforth professor of religion in higher education, and developed a number of relevant courses, duly listed in the practical field. Martin, however, who held an M.A. from Duke and a Ph.D. (1944) in the joint program with Columbia, was a philosopher of religion who had been teaching for many years at Amherst. Hence most of his courses were cross-listed in the theological field, where in fact he did the bulk of his work. When he became head of the department of religion at Columbia in 1967, he continued at Union as adjunct professor of philosophy of religion.

The School of Sacred Music shared in the mood of expansion that characterized the Van Dusen era, reaching its high point of enrollment at 113 in 1954–55. Clarence Dickinson retired as its director in 1945, but continued as a lecturer for eight more years. His successor had previously been in his courses: Hugh Porter, a graduate of the school's first class in 1930, and 14 year later a recipient of its doctorate in sacred music (S.M.D.). Soon after taking office, he was named as the first Clarence and Helen Dickinson professor of sacred music. Though much of the instruction in the school was provided by a long list of guest lecturers which read like a "who's who" of church music in New York at the time, there were some important additions to the full-time faculty. Robert S. Tangeman, holder of a Ph.D. in music from his alma mater, Harvard, came from the Juilliard school in 1953 to the faculty, in five years becoming Harkness professor and later assuming the role of director of graduate studies. Other additions came when Earl F. Berg (S.M.M., 1950) was called in 1959 as associate professor, primarily to teach voice and choral music, followed in two years by Charles L. Hickman, of the same class, who later became associate dean. Also in 1961, much like the way prominent preachers were named part-time associate professors, two talented musicians, Vernon de Tar (organ) and Alec Wyton (boy choir) were ranked as associate professors of sacred music.

The facilities of the school were also expanded. In 1953 a grant of $200,000 from the James Foundation enabled the interior of the James Chapel tower to be finished so that a classroom, a library, a director's studio, and 16 practice rooms supplied with new or rebuilt practice organs or pianos became available. Although a committee of directors had once referred to the school's faculty and students as "musical martyrs" struggling in the "catacombs of Seminary basements," now, in the president's rhetoric, they were "blessed with superbly designed and equipped work-rooms."[20] Further improvement came at the end of the decade with the completion of Dickinson Hall and its new headquarters for the school.

A sad time for the school and the seminary came on a September day in 1960 when trouble with one of the chapel organ pipes sent Dr. Porter up into the loft. He fixed it, and called down, "It's all right. Carry on"—and died there of a heart attack.[21] A gentle man, splendid organist, and competent administrator, he was greatly missed. His successor, Robert S. Baker, also a well-known organist, holder of both degrees of the school (1940, 1944), was named director and Dickinson professor the following year. The presence of the school of music continued to provide an important dimension to the life of the seminary, felt daily in the chapel and at special occasions, such as annual Christmas candle-light services for which there was standing room only.

To understand fully the scope of Union in this period of ecumenicity and expansion, one must glance at least briefly at some of the various activities beyond the curriculum and special programs in which the seminary was involved, directly or indirectly. There had been various efforts in the seminary's history to provide what was often called "extension" work so that laypersons could have some way to hear presentations by the faculty. One of the most successful of these enterprises began in 1952 as the annual "January Lectures"

Faculty members planning their work for a Ministers' Conference in Cleveland, 1954: l. to r: Professors Charles Mathews, Paul Hoon, John Bennett, Paul Scherer, Mary Ely Lyman, Henry Van Dusen, Edwin Kennedy.

which still continue, though the time was later changed to the fall because weather conditions were more favorable. The project developed as the first major effort of the newly formed Women's Committee, the idea for which can be traced back to the enthusiasm of Union's first woman to serve on the board, Elizabeth C. Morrow, and which was established in 1951 primarily through the efforts of Elizabeth M. Barclay, secretary for public relations. Elinor M. Lamont, who also became a board member, was the first chair of the new committee.

To the surprise of many, the lectures by Union professors around a selected theme filled James Chapel to capacity with a broad spectrum of women from the metropolitan area; the late comers could follow the lectures on closed-circuit TV in the Social Hall. Some local churches hired buses to enable groups of their members to attend. Many of the lectures were published in one form or another; for example, Van Dusen edited and was a contributor to a book, *Christianity on the March* (1963), based on lectures given in 1962 along with some others from previous series. The Women's Committee ventured on to some other smaller educational projects, and contributed significantly to the beautification of the quadrangle's courtyard. Its work aroused the interest of many women in the seminary, among them a future chair of the board, Rosalind E. Havemeyer, who came into contact with the seminary through the committee's major project, the annual lecture series.

An interesting facet of Union's life at this time was its active participation in Morningside Heights, Inc., a nonprofit corporation set up in 1947. Its members were nine of the educational, religious, and medical institutions on the hill. It was an effort to try to resist the deterioration of the area, work for improvements in the public schools, deal with problems of public safety, and strive toward slum clearance and the erection of two types of housing developments. One of these was for cooperative, middle-income apartments to be known as Morningside Gardens, across Broadway and north of Jewish Theological Seminary, the other for low-income public housing farther down toward 125th St, the General Grant Houses. The Union board supported these developments and invested in Morningside Gardens, for which ground was broken in 1954. As so often happens in such situations, there was considerable community resistance to the tearing down of the old structures and the way relocation was handled, and Union students and faculty became involved in the debates. The chairman of the student Social Action Committee, Russell S. Williams—decades later to become a board member—discussed "The Housing Problem On Our Doorstep" in a forum at the seminary, presenting the pros and cons of the situation.[22] What role a school like Union should play in its surrounding community was the subject of many informal conversations and class discussions.

One of the most remarkable developments of the period was the founding (1948), growth, and ministry of the East Harlem Protestant Parish (EHPP). Determined to put the gospel to work in one of the most crowded slums of the world, plagued with the problems of poverty, disease, drugs, and crime, J. Archie Hargraves (1948), George W. Webber (1948), and Donald L. Benedict (1949) gathered some funds from denominational and interdenominational sources. They leased storefronts in East Harlem, in the area where Union Settlement was still carrying on its activities, refurbished them into churches, and began regular religious services and ministered to the needs of those they could reach and who could reach them. It was discouraging yet fruitful work. The secret of the early growth of the parish was its group ministry, with its four disciplines: devotional (daily prayer, common Bible readings, retreats), economic (pay according to need), vocational (a commitment to their common calling to proclaim the gospel in the city slums), and political (working on legislative issues affecting East Harlem). The founders and those who joined the group ministry sought to identify themselves with the people, which included living in tenements in the area. Webber, with growing responsibilities at Union in the dean of students' office, made an agreement that allowed him to divide his time between seminary and parish. "It was mainly through him," wrote Bruce Kenrick in his moving story of the parish's spiritual and social ministry, "that more than five hundred students were to do field work in East Harlem, and over twenty were to commit themselves to a long-term ministry there."[23] In the 1950s the inner city ministry in this and other forms became a compelling vocational commitment of many students, while others learned a great deal from their field work at the parish.

One such student was Frederick Buechner, who later described his experiences in staffing an "employment clinic." His portrayal of the group ministry was remarkable. He saw the human problems, the tendencies to self-righteousness, and occasional glimpses of bitterness. "But be all that as it may," he concluded, "they nevertheless seemed, at their best, closer to being saints than any other people I had ever come across; and the quality of their saintness, the face it wore, the effect it produced, struck me as revealing something not only about themselves but about Christ, whose saints they were."[24] The parish was constantly growing and changing in those years. Two of the founders left to start similar ministries in Chicago and Cleveland, but in 1957 Webber focused his major attention on the parish, continuing to teach part-time at Union as associate professor. Though never formally related to Union, EHPP played an important part in the life of the seminary, especially for students—not only those who did field work there, but also those who knew it through conversation, visits, and study. As a parish that was led by ministers of various denominations and was assisted by both denominational and interdenominational agencies, it provided an example of an ecumenical ministry in a local, inner-city setting.

Several projects of a quite different nature were also very close to the seminary but with no official ties. These were scholarly and ecumenical publishing ventures in which Union faculty and graduate students were deeply involved. *The Interpreter's Bible* began when George A. Buttrick was asked what might be the most significant new religious publications that could be thought of and developed, and he answered by saying a new biblical commentary which would enlist the work of the best scholars and preachers of the English-speaking world. It was not to be primarily a critical commentary, but to be of direct help to pastors and religious leaders, seeking to put together scholarly introductions, accurate exegeses, and effective expositions for practical life. The editorial board of six was headed by Buttrick as commentary editor and made up of four associate editors who were all from Union (Bowie, Knox, Scherer, and Terrien), and the editor of Abingdon-Cokesbury Press, which published the twelve-volume set. Editorial offices were set up in Reed House, just across the street from the seminary. As the project unfolded, a quarter of the more than one hundred contributors selected for the commentary were members of the Union faculty or alumni/ae body; among them was Coffin, who listed the others in his informal history. Like all such efforts, *The Interpreter's Bible* (1951–57) reflected the state of the biblical and theological scholarship of its time, but has been widely used in many circles. By the summer of 1985, 2,641,716 volumes had been sold.

Another series of books, the Library of Christian Classics, was planned and edited by Van Dusen, John McNeill, and John Baillie. Published by Westminster and SCM presses (1953–69), the 26 volumes provided newly edited and translated versions of major treatises of Christian history. The first volume, *Early Christian Classics*, was edited by Cyril Richardson. John McNeill also provided a new translation of Calvin's *Institutes*, while Wilhelm Pauck prepared the translation of Luther's *Lectures on Romans* and edited the volume on *Melanchthon and Bucer.*

The involvement of Union directors and faculty members in the various branches of the ecumenical movement in their capacity as church leaders was usually formally unrelated to their roles at the seminary, but their participation in the ecumenical stream along with many graduates and some students was conspicuous. This was evident at many levels of the then burgeoning movement, but became especially visible at the assemblies of the World Council of Churches. None was more quick to recognize or to capitalize on this than Van Dusen, who was himself a prominent, articulate figure at these sessions. His ecumenical, democratic, and Presbyterian proclivities conjoined in what his colleague Daniel Williams once called his "marvelous sense of the order, the dignity, and significance of deliberative bodies."[25] For him the WCC assemblies pointed the way toward a viable conciliar ecumenical future, and he devoted much attention to them, as his papers in the seminary archives abundantly show. He was delighted to discover that 87 persons with Union connections were at Amsterdam in the late summer of 1948 when the World Council, which had been "in process of formation" for a decade, was officially founded. A Union lunch on August 29 attracted 53 of them, including such figures as Bennett, Brunner, Cavert, Dulles, Niebuhr, Parlin, Sockman, and Van Dusen himself. In reporting to the board in the fall, the president exulted, "No other educational institution in the world, not even the great universities of Oxford and Cambridge, had so numerous a representation in either the membership or the leadership of the Assembly."[26]

Union also became deeply involved in the preparations for the second assembly at Evanston in 1954, in connection with which Van Dusen was pictured on the cover of the Easter issue of *Time*. A suggestion he had made earlier that a special commission of 25 prepare a document on the theme of the assembly, "The Hope of the World," was accepted, and he found himself on it with such persons with Union connections as Baillie, Brunner, Florovsky, and Niebuhr. As the assembly drew near, Union's involvement increased as the WCC general secretary, W. A. Visser 't Hooft, and some of his staff resided at the seminary for much of the summer before the meeting, and various guests from abroad were entertained on their way to and from Evanston. When the report of the commission touched off one of the sharpest debates of the assembly, Van Dusen's skills in presiding and mediation were much in evidence; characteristically, he interpreted the theological wrangle as a healthy sign of vitality. He was pleased to call attention to the fact that among the some 1500 persons at the second assembly, 133 were identified in some way with Union among the accredited visitors, consultants, observers, press, staff, and delegates. Van Dusen was again especially prominent at the third assembly at New Delhi in 1961; he had chaired the joint commission to plan for the union of the WCC and the International Missionary Council which then came to a successful conclusion.[27] Though Union's commitment to the ecumenical ideal was often illustrated by reference to its role in the World Council and its assemblies, it was also expressed through the participation of many of its sons and daughters in various other channels, such as in regional, national, state, and local agencies of Christian unity, and their sermons, writings, and actions.

In the fall of 1961, following the New Delhi assembly, a tired president announced to the board that he intended to retire as of June 30, 1963. The question of the seminary's future quickly arose in many minds. When the board met again early in January 1962, the chair, John Irwin, indicated that he had appointed a committee to nominate a successor. A well-earned tribute to the president was given as the board unanimously voted that the new residence building rising on Riverside Drive be named Van Dusen Hall. A tribute of a different sort was given at the same time in the remarks of his colleague Daniel Williams as a member of a panel on Union's future. In his statement, Williams pointed out that Union was a place of increasing diversity, in part because of its intellectual, social, international, and ecumenical concerns. The wide-ranging dialogues between Protestants and Roman Catholics during the pontificate of John XXIII was beginning to have an impact on theological education. But Williams believed that the seminary was open to the new currents yet kept as its primary responsibility the training of a Protestant ministry, and maintained a level of excellence in its teaching. He stressed the importance of strengthening the quality of the basic pattern of education for the ministry while not extending it quantitatively, but argued that the seminary's proliferation of curriculum in recent years reflected an attempt to respond to the demands of the ministry. His statement was a thoughtful endorsement of much of what had happened in the Van Dusen era of ecumenicity and expansion as he called the seminary to maintain its excellence in theological education and to continue to be at the center of both intellectual inquiry and religious leadership.[28]

Williams anticipated what became the general mood as an impressive administration of 18 years came to an end. A long series of farewell events celebrated the occasion. They were marked by many expressions of appreciation for Van Dusen's strong leadership and for all that he had done, not only as president but also as a faculty member for 37 years. The transfer of leadership, however, was not the simple matter it had been when he had taken over from Coffin. Though the search committee had been working for a year and a half, it had not yet arrived at a nomination. As the Van Dusens moved to their new home in Princeton, the dean of the faculty, John C. Bennett, assumed the role of acting president.

CHAPTER NINE

Turmoil and Transition
(1963–1975)

THE STORMY SIXTIES

When the presidential search committee held its first meeting on January 4, 1962, it elected to the chair one of Union's best-known graduates, Samuel McCrea Cavert (1915), former general secretary of the Federal and then National Council of Churches, and one of the board's own vice chairmen. The situation the committee faced was quite different from that of its predecessor, which had selected Van Dusen. It had no such obvious choice, and decided to spread a wide net, to consult many persons knowledgeable in theological education, and to compile a long list of possible candidates. The list grew quickly. It soon included a number of Union faculty and graduates, notable pastors, prominent ecumenists, seminary presidents, and professors across the world. Despite the benefits of this type of approach, it can be costly and time-consuming. It had taken two meetings of the previous search committee to decide to nominate Van Dusen to the board; it was at the 47th meeting that this one finally, and unanimously, decided on a nominee who was willing to accept. At one of its meetings, about midway in its course of almost two years, the secretary was instructed to destroy the records and pro-

vide a summary report, but for some reason this was not done, and
the records remain.[1] As the process unfolded, names discussed often
moved out of the spotlight as new ones appeared. Many potential
candidates were interviewed. Some did not wish to be considered
further; at least two were asked to accept the nomination but declined. By December of 1963 the faculty was getting impatient, and
on the 11th of that month the committee voted to bring the name of
the dean of the faculty and acting president, John Coleman Bennett
(1927), to the board, and he was unanimously elected. Few were
surprised, for most of the faculty and the president emeritus had come
to the same conclusion during the process, even though they knew
that Bennett's term would not be a long one, since he was scheduled
to retire in 1970.

      In the president's chair, Bennett remained a soft-spoken,
shy, friendly, genuinely humble and democratic person, who continued to be forceful in speaking against social, economic, and racial
injustice. Having known the Union of Coffin and Van Dusen, he
moved into the structures they had inherited and elaborated, with the
president's office at the center of the making of decisions—not only
of the major ones (in cooperation with the board), but also many of
the minor ones. He presented no big plan to the board at its next
meeting, observing that there was no need to increase the number of
students or erect any more buildings, but he emphasized the importance of the graduate, music, and B.D. programs (especially the latter's practical aspects), the continuation of the seminary's ecumenical
commitment, and the stabilization of the special programs in psychiatry and religion and in drama. The pattern of faculty members
serving as directors of studies and of graduate studies was continued,
except they were soon made deans; Roger Shinn moved into the first
as dean of instruction, while Cyril Richardson continued as dean of
graduate studies. Instead of naming a dean of women when Helen
Sherrill retired in 1966, Bennett appointed an alumna and doctoral
candidate, Beverly Wildung Harrison, M.R.E. (1956), as assistant
dean of students and instructor in Christian ethics. Her competence
in both areas was soon recognized as she was promoted to assistant
professor and named as acting dean of students for the fall of 1969.

      On the whole Bennett carried on the Coffin–Van Dusen
tradition. In reflecting on his presidency years later, John Bennett

Newly inaugurated President Bennett flanked by Faculty colleagues, l., Wilhelm Pauck, John Knox, r. Cyril Richardson.

explained that "I really wanted to firm up the things which were already in principle a part of the structure and purpose of Union Seminary."[2] At his formal inauguration at the Riverside Church on April 10, 1964, he boasted only of his predecessors: "Indeed as I contemplate this succession I am greatly inspired and even more humbled." Observing that Union "is always in danger of trying the patience of other institutions by making claims to uniqueness," he affirmed three main characteristics of the seminary: a combination of freedom and involvement, a commitment to being both a professional school to educate ministers and a graduate school to equip scholars, and a relationship with churches in many countries and with the ecumenical movement. The bulk of his address, however, was not focused primarily on the seminary but on trends in the church and in the world, both promising and threatening. He pointed to the need for reforms: in the church, in city and suburb, and in civil rights. On the latter point, however, he was glad to recognize a resurgent activism at Union that reminded him of the depression decade, except that "there is much more of a common mind among students, faculty and directors than there was in the 1930's." He did not need to mention Martin Luther King's famous "I have a dream" speech at the Washington Monument the previous summer or the civil rights movement of which it was a part, for they had helped to form that common mind. Rejoicing that this "American form of the world-wide social revolution is very close to Union Seminary," he promised that "I shall do all that I can to help our students prepare to participate in it wherever they are."[3]

Though his style and temperament were quite different from those of his predecessor, in one respect he followed Van Dusen's pattern by continuing to expand the faculty. In the academic year that he became president, the official faculty roster listed 50 names; in his last year it had 55. Many of those added came as instructors or assistant professors. There were three of the latter when he took office, twelve in his final year. Many of them remained at Union for a relatively short time; only a few became tenured members of the faculty. Of the nearly thirty appointments made during the Bennett period, only five were called from the outside as full professors. Though the size of the faculty grew slightly, its composition changed considerably as the average age of faculty members decreased.

Bennett had pledged to sustain the ecumenical emphasis at Union. The historic tension between Catholics and Protestants had been markedly reduced during the pontificate of John XXIII and by the role played by John F. Kennedy as America's first Roman Catholic president. The latter was mourned at a special chapel service on the day of the assassination in November 1963. Bennett's inaugural address contained many references to the growing Roman Catholic participation in ecumenism under the stimulus of the Second Vatican Council (1962–65). In the presence of 340 official delegates, many of whom were Catholics, he expressed his hope that a Catholic scholar would soon be on Union's faculty. One of those who brought greetings was the president of Fordham University, Vincent T. O'Keefe, S.J., who exclaimed:

It is indeed a wonderful and wondrous sign of the spirit of our day that a son of the Roman Catholic Church and a brother of Robert Bellarmine and of Peter Canisius shares with full heart in the inauguration of the President of this illustrious Seminary. This same spirit of union in our restless quest for truth was evidenced by the fact that no so long ago the Robert Bellarmine Lecture at one of our Jesuit Seminaries was given by Dr. Bennett.[4]

In the following year, special relations between the seminary and the graduate department of theology at Fordham were worked out so that the academic credits of both institutions were mutually recognized and there was some faculty exchange as professors from one school taught in the other. The distance between Fordham's Rose Hill campus and Union proved to be a limiting factor in establishing a growing relationship, but it was of great value for some graduate students.

A much closer relationship was developed with Woodstock College, a Jesuit seminary in Maryland, which decided to locate near a university in an urban setting. A basis of understanding between the two schools had grown out of regular meetings over many years of Bennett and Niebuhr with two of Woodstock's prominent professors, Gustave Weigel and John Courtney Murray, both of whom had been active in ecumenical activities.[5] Pulled in several directions, Woodstock finally came to Morningside Heights. An agreement concerning the exchange of credits had been worked out in 1967, but it was not until 1970 that the entire college moved to New York. Its main offices and classrooms were located across the street from Union at the Interchurch Center, while its several residences were scattered from 98th to 125th Streets, with its fine library housed on the latter street. Some classes were taught at Union, and Woodstock students and faculty became familiar figures, not only in classes but also in committees and informal discussions and activities.

It was in cooperation with Woodstock that Union appointed its first ordained Catholic scholar to the regular faculty. In 1967 there were no less than three visiting professors from the Catholic world: Raymond E. Brown, professor of Sacred Scripture at St. Mary's Seminary in Baltimore, as visiting professor of New Testament; Bernard Häring, professor of systematic moral theology at the Lateran University in Rome, and Hans Küng, dean of the Catholic theological faculty of the University of Tübingen. The latter two were at Union as Fosdick visiting professors. This provided for some remarkable ecumenical exchanges at a time when the excitement and enthusiasm generated by the Vatican Council was very high. One of Küng's courses, which was open to the public, had to be moved to Riverside Church, where 1600 people attended his first lecture. With Woodstock's coming, the stage was set for a joint appointment. It was engineered from Union's side by Bennett with the help of Auburn, so that in 1971 Raymond Brown became Auburn professor of biblical studies. The holder of many degrees, Brown was ordained a priest in 1953, earned an S.T.D. from St. Mary's Seminary two years later,

and three years after that a Ph.D. from Johns Hopkins. A member
of the Society of St. Sulpice, whose members devote themselves to
seminary work, Brown had already written many books when he came
to teach biblical studies under this joint appointment, and many more
were to appear.

The arrangement with Woodstock College was unfortunately short-lived. Confronted with too many seminaries as vocations
began to decline following Vatican II, the Jesuit provincials decided
to close Woodstock College and relocate some aspects of its program
in Washington. Thus 1973–74 was the last full year of what had
been a stimulating relationship that had significantly increased the
resources for theological education on Morningside Heights. Though
the Woodstock experience began just as Bennett retired, it was he
who had patiently prepared the way for it. Happily for Union, arrangements had been made so that Brown was able to continue as a
permanent member of the Union faculty after Woodstock's closure
as a seminary.

Bennett had other ecumenical interests, however, one of
which was furthering Jewish-Christian relationships. Among those who
brought greetings at his inauguration was Chancellor Louis Finkelstein of the Jewish Theological Seminary of America, a very near
neighbor. Finkelstein mentioned not only the new president's two
predecessors, but also Reinhold Niebuhr, "to whom our Jewish Seminary is also indebted for endless friendship and affection."[6] It was at
a joint evening of the faculties of the two seminaries in 1957 that
Niebuhr had given his famous but controversial address, "The Relations of Christians and Jews in Western Civilization" in which he
argued that it was wrong for Christians to carry on missionary activity
among Jews "because the two faiths despite differences are sufficiently
alike for the Jew to find God more easily in terms of his own religious
heritage than by subjecting himself to the hazards of guilt feeling
involved in conversion to a faith."[7]

Bennett quickly set to work to build on the foundations
that had been laid. Arrangements were made to exchange some academic credits between the Rabbinical School of J.T.S. and U.T.S.
in 1964. The next year Union welcomed one of Jewish Seminary's
most distinguished scholars as its Fosdick visiting professor—Rabbi
Abraham Joshua Heschel, a profound thinker and conspicuous activ-

ist. Since Union's constitution required that professors be members of Christian churches, a slight change was made by the board so that this did not apply to visiting professors. There had long been occasional joint gatherings of the two faculties, and a joint student discussion group was a regular feature of seminary life, but in the sixties more contacts developed as a result of the common struggle for civil rights and the opposition to the undeclared war in Vietnam.

To understand the growing strength of these protest movements at Union, one should be aware of the initiative, determination, and creativity of increasing numbers of students involved in them without minimizing the role played by the president and members of the faculty. There was a large pool of students available, for enrollment remained high during this period, reaching an all-time peak of 793 in 1967–68—a number which included a record of 134 students from other institutions who were enrolled in Union courses. A significant change in patterns of student financing in 1964 seemed not to affect enrollment. In that year the former italicized catalog statement that B.D. and M.R.E. students making their best efforts toward self-support would receive sufficient scholarship assistance to undertake and complete seminary work was now changed to read "*shall receive sufficient financial assistance in the form of a grant, loan, and/or work scholarship*" to undertake and complete their work. This large student body was more diverse in age, denominational affiliation, and cultural and educational background that it had once been.

A growing concern for racial justice helped to unify this diversified group. This manifested itself in various ways, one of which was the organization of the Student Interracial Ministry (SIM) in the fall of 1960 after four white students had spent the summer serving as assistant pastors in southern black churches and becoming involved in the life of these communities. Faculty sponsorship was provided by Roger Shinn, who took part in the freedom rides of that phase of the civil rights movement, and was arrested. The movement grew rapidly until by 1965 about 50 students were at work in the movement in the summer, and nearly 20 spent the winter as interns who were taking a year away from the seminary while earning some academic credit under faculty direction. The SIM did much of its work through the Southwest Georgia Project in which the leadership of Charles Sherrod, S.T.M. (1966), was instrumental. Toward the end of the decade, as the integrationist stage of the civil rights struggle faded, SIM dissolved. But during the peak of its activity under student leadership, as two of them put it, "there was almost universal support for civil rights in the seminary, although only a minority of students directly participated in the Student Interracial Ministry and the Southwest Georgia Project."[8]

The seminarians' Civil Rights Vigil at the Lincoln Memorial in Washington was launched at Union. Under the leadership of Tom Leatherwood (1967), a student committee brought Protestant, Catholic, and Jewish seminarians from across the country to maintain the vigil. It began in April and ran continuously around the clock for 64 days until the Civil Rights Bill of 1964 passed in June. Some faculty members supported it by taking a turn. Estimates of the vigil's actual significance varied, but it was very popular at Union and was a unifying force in seminary life and illustrated a mounting student momentum for change.

Though the focus of social concern in the later 1960s became opposition to the Vietnam war, neither students nor faculty turned away from issues of racial justice. There was a growing awareness that it was working-class youth, including many blacks, who were especially vulnerable to the draft while the children of middle and upper class families qualified for student deferments while attending college and graduate school. Bennett and others were deeply concerned that there were no blacks on the regular faculty, and the president was instrumental in the appointment of three. The deans of students had long played an important role; one student of the Union scene during that period wrote, "It is paradoxical that the rather extensive services of the Deans of Students, in one of the most comprehensive programs of student personnel work among Protestant seminaries in America, are not mentioned at any point in the Seminary catalog."[9] When James Ault left that office to become director of field education, the vacancy was filled by Lawrence N. Jones, who had earned a B.S. at West Virginia State College, an M.A. at the University of Chicago, a B.D. at Oberlin, and a Ph.D. at Yale; and who had had a varied career in military service and education. He filled the dean's role ably for five years, doing some teaching in church history and religion in higher education, and in 1970 was named professor of Afro-American church history.

The new dean was not to remain the only black faculty member; in 1967 Union was fortunate to have secured as its professor of sociology and religion C. Eric Lincoln, a man with degrees from LeMoyne (B.A.), Fisk (M.A.), Chicago Theological (B.D.), and Boston University (Ph.D.). He had held various educational and administrative posts. Gifted with poetic as well as with research, writing, and teaching talents, he was director and founding president of the Black Academy of Arts and Letters during his Union years. In 1969, as Bennett began his last year, a young man destined to become very visible at Union and beyond, James H. Cone, was named assistant professor of theology. A graduate of Philander Smith College with a B.D. from Garrett and a Ph.D. from Northwestern, Cone already had five years of teaching experience when he came to New York. His first book, *Black Theology and Black Power* (1969) marked him as the principal founder of the field of black theology and an interpreter of the black power movement. Cone was receiving many teaching offers at this time, and in a "spiritual autobiography" explains why he came to the seminary:

I chose Union over the others because it was located near the largest black community in the United States (Harlem), and because it symbolized the major intellectual forces of white theology. It was the seminary where Reinhold Niebuhr and Paul Tillich had taught, and the place where Daniel Day Williams, Paul Lehmann, John Macquarrie, John Bennett, and Roger Shinn were currently teaching. What other place could I have gone that would have presented the most challenging side of the black and white worlds? I wanted to see if I could make a case for black theology among some of the most respected white theological minds in the country.[10]

At Union he became prominent as a tireless speaker and prolific author.

As the Vietnam war was escalated in the middle 1960s, a national seminarians protest effort, called Theological Students for Peace in Vietnam, was centered at Union. Less sweeping in its popularity than the previous effort, it did contribute to the growing opposition to the undeclared war in Asia by maintaining watches for peace in varius cities. The cause of peace was also vigorously supported by Union's president and most of the faculty. In early 1967 a board member who was also a lecturer in homiletics, Avery Post, then pastor of a church in Scarsdale, reported that there was a massive preoccupation with the Vietnam war in the student body.

At a time of a deepening national crisis over an increasingly unpopular war, many young persons found seminary something of a sanctuary where they had freedom to explore various options toward the future—and to protest what they perceived to be a disastrous military involvement. By October, sparked in part by a dramatic appearance at the seminary by William Sloane Coffin, then chaplain at Yale, a number of students became part of the draft resistance movement—26 turned in their draft cards that month. Support for this form of protest was expressed in chapel services that preceded arrests. As he came out of such a service, for example, David R. Hawk (who graduated in 1972 after devoting several years to the resistance movement) was arrested on the chapel steps. When Vincent F. McGee Jr. resisted the draft in the fall of 1968, his case was unsuccessfully appealed to the Supreme Court, and it was not until 1971 that he served a term at Lewisburg Penitentiary.[11]

Another illustration of student leadership in this period was demonstrated by a movement to convince the seminary and denominational boards not to invest their funds in banks which were loaning money to South Africa, thereby strengthening the government's rigid apartheid policies. Union began to wrestle with this complex question when two students of the class of 1966, David Hornbeck and Charles W. Powers, returned from their middler year at Oxford, where they had become aware of the South African situation. Upon returning to New York they enrolled as seminary students in the International Fellows Program at Columbia, a special one-year interdisciplinary program on American foreign policy, and focused their research on Africa. Discovering that the First National City Bank was part of a consortium of banks providing a large loan pool to benefit the South African government, they withdrew their own funds from a local branch at Broadway and 111th St., and formed a committee to urge the faculty and student body to remove their funds from the bank until its policy changed. They also began to pressure the Board of Directors to take similar action.

A high point in the early phase of this effort was a march of more than 300 students, faculty, and other members of the community down Broadway to 111th St. on April 20, 1966, where some withdrew their funds and others laid a statement of protest on the counter. Some board members thought that it was not the students' business to get involved in such controversial questions; others believed that a weakening of the South African economy would only make it harder for the blacks. A board committee to explore the issue further with students and faculty was appointed. A discussion about the moral and social aspects of investments began. It sporadically continued, and eventually led to some specific divestment decisions. The wider movement soon became permanently organized outside the seminary with some continuing leadership and support from persons with Union connections, such as Timothy H. Smith (1971).

During this period both faculty and students expressed a concern to improve the curriculum, particularly for the B.D. program, which was foundational to most of the others. One major step that was engineered by Bennett when he was dean came into effect as he moved into the president's office: the B.D. degree requirement was shifted from 90 to 78 curriculum points, about three-quarters of them required as designated courses or in fulfillment of field minimums. The big, basic introductory courses were henceforth taught not four but three times a week, and more time was expected for outside preparation. This allowed time for greater depth in reading and writing, and made the first year a little less formidable for students who had enjoyed considerable freedom of choice in their last college years.

Another effort at curriculum reform was sparked by Bennett's concern to make the practical field offerings more coherent. Ellis Nelson of the religious education department was instrumental in designing a pilot project that had begun to orient practical training for ministry around field education with the assistance of ministers of churches as "pastoral associates." The experimental program was developed over several years, with the results carefully evaluated by educational experts, and its basic approach was refined and accepted. In the fall of 1966 a former set of required courses in the practical field was replaced by a year course taught by a large teaching team and oriented to the student's required field experience.

Former dean of students James Ault had become director of field education and professor of practical theology in 1964, and was strongly behind the new effort. When he resigned to become dean of Drew Seminary in 1968, he was succeeded by one of his staff, James W. Bergland, a graduate of United Theological Seminary in Dayton, who had also earned an S.T.M. and later a Th.D. at Union. Associated with him was William E. Barrick, an alumnus of Garrett, who had undertaken further graduate study at Union and Teachers College. Also participating in the teaching team was Sidney D. Skirvin, a graduate of San Francisco Theological Seminary, who had served in several Presbyterian pastorates before coming to Union in 1966, primarily as placement officer, but with faculty rank in the practical field. At a time when many students were troubled by vocational indecision, he was very helpful to those who came to him for an assessment of their strengths and limitations and for guidance to suitable positions. The new arrangement brought some improvement to the curriculum of the practical field, and its basic patterns were effective until the middle 1970s.

By 1967, students were effectively pressing for representation on major committees that affected the curriculum and other aspects of the seminary's life. When John L. Quigley (1967) as chair of the student curriculum committee had been invited to meet regularly with a faculty committee, he demonstrated how resourceful and helpful students could be to such committees. The faculty voted on March 18, 1967 to include them on most committees. In part because of student efforts, the faculty allowed a student to complete work in some major introductory areas by working independently through a syllabus that covered the same ground and taking a competency examination rather than choosing a course for regular credit. The syllabus unit plan, as it was called, was passed but its form was considerably modified, which provoked some sharp student reaction. It did not prove to be very significant academically in the long run.

At about this same time the special programs were incorporated into the regular curriculum as part of the practical field. They were paid for now out of the annual budget, putting increased pressure on it. Courses in religious drama were included in the department renamed speech, drama, and communication. The program in psychiatry and religion continued as a regular department with Jack

John L. Quigley (in chair) participating in the march against apartheid down Broadway, 1966.

Greenawalt as director. A new faculty member was added to it in 1966 when Ann Belford Ulanov was named instructor. A graduate of Radcliffe and of Union (B.D. 1962), she had been a resident psychotherapist at the American Foundation for Religion and Psychiatry for three years, opened a private practice in 1965, and two years later—after graduating with a Th.D. from Union and also from the Jung Institute for Analytical Psychology—became an assistant professor. The department continued to draw many students from various degree programs, including the Th.D.

The Program of Advanced Religious Studies was terminated in 1965, but features of it were built into the smaller Ecumenical Fellowship Program. Its courses were usually listed in the "Christianity in its World-Wide Relations" section of the practical field. The president guided a special course for the fellows on several occasions. When M. Searle Bates retired in 1965, his successor as professor of missions, Johannes C. Hoekendijk, became an important influence in the modified program. He had studied at the universities of Leiden and Utrecht, and had had a varied career as missionary educator and administrator, chaplain, World Council secretary for evangelism, and professor at Utrecht. His contribution to Union was tragically cut short by his death in 1975.

Early in 1967 an impressive group of nine educators representing the American Association of Theological Schools, the Middle States Association of Colleges and Secondary Schools, and the National Association of Schools of Music spent a few days at the seminary for the usual ten-year evaluation to maintain accreditation. They were thoroughly briefed by a lengthy report prepared by "The President and Faculty," for which much of the spadework had been done by Ellis Nelson. The report of the team was strongly favorable. It contained such sentences as "The Committee, impressed by a distinguished faculty and an intelligent student body, especially commends Union's awareness of problems associated with an institution 'committed to the Christian faith, even though it emphasizes freedom of teaching and is hospitable to students who have no such commitment or are adherents of other faiths.' " But the report urged long-range planning so that the seminary could prepare for coming changes in church and world, and suggested that an educational policy committee of faculty and administration face basic questions honestly lest the school be victimized by the future. The various administrative bailiwicks and functions needed to be spelled out in print, the report stated, and the whole structure of the B.D. program needed a most careful and painstaking reevaluation. Indicating awareness that "Union is at present far from rudderless; in fact, we consider the administration of the school laudable," the evaluators still reported a mild discontent with certain administrative practices and urged an examination of traditional procedures and their effectiveness. The School of Sacred Music's S.M.M. program was evaluated as particularly strong, but the report asked if the doctoral courses were sufficiently sophisticated, and noted that more space and better facilities for specialized instruction were needed. The library, with its staff of 15 full-time and 47 part-time employees, was strongly commended as one of the strengths of the seminary.[12]

During the following year, however, not mild but radical discontent was voiced by many Union students. With his characteristic perceptiveness, Bennett had told the board late in 1965 that if the war lasted in Vietnam, "I am sure we will have serious crises at Union, and at other seminaries, as well as in colleges and universities."[13] The free speech movement in Berkeley had already started, and signs of discontent were rising in many quarters as what has been labeled in an oversimplified way a "counterculture" was developing in sharp opposition to the military-industrial establishment. A number of civil rights leaders, notably Martin Luther King Jr., spoke out against the Vietnam war. In 1965 Bennett did not know what form a crisis might take, but he anticipated it would stir controversy. It came suddenly near the end of the spring semester in 1968—and it stirred extensive controversy.

The story of the occupation of Columbia buildings by students in 1968 has been told many times. Accounts written soon after the events convey something of the mood and excitement of the period. They show that the whole affair was a complex one, which had been brewing for some time and which had caused a number of campus disturbances before the dramatic occurrences of April 23–30. Two organizations, Students for a Democratic Society (SDS) and Students Afro-American Society (SAS), led some 700 to 1000 students in the seizure of five university buildings. Three main issues excited students' attention: 1.) Plans for a gym in Morningside Park with a lower, "public" building open to Harlem and an upper private structure for University use—the whole complex to be on public land. This seemed to symbolize the shortcomings of the university's attitude toward its black neighbors. 2.) University connections with the Institute of Defense Analysis (IDA), symbolizing complicity with the Vietnam war. 3.) The disciplining of six SDS leaders without a formal hearing. Behind the whole upsurge of demonstrations at Columbia and many other campuses was the war. As the fact-finding commission summarized it, "The Vietnam war is the overriding concern of nearly all students. For them it is a matter of life or death—to kill or be killed."[14]

There was considerable sympathy among Union students for those who occupied the buildings, and of course those in joint degree programs were officially also Columbia students. A Union student, Daniel E. Pellegrom (1969), had recently become president of the Columbia University Student Council, and was trying to get more persons from the seminary community to become involved in the crisis. While a meeting at Union to plan such involvement was still going on after midnight in the very early hours of Tuesday, April 30, news came that a police "bust" was imminent. Some hundred or so Union students went over to Columbia and were there when riot police marched onto the campus with flailing nightsticks. Some 147 persons were injured, a number of UTS students among them, and in all 711 were arrested.

The seminary community was appalled by what had happened, and sought to find a way to take appropriate action. At a mass meeting under the leadership of students on the morning of May 1 there was a positive response to the suggestion that the best way would be to concentrate on Union's own problems. It was voted 340 to 40 to call off the week of classes that remained. A. Theodore ("Ted") Kachel (1965), a doctoral student in the joint program, suggested a full investigation of the seminary situation in a rather loose structure which he called a "free university." In a community-wide meeting on May 2, he was elected to chair the new effort, and proposed that there be "task forces" on decision making, educational policy, and community relations. On that same day the faculty met at 9:00 A.M., agreed to discontinue the several remaining days of scheduled classes, and appointed a committee to be in touch with the student leaders in an effort to understand their concerns. The faculty continued to meet briefly each morning during the following week; some of the younger faculty members became more articulate than they had traditionally been as they sought to interpret the words and actions of students. Various faculty members participated in the "free university" task forces that had been set up and that often met for many hours at a time and proliferated subcommittees. Some also attended the lengthy evening meetings when reports from the groups were given and decisions made.

Divisions within the student body appeared during the two weeks of the "free university" period. A radical caucus formed, its members anxious to capitalize on the momentum for change and willing to use political tactics toward that end. Various rumors spread, however, that the caucus was planning such disruptive tactics as dumping the library card catalog files on the floor or destroying student transcripts. Caucus leaders later denied that such actions were ever seriously considered by the group; some individuals may have. A black caucus was also formed to press for a black church recruitment program and a black church studies program. A small caucus which took the name Students for a Sane Seminary pressed for return to normalcy.

Ted Kachel proved to be an effective leader of the large evening community meetings, not allowing any one faction to take over the rather free-floating movement, yet keeping the floor open. The whole experience was of course highly controversial; among both students and faculty were elements who were either disgusted with the whole thing or thought it had not gone far enough. The large majority were willing to accept what had happened as an opportunity to effect some needed reforms and move ahead. On that note the "free university" came to an end on Wednesday, May 15. It was decided that the work of systematically continuing the examination of the seminary's structures and proposing changes would be entrusted in the fall to a Union Commission with representatives from students, faculty, board, alumni/ae, and staff. Plans were made to experiment with what were called core groups: small groups of students meeting with faculty advisors would determine their own syllabi and academic requirements for a year's work with full credit. The faculty agreed to grant extensions until early fall for work left uncompleted to those who asked for them, but the great majority of the students, especially those who were planning to graduate, did complete their work—even those who had been deeply involved in the free university and its task forces. Commencement was held on schedule, and the summer session, which as usual drew many students from other seminaries, passed without incident.

As the fall semester of 1968 approached, some feared that the reforming impulse would be frittered away or co-opted, while others were troubled that it might create further disturbances. A number of students who entered that autumn had been involved in demonstrations on the campuses from which they had come and were interested in increasing student power so that they could, in the familiar language of that period, participate in the decisions that affected their future. Some of them were greatly interested in the core group experiment, which provided an alternative to the prescribed curriculum as the group planned its own work for the year, usually auditing some courses and inviting professors in for a session or two, but shaping its own agenda, often across disciplinary lines. Jeffrey W. Rowthorn arrived from England as an instructor in theology. After he had won his B.D. from Union in 1961, he received a Cambridge M.A., studied at Cuddeston Theological College, where he later did some teaching, and served several Anglican parishes. He was effective in getting the first full-time core group to work together early in the semester, and worked with a second one in the following year, when there were also two others taught by lecturers. His versatility was displayed in other ways: he served for two years as the seminary chaplain (1969–71), developed courses in worship, became assistant professor of pastoral theology, and was later named dean of instruction. The core groups continued for several more years under lecturers, but both their expense and changing student interests led to their discontinuance.

It took a little longer for the Union Commission to begin its work, which it did at a weekend retreat at a conference center in Warwick, New York, October 25–26, 1969. The student body and the faculty each elected 12 members, the board 6, the alumni/ae 4, which along with the Comptroller and a representative each from the secretarial and maintenance staffs, made up a body of 37. Alternates were also chosen, so that attendance could and did remain high. One of the first compromises as the commission set to work under Ted Kachel's temporary leadership was whether a student or faculty member would chair the commission. Instead, Charles W. Powers, a recent alumnus then doing some teaching at Princeton while completing a doctorate at Yale, was chosen. It proved to be a good choice. He guided the body through many meetings, some of them day-long, with a balance of flexibility and firmness. There were two vice-chairs: a doctoral candidate, Horace T. Allen Jr., and a faculty member, Robert Seaver. A B.D. student, Jeffrey Slade, became secretary and a board member, Mary Lindsay, treasurer. The president sat as one of the faculty representatives. An executive committee was composed of the officers and four members at large.

The first three months of the commisson's life were largely exploratory. Three subgroups set to work with agendas much too large, as every aspect of the seminary's life came under examination and a great variety of proposals for change were put forth. Meetings at the seminary were normally around tables arranged in a square in the social hall. The meetings were open, but few outside the membership came unless they were there to make a presentation of some kind. The commission was unique in that representatives of many aspects of the seminary's life sat as equals in voice and voting, yet it had no governing power of its own—its task was to present a report which it hoped the various official bodies would adopt. In addition to the meetings of the commission and its groups, various seminary-wide "hearings" on major issues were held from time to time.

During its first day-long meeting since the retreat, February 1, 1969, an important turning point was reached. The commission decided to avoid getting entangled further in decisions being made through the seminary's regular channels of governance—as, for example, by the board's search committee for a new president—and to focus its remaining time on two main tasks: preparing a new plan of governance for the seminary under the board, and offering proposals for specific curriculum changes and experiments for the coming academic year with recommendations for the year after that and beyond. The work was refocused around two main standing committees.

One of them, nicknamed Committee A, dealt with internal decision-making, or governance, as it was popularly called.

The main tension was between plans that retained a central place for the faculty with student representation on most of the important committees and those that made a council representing faculty and students the major internal governing body. The debate was intense and was carried out not only within the commission but in the seminary at large. A compromise plan provided for an assembly which would include all the faculty and one half as many students—a body of some 70 people. This idea broke the log-jam, and opened the way for a series of other compromises in both Committee A and finally in the commission itself. The new governance plan was clearly labeled as transitional; it was to be replaced by January 1972 unless the Assembly itself extended its life. It provided for two large representative subordinate councils, one on academic affairs and the other on community affairs. It also created a new administrative position, dean of the seminary, to be appointed by the president in consultation with assembly and board, to be an administrative enabler for the work of the assembly and the academic affairs council.

Meanwhile, Committee B, which considered the nature and purpose of theological education, proposed that all specific course requirements for the B.D. be given up, except the introductory course in the practical field oriented to field education. In effect, this meant a return to the B.D. curriculum situation before 1945 when there were no specific course requirements but only general field requirements. The committee also recommended that there be a core group for each of the three B.D. years, urged simplified requirements for the M.R.E, and proposed a grading plan that gave up the traditional A–F letter grades for an Honors/Satisfactory/Unsatisfactory scale, to be accompanied by the professor's written evaluations of each student's work in a course. The commission was able to complete its work as directors, students, faculty, and staff learned to work together and to make compromises across constituency lines. A final report was hammered out of the two committee reports and the commission (after meeting seven times in April) went out of existence on April 30.[15] Before it was adopted with some modifications by faculty and board in May and June, several controversial events took place.

Beneath the surface of the compromises and working agreements that made a final report possible, there were continuing and deepening tensions. The student body included those who had little interest in what was going on for different reasons—some because they saw it as merely reformist and not providing for sufficient change, others because they were absorbed in academic and other projects and did not get seriously involved in commission debates. In the faculty the tension persisted between those who were ready to accept the sharing of power in an assembly and those who felt it was a downgrading of the role of the faculty. Then several highly controversial happenings in the spring of 1969 came to a head and intensified growing rifts within the faculty, and the ability to disagree over issues without lowering levels of trust and threatening friendships eroded.

The first of these tumultuous happenings was an explosion over an action of the selection committee for a new president, which had held its first meeting on March 12, 1968, well before the Columbia bust. It was at first composed only of board members and was chaired by William C. Schram (1949), a Presbyterian pastor. Parallel faculty and student committees were also formed and arrangements made to have them represented at the gatherings of the board's committee. The latter consulted with many persons, including potential candidates and leaders in the field of theological education. Many names were added to a growing list. By late fall two faculty members and two students had become voting members of the board's committee, in part because of student pressure. Faculty opinion tilted toward the selection of a person from the outside.

On March 11, 1969—the selection committee had been at its task for a year at that point—a decision was made. One of the leading names that had long been before the committee was that of John D. Maguire, Yale B.D. and Ph.D., a theologian and civil rights activist who as associate provost of Wesleyan University had been instrumental in a policy study that led to the reintroduction of coeducation, a limit on additional Ph.D. programs, and a general university reorganization. He had other offers and needed to hear some kind of decision. The students strongly supported his candidacy, but the faculty committee was divided in its opinion, and had recently voted 6–5 not to make a decision at that time.

The board's committee, with the student and faculty representatives present and voting, did decide to present Maguire's name to the board, and he was told that and invited to come to the seminary. The committee had previously decided to work quietly, however, not publicizing the names before it. Hence a number of the faculty outside of the process had not even previously heard the candidate's name, and learned with some surprise that the committee had come to a decision. Some of those on the faculty committee, including several of the most senior professors, were sharply opposed to the young candidate, and vehemently made their feelings known. Comments from Maguire's opponents ranged from criticism of his youth to his reported "toughness" and to the fact that he was a layman. There were accusations that some of the younger members of the faculty were trying to change the character of the seminary, and counter-charges that the seniors were using unfair and unreasonable tactics in an effort to veto a choice unacceptable to them. Many strongly pro-Maguire students saw in the whole emotional storm a further reason to distrust the faculty. The Union Commission's Committee A was thrown off stride for several weeks as a number of the principals on both sides of the bitter dispute were busy elsewhere. "Some of the faculty, I'd have to say," reflected John Bennett later, "were almost fanatical on the subject for no very adequate reason." [16]

When Maguire visited the seminary and talked with various people, he came to the conclusion that his candidacy was indeed not viable, and in a note of March 19 to the board's committee observed that "My imagination was fired by a vision of the possibilities for the Seminary in the future and I welcomed your selection with enthusiasm." He regretfully concluded, "Having now visited the Seminary and taken the measure of the situation and the sentiments in certain critical quarters of the faculty, I find it impossible to accept your invitation to the Presidency." [17] That did not quite end the incident, however, for some continued to press his name as the best candidate, and a widely circulated open letter from an alumnus in early May urged the board's committee to fight for its candidate. The scars from this episode, which was marked by bitterness and name-calling, did not disappear easily, and surfaced again in later difficulties. The search was to go on for another year before the new president was named.

Later in the spring of 1969 came another unprecedented and startling event. The black power movement was being strongly felt, and one of its organizational vehicles was a newly formed National Black Economic Development Conference (NBEDC). Speaking for it on Sunday, May 4, James Forman led a group down the aisle of Riverside Church and interrupted the service to read the conference's statement of purpose, *The Black Manifesto*, and to make extensive demands on the congregation in the name of reparations for centuries of slavery and oppression. Wanting to do something significant in support of Forman on behalf of black people, a group of Union's students late Sunday evening, May 11, demanded that President Bennett immediately phone the chair of the Board of Directors, John N. Irwin, and have him call an emergency meeting of the board to provide funds for the NBEDC. Bennett refused to call that late and about 75 or 80 students in all thereupon occupied the administration building, and barricaded it so that people arriving on Monday morning found the entrances blocked. After the demonstrators held a news conference at 11:00 A.M., President Bennett arranged for a board meeting on Thursday evening (the earliest time it could be held because of a legal provision for a three-day notification period). Those who had sat in left the administration building in good order, but continued their demonstration in the chapel in order to keep up the pressure.

The reaction among both faculty and student body to the takeover was greatly divided. Some feared that such a strong action jeopardized the channels of communication between faculty and students that the commission had so patiently cultivated. An emotional, protracted service in the chapel Tuesday evening won many students to the cause of reparations, and at a noon service on the following day more than $5000 in pledges were raised for the National Black Economic Development Conference.

On Thursday, May 14, the board met in the president's apartment in Knox Hall. The location was deliberately chosen, for the apartment had several exits and board members could not easily be blockaded, as had happened on several other campuses. A student negotiating team presented a case for contributions to the NBEDC through its sponsoring organization, the Interreligious Foundation for Community Organization (IFCO). In executive session, board members present pledged more than $100,000 for black development, and then indicated to the students that they would further invest half a million in endowment funds for black enterprises in Harlem, and promised to try to raise a million more for black causes. The negotiating team walked out, explaining that its demands had not been met. About 4:00 A..M. one of the negotiators returned to Bennett's apartment to say that the depth of the board's consideration was appreciated, but that the response was inadequate. After several days' discussion, however, and hearing a variety of reactions including those of black leaders, they decided to accept the offer. When the board held its regular meeting on May 20, one prominent member who had not been present on the 15th disassociated himself from the board's action and resigned. A delegation of students from the sit-in appeared before the board and indicated that they saw the action as a compromise that gave hope of ultimate reconciliation, and were told that the board had not condoned the building takeover. Actually, compared with some of the demonstrations on some other campuses, these episodes at Union were brief and did little physical damage, but they received much publicity, in part because of the seminary's prominence and its New York location.

Dean Lawrence Jones was instrumental in gathering the committee to be responsible for channeling the funds. In less than a year he reported that most of the $103,000 contributed by the board had been distributed, including $25,000 granted outright to NBEDC through IFCO. More than half of the $500,000 for investment in black enterprises had been so used—for example, $100,000 each for Freedom National Bank and Carver Federal Savings and Loan Association—and the black steering committee was providing a list of suitable investments to advise the board on distributing the rest. Of the additional million the board had indicated its willingness to try to raise, about a third was then in view; a report made by the committee in the middle of 1974 showed that roughly three-quarters of it had been raised, the bulk of it contributed by a committed board member. The funds were used for a variety of approved causes, including scholarships for black students.[18]

From the perspective of later, calmer times the events of 1968 and 1969 seem to be almost unbelievable to some. Questions as to whether the board and faculty should have yielded to student pressure as it did were often discussed, then and after. Many years later, the person in the very center of the tangle, John Bennett, reflected on his role:

I'm sure if I had been Henry Pitney Van Dusen I would have laid the law down, but I'm not sure what would have happened. I think you would have had a situation that was so brittle that things would have broken. I don't know. At any rate, I tried to moderate the process at each stage. I had some sympathy with it; I had some sympathy with the emphasis on student power at that time, more than I would have now, I would think. . . . Yet, at the time I felt that we didn't do anything that could have been avoided.[19]

So board, faculty, students, staff, and alumni/ae compromised in ways less than satisfactory to most in the brittle time from the "free university" through the Union Commission to the building takeover and its aftermath—and things did not break apart. Many of the compromises were creative. But mounting bitterness and polarization in the faculty showed that a price had been paid, and there was more to come.

The takeover occurred when the report of the commission had just received almost unanimous support by a student referendum, but was still before the faculty, board, alumni council, and staff. Some feared that what had happened would negate the patient work of the commission. But the faculty approved the report later in May, except for the proposal on grading, which it turned over to the new assembly, which would meet in the fall, for further discussion and action. At a special meeting on June 4, the board also accepted the report, applying its own quorum requirement of 33⅓ percent to the assembly, its electorates, and its subordinate units. The alumni council agreed on June 11, and the several support staffs at their meetings. Thus the new assembly was legitimated as the seminary's main governance body under the board.

The first meeting of the assembly took place on October 8, 1969 in rooms 207–205, with chairs gathered around a central table and podium in a U-shaped pattern for members of the assembly and rows of chairs on the edges and in 205 for auditors. The meetings were open; the number from the community that came varied with the issues on the agenda, and noise from the "galleries" often indicated support or disapproval of an assembly member's remarks. President Bennett opened the first assembly with prayer and after introductory remarks asked the new dean of the seminary, Ellis Nelson, to preside as his administrative enabler for the assembly. Meetings were conducted formally with agenda prepared by the steering committee and circulated in advance, and rules of order were closely followed as a parliamentarian was elected.

Among the first items of business was the announcement that Professor Macquarrie would be leaving at the end of the year to become Lady Margaret professor of divinity at Oxford. His colleague Daniel Day Williams spoke highly of his great contributions to Union, and the several hundred persons present joined in appreciative applause for a highly respected scholar. The assembly then declared a vacancy in the theological field, and the president indicated that he had already carried on a number of consultations in naming a search committee of five. Next followed long parliamentary wrangles over the proper wording of a resolution in support of the October 15 moratorium against America's participation in the Vietnam war, but a version was finally adopted and classes suspended for that day. As the meeting ran long, a problem that was to trouble the assembly many times surfaced: the maintaining of a quorum, especially of faculty. At the January 1970 assembly a proposal to increase the tuition for B.D., M.R.E., S.T.M., and S.M.M. degrees from $1200 to $1400 led to a long discussion of student aid, and the financial aid officer, Robert E. Broadwell, indicated that over 50 percent of increased income thus generated would be used for scholarship assistance.

As the meetings continued, it became apparent that the new governance system was a complex one, for the academic affairs and community relations councils which reported to the assembly each had heavy agendas of their own. The transitional plan of governance also provided for 11 operating committees with a three-student to four-faculty balance, which along with search committees could request time at assembly meetings. Financial pressures were beginning to be felt as budget deficits loomed; on March 4 the assembly passed a motion introduced by the Finance Committee "that no proposal from a council or committee should come before the Assembly without a budgetary projection attached."[20] It was later reported that the deficit for the year 1969–70, after transfers from the unrestricted endowment of $400,000, was still more than $60,000. As the budget for that year was just over $3 million, the total deficit of nearly half a million dollars was formidable. The problems of maintaining the special programs without endowments for them when grants ended, multiplied by the failure to have a capital funds campaign in the 1960s to increase endowment, were mounting.

The most controversial issue to come before the assembly in its first year was a resolution presented by an ad hoc committee on civil liberties at a special meeting called on March 13, 1970. Some members of a political entity, the Black Panther Party, had been jailed and what seemed to many persons as excessively high bail had been set, thereby raising a question of civil liberties. The resolution asked the Board of Directors to make available four percent, or about $400,000 of the seminary's unrestricted endowment, as collateral for bail for the jailed Panthers. For an hour the assembly sat as a "committee of the whole" to hear extensive information on the issue and opinions concerning it. A lawyer for the Panthers was present and given the opportunity to speak. The debate was long and intense. Some, including Bennett and most faculty members, argued that funds given for the purposes of theological education could not morally be diverted to other uses, however important. Others declared that while donors of the past might not regard this use of funds as theological education, in the present situation it served important educational purposes and made a witness to the importance of fair, equal, and just treatment for all accused persons. The final vote at 6:30 P.M. was 29 for the resolution and 11 against, with 2 abstaining.

The matter came before the board four days later; a number of persons who had voted on opposite sides of the assembly's debate were present at the beginning as guests to make their viewpoints known. Then, in executive session, the board passed the following 30 to 2: "RESOLVED that Seminary funds should not be used for purposes not directly concerned with the educational purposes of the Seminary." At a news conference following the meeting, Bennett read a statement declaring that the directors shared the concern of the assembly for the defense of civil liberties, but that their primary responsibility was to strengthen the seminary, believing that "one of the effects of the theological education provided at Union will be that the seminary will make an important and continuing contribution to the maintenance of civil liberties through the teaching of its alumni."[21] Though there were continuing conversations between committees of the board and the assembly, there the matter rested. Some of the Panthers did later jump bail.

By this time the presidential selection committee had completed its work. It was a while before momentum was regained after the difficulties of the previous spring, but it continued to discuss old and new names and to conduct interviews, keeping in close touch with both student and faculty committees. One prominent alumnus was offered the position but declined it. Not until December did the name of the person finally selected come to the serious attention of the committee—J. Brooke Mosley. He was no stranger to Union, for he had become a board member in 1966, and had spent a leave of absence at the seminary. While serving as Episcopal Bishop of Delaware he had become conspicuous in ecumenical circles as co-chair of an international Conference on the Church and Society in Geneva under the auspices of the World Council of Churches in July 1966, and had written the study book that came out of it, *Christians in the Technical and Social Revolutions of Our Time: Suggestions for Study and Action* (1966). He was known as a friendly, personable man and a competent presiding officer. The three committees interviewed him, and compared him with another possibility whose name had come high on the list at about the same time.

A graduate of Temple University and the Episcopal seminary in Cambridge (1940), Mosley had served in several parishes, as director of the department of social relations of the diocese of Washington, DC, as dean of the cathedral church in Wilmington before becoming the Episcopal bishop of Delaware (1954–68), and then the Deputy to the Presiding Bishop for Overseas Relations at his church's national headquarters in New York. It was recognized by the committees that he was not a scholar, was not well-known as speaker or writer, and had not been a theological educator. But reports from posts he had served indicated he was a good administrator, and was interested in governmental process. After a large majority of the student committee came to favor him, and the faculty committee did so unanimously, on March 15, 1970, at its 46th meeting, the board's committee indicated its approval.

By the time of a special board meeting on the 31st, however, a sizable group in the student body were having second thoughts. Some had gotten word that there had been problems in his leadership in Delaware—a rumor probably arising out of opposition to him because of his stand for racial equality. A petition signed by some 150 students asked for delay until the larger community at Union could talk with the bishop. When the board met, a group of protesting students gathered outside of the Auburn library where the board was meeting to urge further reflection, and two student speakers addressed the board, one representing the student committee and the other the dissenting group. In executive session, the board did unanimously elect Mosley. As he was not able to arrange to commence his new work until December 1, Lawrence N. Jones was later named acting president for the five-month interim period. So the long, troubled search, which in many ways reflected the conflicts and difficulties of that stormy period, came to a conclusion.

Although much attention, energy, and publicity was given to the encounters and controversies of the last several years of the period of Bennett's presidency, the main educational life of the school went on steadily. Classes were actually interrupted on only a few occasions, and the quality of papers and examinations remained high. Indeed, the attention that had been focused on the nature of theological education led to certain variations and improvements in both the method and content of various courses. The partnership with Auburn was flourishing; an important addition came in 1965 when John H. Hendrickson (1948), who had been pastor of three Presbyterian congregations, was named director of continuing education with the rank of associate professor, serving both Union and Auburn effectively in his new position. The Monday lectures were doing well; an attendance record of 820 was set on January 8, 1968, when Paul Lehmann lectured on Dietrich Bonhoeffer.

Faculty appointments continued to be made throughout the period. The School of Sacred Music had suffered a great loss in the untimely death of Professor Tangeman at the beginning of the academic year 1964–65. Richard F. French was immediately brought in as a lecturer and soon was named the first Robert S. Tangeman professor of sacred music; he also succeeded his distinguished predecessor as director of graduate studies for the music school. The holder of several degrees from Harvard, French had taught there, worked in music publishing, and served as president of New York's Pro Musica before coming to Union. In the biblical field the retirements of Muilenburg and Knox left major vacancies which were filled by James A. Sanders and Reginald A. Fuller. A graduate of Vanderbilt University and its Divinity School, Sanders had received his Ph.D. from Hebrew Union College and had taught at Colgate Rochester. Well-known for his work on the Dead Sea scrolls and other writings, he came as professor of Old Testament in 1965. A year later Fuller, a prominent New Testament scholar, was named Baldwin professor of sacred literature. A graduate of Cambridge, he had taught in England and Wales before coming to the United States to serve for 11 years at Seabury-Western in Evanston.

The majority of those appointed as instructors or assistant professors in that period served relatively short terms, but some were promoted to serve for a number of years. In 1967, Walter P. Wink (1959) was brought back to the seminary as assistant professor of New Testament; a graduate of Southern Methodist University, he had earned his B.D. and Th.D. (1963) degrees at Union. The next year David W. Lotz, while still a candidate for the Th.D., was named instructor in church history, primarily to teach the late medieval and reformation periods following the retirement of Wilhelm Pauck. A graduate of Concordia Senior College in Fort Wayne and Concordia Theological Seminary in St. Louis, Lotz earned the M.A. at Washington University in 1964 and the Union S.T.M. the following year. Soon promoted to assistant professor, he earned the Th.D. in 1971 with a dissertation later published in revised form as *Ritschl and Luther: A Fresh Perspective on Albrecht Ritschl's Theology in the Light of His Luther Study* (1974).

While the academic life of the school was surprisingly little affected by the turmoil of the times, there were major changes in its life of worship. By 1966 the president was sharing with the board his concern over the sharp decline in attendance at 8:30 A.M. chapel, and quoted a student who spoke for his generation as saying "we are night people." Hence in the fall of that year a longer (50-minute) chapel service was scheduled each Wednesday at noon, which went well. The much shorter 8:30 service was continued three days a week, but steadily declined until only a handful of students and faculty were attending, and it was given up in 1968. At a time when certain trends of the sixties for "secular" and "death of God" theology had their followings, some students and faculty put less emphasis on the importance of worship. And though it had never attracted many students, there was noticeable decline in attendance at the service in James Chapel on Sunday at 11:00 conducted largely by faculty members—the days when a Niebuhr or a Tillich could draw a full house were clearly over. There had been an internal debate about that service for years because it was not related to the life of a congregation, and it was at last discontinued in 1969.[22]

As President Bennett's term drew to an end, the seminary was once again thrown into turmoil, this time because of the extension of the Vietnam War into Cambodia, a move sharply criticized at the seminary. A special meeting of the assembly was called, and it was agreed that because many persons at Union felt a responsibility to act on behalf of their views at a time of crisis, deadlines for ex-

A light moment at the end of a hard year: the *Union Seminary Quarterly Review* staff says goodbye to the helmeted outgoing editor, Robert Harsh (1970), and welcomes successor Willis Logan (1971), at top.

aminations and papers were extended until fall, though those wishing to complete them for graduation could do so. The assembly strongly recommended that members of the Union community participate in action groups, of which eight were set up. On the following day, its last regularly scheduled meeting, the assembly adopted a resolution which had been drafted by Bennett and which in its final form opened with these words:

Our country for many years has been engaged in a cruel and immoral war destroying the people and the communities and the land of Vietnam. Now the administration has made us invaders of another nation; has brought into Cambodia our massive powers to destroy. Our President has followed the advice of those who have always sought the impossible goal of a military solution in Vietnam. . . . How many more victims must be sacrificed to the Moloch of American pride, how much more territory must be laid waste? How many Americans, North and South Vietnamese, Laotians, and Cambodians must die?[23]

The resolution concluded by urging the nation to turn from moral failure and death to peace and life. It was agreed that the graduation exercises on May 19 would relate to the national emergency and to the repression of political dissent in this country (the killing of four persons at Kent State University by a national guard unit had occurred on May 5). Commencement at Riverside was held in a solemn setting of mourning; there was no address, but some farewell words by President Bennett.

His role throughout the last several years of stress was widely appreciated. His willingness to sit through the long meetings of the commission as one among equals was greatly respected, and at its last session it was so noted and he was roundly applauded. As he retired, a *festschrift* was presented to him which contained essays on his person and thought by two close colleagues, Daniel Williams and Reinhold Niebuhr. The latter concluded his essay by saying:

As an old man, who in his age regrets the polemical spirit of his youth, I wish I had profited a little earlier by noting the unpolemical genius of my— then young—friend, with whom I maintained a personal, academic, and journalistic partnership without friction for four decades. His unpolemical wisdom accounts for much of his success as a scholar. He always was fair to opinions with which he disagreed. It also explains his remarkable success as seminary president and ecumenical statesman.[24]

In later years one of Bennett's former students, Mark Juergensmeyer (1965), prefaced his published interviews with the president emeritus by saying, "By reading these reflections on his life, perhaps those who do not know John Bennett well will come to understand why he has become a sort of quiet hero for many of us, a model of concerned and yet objectively fair judgment, a man with a passion for justice tempered with a gentle decency." [25] His active career of teaching and writing continued for many years after he moved to the West Coast, but his name will always be associated with the seminary from which he graduated and served so well for many years, climaxing in a presidency during a stormy time.

A HALF DECADE OF CONTRASTS

There were many good happenings in the five academic years from July 1, 1970 to June 30, 1975. The quality of students in the various degree programs remained high despite the turmoil of the time; numbers declined but a challenging diversity increased as a larger percentage of those who were then thought of as "minority" persons were welcomed. Though the famous theological giants of the past had gone, widely recognized scholars and rising younger teachers in every field maintained a high level of classroom instruction. Several venturesome if controversial educational experiments were tested, some of which met particular needs of that time and were discontinued, while others were adapted and retained. The governance system that had risen out of the crises of the sixties showed limitations and the seminary returned to more familiar ways, but the importance and value of student membership on most councils and committees, both for them and for the school, was accepted.

It was clear, however, that the years of expansion were over. For the last half of the sixties total enrollment had remained above 700, but then year by year it dropped: 676, 628, 535, 469, 456. Union had a bad press for several years after 1968, rumors of inner dissension rendered the school less attractive to applicants, and the problems of New York city were mounting. The faculty also decreased in size by intention; in 1970–71 the inclusive faculty list, including adjuncts and visiting professors, was 55; just four years later in 1974–75 the comparable figure was 35. The reality of reduced numbers had an effect on various aspects of seminary life and an impact on some crucial decisions. Though in face value the income and the budget of the seminary increased through most of these years, the actual purchasing power of dollars received from tuition, fees, gifts, grants, and income from endowment decreased because of the agonizing pressures of inflation. The endowment also lessened as its unrestricted parts were drawn on to cover deficits.

The way Union responded to challenges to some of its familiar patterns continued to evoke controversy. Union had long thought of itself, and had been widely regarded, as a leader in church life and theological education in such areas as critical scholarship, preparation through field experience for urban ministry, ecumenical leadership, and civil rights. Now it was involved in the crises of the liberal causes for which it had long stood. It had championed excellence in education, but now representatives of minorities, including black persons from its own board, faculty, and student body, reported that its definitions of excellence were influenced more than it had recognized by the patterns of economic class and racial identity. It had long had women in its student body and finally on its board and faculty, but now some of them had begun with fresh intensity to point out how its patterns of thought and language had been strongly shaped by the male-oriented, patriarchal patterns of Western life. The formation of a women's caucus in 1969 and the designation of Knox 1W as a Women's Center four years later (with its Women's Counseling Team) provided important channels for the growing influence of women in Union's life. Many welcomed the new perspective and practices, while others were slow to accept them.

Another important shift created other challenges for the seminary. It had long served primarily the large, ecumenical, "mainline" denominations, but their memberships were largely static or in some cases declining, and the liberal consensus that had long characterized these churches was eroding as inner diversities multiplied. Religious vitality was resurgent in many conservative evangelical, black, and pentecostalist churches and movements. Faculty and students from these traditions began to find a larger place at Union and contributed significantly to its life along with the others, but it was not easy for everyone to accept the new perspectives. In matters of curriculum, certain proposed educational changes were welcomed by some but were regarded as undermining a tested and effective system by others. These challenges had been known at Union in the late sixties, but their insistent pressure was felt in the seminary's continuing effort to redefine itself for new tasks. Responses to them that proposed certain changes in the seminary's life were found by some to be creative while they were regarded by others as either hasty or dubious.

There was not only a change in the presidency at the beginning of this half-decade, but also a shift in board leadership. John Irwin, appointed as Under Secretary of State, resigned in the fall of 1970 after having chaired the Board of Directors for nine years. Bennett later spoke of him as representing "an entirely different background from mine, a person of very great wealth; but I saw him as a man of extraordinary Christian sensitivity and I don't think during the seven years we were together that we ever differed seriously on policy." When Bennett was arrested in front of the White House for protesting the war in 1970, he got no word of criticism from Irwin, "only concern whether I had suffered any harm, whether I had been mistreated in any way." [26] His successor was the board's first chairwoman, Rosalind E. Havemeyer, who had been a member of the women's committee for a quarter century, and its former head. An Episcopal laywoman, she was active in community affairs on Long Island, and member of committees related to Drew and Japan International Christian universities.

As the assembly swung into its second year in the fall of 1970, Lawrence Jones chaired the meeting as acting president. Ellis Nelson was thanked warmly for his services to the assembly as he had left the post of dean of the seminary, now filled by Robert Handy. Jones asked the vice-chairman, student Frank Chong (1971), to preside over the next meeting, thereby setting a precedent of alternation that continued for the life of the assembly. A resolution passed unanimously at that session declared "That there will not be discrimination as to race or sex in the recommendation of a candidate for employment or placement in education training programs." At the third meeting the new president was introduced and took the chair, quickly displaying his skill at presiding and his knowledge of parliamentary procedure. He was not long in discovering the complexity of the governance structures that were in operation. Reporting to the board after seven weeks in office, he explained,

> Since my arrival, I have attended some meetings, such as those of the Seminary Assembly, the Academic Affairs Council, the Community Affairs Council, the Faculty, the Assembly staff, the Alumni Council, a faculty retreat . . . and a Barth Colloquium. Sometimes, like daily, there are also committee meetings. So I have tuned in on the Executive Committee, the Nominating Committee, the By-laws Committee, the Finance Committee, the Budget Committee, the Appointments Committee, the Planning Committee, the Steering Committee, the Priorities Sub-committee and a few others. Fortunately, they meet frequently enough so that I have been able to be at more than one meeting of each.[27]

At some of these meetings basic changes in degree nomenclature were worked out and sent to the board which approved them early in 1971 and arranged through the proper educational channels that the B.D. become the M.Div., in accord with a national trend, and the M.R.E. the M.A.E.T.S. (Master of Arts in Education and Theological Studies), changes that became effective in 1972.

The grading issue was finally settled after much discussion in the spring of 1971. The academic affairs council brought to the assembly a plan, adapted from the commission's report, to replace the familiar letter-grade system with a credit/no-credit designation for each course, to be accompanied by a written evaluation of each student's work. Those supporting the plan were trying to reduce the competitiveness bred by letter grades and to improve the pedagogical values of grading, in part by helping the students to assess their own academic progress and learn where their strengths and weaknesses were. The debate was intense; some argued that the transcript (for the evaluations were for the student's eyes only and did not become part of the transcript) would then lose much of its meaning, and handicap those students who wanted to continued on in further graduate study. Others, especially those who taught large courses, felt the work of preparing the evaluations would be much too heavy. It was, however, finally passed by the assembly, and continues in effect at the present writing. There were, of course, exceptions: as Columbia remained on a letter-grade system, students in joint programs were not affected. The mark of "credit with distinction" was added later.

That was a partial return to the older system, but did help those seeking entrance to other schools.

Unfortunately, the long shadow of the growing deficits hung over the meetings of assembly, councils, and committees. One of the latter reported to the assembly early in 1971 that service in the refectory had been discontinued because too high a subsidy was required by the food service that had been operating it, and what had long been an important center of community life was closed. There were five additions to the faculty that year, but only one as full professor—Raymond Brown in conjunction with Woodstock. The others were instructors or assistant professors, and their terms at Union were short, in most cases because of financial limitations. Only one of them served past mid-decade: Marcia Weinstein, assistant professor of Greek. A graduate of Brown University with a Ph.D. from Harvard, she was a good linguist and a popular teacher during her six years at the seminary.

Another sign of change was the end of the six-week academic summer session after more than forty years. Its attendance had been declining for a variety of reasons, among them the changing reputation of New York because of increasing problems of security. When enrollment decreased to 70 in 1971, and no funds were available to rethink and reshape the program, it was discontinued. The short-term, non-credit summer ministers' conferences, however, were continued. In the fall of the year came more bad news. The president announced a freeze on all searches for faculty replacements. He was under board mandate to reduce the size of the faculty, a very difficult task which he carried out, inevitably facing criticism as hard choices had to be made. During the spring of 1971 Mosley had worked out with the board and the assembly a way to face Union's problems boldly with the appointment of a long-range Planning Group of six faculty members, five students, three "at large" members from outside of the immediate Union community, and five ex-officio members without vote. Named by the board in late May, its members began their work immediately so as to have its report ready in a year. As the Planning Group, ably chaired by Beverly Harrison, set to work, many persons were involved in its labors. A questionnaire was sent to all 7200 living alumni/ae; there were 350 written responses, and further input came from 42 meetings of graduates in different parts of the country. No less than six task forces were formed to prepare reports relating to aspects of the group's work, involving many students and faculty, and a seventh student-initiated one addressed pedagogical method. The president worked very closely with the Planning Group as one of its ex-officio members. So did Lawrence Jones, who had succeeded Handy as dean of the seminary. The assembly was kept in touch with the group's processes, and sponsored an open hearing on the task-force reports. A great deal of attention and energy was given to this major effort.

The group's mimeographed report in three parts appeared in May 1972. The important Part I contained its recommendations; the other two parts provided background material and a brief history of the group. The recommendations were prefaced by a statement that "The Planning Group affirms that Christian theology is the reflection of the church on the meaning of God's activity in the world in the light of what God has revealed in the life, death, and resurrection of Jesus Christ, and of what the Holy Spirit continues to bring before the church as truth, as power, and as hope." It declared that Union "should embody in its life, worship, and work, an interpretation of the gospel that speaks directly to the felt needs of the oppressed," meaning that representatives of such groups should be present at the seminary. Its first main recommendation was that Union move toward a collegial mode of education and research so that the wealth of the theological disciplines might be shared in common, and all faculty, students, administration, and staff could work together at bringing their individualized researches and specialized knowledge to bear on the critical problems before church and world. This was rather general, and since nobody was against collegiality as such, it readily passed by the assembly at its meetings on May 15 and 17 and by the board on May 30–31.

The second recommendation, however, on new constituencies, was the most controversial of them all, for it proposed three things: 1. That "the Seminary take steps immediately to recruit and admit students so that Black persons will number at least one-third of the total; so that other minority groups and other countries will be significantly represented; and so that women (including Black women and those of other minorities) number at least one half the total." 2.

That all appointments and hiring to board, faculty, and staff be conducted so that those groups "will attain to comparable constituting proportions of the several totals as rapidly as possible" consonant with the goals of the seminary. 3. That a faculty member be appointed in practical theology to be responsible "to the needs of persons engaged in the practice of ministry in the Black community, and the development of a program for the recruitment of Black students."

Some assembly members believed that it was unrealistic to expect that a student body which had about 20 percent women and 3 percent blacks could change very quickly, and that in view of tenure the faculty could change only slowly over a long period of time. It was argued that these rather idealistic goals would be interpreted as quotas. The recommendation did cause a furor within the world of theological education. There were those at Union and beyond who thought that the seminary was abandoning its historical commitment to academic excellence, and could not see it as a step in the direction of a wider definition of excellence. But the recommendation was passed decisively.

The great majority of the board, faculty, and student body continued strongly to reaffirm "the constituency decision" in succeeding years, knowing it would take a long time to be realized. It made Union more visible to many Christians in the "third world." The one regular faculty appointment made from 1972 to 1975 was of a black recruiter and educator, Bobby Joe Saucer, a graduate of Colgate Rochester Divinity School and a doctoral student at Brandeis University, who served at Union for three years before being called to a deanship.

Most of the other recommendations were accepted; for example, that educational priority be given to the M.Div. and to both the Union and the joint doctoral programs. The Planning Group did not have time to work further on the specifics of these programs. It therefore recommended that what came to be called the M.Div. Design Team be created to redesign the program for that degree. It referred detailed reconsideration of doctoral work to a continuing faculty committee on collegiality, which became so deeply involved in internal faculty problems that it never fulfilled that part of its assignment. But the Planning Group's suggestion that the board petition the Board of Regents to change the Th.D. to a Ph.D., consistent with the practice of the university divinity schools, was accepted. The change was accomplished by 1974.

One of the most difficult decisions of the Planning Group was to have to recommend the closing of the School of Sacred Music. In a long memorandum of March 7, 1972, followed up by a presentation to the group six days later, Dean Robert S. Baker pointed out that the school had been living on a shoestring for too long, had not replaced three younger faculty members, and had seen its practice equipment become obsolete and worn. The results of years of deferred maintenance could no longer be avoided. In his view, to make it a first-rate school would involve between $350,000 to $400,000 yearly, with a similar amount for capital investment. Enrollment, which had averaged 94 for the ten years prior to 1968–69, had dropped to the low 70s, and though there were many good students among the entrants, they were coming increasingly from smaller schools, rather than the major ones from which the school had once drawn. Matters had reached the point where, in his judgment, the program could not really be justified for incoming students. Baker therefore recommended that no more incoming students be accepted, and that the school be closed at the end of 1972–73, leaving enough resources to see the few remaining degree candidates through.

The Planning Group regretfully recommended the closing of the school, and suggested that the M.Div Design Team deal further with the question of music and other arts at the seminary. When the assembly accepted the verdict, Professor Williams observed that "its removal will cause a very aching void in the community." At the same time that the assembly was adopting the group's report, however, Mosley was negotiating with Yale University and with one of the school's donors, J. Irwin Miller, so that the work of the school and its faculty could be continued in a different location. This led to the founding of Yale's Institute of Sacred Music, based in the university's School of Music and Divinity School. Two of the three tenured members of Union's music faculty, Baker and French, became professors there, and, as a pastoral theologian was needed at the new institute, so did Jeffery Rowthorn. A settlement was made with Earl Berg, who had requested early retirement. All endowment funds expressly related to the former School of Sacred Music, including the endowment for the Tangeman chair of sacred music, were transferred to the institute in New Haven. These negotiations were known to the board when it accepted the Planning Group's report at its two-day meeting at the end of May 1972.

Various other recommendations of the long report relating to the continuation of other degree programs, the strengthening of the library, the improvement of inter-institutional relationships, and the maintenance of an international presence at Union were duly passed. More controversial were several recommendations concerning the faculty: that reviews of faculty resources and of departments, fields, and programs be undertaken in case further retrenchment was needed, and that the retirement age be fixed at 65 (with financial assistance to those who had expected to serve to the customary age of 68). The assembly perfunctorily and the board carefully approved the setting aside of seminary funds in an "implementation budget" outside of the annual budgets to carry out the recommendations adopted: a total of $1,204,500, including seed money for a capital funds campaign.[28]

The Planning Group had taken a close look at many aspects of the seminary's life, had involved many persons outside its ranks while doing its work, had come up with prophetic but controversial proposals (especially on the new constituencies), and had recommended some hard decisions (notably the closing of the School of Sacred Music). It was a remarkable performance. But to a number of board, faculty, and staff members who had been through the excitement of the Union Commission and the launching of the transitional plan of governance—which had already had its term extended once— it came too soon on the heels of the year of the commission with all its subcommittees and the inauguration of the assembly with its network of satellite structures, and left some tired and wary people. The experience widened gaps among faculty members. Some were eager for continued experimentation and new ways, while others felt that certain tested and historic commitments of the seminary were not being given sufficient attention. There were, however, hopes that as the seminary followed up the work laid out by the Planning Group relating to curriculum design and collegiality, some of the tensions might be relieved and new understandings emerge.

One of the persons who was an important to the Planning Group's work was comptroller Randolph H. Dyer, who devoted much of his last year at Union to working with it. During his 22 years of effective service at Union he had earned the respect of students and staff, of faculty, board, and administration. Many persons facing crises, particularly the bereaved, learned that they could depend on him for advice and help in time of need. Upon his retirement in 1972, the position of comptroller was filled by Raymond Hahn Jr.

The academic year 1972–73 began with an innovation: opening right after Labor Day. For generations it had opened in late September, but the adoption of an early opening by Columbia made it advisable for Union to do the same, and it had the added advantage of clearing January for an intersession in which biblical languages could be taught in a concentrated way. Considerable attention during that and the following academic year was given to the work of the M.Div. Design Team. The director of field work, James W. Bergland, agreed to chair it as it met for the better part of two academic years, often weekly. Its composition changed somewhat from time to time as members resigned and others were added; an early membership list showed a total of 21 names representing faculty, graduates, administrative staff, and students. Even as the assembly confirmed the names in September, there was criticism of the large size of the team and the way it had been appointed. Barbara Wheeler, who had done much office, coordinating, and secretarial work for the Planning Group, did the same for the new effort. The meetings were open, and observers were often present, usually to give or respond to a particular report. The team spawned a number of subcommittees and liaison groups of various size and duration. Its discussions were often wide-ranging; many of its members were pressing to find a fresh pattern for foundational theological education. One result of this procedure was that rumors about what the team was about filtered through the seminary and produced some negative reactions. Regular reports to the assembly did not always alleviate this problem. There was some disappointment when it became clear that the team would not have its final report ready until the spring of 1974. Even then, much of the report was in quite general and theoretical terms. Its actual proposals were quite modest—it had discovered how difficult a revision of an ongoing curriculum with a long history behind it is.

The final report was brought before the assembly on March 27, 1974, but only certain recommendations requiring action were actually presented—and they did not fare well. Brief recommendations for the M.Div. work of each of four academic fields had been prepared but with a single exception were not accepted. An attempt to retitle and reform the practical field under the heading "Ministry: Church, Society, and Personality" failed by a vote of 28 to 20 with 4 abstentions—this broke the back of the team's report. A recommendation that the advisement process be formalized and given a total of 3 academic points failed. One salvaged item was a proposal for experimentation in field-based theological study. It was an effort to center a semester or two of M.Div. theological education in local congregations where there would be opportunity for both supervised practical experience and disciplined academic study of the local church and ministry. Three Union students were already involved in such an experimental program centered in Presbyterian churches in and around Oneonta, New York—the Susquehanna Valley Project. The assembly's action in approving continuing experimentation did not alter the M.Div. curriculum at all, except for allowing a few students an alternative way of earning a year's credit, as the core groups had done. One outcome was a program that ran for nine years sponsored in cooperation with other New York and New Haven seminaries entitled "Inter-Seminary Theological Education for Ministry" (IS-TEM), directed by T. Richard Snyder, a B.D./Th.D. graduate of Princeton Seminary who had considerable experience in inner-city ministry.

The rejection of the main recommendations of the M.Div. Design Team was widely regarded as a defeat not only for the team but for the administration as well, although the president had not been active in it as he had in the Planning Group. The board was at once disappointed and puzzled by what had happened. There were several causes: both the commission and the planning group had learned to focus on certain rather specific matters, and completed their reports on time, but when the design team finally got around to framing some specific recommendations they were not founded on a clear, coherent pattern. By this time the method of dealing with serious problems by assigning them to a large special group was wearing thin. Also working against a successful conclusion for its task was a growing polarity in the faculty, sharpened by a growing opposition among the membership to the president and his way of working.

The mounting tension showed itself in other areas of faculty life. There was a lot of talk about collegiality, for example, and in accordance with the Planning Group's mandate a small faculty committee was appointed to work on it. But the very search for collegiality revealed how the deep division in the faculty was frustrating its realization. The committee for 1972–73, elected by the faculty, was chaired by Louis Martyn with Richard French, Paul Lehmann, and Jeffery Rowthorn as its other members. It arranged for meetings of three small groups of faculty members to further the collegial spirit. But it soon came into conflict with the president over statements in his newsletter of November 13, of which the committee had had no advance knowledge. In the letter, Mosley looked forward to a standing committee on collegiality and noted that "the present committee of four, . . . has done well since spring in preparing the way for this next step and we owe it our thanks."

The small committee thereupon resigned, but the faculty unanimously voted that it reconsider. It did, and prepared a paper on collegiality that was the basis of discussion at a faculty retreat between semesters. The paper took a strong theological stance, arguing that collegiality is "a fruit of the event of grace in a community of theological discipline and, as such, must be carefully distinguished from the practice of collegiality as an operational life style and/or educational method." That second form of collegiality, the authors declared, is an administrative device which may emerge from a variety of institutional or instructional goals, "but which commend themselves chiefly as institutional, bureaucratic, or pedagogical innovations—innovations, one must add, which can be readily prone to the confusion of creativity with novelty."

The paper expressed a strong negative reaction to the style of the administration, and to differences in the way colleagues assessed the situation. Those who responded to the paper expressed appreciation for it, but several found that the gap it had opened between the two types of collegiality was overemphasized, one arguing that "the two types should be kept in intimate relation and tension," the other reporting that the words "institutional," "bureaucratic," and "pedagogical" are all honorable ones, and protesting their pejorative and polemical use in the paper. Hence this effort to enrich faculty collegiality illustrated how deep certain tensions within the faculty were and showed a widening gap between some of its members and the administration.[29] A new committee was elected for the following year with Daniel Williams as its chair and with student members added, but his tragic death on December 3, 1973 interrupted its work— and took from the faculty a loved member, among whose books was one on *The Spirit and the Forms of Love* (1968), and who was sincerely trying to be a reconciler in a difficult time.

Differences among the faculty also contributed to the delay in working out a new form of governance, though that was not the only reason, for heavy tasks had been placed on busy people, and some students were worried that a change might mean a decline in their power. The transitional plan was supposed to have been replaced after two and a half years, but as a satisfactory alternative had not been worked out, its life was extended several times. There was less and less enthusiasm for it as time went on. A new plan, "Rules for a Collegial Form of Education," developed by the assembly's planning committee, was to be voted on at the assembly meeting of October 24, 1973, but instead Jim Sanders, Old Testament professor, who had been away on sabbatical the previous year, gave an impassioned address, which included these sentences:

I arrived back on campus five weeks ago, after 15 months absence, to find the Seminary in a state of shock, . . . "Malaise" and "unhappiness" were the most frequently occurring words among my colleagues as well as among administrative and library staff. I soon found that this had nothing to do with the students; . . . The malaise and unhappiness which I perceive is due rather to poor communication among faculty and administration.[30]

When he got a copy of the "Rules" he found "at least some of the reasons for the low level of morale on the part of the faculty," for he had very basic objections to the structure of governance proposed, and he found that others did also. He pled for beginning with an exploration of the theological grounds of the proposal by the assembly over a number of sessions.

Meanwhile, the executive committee of the board decided the matter had to come to a head as other decisions that had to be made were being held up by the delay in reforming the governance system. Early in January it asked the president to present a plan for decision-making. He responded on January 15, 1974 by commenting quite fully on the "Rules," suggesting many changes, some of them quite substantive. The next day he reported this to the planning committee, which responded with some surprise at this short-circuiting of the process. Negotiation led to the executive committee's request of January 28 that the planning committee present proposals for a new form of governance, taking the president's plan into account, and get it through the assembly in April so that the board could accept it in May, when the transitional plan would expire. This was done as the committee prepared "Agreements for Governance" framing a decentralized structure which was in force for only a year. Nothing was said about its theological basis.[31]

The transitional plan of governance devised by the Union Commission thus came to an end after five years, though some of the features it introduced were retained in later arrangements. The board's decisive action had played an important role in pressing for the new "agreements." It was at the same time pursuing another matter that also led to a firm decision. When Mosley became president, he requested a regular review of the president's work by the board. A committee of eight met with him on October 15, 1973 with Avery Post presiding, and after the meeting both Post and the president agreed that "it had been an exhilarating and nourishing experience" which laid the groundwork for a continuing evaluative process. After the events of the winter, the committee met again under the leadership of T. Guthrie Speers Jr. (1953), a Presbyterian pastor in New Canaan, who replaced Post. It was widely known by then that a number of the faculty were displeased by various remarks and doings of the president, and had communicated their feelings to him in person and in writing. In at least one case, copies of the letter were sent to the executive committee of the board.

The review committee looked into the matter with some care, and on June 4 Speers presented its report to the executive committee, opening with the words, "After full and frank consultation with faculty, students, administrative officers, and with President Mosley himself, the Seminary Review Committee believes that in five years the President can make his best contributions to Union and that therefore upon his completion of five years in office on November 1,

1975, a new president should be installed." The report went on to note that Mosley's style of leadership had been especially suited to the turbulent times in which he came, that he had been able to work through a cumbersome form of government, had helped the seminary to face the realities of budget problems, and had guided it into the *Plans for the Future* with its challenging goals. Mosley expressed his disagreement with the committee's conclusion, but submitted his resignation, to be effective no later than November 1, 1975. It was, however, agreed that either he or the board could move the termination to an earlier date.[32]

Though the matter did not become final until the board met on June 25, the termination became widely known in advance through a press release. Mosley referred to his resignation as a forced one. He was deeply disappointed by the board's action, for he felt that the steps that had been taken during his administration were leading to a resolution of many of the difficulties faced by the seminary. Reflecting on his successor's difficulties, John Bennett mentioned those relating to educational policy, saying that "his lack of experience in theological education may have been a real handicap at that point." Some criticized him for not having taken an academic chair, as presidents customarily had done. Mosley had not spent his life in academia, and did not think it appropriate to accept a chair, and hence did not seem to be identifying himself closely with the faculty. When some of his colleagues concluded that Mosley was not hearing them, they responded rather ungraciously, talking behind his back both at the seminary and beyond. Union's reputation suffered because of some of the reports and rumors that were being widely repeated.

The situation was further complicated by the growing financial problem—not only the mounting deficits, but the shrinking endowment as well. Bennett, who had been one of Mosley's early supporters, thinking that he had the gifts for just such a time, was candid enough to speculate that had his own term been extended, "there's one thing that would have defeated me. And that was the financial crunch."[33] The decline in the market coupled with increasing inflation was a major concern to the board.

In part because of internal pressure, the time of departure was shortened. Samuel Terrien, elected faculty representative to

the board's executive committee, with the chair of the student house
who also attended, circulated a letter to executive committee members on June 13, indicating that they had consulted as widely as possible with their constituencies at a quiet time of year, and pointing
to "the disastrous consequences which may prevail over the spiritual,
moral, intellectual, and financial state of this institution in the event
that the President's resignation does not take effect at once." There
were a number of sharp responses, both from within and outside the
seminary community, to these and other charges. The letter did not
sit well with the board. But Mosley decided to resign in early September of 1974. A financial settlement was worked out with him. He
soon became assistant bishop of the Episcopal diocese of Pennsylvania.

The board chose Roger Shinn, then dean of graduate
studies, as acting president. Working closely with him were Robert
Seaver as dean of first degree studies and Robert Handy in the deanship Shinn had occupied. "When this Board of Directors last met in
June, I was in Bucharest, . . ." the new president said in his first
report to the board, noting that though he knew about the meeting,
he did not know the agenda. "And I had not the slightest notion that
at your next meeting I should be reporting to you as Acting President." Admitting a fair share of breathless days and short nights, he
continued:

I've felt the urgency of the pace and the awesomeness of the responsibility
of this job. I can say honestly that I have been supported, beyond what I
had any right to expect, by the immediate community of faculty and students, by alumni across the country and overseas, by Brooke Mosley, and
by the Directors including, above all, your Chairperson, Rossie Havemeyer. . . .

I should mention, if only briefly, what I have learned about
how much people care about Union Seminary. They support us in our
ministry, worry with us in our turmoils, express their loyalty to us in count-
less ways.

Many persons had written to him stressing the importance of Union
in theological education; alumni/ae and friends often promised continuing support—and delivered.

Shinn then set the tone for what proved to be a time of
healing, of quiet advance, and of preparation for a new administra-

tion. He urged resistance to the temptations either to retreat into the familiar or to devise and publicize new programs that were "more impressive in rhetoric than in reality." Experimentation should continue, but preferably in pilot projects. He perceived and encouraged an important change in mood:

We should air openly the differences of judgment among us, in the confidence that controversy can be creative. It is not always so; it has not always been so in recent times at Union. But I see signs that we have learned from our controversies and that we can continue them in good faith and good will.

He devoted a major section of the report to the financial crisis, noting the merciless pressure of inflation and calling for a pledge to work toward a budget for the following year that would move significantly toward balance.

Shinn offered a timely reminder to the board—and others, for the report was duplicated and circulated—of the seminary's solid strengths:

(1) a sizable endowment (about $24 million dollars even in today's depressed market); (2) a superb library; (3) a physical plant which, though expensive to maintain, is adequate to most of our needs; (4) a host of loyal supporters who make annual gifts greater than those to any other Seminary in the country; (5) a faculty of distinction; (6) a student body that continually excites the faculty including visiting professors; (7) a legion of faithful alumni and friends; (8) a reputation that, though damaged in some circles; is still high; (9) a location, expensive and difficult in many ways, but strategic to many of our purposes; (10) a mission that enlists devoted people, including this Board of Directors.[34]

He proposed to carry on the tasks before the seminary relying primarily on the established committees of students, faculty, and directors, for "we have had enough of extraordinarily appointed committees," but characteristically he appreciated the fact that they had worked loyally and often well.

The interim year was one of strategic withdrawals to prepare the way for advance, a year of rebuilding trust and confidence. The most difficult job by far was to shrink the budget rather than to increase deficits. It was a trying business, and many people were involved in it. Midway through the year the treasurer and business manager, Raymond Hahn, resigned to take another position, and was replaced by H. Leroy Brininger. Budget stringency meant that the social hall and refectory went unheated, that library services were reduced, that Reed House was sold, that tuition was raised (to $2300 for M.Div. and S.T.M students), that faculty salaries were almost frozen and certain benefits reduced—all this at a time when inflation was hard on everyone. It meant the termination of several important nonfaculty administrative positions, and the reduction of support staffs. But it did reverse the trend, setting a budget for 1975–76 with a reduced deficit that gave some promise of a balanced budget for the next year. In summarizing his second report to the board, focused on the budget, Shinn declared that the outcome of the struggle "is a victory—with great costs. It is a victory of integrity, a victory of responsibility." It was a modest one, he noted, yet one "that gives a fair opportunity to a new administration to develop its own program without the terrible weight of a huge deficit."[35]

Another achievement of the year was also built on hard decisions—the fixing of a table of organization for the faculty. The work was done largely by the faculty-student curriculum committees and arrived at a total figure of 27 teaching faculty: 6 in the biblical field, 4 in the historical, 7 in the theological, and 9 in the practical, plus the visiting Luce and Fosdick professors in alternate years. The table did include some faculty who also carried certain administrative responsibilities, such as the deans of first and advanced degree students, but not administrators who also did some teaching, such as the president and the dean of students—a role that Sidney Skirvin had assumed early in the 70s along with his placement responsibilities.

The job that had been done was very important for the future, for faculty strength had slipped seriously, and a design for its rebuilding that would maintain necessary teaching resources for both M.Div. and doctoral programs was much needed. Retirees were Frank O. Reed of Auburn, Mary A. Tully, and James D. Smart in 1971, and Robert F. Beach, Paul L. Lehmann, and Cyril C. Richardson in 1974. The latter was the first one affected by the rigidity of the new rule setting retirement at 65, but happily a way was found to continue his services as a brilliant teacher for two more years as a "Union Scholar." He continued to teach his famous Church History

107 course as a lecturer until his death on November 16, 1976—a continuous career of 45 years at Union since he entered as a graduate student in 1931.

The half decade ended with the retirement of Paul W. Hoon and Edmund A. Steimle, stalwarts in homiletics and worship. In addition, there was a series of departures for other posts by a number of full professors: Reginald Fuller to Virginia Seminary in 1972, Eric Lincoln to Fisk a year later, Ellis Nelson to Louisville Presbyterian as president in 1974, and the following year Robert Lynn to the Lilly Endowment as senior program adviser and Lawrence Jones to Howard University Divinity School as dean. At the end of the first semester of 1974–75, Jack C. Greenawalt left the department of psychiatry and religion to serve on the staff of the National Institute of Religion and Health. In the spring of 1974, in a controversial action sharply criticized by many students, Walter Wink of the New Testament field was denied tenure and his term ended two years later. He continued some teaching in 1976–77 as visiting professor, while focusing his major efforts in his new post as professor of biblical interpretation for Auburn Seminary in the continuing education program. One could staff a first-class seminary with such a group—and there were 16 others, mostly younger faculty, whose terms came to an end in this same period, as well as the death of two of Union's professors of international reputation: Daniel Day Williams on December 3, 1973, and Johannes Hoekendijk on June 25, 1975.

There was obviously an immense amount of faculty rebuilding to be done. That the seminary was able to maintain high academic standards for its various degree programs in the face of such faculty losses was largely because of the competence and industry of those who remained, some deferring sabbaticals and delaying research and publishing projects. Union remained a significant center for theological education through the hard years because of those who effectively carried heavy burdens of teaching. Some of them have just been mentioned, but among those who served on into the next period were such professors as Brown, Landes, Martyn, Sanders, and Weinstein, in the biblical field; Handy and Lotz in the historical; Cone, Driver, Harrison, and Shinn in the theological; and Bergland, Hendrickson, Neale, Seaver, Skirvin, and Ulanov in the practical. As always, adjuncts, visiting professors (including the Luce and Fos-

James H. Cone on the day he was inaugurated full professor, flanked by
Lawrence N. Jones (left) and Roger L. Shinn.

dick appointments), and lecturers were important in maintaining a
suitable spread of educational offerings.

A start at the important task of faculty rebuilding was
begun in the interim year. A doctoral student, Christopher Morse,
who had graduated from Yale Divinity School, served in the pastorate, earned an S.T.M. at Union and had some teaching experience
at Duke, was named assistant professor of systematic theology. He
focused his research and teaching primarily on the formative dogmatic traditions in Christian thought and on the contemporary significance of church doctrines, and completed his Ph.D. dissertation
in 1976, a work later revised and published as *The Logic of Promise
in Moltmann's Theology* (1979).

Meanwhile, the search for a senior theologian led to a

prominent European scholar, Dorothee Sölle, who had received the D.Phil. from Göttingen in 1954. Books of hers that had been translated into English included *Christ the Representative* (1967) and *Political Theology* (1974). Because of family considerations, she chose not to accept a regular appointment but in the fall of 1975 came for two years as a visiting professor. Her courses on religious responses to the challenges of modern philosophical, cultural, and political life, on problems of women's identity, alienation, and anxiety, and on liberation and political theology met needs of Union students. Agreements were made for her to come on a regular basis for a semester a year as a visiting professor.

Another important appointment at the same time was that of librarian. Since Robert Beach's retirement, William M. Robarts had served as acting librarian until the coming of Robert F. Maloy. Holding a library degree from the University of Chicago and an S.T.D. from the University of Fribourg in Switzerland, Maloy, a Catholic priest of the diocese of Basel, had had a varied career as teacher of both library science and medieval religious studies, and at Union was named librarian and associate professor of church history. One other appointment was made in this interim period, though obligations where he was teaching at Pittsburgh Theological Seminary kept him from accepting until 1976. Samuel K. Roberts, a graduate of Morehouse College who earned his M.Div. at Union (1970) and Ph.D. in the joint program with Columbia (1974), was named assistant professor of sociology and the church. With these appointments, the process of rebuilding had begun, but much remained to be done in order to bring the faculty up to the table of organization that had been designed.

During this interim year of many changes, the board decided to become a smaller, more cohesive, efficient group, and went from over 50 to 29 members. The older provision that the board be composed of half lay and half clergy members was discontinued. By May 15 all members had resigned, and a special nominating committee presented 23 names of former members for the streamlined board, and the alumni council had chosen 4 others. A few weeks later, Havemeyer resigned as chair. A tribute to her leadership referred to the difficulties of her term of service: "For Union it was a time of trial. Our house was divided. To lead in such times was a task which only a few would undertake, and in which she, perhaps alone among us, could have succeeded." [36] She was followed by Walter Burke, who had been a board member since 1969. A graduate of Dartmouth and Columbia Law School, Burke was the retired chair of the board of Fairchild Camera and Instrument Corporation, and president of the Sherman Fairchild Foundation.

In June of 1974 the "old" Board of Directors had appointed a presidential search committee of nine of its members chaired by John B. Coburn (1942), then rector of St. James' Church on Madison Avenue, where meetings were held throughout the year. It asked the faculty and student body to form advisory committees with which it kept in close touch. A list of nearly 400 candidates was drawn up from various sources in response to many letters and calls. Eventually two were selected to come to the seminary in January for conversations and interviews. Both were highly qualified candidates, but when one withdrew his name from further consideration and the committee voted to present the other person's name to the board, this candidate also withdrew. The committee learned that certain widespread impressions that Union was "ungovernable" were impeding the search, and pressed for further modification of the governance structures.

Meanwhile, a number of new names had been suggested. That of Donald W. Shriver Jr. rose to the top. He was then professor of ethics and society and director of the D.Min. program at Candler School of Theology at Emory University in Atlanta. Shriver visited the seminary in late May, meeting with many in the community and with the three search committees. The board committee voted unanimously to recommend his name to the board. The candidate was present at the early part of the board meeting on July 10, and requested two things. Because he wanted to be fully a part of the faculty, he believed he should hold a faculty position. He also asked the board to establish and raise money for a "Research and Experimentation Fund" in the sum of 10 percent of the current annual budget, approximately $380,000, so that an office of educational research could be set up to enable faculty experimentation in teaching methods and course content, provide innovative scholarships, encourage flexibility in educational programs, and prepare the way for a capital funds drive. In executive session, the board unanimously elected him as Union's 13th president, and named him William E. Dodge professor of Applied Christianity, effective September 1, 1975.[37]

The board had already committed itself to a new pattern of governance, and after consultation with student and faculty representatives, adopted a new set of bylaws on August 26. The new document, based on the principles of previous bylaws but continuing the membership of students on most seminary committees, carefully defined the role of the board, the president, the faculty, and the students. The latter were directed to form a student organization and elect representatives to the four standing committees of the seminary, curriculum, community life, library, and advisory finance. A feature of the new bylaws was that the faculty committee on appointments was no longer composed of all the tenured members, but was a smaller group appointed by the president with the approval of the faculty to include both tenured and nontenured members. Students were to be on all search committees. Thus the new bylaws combined both traditional and certain innovative patterns.

In his last report to the board Roger Shinn said, "Since it is natural to think of a school as its students and faculty, I want to mention also the many people on the administrative staff who, in near anonymity, do their jobs so well that we scarcely notice them, although if they were ever to fail we should all realize their importance quickly."[38] There were many of them through the years, and to pick out any names is to remind those who remember those years of a list of others. Very important in maintaining the day to day life of the school in those troubled years were such persons as Norah Wünsche, who played a role in the admissions processes for some forty years and frequently the first person from which applicants heard; Elizabeth Jones, who from her desk in the dean of students office was friend to many in the seminary community; Henrietta Harvin, registrar and recorder of the faculty who died on July 8, 1975, after years of faithful service; Robert E. Broadwell, financial aid officer and informal adviser to many students, faculty, and staff; and Mildred B. Stoerker, executive secretary of advanced studies and later recorder of the faculty, who with Blanche Britton was placed among the faculty emeriti. The steady work of such persons, and many others who carried heavy administrative loads in the library and the business office, and on secretarial and maintenance staffs, contributed mightily to the basic health of the seminary in a difficult and exciting period.

In the student body during that half-decade of contrasts there was a growing interest in the various movements of liberation theology with their intense concerns for freeing oppressed groups at home and abroad. The liberation emphases of such professors as Cone, Harrison, Lehmann, and Sölle were supplemented during this period by such visiting professors as Rubem Alves, Mary Daly, Burgess Carr, and John Mbiti. In the classroom, the chapel, and the wider community the concern for blacks, women, native Americans, and the poor in urban ghettos and third world lands was given expression and helped to shape vocational decisions. The seminary's own time of troubles had not seriously diverted attention from its main commitment to the gospel, the church, and the world.

CHAPTER TEN

Reaffirmation in a Time of Testing (1975–)

W hen Donald W. Shriver Jr. took office as Union's 13th president in September 1975, he was not well-known at the seminary nor did he know it in detail, though he was aware of its reputation and respected its tradition. A graduate of Davidson College, Union Theological Seminary in Virginia, Yale Divinity School (S.T.M.), and Harvard University (Ph.D., 1963), he had exercised his pastoral and educational ministry in the South. After graduation from seminary in 1956 he had served for three years as a southern Presbyterian pastor in Gastonia, North Carolina. As his graduate work at Harvard was drawing to a close in 1962 he took a position as a campus minister of his denomination at North Carolina State University, continuing in that role for five years even as he accepted a teaching post in religion in 1963. He was involved also as director of three special studies under foundation grants, in the areas of religion and society, science and society, and urban policy. He produced a number of articles and books. Especially noticed at Union was a work he edited, *The Unsilent South: Prophetic Preaching in Racial Crisis* (1965), and one he wrote, *Rich Man, Poor Man: Moral Issues in American Economic Life* (1972). In 1972 he assumed the post he was holding when Union had become interested in him—professor of ethics and society and director of the D.Min. program at Emory. In

Donald W. Shriver Jr., Christian ethicist and 13th president.

Atlanta he had developed a number of civic involvements, and was co-authoring a book that took its point of departure from Liston Pope's famous *Millhands and Preachers* (1942), and which appeared as *Spindles and Spires: A Re-Study of Religion and Social Change in Gastonia* in 1976.

After accepting the position on July 10, he did not have much time to prepare for the role he took on a few weeks later, but in his inaugural address at Riverside Church on the following February 11, "The Heart's Love Uttered with the Mind's Conviction," he showed how deeply he had delved into and identified with Union's tradition. He had found that "the genius of Union Seminary in New York, at the symbolic and many other levels, has been the determination of its constituents to join what some others are inclined to put asunder." Typical of his dialogical style, he posed three questions. Observing that "we have traditionally been a school where questions of social justice have been vigorously debated," he asked what its educational role should be in the contemporary move from an imperial toward a more equalitarian way of life, and suggested an answer with a rhetorical question: "What would it mean, for example, to maintain and to improve an ecumenical school in the heart of New York City as *a center of excellence which made no pretensions of pre-eminence?*"

Secondly, he noted that the founders identified "peculiar facilities and advantages for conducting theological education" in New York, and asked what is the continuing advantage for Union of its location in a city a facing serious social problems at a time when it was on the edge of bankruptcy: "What would the Christian advantage be for a school set down in the midst of a shrinking tax base, a declining capital concentration, cutbacks in services to many of the poor and some of the rich, and cutbacks in the pride of a great city having to live for the first time in a world of limited growth, limited power, limited virtue?" The advantage is theologically stupendous, he answered, for "the relations of riches to poverty, power to weakness, injustice to justice—these are the very matrix of circumstances in which the faith of Jews and Christians had its conception, gestation, birth, and maturing." For "to address the large questions of justice and social salvation . . . we *are* in the right place, with some 'peculiar advantages' indeed."

The climactic question was *"What is the service of the love of truth to the truth of love?"* Protesting the dogmatic separation of truth into antiseptic compartments of fact and value as "contrary to the mind and heart of the great Union Seminary tradition" and the one boding most evil for the future of the faith, this newcomer eloquently emphasized a key theme in the seminary's history:

> How then might the truth of love become plain to persons who as scholars devote themselves to the love of truth? One answer is as fundamental to the history of the church as it is to the wisdom of social science: *The conviction that everything is of value to God gets nourished best in a community of people who demonstrate daily their value to each other.*

He concluded by stressing that theology and theological education are communal enterprises: "if any one of us is to engage in the struggle to believe the Gospel, to put our confidence in the God who raised Jesus from the dead, we will require the help of many co-participants in that struggle."[1]

Shriver immediately began to guide and energize the board and the seminary community to bring added strength to the faculty. The naming of new faculty members involved many persons as student-faculty search committees gathered materials and invited candidates to lecture. During Shriver's busy first year, the process worked to bring no less than six new regular appointments (in addition to Samuel K. Roberts, who had been previously named) and four visiting professors for the following academic year.

Robert McAfee Brown (1945) returned to the faculty for the third time, to serve as professor of ecumenics and world Christianity and, with Sydney Brown as co-director, to build a new ecumenical program. He had been extensively involved in ecumenical affairs since the time of Vatican II, was the author (among many other writings) of the prize-winning book *The Ecumenical Revolution: An Interpretation of the Catholic-Protestant Dialogue* (1967), and had been the keynote speaker at the Fifth Assembly of the World Council of Churches at Nairobi in 1975. His current interests were in the ecumenical antecedents of liberation theology, the theological implications of the writings of Elie Wiesel, and theology as narrative.

At the same time Brown returned, so did one of his former students: James A. Forbes (1962) as associate professor of worship and homiletics. After serving as pastor of several Pentecostal churches in the South, concurrently ministering and teaching in various educational settings, Forbes had been director of education at the experimental Inter/Met seminary in Washington for three years, earning a D.Min. from Colgate Rochester in 1975. Already widely known for his pulpit abilities, his reputation rapidly increased, and he was soon listed among the nation's leading black preachers. At Union he worked in the leadership of the chapel program with another new appointee, Linda J. Clark, assistant professor of worship and music. She had earned the S.M.D. at Union in 1973, and later in that year was named director of the music program, experimenting in various ways—many successful—to fill the gap caused by the departure of the School of Sacred Music, and serving as seminary organist. Now given faculty status by administrative appointment, she developed courses in the areas of her expertise.[2]

Those three appointments were all related to the practical field, the biblical and historical fields also gained new members. John T. Koenig, who had earned Union's Th.D. in 1971 and taken a post at Princeton Seminary, returned to Union to teach New Testament for two years before migrating to Chelsea Square to join the faculty of General Seminary. Union was also fortunate to obtain for the parallel nontenurable "third" position in Old Testament Gerald T. Sheppard, a graduate of Fuller Seminary in 1972 who had just completed the Ph.D. at Yale and was to teach at Union until 1985, then accepting an invitation from Emmanuel College, Toronto. James M. Washington, holder of a Harvard M.T.S. who later (1979) completed his Ph.D. at Yale, joined the historical field to focus his work in modern church history, with particular attention to Afro-American religion.

When the academic year 1976–77 opened, therefore, the shrinkage of the faculty had been halted. The visiting professors who taught during that same academic year were a stellar group: Eberhard Bethge, well-known biographer of Dietrich Bonhoeffer, in systematic theology; Gustavo Gutiérrez, notable Catholic exponent of liberation theology at the University of Lima in Peru as Luce professor; Henri Mottu, former faculty member now back in the Fosdick professorship; and Fulbert Steffensky, husband of Dorothee Sölle, as visiting professor of philosophy of education.

New appointments continued to be made yearly through the 1970s to complete the roster and to take care of vacancies left by resignations. In 1977–78 Richard A. Norris Jr. joined the historical field to take on the work in patristics and the early church that Cyril Richardson had carried for so many years. A graduate of General Seminary who had earned the D.Phil. at Oxford, he had taught both theology and history at the Philadelphia Divinity School and at General, wrote many articles and books, and played an active role in ecumenical affairs. Mary D. Pellauer was called to a new position as assistant professor of women-in-ministry. A graduate of Macalester College, she had earned an M.A. in ethics and society at the Divinity School of the University of Chicago and was well along in her doctoral study on religion and feminism. Another post that had not been occupied by a regular teaching member of the faculty for years was filled by a young professor of philosophy of religion: Cornel West, graduate of Harvard with an M.A. from Princeton, where he also earned the Ph.D. Among the visiting professors that year was one of particular importance in the field of religion and education: Thelma C. D. Adair, who helped the seminary to re-think its work in that area and to pave the way for a permanent appointment. In the next academic year, 1978–79, Phyllis Trible taught during the second semester as professor-elect of Old Testament, taking up her full-time work in the fall. A graduate of Meredith College, she had studied at Union in the 1950s and completed her doctoral work in the joint program with Columbia (Ph.D. 1963). She had taught at Wake Forest University and Andover Newton Theological School; her widely cited book on *God and the Rhetoric of Sexuality* appeared in 1978.

The last academic year of the decade, 1979–80, saw five faculty appointments. Ardith S. Hayes, a graduate of Yale Divinity School (B.D., 1959, S.T.M., 1963), competently assumed leadership in field education, renamed professional development, with the rank of associate professor. An ordained Presbyterian minister, she had been filling a similar post at McCormick Seminary in Chicago. Thomas L. Robinson, a graduate of Abilene Christian University and Princeton Theological Seminary, was named instructor in New Testament. Two years later, having completed his doctorate at Harvard, he became an assistant professor. Union reached across the Atlantic for a professor of systematic theology, Geoffrey Wainwright. A graduate of Cambridge with a doctorate in theology from the University of Geneva (1969), Wainwright had taught systematic theology in Yaounde, Cameroon, and at Queen's College, Birmingham, and was active in the Commission on Faith and Order of the World Council. He resigned after four years to take a position at Duke. The two other appointees of that year had also had extensive ecumenical experience. William B. Kennedy, who earned a B.D. at Union in Richmond (where he later taught) and a Ph.D. from Yale, had directed the office of education of the World Council of Churches for six years. He was no stranger to New York's Union, where during a period of postdoctoral study he had written *The Shaping of Protestant Education* (1966). In the second semester, Kosuke Koyama began his work as professor of ecumenics and world Christianity and director of the ecumenical center.

This last appointment followed a decision by Robert and Sydney Brown to return to the West Coast, where the former took a post at Pacific School of Religion. The reasons were complex, and were spelled out in the theologian's *Creative Dislocation—the Movement of Grace*. He had long been involved in ecumenical life, but as he took up his new role on a graduate theological faculty with responsibility to teach and guide study in the complexities of ecumenical developments on many continents and to direct a center with its administrative burdens, he realized that he simply had too much to do. He was too honest not to face the problem directly, saying "I didn't want to fake it." Despite their hopes, the Browns found that the seminary's administrative processes did not leave them free to become genuine co-directors of the center, and that they and the seminary had misinterpreted each other's priorities. As Brown expressed it, while he was moving down the road of "reluctant radicalization," the seminary, "seeking to recover from what it considered the 'onslaught' of the sixties, seemed more interested in recovering the stability of the fifties than exploring radical options for the eighties."[3] There were differences in judgment as to how Union could maintain its commitments to both high academic standards and the search for justice and survive as an institution of theological education. Although the Browns discovered this early in their second year, they agreed to stay a third, in which they laid foundations for the seminary's continuing program in world Christianity, particularly in their outreach to Latin America.

Kosuke Koyama was well qualified to take responsibility for the position in ecumenics and world Christianity. He had extensive ecumenical experience, especially in Asia and in many aspects of the World Council—faith and order, church and society, world mission and evangelism. A native of Japan, he had graduated from Tokyo Union Theological Seminary, earned a B.D. from Drew and a Ph.D. from Princeton seminary in 1959, and taught at Thailand Theological Seminary, South East Asia Graduate School of Theology, and the University of Otago in New Zealand. Such distinctive books as *Waterbuffalo Theology* (1974) and *No Handle on the Cross* (1977) attracted a good deal of attention.

Appointments and promotions were recommended to the board by a small representative faculty committee on appointments which included several untenured members, a feature of the new bylaws. When recommendations concerning tenure were made, they had to be confirmed by a committee on tenure, composed of all the tenured full professors. This system worked until a protracted controversy in 1978 and 1979 upset it.

The dispute was not over a new appointment but about the promotion to full professor of an already tenured (since 1974) associate professor, Beverly W. Harrison. In the spring of 1978 the committee on appointments did not recommend Harrison's promotion to the board. Its action touched off an intense controversy that was marked by long meetings and demonstrations. At that point, she had written a number of important articles but had not published a book, so much of the discussion was on the nature and extent of publication needed for such a promotion in her field. Many pointed out that Harrison was involved in research and writing on recent and controversial matters, such as feminist theology and ethical questions relating to the abortion issue, and that such pioneering work is very time-consuming and is best put forth in the form of articles. She also devoted a great deal of her time to teaching, advising students, and working with the Women's Center. The issue of whether or not there was discrimination against her as a woman also entered into the debates, during which some forgot that the question of tenure was not involved.

The matter was discussed by the faculty in the fall and again it came before the committee on appointments, which reviewed it thoroughly and at its meeting on January 31, 1979 again said no. As before, there was strong protest in the seminary, including some disruption of registration for second-semester classes. When the board's educational policy committee met on February 5, without consultation with the faculty's committee on appointments it did recommend the promotion to the board, which so voted on the same day. It was an unprecedented action for the board to give such a promotion when it had not been recommended by the appropriate faculty committee. A number of faculty members were deeply disturbed by it, while others—along with many students—felt that the action was within the power of the board and had corrected a committee mistake, for they respected the quality of her teaching and the freshness of her ethical thought. One of the upshots of the affair was the amending of the seminary's bylaws so that the committee on appointments again became a much larger body—all the tenured professors as had long been the case—and an appeals process was formalized. The faculty also revised its criteria for appointment and promotion. Harrison's first book appeared in 1983, *Our Right to Choose: Towards a New Ethic of Abortion.*

A great strength of Union has always been the quality of its student body, and the rebuilding of the faculty helped to attract and hold an increasingly diverse but remarkably able and industrious group. The low year in enrollment was Shriver's first, as it fell to a total of 396. Though the number did not return to previous highs, in the first ten years of the new administration it averaged 431. The percentage of part-time students increased, in great measure because of their need for gainful employment. The goal of having a student body of about half women had been realized; a statistical analysis early in the first semester of 1984–85 showed that M.Div. student body had 159 men and 164 women; total enrollment was 215 men and 207 women. The number of black students (not including those from overseas unless they were permanent resident aliens) was then 33 men and 20 women. Though many factors contribute to shifts in student morale, the reopening of the refectory for lunch early in 1976 after five years of only occasional use was a positive factor, not only for the students but for the wider community.

Clearly, however, the educational needs, interests, and backgrounds of those applying to Union (as to other seminaries) was changing, and one of the president's concerns in accepting his appointment was to find out more about that and how to deal with it through an office of educational research. In explaining the plans for that three-year program to Union graduates and friends, Shriver wrote, "The *long range aim* of the program is to build 'research capability' into every nook and cranny of the school; to further the development of an educational culture which already has profound precedent in Union's own past—a culture that encourages its members to ask 'why?' of almost everything; to fortify the ability of every part of the Union community to take account of its actual impacts upon other parts; and thereby to fortify the capacity of us all to be salty Christians who actually add tastable flavor to the earth."[4]

Malcolm L. Warford, a graduate of Andover Newton who

Tribute to a beloved professor: Donald Shriver and Henry J. Stern, member of the City Council, appreciating the new name of the west end of 120th Street. DON B. MERIWETHER had been minister of several United Church of Christ congregations and had completed the Ed.D. in the cooperative program of Union Seminary, Teachers College and Columbia University (1973), was chosen to head the new office. He had taught religion and education at St. Louis University for four years before accepting the invitation to the new post as director of educational research and associate professor of religion and education in 1976.

Assisted by several part-time research associates, Warford launched a number of projects. He gathered information on Union graduates since 1970, studied the work habits and financial arrangements of current students, undertook a "longitudinal study" of selected groups of M.Div. and Ph.D. students, interviewed all faculty members about their attitudes and expectations concerning the seminary, and provided a content analysis of the curriculum and an evaluation of some of its components. His studies were immediately useful to the work of the board and of various committees. An early document produced by the office was a statistical faculty analysis; it was of great help in planning for the appointments that have already been discussed. The gist of the interviews with faculty members were circulated in notebook form; they showed the firm commitments of Union's teachers, variously expressed, to theology and the church, to high educational standards, to their own disciplines, to their hopes for reform and change, and to their acceptance of growing diversity and the challenges that were coming with it. Spiritual depth was displayed in a number of the interviews, and one was encouraged to find that on the whole there was a creative facing of the tensions that were a part of the life of a relatively small and overloaded ecumenical faculty.

After the three-year term of the program was completed, Warford remained as advisor to board and president. Then he completed the report of the five-year longitudinal study, entitled "Stirring Muddy Waters" from a comment of a student who observed that "It's amazing, the means by which this seminary as a whole with all its talented individuals . . . moved into my psyche and consciousness and, not disrupted, but stirred the muddy water a bit and allowed things to settle." Warford's interpretation of the five-year studies of individuals indicated that "the overwhelming fact reflected in the study is that the church is a real and powerful presence in the theological education of students at Union Seminary," but insisted that better ways had to be found to let the many different values and perspectives within a diverse student body find expression and serious considera- tion: "hospitality is an educational virtue necessary for the integrity of the seminary." In 1981 Warford left to become president of Eden Seminary in Missouri.

In a printed "progress report" at the end of his second year (1976–77), the president discussed "the implementation of some important but not radical reorganizations of administrative structures of the school." The method was to devolve considerable day to day responsibility for various aspects of the school's life to a circle of ad- ministrators: the academic dean, the vice-president for administration (including the previous office of treasurer and business manager), the vice-president for seminary relations (later renamed vice-president for development), the librarian, and (by 1980), the dean of seminary life.

The various functions that had been carried out by the two part-time deans of first-degree and graduate studies, the dean of students, the registration, the admissions, placement, and financial aid personnel were brought under one academic office, with Robert T. Handy as academic dean, Roger L. Shinn as counselor to gradu- ate students, Sidney D. Skirvin as dean of students, and Mildred B. Stoerker as executive secretary of academic programs. A timely test for the new office and for the seminary came when the decennial visit of the accrediting team representing the Association of Theo- logical Schools (ATS) and the Middle States Association of Colleges and Secondary Schools (MSA) drew near. It was originally scheduled for 1976, but in view of all the recent changes at Union the ATS and MSA readily agreed to November 1977 as a time for the visit. To prepare, the seminary was required to undertake a self-study, which was done under the direction of a steering committee chaired by the academic dean. The self-study gathered together, reconsidered, re- vised, and updated the statements of educational goals and methods that been prepared in connection with the work of the Union Assem- bly and the Planning Group in the earlier 1970s. The new office of educational research proved itself as an invaluable resource in gath- ering the documents and statistics required by the evaluators.

There was considerable interest not only at Union but in the wider world of theological education as to the outcome of the reaccrediation process, for many wondered if educational and academic standards had been seriously damaged by the storms of Union's recent history. Co-chaired by Sara Little of Union in Virginia and Morley Mays of Albright College, the team was thorough, probing into many aspects of what Union was about, and its report was positive. Its report declared,

Without hesitation, the Team reports that the progress which has been made seems almost incredible. Faculty is being rebuilt, morale is improving, the budget is balanced. It is now possible to move into the future with hope.

The team also affirmed the high quality of the doctoral program, and found that " 'scholarship' has *not* been sacrificed for 'relevance.' " It did point to the need for more courses directly related to the practice of ministry, additional faculty in religion and education, and a clearer articulation of the institution's focus on urban and global mission. It found that the president "has the temperament and vision of a prophet and pastor, the operational and planning skills of an administrator," and discerned a "renewal in spirit and perspective." The value of the office of educational research was emphasized.[5]

When Handy decided to return to full-time teaching, the search for a successor led to Milton McCormick Gatch Jr. who assumed the academic dean's responsibilities in September 1978. A graduate of what was then Episcopal Theological School in Cambridge in 1960, Gatch earned the Ph.D. at Yale three years later. After teaching at several institutions, he served for ten years at the University of Missouri, becoming professor of English. Focusing his research and teaching in the religious literature of the middle ages, especially in Anglo-Saxon England, he had written many articles and three books: *Death: Meaning and Mortality in Christian Thought and Contemporary Culture* (1969), *Loyalties and Traditions: Man and His World in Old English Literature* (1971), and *Preaching and Theology in Anglo-Saxon England: Aelfric and Wulfstan* (1977). In addition to his administrative role, he was made professor of church history and taught courses in the history of liturgy, spirituality and literature in the middle ages, and ecclesiastical Latin.

As academic dean, Gatch devoted a good deal of attention to curricular matters, curriculum, working with appropriate committees and the four fields to bring greater coherence into the

M.Div. program without returning to a rigid set of course requirements. An elaborate memorandum from the curriculum committee
to the faculty in January 1980 paved the way for a reform that answered satisfactorily the few questions that the accreditation team had
raised. The changes meant that M.Div. students would normally take
certain of the basic introductory courses (or designated options) in
each of the four fields. Dean Gatch also worked closely with the
fields in a 1980–81 study of the Ph.D. program, with Professor Jaroslav Pelikan of Yale serving as observer and advisor. The review led
to some helpful improvements in the programs of study leading to
Union's highest degree. The wider educational significance of Union's
doctoral programs, including the joint one with Columbia, was demonstrated in a survey of the sources from which faculty in Protestant,
Orthodox, interdenominational, and nondenominational seminaries
in the United States and Canada had received their doctoral degrees.
It reported that in 1981 as in 1971 more faculty members had come
from the Columbia/Union Th.D., Ph.D., and Ed.D. programs than
any other sources.[6] The dean served as acting president when Shriver
was away. Gatch was also instrumental in working out with Columbia University's School of Social Work a plan by which qualified
students could receive both the M.Div. and the Master of Science in
Social Work (M.S.S.W.) over a four year period—a program which
quickly grew in popularity.

Union's first vice-president for administration, Georgina
F. Pesante, became responsible for nonacademic administration with
major emphasis on budgetary and personnel matters in August of
1976. She had earned academic degrees in business administration
from the University of California-Berkeley, Harvard Business School,
and the Business School of the University of Puerto Rico. A woman
of great energy, she reorganized administrative patterns. She built on
the work that had been done in the previous several years so that the
budget could at last be balanced—a real victory in a time of inflation.
After ten years of deficits, the books for 1976–77 closed in the black.
The income for current expenses of just over $4,250,000, leaving a
surplus of just over $2000. It was done even as direct spending for
academic programs increased substantially, with some increases in
student services and aid, but with a reduction of overall administrative expenses of more than $100,000. For the rest of the decade an-

nual budgets—approximately $5.5 million by 1978–79—remained balanced, at a cost of the continued deferral of certain maintenance needs.

After three years Pesante resigned, and was replaced in the vice-presidency by Judith Cooper Guido. Trained in both history and business management, she had earned the M.A. at Manhattanville College and had been treasurer and business manager at Elizabeth Seton College in Yonkers for five years. The office expanded somewhat under her able leadership, and effective budget control was instituted. Some of her reports, such as those on the financial status of Union and its complex and aging physical plant, combined a scholarly dimension with financial and administrative precision.

A third feature of administrative reorganization was the appointment in 1976 of Norman D. Stanton (1964) as vice-president for seminary relations to head an office combining development, fund raising, publications, and alumni/ae affairs. A former board member, Stanton had provided executive leadership for neighborhood centers in Scranton, Pennsylvania and served as associate minister of Madison Avenue Presbyterian Church. The work of the newly enlarged office was a factor in balancing the budget, as total giving for 1976–77 was then one of the best in seminary history: $1,233,504. An important slice of that ($470,000) was provided by the annual fund, about a quarter of which had been contributed by graduates, breaking all previous records. They were soon broken again; the annual fund for 1979–80 topped half a million, with alumni/ae contributions at a new high of $132,042.

The work of the dean of students had been placed in the new academic office in 1976, but this proved to be somewhat cumbersome, so in 1980 a new office of seminary life was created. Headed by Sidney Skirvin, the new unit was responsible for recruitment, first [theological] degree admissions, financial aid, housing, and student services. Academic guidance of first-degree students came under the direction of a faculty member as counselor, a position capably filled by Robert Seaver. Bonnie Rosborough (1976), associate pastor of a church in Connecticut, was named coordinator of recruitment. A year and a half later she found herself also filling the role of acting dean of seminary life when Skirvin resigned to become pastor of the Church of the Pilgrims in Washington. The search for a new dean led in 1982 to Jualynne E. Dodson, who was working on a Ph.D. in sociology at the University of California at Berkeley and teaching at the School of Social Work of Atlanta University. With special interests in the social and cultural dynamics of the institutional church and in the history and life of African-American women, she became associate professor when she completed the doctorate in 1984.

After the administration was reorganized and the budget balanced, the way was clear for the Board of Directors to proceed with a capital gifts campaign. A goal of $9 million was set, of which $600,000 was for refurbishing the chapel and installing a new organ; $2.4 million for renovating the library; and $6 million for endowment to be used for increasing faculty support, improving student aid, strengthening ecumenical programs, and conserving buildings. Advance gifts and pledges from board members, major donors, and foundations assured more than a third of the goal when national solicitation of alumni/ae and friends was undertaken in the fall of 1979. Even as the funds were being raised, the fruits of the ultimately successful campaign began to be felt, from increases in faculty salaries and financial assistance for students to very visible renovations in parts of the quadrangle.

Attendance at chapel services increased in the late 1970s, as the imaginative leadership of Professors Clark and Forbes—with frequent help from Seaver—stimulated fresh interest in worship at a time when there was a growing concern for matters of the spirit. Many were restive with the fixed pews that limited variety and movement. There was a concern for both historic and contemporary liturgies, not all of which fit comfortably in the chapel as it was, and a mounting appreciation for the dance as an expression of devotion. The body movement and dance courses of Carolyn Bilderback, named an adjunct professor in 1977, provided important resources for this aspect of the religious life.

Committees set to work with architect Philip Ives to redesign the chapel. What they developed proved to be quite controversial as the renovation proceeded. As room 207 served as a temporary place for worship, the pews and chancel furniture were removed from James Chapel and the walls were stripped of the dark paneling, leaving the basic Gothic shell; movable chairs on a stone floor replaced the old pews and a new Holtkamp organ was installed in the center

Worship in the renovated James Memorial Chapel

of the chancel, walling off entirely the "Great Commission" window. Early in 1980 a whole series of dedicatory events showed the new versatility of James Chapel. Services of worship, a number of organ recitals and inaugural lectures, along with choral, dramatic, and dance activities, could all be accommodated, with the chapel set at one time as an auditorium, another as a church in the round or in the square, or again largely cleared for various liturgical purposes.

Some did not like the renovated chapel at first. As they worshipped there, however, many came to appreciate the flexibility the new setting offered with its movable chairs, lecterns, and communion table. Some did not relish the changes, however, and continued to feel that a mistake had been made. It was decided to hold regular chapel services of thirty minutes duration at noon, Monday through Thursday. Faculty members and various student-faculty groups regularly accepted responsibility for services for a week. When Linda Clark accepted an appointment at Boston University School of Theology just as the chapel was reopened, Janet Walton was named as coordinator of worship in 1980 with the rank of assistant (later associate) professor. A skilled pianist with an M.M. from Indiana University and an Ed.D. in religion and the arts from Columbia, she moved into her new role with genuine effectiveness. As a teacher in worship and the arts and music in church, this Catholic sister showed deep ecumenical sensitivities in enabling persons from many backgrounds and perspectives to participate meaningfully as leaders and worshippers in the daily services. Though attendance fluctuated, in part because of the rhythms of academic life, it increased noticeably by the middle 1980s. The depth of student concerns—for peace with justice, for the oppressed persons of the world, for authenticity in religion—could often be more clearly perceived in the chapel than in any other single part of seminary life.

One of the president's special concerns was to make the refectory more directly available to the chapel. This was accomplished by cutting a door from the narthex directly into the refectory. It proved to be a worthwhile feature, and it became a familiar sight to see persons moving together from chapel to lunch. Furthermore, special occasions in the chapel were often followed by receptions in the refectory. This could happen, for example, after the celebrational events of an inaugural lecture, or after a special lectureship. The

Cyril C. Richardson Memorial Lectures, for example, supported by an endowed fund established by friends and former students of a great teacher who had served for 42 years on the faculty, had been launched in 1979 in room 214, but the popular event, repeated biennially by such distinguished scholars as Robert M. Grant (1941) of Chicago, George H. Williams, Th.D. (1946) of Harvard, and Jaroslav Pelikan of Yale, continued to draw large numbers and was moved to the chapel.

The chapel was also the place where crowds gathered for presentation of the seminary's highest award, the Union Medal, instituted in 1981 to honor men and women whose lives reflect the values for which the school stands. Recipients have included Andrew Young, mayor of Atlanta and former ambassador to the United Nations; George Kennan, diplomat, scholar, and opponent of the nuclear arms race; Ok-gill Kim, president emerita of Ewha Women's University in Korea and defender of human rights; Rachel Henderlite, Presbyterian educator and ecumenist; Eberhard Bethge, participant with Bonhoeffer in resistance to the Nazis and later his biographer; and Gardner Taylor, often called the "dean of black preachers." Thus James Chapel's flexibility has made it useful for many purposes, including a rare common meal, and in 1985 it provided the setting for the first two weeks of the historic exhibit of photographs and documents illustrating the life of Anne Frank. One presentation of the Union Medal was not there, however, for early in 1986 it was awarded to Anne and John Bennett at their place of retirement on the West Coast.

A more extensive and expensive reconstruction project was that of the library, which with its more than half-million volumes is the preeminent theological library in the western hemisphere. A number of changes had already been made in library procedures; for example, in 1975 books began to be classified under the Library of Congress numbers and microfiche readers replaced the old card file for new accessions. Two years later Union became a charter member of the New York Area Theological Library Association, which soon had 18 members. The capital campaign, thanks in part to a challenge grant of $600,000 from the National Endowment for the Humanities which called the library a "national treasure," and one of $250,000 from the Kresge Foundation, along with those from many other sources, provided the funds for the project that cost more than three million dollars. The planning process for the reconstruction was started by Librarian Maloy, who left in 1979 to become director of the Smithsonian libraries in Washington, D.C.

His successor, Richard Spoor, had been on the staff since 1970, most recently as associate librarian for research and planning. He had earned M.A. and M.S. degrees from Columbia, and continued in the doctoral program in library science as he was named director of the library with the rank of associate professor. A considerable slice of his time in his new position was spent in dealing with and explaining to others various delays in library reconstruction. It was a complex operation to rebuild a library that was in use, and the plan included the refitting of Brown Tower, where the Missionary Research Library materials had long been kept, as a place for rare books and archival materials. Users of the library confronted difficulties as the familiar third-floor entrance hall was closed, and the circulation desk was moved temporarily to the gate room between the library and Hastings Hall. Many researchers were disadvantaged as certain materials were stored, and other shelved in areas not contiguous with the library. Various obstacles to completing the work were faced as old blueprints proved to be erroneous and building deadlines were often missed. When the rebuilt sections of the library were finally opened, *The Union News* for April, 1983 carried the appropriate headline in bold letters, "UNION SEMINARY LIBRARY REDEDI-CATED; AT LAST!"

Those coming to see the reconstructed library for the first time were often surprised to discover the entrance directly off the rotunda where the General Office and Book Service had long been, and to find themselves moving between the circulation desk and a new small reading room. Periodicals and new books were now located on the second floor, with library offices, reference desk, conference room, and the familiar large reading room—now redecorated—on the third, and seminar rooms, carrells, and microform readers on the fourth. A new glassed-in stairway facing the quad was built to link the floors. The project won a 1984 award of the New York chapter of the American Institute of Architects.

The rededication ceremonies included a major evening address by Frederick Buechner (1958), and "A Festival of Word,

Symbol, and Space" created by Robert Seaver. It was announced that the renovated library had been named for Walter Burke, who had retired as chair of the Board of Directors late in 1982. He had worked consistently and generously for the seminary since he had first joined the board in 1969. His unostentatious leadership had much to do with the achievements that marked the seven years he presided over the board. One of the happy notes of his final year in that office was his announcement that the capital fund campaign had not only reached its goal (which had been reset at $9.2 million) but went over it by some $600,000.

Though not as conspicuous or expensive as the major chapel and library renovations, some other spaces in the seminary were also redone, some as byproducts of the Burke Library project. The problems caused by the displacement of the Book Service and General Office were solved by widening the central corridor on the lower level of Auburn Hall and turning it into the snack area (affectionately known as "the pit") with seminary mailboxes on one wall, and by remodeling an adjoining classroom into an attractive setting for the Book Service. The social hall was redecorated through funds that came through the alertness of Chancellor Gerson Cohen of the Jewish Theological Seminary. Those responsible for settling the estate of Mr. and Mrs. Fred Ziprik were required to find a "Christian charity" for a stated sum, and the chancellor suggested Union. The result was a refurbished room more usable for receptions and other occasions.

Another striking rejuvenated space was dedicated on alumni/ae "Union Day," April 11, 1984. The "gate room" above the entrance to the quadrangle, which a half century before had been the location of the "prophets' chamber," and then the tutors' office and afterward the temporary location of the library card catalog and circulation desk, was overhauled and made into the beautiful "Bonhoeffer Room" for seminars, small conferences and meetings, and special events. It was while he was resident in the prophets' chamber for three weeks in 1939 that Dietrich Bonhoeffer made his fateful decision to return to Germany to identify himself with his people and continue his role in the movement of resistance to Hitler. The room was dedicated in his memory on the same day that Eberhard Bethge received the Union Medal.

In the early 1980s Auburn Seminary also took the opportunity to reconstruct its suite of offices on the third floor of Auburn Hall and to redecorate its library on the fourth. After a period
of study and reflection, Auburn had reorganized. At the beginning of
the 1980–81 academic year Barbara G. Wheeler took office as the
seminary's president. She was a familiar figure, having done staff work
for several of Union's planning and search efforts. She had also been
consultant to two presidents and to other institutions. Auburn continued to serve Presbyterian students at Union, to carry on a series of
programs in continuing education, drawing on its own largely part-
time teaching staff and various Union faculty members in its activities on behalf of the churches.[7]

While Union students, faculty, and staff were profiting
from the improvement in seminary morale, the balanced budget, and
the renovated facilities, the administration foresaw that the school
would soon again be facing financial difficulties again. At its meeting
of April 14–15, 1980, the Board of Directors authorized the appointment of a committee on educational excellence in the eighties. Its
task was to advise the board concerning specific budgetary priorities
and strategies that would most help the seminary to maintain educational excellence over the next decade, a time of predictable financial
stress. The committee was composed of three board members appointed by the chair and three elected by the faculty. It was chaired
by board member John F. Wilson (1957, Ph.D. 1962) and became
known as the "Wilson committee," somewhat to the chair's chagrin,
for the group was asked to do a very difficult job as it faced the overall
problems of the seminary while many viewed it from more limited
perspectives.

The committee consulted with members of the student
body, staff, and faculty. Its major agenda was provided by a battery
of 32 pointed questions posed by the president based on his experience as budget builder. It faced the difficult problems of maintaining
a sufficiently large and highly qualified faculty in the face of a steadily mounting budget caused in part by inflation. Its report, presented
to the board on February 17, 1981, observed that "never before has
Union been called to do so much more with so much less." Its objectives for the seminary, hopefully to be reached by the end of the
150th academic year, 1985–86, included a larger enrollment, espe-

cially of M.Div. students, and an increase of net tuition income (tuition income less financial aid) from 6 to 12 percent. The report called on the faculty to reduce its table of organization by up to six positions, while it advocated increasing faculty compensation to compare favorably with salaries at university divinity schools. It also introduced merit considerations in setting salaries through annual review procedures. A reduction of eight to ten staff and administrative positions was also recommended. A carefully conceived program of preventive maintenance was judged to be a worthwhile investment. The president and board "must be prepared to continue active fund raising beyond the conclusion of the current capital campaign with the minimum objective of securing an additional ten million dollars for endowment by 1986." The report concluded with the words, "For all the concern which gave rise to the Committee and the caution expressed in its Report, however, we are unreserved in our recommendations and confident about the distinguished future we look forward to for Union."[8]

When the board did accept the report of its committee

A group of women Faculty members in the 1980s: l. to r., Professors Jualynne Dodson, Ann Ulanov, Phyllis Trible, Janet Walton, Beverly Harrison, Ardith Hayes, Dorothee Sölle.

on educational excellence on that February day, it passed a resolution that called for its standing committees, the faculty, and other governance structures of the seminary to refine the proposals and make recommendations for action by December 1. Once again, it reaffirmed "its commitment to the goal of a student body and faculty one-third of whom will be members of America's racial minorities and one-half women," and resolved that in the implementation of the report "no steps will be taken that adversely impact on the achievement of this goal."[9] To accept the report was not an easy or merely formal decision of the board, for it meant an already "working" board would need to increase its efforts.

Though the seminary community had been involved in the work of the committee, the circulation of the finished report generated much discussion. Criticism of the report was expressed in open meetings with members of the committee and gatherings of faculty and students. It was often asked if the efforts to stress educational excellence and yet reduce faculty size were consistent. Both students and faculty expressed anxieties over the policy of requiring student loans before granting student aid, especially as many students began their seminary careers already carrying educational debts. The prospect of steadily increasing tuition was troublesome; students expressed their serious concerns, and suggested other options.[10] Tuition for first theological degrees had already climbed from $2300 to $3100 per year between 1975–76 and 1980–81 while doctoral tuition rose from $3550 to $5730. The road ahead, however, proved to be even steeper; by 1985–86 the figures were $6250 and $10,400, which did bring net tuition income to 12 percent of total revenues by 1985. Help for students came early in 1982 through an anonymous gift of one million dollars, half to be used for special grants and half for a revolving loan fund.

The faculty agonized over the reduction of its table of organization by as many as six positions by 1986. Several positions were eliminated and others consolidated. In the theological field, the number of systematic theologians was reduced from four to three. For the historical field, the positions in modern and Afro-American church history were to be combined when they became vacant. The practical field was doubly disadvantaged, for no full-time appointment in speech and drama was to be made when a vacancy occurred, and the positions in church and society and women in ministry were combined. It was also decided not to continue the Fosdick visiting professorship but to reallocate its endowment income to some other aspect of faculty support. (An anonymous gift, however, made it possible to continue to invite Dorothee Sölle as visiting professor for a semester a year outside the table of organization.) The faculty hoped that the reductions could stop there, but stood ready to identify a sixth position if absolutely necessary. The new plan provided for a general increase in faculty salaries, with merit increases which promised to help Union remain competitive in holding leading scholars and teachers.

As positions on the reduced table of organization became vacant, search committees were appointed, and in 1985, for the first time in five years, two new regular members of the faculty were welcomed. Eleanor Scott Meyers took the newly defined position as assistant professor of church and society. An ordained minister of the Christian Church (Disciples of Christ), she had earned the M.A.R. from Yale and the Ph.D. in sociology at the University of Wisconsin at Madison, with emphasis on complex organizations and religious institutions. Her courses on the church as social institution, ministry on the campus, the politics of power in the local congregation, and the culture of the urban congregation filled important educational needs. Peter H. Van Ness was no stranger to Morningside Heights when he accepted the position as assistant professor of the philosophy of religion, for he had graduated from Columbia College ten years before. He completed his graduate studies at the Divinity School of the University of Chicago with a Ph.D. in 1983, and taught religion and philosophy at the college level for several years, devoting some of his writing to the current dialogue between religion and science.

The board soon found that its committee on educational excellence had been right on many counts. The day of deficits was again at hand, for in the very year the report was accepted, the shortfall was $329,000. In a 1985 review of the report of that committee, however, the vice-president for finance and administration estimated that deficits would have been very much higher except for the economies and strategies that had been suggested. A followup review in January 1986, however, showed that only a few of the objectives of the committee on excellence would be fully met by the end of the academic year. M.Div. enrollment had not significantly increased, though tuition income from all degree programs was at or close to 12 percent of total revenues. Faculty and staff salaries had been increased. The size of the faculty had been somewhat reduced (by four as of July 1, 1986), while eleven positions had been cut from the staff. A basic, manual preventive maintenance program was in process, but it was not the sophisticated program envisioned by the committee. While there had been some increase in the endowment through gifts, the board was still working out a plan to enlarge it substantially. Other plans for facing the financial problem squarely were being shaped by the administration and the board.

One of the hard-working members of the committee on excellence succeeded Walter Burke as board chair in 1982: Thomas S. Johnson, then senior executive vice president of Chemical Bank, soon president. Holder of an M.B.A. from Harvard, Johnson, the first Roman Catholic to head the board, had taught finance at the Graduate School of Business at Ateneo de Manila University in the Philippines.

Under his leadership, early in 1984 the Board of Directors became conscious of mounting deficits and realized that despite the slower rate of inflation the seminary's budget would indeed top $8 million by 1986. The board decided to seek to ensure Union's future by a renewed emphasis on development in an effort to increase the endowment significantly. To that end it took the risk of drawing on the unrestricted endowment to the tune of well over a million dollars for a variety of interrelated purposes: to increase the development staff, to take care of long-deferred maintenance needs, and to provide for new educational initiatives, often in the form of bringing special speakers to Union, organizing special symposia and conferences, increasing ecumenical exchanges of students and faculty, and enhancing the worship program and extending its educational values to churches.[11] Meanwhile, in 1983 a new vice-president for development had been secured: Mary Jordan Cox. A graduate of Barnard College, she had experience in editing and publishing before serving as vice-president for development at Radcliffe College, there compiling an enviable record in doubling gifts to the annual fund, guiding a major capital campaign, and attracting foundation grants. Under

her direction the annual fund once again broke records as it topped
$750,000 in 1985.

As Union's sesquicentennial approached, the seminary
had come a long way from its small faculty and first inadequate plant
at University Place, but was still seeking to use its human, financial,
and building resources for the betterment of its students, of theological education and scholarship, and of the Christian churches.
Union on Morningside Heights in the 1980s was vastly more diversified as a community than when it was at University Place or Park
Avenue, or when it was on Broadway at the time of the large enrollments in the Van Dusen and Bennett eras. It repeatedly reaffirmed
the historic decision of 1972 to seek a community half of which would
consist of women, one-third of minorities. Though that goal was more
immediately obtainable in the short run in an ever changing student
body than on a heavily tenured faculty, it continued to reach out to
persons of widely varied backgrounds. As James Cone, one of Union's
internal monitors of that important commitment, summed up the
matter:

Far more than I anticipated, Union has made a genuine effort to define
theological education in such a manner that it explicitly includes persons
who are concerned for the liberation of the poor. I would be the first to
admit that Union has not gone as far in this direction as it should. But
when Union is compared with other white seminaries like it, no school, to
my knowledge, has ever come close to making the commitment that Union
has. It is the only white seminary that I know of that seeks to include Third
World people's culture, history, and theology at the center of the educational process along with the traditional European models.[12]

The increasing diversity of students from North America, including
those of various racial and ethnic backgrounds, educational and vocational experience, and sexual preference, went beyond the expectations of 1972.

To be sure, with a student body smaller than it had been,
the increase in opportunities for theological education for overseas
students on their own continents, and the mounting difficulty of financing them in view of travel expense and limitations on their gainful employment, there was a smaller percentage of them than for-

merly. Nevertheless, there was no decrease in community concern for persons across the world. Ecumenical fellowships continued to bring students annually from other countries, four to six a year. Some students from abroad came on other resources, and others were recently arrived new residents in America.

The Ecumenical and World Christianity center, under the direction of Professor Kosuke Koyama with Grace Keefer Parker (1950) as administrative assistant, arranged for programs to express Union's commitment to ecumenical theology and life, to deepen insights into other theologies and cultures across the world, and to provide opportunities for Union students to travel and study abroad. Connections for a semester's academic work outside the United States were developed for Costa Rica and Korea, while shorter-term opportunities were made available in Asia, Africa, and Latin America. An annual travel seminar during January intersession which focused on the church in the Caribbean proved to have high educational value.

The Luce visiting professorships helped to enrich the international dimensions of theological education. Early in 1982 Younghak Hyun, an alumnus of the PARS program, holder of a Union S.T.M., and former professor at Ewha Women's University in Seoul until forced to resign for advocating governmental reforms, reached Union after long delays because of difficulties of getting the South Korean government to grant visas. His courses and other presentations on the "Minjung theology" of Korean people were well received. In the fall of 1985 the Luce professor was Sergio Arce Martinez from Cuba. A graduate of Princeton seminary with a Ph.D. from the University of Havana, his courses focused on theology in revolutionary situations. The Luce Foundation also made an additional grant for a three-year program to expand ecumenical exchanges so that professors and doctoral students might have the experience of working for a semester in an Asian country while a team from there would visit Union.

The increasing diversity of the student body can be glimpsed from the caucuses formed to express the interests of various groups within it and to enrich thereby the education of all. Among the active student caucuses and groups at Union in the early 1980s were the black caucus, the black women's caucus, the Hispanic caucus, the international students caucus, the lesbian and gay caucus, the Oikumene committee, and the women's caucus. As they responded to the invitation to take the lead in daily chapel, such groups often chose to share their perspectives and concerns in the context of worship. Learning, teaching, and living in such a setting stretched the mind, heart, and vision of many within the Union community. A few found it too intense and left primarily for that reason, in some cases finding themselves drawn back once again to study amid the realities of its pluralistic atmosphere.

Behind the diversities, however, was the presence of widely shared unities which persons were free to express in word and deed in various ways, unities that often were late-twentieth-century forms of the aims that brought the seminary into existence in 1836. The way that they should be articulated and acted out often caused controversy.

There was, for example, the continuing concern for peace, a cause served in various ways when students and faculty opposed the Vietnam war, a cause renewed in the growing resistance to nuclear weaponry, as in a statement that was published in the *New York Times* and elsewhere: "To End the Arms Race," signed by some 350 persons connected with Union, including members of the board, faculty, staff, alumni/ae, and students.[13]

Another major concern that operated as a unitive force was for racial equality in America and the world. It was pressed with particular vigor by students in the drive for divestment in South Africa. Continued investment in that nation seemed to many to provide support for a government committed to apartheid, while others argued that responsible investment by those who pressed for changes in its basic national policy in the direction of reform was an acceptable strategy to follow. There were various meetings of student groups with subcommittees of the board; in 1979, for example, a coalition of student caucuses pressed the board to divest, making it clear that they did not find other options sufficient. A board resolution on February 6, 1979, took the discussions with students seriously. The board was not then ready to take the step of total divestment but, in accordance with the suggestions of its committee on social responsibility in investments, it planned selective divestment and recommended that the seminary, in cooperation with others, petition our government to set regulations concerning activities of American institutions in South Africa.[14]

Three years later the board's committee recommended divestment as a strategy of last resort. Growing concern over the issue came to a head in 1984–85. In October 1984 well-known South African opponents of apartheid spoke at Union: Allan Boesak, president of the World Alliance of Reformed Churches, who had attended some classes at Union a decade earlier; and Desmond Tutu, Anglican Bishop of Johannesburg and winner of the 1984 Nobel Peace Prize. A resolution drawn up by students, which labeled apartheid as a sin, was signed by many of them and by other members of the Union community; it was read at the event on October 25 and widely circulated. At about the same time Shriver named a new policy research group on seminary investments. Chaired by Roger Shinn, it probed deeply into many issues.

While the committee was nearing the end of its work, students, led by Clarke Evans and Walter Parrish, organized a demonstration—one of a series in which groups of many kinds participated—at the South African consulate on Park Avenue to protest racism and apartheid on April 3, 1985. An estimated 200 members of the community went down to the site together, gathering in a legal vigil and celebrating the Lord's Supper under the leadership of Professors Forbes and Kennedy. Then 91 of the group participated in civil disobedience by blocking the doors. President Shriver read a statement which declared that the demonstration was a way of showing support for "our brothers and sisters of the earth who suffer the injustice of racism." The group, including the president, the academic dean, and eight other faculty members, was then arrested and driven in paddy wagons to precinct headquarters for booking. They were required to appear in court on May 13, where the charges were dismissed on the ground that they were exercising First Amendment rights. Though there were those in the community who had some questions about the value or the significance of the action, it did witness to one of the unities that helps to bind a diverse group. As student Wendy McCormick concluded in her *Union News* story, "Participants described the demonstration experience as a powerful and deeply moving one, not only in the opportunity to make public witness against apartheid but also in the strong sense of Union's community as so many stood together that day in a statement for freedom for all the people of South Africa."[15]

The patient work of the research group paved the way for the board at its April 22, 1985 meeting to "accept the principle of divestment of its stock in companies that have major direct involvement in South Africa," choosing that option to the alternate one of exercising stockholders' opportunities to influence management as the clearer action. The group's report to the board noted that such action "may alienate some potential donors, as our actions in the past have sometimes done," but concluded that "we cannot cultivate public approval by ceasing to be Union."[16]

Another unifying force in a diverse community has been concern for neglected and unjustly treated persons. Although often expressed in generalities, that spirit has manifested itself also in practical ways. In February 1982, for example, two students, David Gordon and Donna Buyske, took the lead in gaining support among students, staff, and faculty for the operation once a week of a soup kitchen at Broadway Presybterian Church. Conducted largely by volunteers, this soup kitchen like others filled an important need at a time when homeless and hungry people were frequently to be seen on New York's Upper West Side. "The Soup Kitchen balances out the ivory tower nature of Union," one participant, Amy Greene, put it. "It is one way to get involved in the life of the neighborhood . . . these people are our neighbors."[17]

The most pervasive force for unity at the seminary has been its educational task, defined as the continuing search for truth in freedom. When the third home of Union on Morningside Heights was dedicated in 1910, Francis Brown was referring primarily to the faculty when he said:

Most of our work is very quiet, apart from public gaze. We publish some books; . . . We offer some public lectures, some courses of sermons, occasional indications of our presence in the community; but after all our real steady work is quite out of sight, . . .

The continuing, everyday work of Union has always been centered in what goes on in lecture halls, seminar rooms, library, chapel, and offices in the ceaseless quest for a larger vision of Christian faith and a deeper knowledge of the life and thought of the church. Though exchanges in the classrooms and halls are often sharp, barriers between persons of different backgrounds are pierced in the common effort to get to the heart of issues. The work of research, teaching, and writing is rarely newsworthy, except, as Brown noted, "as its result appears at some remove in time and space from our workshop."[18] Union's intellectual work becomes public on those occasions when students, graduates, and faculty members lead groups, deliver lectures and sermons, and publish articles and books in which appear the results of months and years of probing and reflection. Though interests, approaches, and conclusions vary greatly, the common search for truth has continued to serve as a unifying force throughout the seminary's history.

During Union's 150 years, amid many changes and increasing diversities, it has been the power of faith seeking understanding that has brought faculty and students together in the quest for the things that are true, just, and loving. In varied but appropriate ways in classroom and refectory, in chapel and library the spiritual and the intellectual quests have reinforced each other. The great variety of traditions and backgrounds have brought enrichment in the struggle to understand the gospel and its meaning. The very location of an ecumenical seminary between a great university and a towering church symolizes the effort to love God with both mind and heart.

Many graduates have looked back on the time when they were at Union as its "golden age." Timothy Light (1965) has written that as a student he "found the Seminary enormously exciting, challenging, caring, and supportive. . . . It was at Union that I learned the meaning of social action, the power of liturgy, the sense that the Bible and its inspiration permeate our lives, a feeling for the movement of God in history, the power of both God's love and God's justice—in short, it was at Union that I learned about the Christian faith as needed by educated Western people in the latter half of this century." In 1985 as a member of the Board of Directors he declared that "as magnificent and as important as Union was for me at that time and as important as the Union of that time remains for me now, I am convinced by my somewhat remote acquaintance with the place that it is even greater now than it was then." He found that harder to characterize now in a "current time of explicit and celebrated di-

versity" than in the earlier period, and concluded that "Somehow—
I guess that 'somehow' equals the work of the Holy Spirit—Union of
today has taken that diversity and diffusion and, without in any way
perverting that diversity, has made of it something that is far greater
than the sum of its parts." Among the many factors that have joined
to cause this he cited the faculty, its leadership, the library, and the
students, who "are that diversity captured by a common divine vision
which charges them with an intensity that is unmistakably Union."[19]

That is Union at its best as interpreted by one who knows
it well. Many others throughout the seminary's history have expressed
something quite similar in different words. Union has not always
been at its best throughout its 150 years, but something in its dynamic guiding vision has brought it back on course again and again.
The story of the seminary's past can encourage those of the Union
family and its many friends to look forward to its work in the twenty-
first century with faith and hope, as it seeks to hold in dynamic balance the words of the motto on its seal: Unitas—Veritas—Caritas.

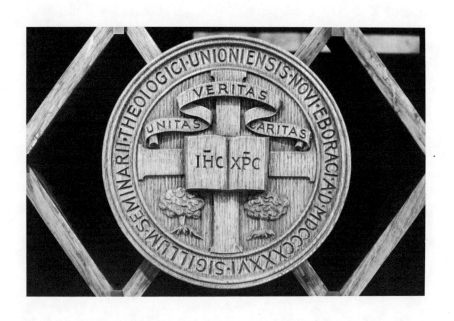

Notes

1. Embodying a Vision

1. George Lewis Prentiss, *The Union Theological Seminary in the City of New York: Historical and Biographical Sketches of its First Fifty Years* (New York, 1889), p. 9. (Henceforth Prentiss, *Fifty Years of Union.*)

2. Ibid., p. 15.

3. The Westminster Confession, prepared by the Westminster Assembly in the 1640s during the English civil wars, was a notable expression of Calvinist faith, and became the basic standard of Scottish and American Presbyterianism.

4. *Extracts from the Minutes of the General Assembly, of the Presbyterian Church, in the United States of America*, 1817, p. 27.

5. Robert Wood Lynn, "Notes toward a History: Theological Encyclopedia and the Evolution of Protestant Seminary Curriculum, 1808–1869," *Theological Education* (Spring 1981) 17:118–44. A brief, older historical survey can be found in ch. 7 of William Adams Brown, *Ministerial Education in America: Summary and Interpretation* (New York, 1934), vol. 1 of Brown, Mark A. May, and Frank K. Shuttleworth, *The Education of American Ministers* (4 vols., New York, 1934).

6. Stuart Henry, *Unvanquished Puritan: A Portrait of Lyman Beecher* (Grand Rapids, 1973), pp. 214, 221.

7. Prentiss, *Fifty Years of Union*, pp. 43–44.

8. Arthur C. McGiffert, Jr., *No Ivory Tower: The Story of The Chicago Theological Seminary* (Chicago, 1965), p. 32.

9. The Preamble has been reprinted numerous times; the original is appended to the bound Minutes of the Board of Directors, January 18, 1836, in the archives of Union Theological Seminary, New York.

10. The larger part of the letter is reprinted in Prentiss, *Fifty Years of Union*, pp. 246–49.

11. Edward Robinson, *Biblical Researches in Palestine, Mount Sinai and Arabia Petraea: A Journal of Travels in the Year 1838 by E. Robinson and E. Smith, Undertaken in Reference to Biblical Geography* (3 vols., Boston, 1841; reprint, New York, 1977).

12. Jerry Wayne Brown, *The Rise of Biblical Criticism in America, 1800–1870:*

The New England Scholars (Middletown, Conn., 1969), p. 111.

13. George Bowen, as quoted by Robert E. Speer, *George Bowen of Bombay* (New York, 1938), p. 102.

14. Henry Sloane Coffin, A *Half Century of Union Theological Seminary, 1896–1945: An Informal History* (New York, 1954), pp. 207–13.

15. As quoted by Charles R. Gillett, "Detailed History of the Union Theological Seminary in the City of New York" (3 vols., typescript, [1937?], 3:1019.

16. *Services in Adams Chapel at the Dedication of the New Buildings of the Union Theological Seminary, 1200 Park Avenue, New York City. December 9, 1884* (New York, 1885), p. 11. (Henceforth *Dedication, 1884.*)

17. Edwin F. Hatfield, *The Early Annals of Union Theological Seminary in the City of New York* (New York, 1876), p. 16.

18. Minutes of the Board of Directors, October 28, 1839.

19. Ellouise W. Skinner, *Sacred Music at Union Theological Seminary, 1836–1953: An Informal History* (New York, 1953), pp. 13–14.

20. As quoted by Prentiss, *Fifty Years of Union*, p. 69.

21. Elizabeth L. Smith, ed., *Henry Boynton Smith: His Life and Work* (New York, 1881), p. 159.

22. Channing R. Jeschke, "The Briggs Case: The Focus of a Study in Nineteenth Century Presbyterian History" (Ph.D. thesis, University of Chicago, 1966), pp. 96–103.

23. Gillett, "Detailed History of Union Theological Seminary," 3:1029.

24. Speer, *Bowen*, p. 101.

2. Strengthening the Seminary's Identity

1. Lewis F. Stearns, *Henry Boynton Smith* (Boston, 1892), p. 146.

2. George M. Marsden, *The Evangelical Mind and the New School Presbyterian Experience: A Case Study of Thought and Theology in Nineteenth-Century America* (New Haven, 1970), p. 156.

3. As quoted by Stearns, *Smith*, p. 12.

4. William K. B. Stoever, "Henry Boynton Smith and the German Theology of History," *Union Seminary Quarterly Review* (Fall 1968), 12:69–89.

5. Horace Bushnell, *God in Christ* (Hartford, 1849), pp. 279–356.

6. The Andover address is reprinted in Henry B. Smith, *Faith and Philosophy: Discourses and Essays*, ed. George L. Prentiss (New York, 1886); quotations on pp. 4, 20, 24, 35, 45.

7. As quoted by Stearns, *Smith*, pp. 138–39.

8. For brief treatments of Smith's theological role in nineteenth-century theological history, see Jurgen Herbst, *The German Historical School in American Scholarship: A Study in the Transfer of Culture* (Ithaca, NY, 1965), pp. 14–15, 92–94, and a paper by Mark A. Noll, "Jonathan Edwards and Nineteenth-Century Theology," Wheaton College, Ill., 1984, pp. 14–19.

9. The inaugural address is reprinted in Smith, *Faith and Philosophy*, pp. 49–86, quotations on pp. 49, 50, 52, 57, 61, 65.

10. For an interpretation of the origins and history of the fourfold pattern of theological education in Europe and America, see Edward Farley, *Theologia: The Fragmentation and Unity of Theological Education* (Philadelphia, 1983).

11. Prentiss, *Fifty Years of Union*, pp. 53–54, 97–99.

12. As quoted by Gillett, "Detailed History of Union," 3:1024.

13. James Hastings Nichols, *Romanticism In American Theology: Nevin and Schaff at Mercersburg* (Chicago, 1961), p. 3.

14. The 1855 address in reprinted in Smith, *Faith and Philosophy*, pp. 125–66; quotations on pp. 136, 132, 163.

15. Stearns, *Smith*, p. 235.

16. Prentiss, *Fifty Years of Union*, pp. 280, 282.

17. Roswell D. Hitchcock, "Address," *Dedication, 1884*, p. 20.

18. Coffin, *A Half Century of Union*, p. 209.

19. Minutes of the Board of Directors, January 6, 1857.

20. Marsden, *The Evangelical Mind and the New School Presbyterian Experience*, p. 199.

21. Arthur C. McGiffert, "The Seminary and the War," *Union Theological Seminary Bulletin* (November 1917) 1(1):5.

22. The discourse is reprinted in Smith, *Faith and Philosophy*, pp. 265–96; quotations on pp. 275, 278, 284.

23. Lefferts A. Loetscher, *The Broadening Church: A Study of Theological Issues in the Presbyterian Church since 1869* (Philadelphia, 1954), p. 21. Loetscher provides a brief interpretation of the reunion of 1869, as does Marsden; for fuller accounts see Lewis G. Vander Velde, *The Presbyterian Churches and the Federal Union, 1861–1869* (Cambridge, Mass., 1932), part 6, and William Adams, "The Reunion," in *Presbyterian Reunion Memorial Volume* (New York, 1871), pp. 246–315.

24. The Patton quotation is in Prentiss, *Fifty Years of Union*, p. 264; the Loetscher remark in his *The Broadening Church*, p. 26.

25. As quoted by William Adams, "The Reunion," p. 312 (see note 23).

26. Hitchcock, "Address," *Dedication, 1884*, p. 25.

3. Union as a Denominational Seminary

1. Prentiss, *The Union Theological Seminary in the City of New York; Its Design and Another Decade of its History* (Asbury Park, NJ, 1899) p. 78. (Henceforth Prentiss, *Another Decade.*) A chart of seminary enrollments from 1838–39 to 1890–91 is provided (pp. 78–79).

2. The trial is discussed by George H. Shriver, "Philip Schaff: Heresy at Mercersburg," in Shriver, ed., *American Religious Heretics: Formal and Informal Trials* (Nashville, 1966), pp. 18–55.

3. For a full discussion, see Klaus Penzel, "Church History in Context: The Case of Philip Schaff," in John Deschner, Leroy Howe, and Klaus Penzel, eds. *Our Common History as Christians: Essays in Honor of Albert C. Outler* (New York, 1975), pp. 217–60; also his "Church History and the Ecumenical Quest: A Study of the German Background and Thought of Philip Schaff" (Th.D. dissertation, Union Theological Seminary, N.Y., 1962).

4. Perry Miller introduced and edited the work under the title *America: A Sketch of Its Political, Social, and Religious Character* (Cambridge, Mass.: 1961).

5. This is discussed by Nichols, *Romanticism in American Theology*, esp. chaps. 3, 5, and 7.

6. David S. Schaff, *The Life of Philip Schaff: in part Autobiographical* (New York, 1897), p. 287.

7. Prentiss, *Another Decade*, pp. 421–22.

8. Roswell D. Hitchcock, "Address," *Dedication, 1884*, p. 28.

9. Charles A. Briggs to Marvin Briggs, Jan. 8, 1867, The Dr. Charles A. Briggs Transcripts, 1:34, #3170. The transcripts were copied in longhand from his manuscripts by his daughter, Emilie Grace Briggs. (Henceforth Briggs Transcripts.) Many letters from and to

him are included in the twelve volumes in the Union Seminary archives. Comparisons with other materials attest to the trustworthiness of the transcripts.

10. Arthur C. McGiffert Jr., *No Ivory Tower*, p. 32.

11. Ernest W. Saunders, *Searching the Scriptures: A History of the Society of Biblical Literature, 1880–1980* (Chico, Ca, 1982), pp. 3–4, 117.

12. Philip D. Jordan, *The Evangelical Alliance for the United States of America, 1847–1900: Ecumenism, Identity and the Religion of the Republic* (Lewiston, N.Y., 1982), esp. pp. 69–97; quotations on pp. 69 and 93.

13. Philip Schaff, "Diary of 1884," entry for September 22. I am grateful to George H. Shriver, a biographer of Schaff, for calling this to my attention.

14. *Dedication, 1884*, p. 8.

15. Schaff, *Life of Philip Schaff*, p. 289.

16. Gillett, "Detailed History," 3:815.

17. Prentiss, *Another Decade*, p. 311.

18. Jeschke, "The Briggs Case," p. 137.

19. Charles A. Briggs to Marvin Briggs, Jan. 8, 1867, Briggs Transcripts, 1:39, #3170.

20. William Adams Brown, *A Teacher and His Times: A Story of Two Worlds* (New York, 1940), pp. 77–78.

21. Jeschke, "The Briggs Case," p. 140.

22. James A. Ludlow to Briggs, Sept. 30, 1889, Briggs Transcripts, 7:496, #3723. "Hodgeolators" were those devoted to the strict interpretation of the Westminster Confession and the doctrine of biblical inerrancy as taught by the famous Princeton Seminary theologian Charles Hodge.

23. Jeschke, "The Briggs Case," p. 174; cf. pp. 142–48.

24. As quoted by Archibald A. Hodge, *The Life of Charles Hodge* (London, 1881), p. 521.

25. Max G. Rogers, "Charles Augustus Briggs: Heresy at Union," in Shriver, ed., *American Religious Heretics*, p. 93. A full treatment of the series is in Jeschke, "The Briggs Case," pp. 170–272.

26. Prentiss, *Another Decade*, pp. 328–34; quotation on p. 330.

4. The Trials of Charles Briggs

1. Prentiss, *Another Decade*, p. 311. The primary sources on the Briggs case are extensive; e.g., besides the 12 volumes of the Briggs Transcripts in the Union Library, there are also the Briggs Scrapbook of newspaper clippings and the Thomas S. Hastings Scrapbook. A vast amount of printed material representing various viewpoints was generated by the whole affair, of major importance are the *Minutes of the General Assembly of the Presbyterian Church in the United States of America* (henceforth *Minutes of the General Assembly*) for the years 1891, 1892, and 1893. The church also published many official documents relating to the trials and appeals before presbytery and assembly. Two good brief historical interpretations are by Lefferts A. Loetscher, "C. A. Briggs in the Retrospect of Half a Century," *Theology Today* (1955) 12:27–42, and ch. 6 of his *The Broadening Church*, and by Rogers in Shriver, ed., *American Religious Heretics*, ch. 3. Thorough dissertations are by Jeschke, "The Briggs Case," which focuses on the historical setting of the affair within Presbyterianism, and by Max Gray Rogers, "Charles Augustus Briggs: Conservative Heretic" (Ph.D. dissertation, Columbia University, 1964), which traces in detail the story of the events of 1891–93, and discusses Briggs'

later career. Carl E. Hatch, *The Charles A. Briggs Heresy Trial: Prologue to Twentieth-Century Liberal Protestantism* (New York, 1969), deals only with the veto and the first presbytery trial of 1891.

    2. As quoted in Prentiss, *Another Decade*, p. 332.

    3. Charles A. Briggs, *The Authority of Holy Scripture: An Inaugural Address* (2d. ed., New York, 1891), quotations on pp. 29–34, 36–38, 54, 61, 64.

    4. Loetscher, *The Broadening Church*, p. 52.

    5. Minutes of the Board of Directors, May 19, 1891; Prentiss, *Another Decade*, pp. 549–50.

    6. Briggs to Francis Brown, May 21, 1891, Briggs Transcripts, 8:183–84, #4114.

    7. Briggs, *The Authority of Holy Scripture*, 2d. ed., p. 161.

    8. Prentiss, *Another Decade*, pp. 262–67.

    9. Philip Schaff, "Other Heresy Trials and the Briggs Case," *The Forum* (Jan. 1892) 12:626–27.

    10. Briggs to Francis Brown, June 5, 1892, Briggs Transcripts, 8:361, #4501.

    11. *Minutes of the General Assembly*, 1892, pp. 66–67.

    12. Ibid., p. 179.

    13. Minutes of the Board of Directors, October 13, 1892.

    14. Prentiss, *Another Decade*, pp. 280–85.

    15. *Presbytery of New York. The Presbyterian Church in the United States of America Against the Rev. Charles A. Briggs, D.D. Argument of Rev. George W. F. Birch, D.D.* (New York, n.d. [1892?]), p. 41.

    16. [Charles A. Briggs] *The Defence of Professor Briggs before The Presbytery of New York, December, 13, 14, 15, and 19, 1892* (New York, 1893), p. 122.

    17. Ibid., p. 189.

    18. William Adams Brown, *A Teacher and His Times*, p. 99.

    19. There is an analysis of the vote in Jeschke, "The Briggs Trial," pp. 338–42.

    20. *One Hundred and Fifth General Assembly of the Presbyterian Church . . . 1893. The Presbyterian Church in the United States of America Against The Rev. Charles A. Briggs, D.D.: Notice of Appeal* (New York, [1893]), pp. 13–15.

    21. Loetscher, *The Broadening Church*, pp. 58–59.

    22. William Adams Brown, *A Teacher in His Times*, p. 157.

    23. John Crosby Brown to Briggs, May 27, 1893, and Charles Butler to Briggs, May 29, 1893, Briggs Transcripts, 9:12, #4840, and 9:15, #4843.

    24. *One Hundred and Fifth General Assembly of the Presbyterian Church . . . 1893. The Presbyterian Church in the United States of America, Apellant, Against The Rev. Charles A. Briggs, D.D., Appellee. Argument of Rev. Joseph J. Lampe, D.D.* (New York, [1893]), pp. 18–19.

    25. John J. McCook, comp., *The Appeal in the Briggs Heresy Case* (New York, 1893), p. 363.

    26. Minutes of the General Assembly, 1893, p. 165.

    27. Ibid., p. 169.

    28. D. Willis James to Charles Butler, June 3, 1893, Briggs Transcripts, 9:39, #4909.

    29. Minutes of the Board of Directors, June 13, 1893.

    30. As quoted by Prentiss, *Another Decade*, p. 362.

    31. Bound typescript in the Union Library, "Dedication Ceremonies, November 28th, 1910," p. 16. Brown repeated these words in his address at the Centennial, "A Century in Retrospect," *One Hundredth Anniversary, 1836–1936* (New York, 1936), p. 31.

32. B. A. Garside, *One Increasing Purpose: The Life of Henry Winters Luce* (New York, 1948), p. 39.

33. Henry H. Ranck to Mary H. Byrne, October 30, 1892, in the collection of Ranck letters of 1892–93 in the Union archives.

34. Schaff to Butler, June 29, 1893, and S. D. F. Salmond to Briggs, June 26, 1893, Briggs Transcripts, 9: 76–77, #4991, and 9:74, #4984.

35. Prentiss, *Another Decade*, p. 296.

36. Loetscher, *The Broadening Church*, p. 62.

37. Philip Schaff, *The Reunion of Christendom: A Paper Prepared for the Parliament of Religions and the National Conference of the Evangelical Alliance Held in Chicago, September and October, 1893* (New York, 1893), pp. 13, 31, 38.

38. Morgan Phelps Noyes, *Henry Sloane Coffin: The Man and His Ministry* (New York, 1964), p. 62.

39. In his sermon at the Centennial, *One Hundredth Anniversary*, p. 21. See ch. 7.

5. Liberal Evangelicalism

1. Robert W. Patterson to Thomas S. Hastings, July 4, 1893, Prentiss, *Another Decade*, pp. 323, 325.

2. Enrollment in 1894–95 was 142, of whom 120 were in the regular three-year theological course. Of the rest, 2 were winners of the traveling fellowship studying abroad, 12 were classed as "graduates"—usually those who came with a theological education but were doing advanced study and often earned a Union diploma, and 8 were special students who were taking selected courses.

3. Gillett, "Detailed History," 3:878–89.

4. Ibid., p. 817.

5. As quoted in unidentified newspaper clippings in Julie V. [Mrs. Charles A.] Briggs Scrapbook, in Charles A. Briggs Papers, Union Theological Seminary Archives.

6. Coffin, *A Half Century of Union*, p. 32.

7. Sherwood Eddy, *Eighty Adventurous Years: An Autobiography* (New York, 1955), pp. 28–29; cf. Coffin, *A Half Century of Union*, pp. 213–14, who also lists other graduates of the period who became missionaries.

8. "A Sketch of the Life and Public Services of Charles Butler, LL.D." is Part 5 of Prentiss, *Another Decade*, pp. 427–531.

9. Union Theological Seminary, *The Inauguration of the Rev. Charles Cuthbert Hall, D.D. . . . February Eighth, 1898* (New York, 1908), pp. 11–13, 27, 29, 31, 33–34, 36.

10. Coffin, *A Half Century of Union*, p. 43.

11. Basil Douglas Hall, *The Life of Charles Cuthbert Hall: "One Among a Thousand"* (New York, 1965), p. 146.

12. Coffin, *A Half Century of Union*, pp. 49–50.

13. Ibid., pp. 23, 51.

14. As quoted by Hall, *Hall*, p. 256.

15. Coffin, *A Half Century of Union*, p. 23.

16. Ibid., p. 129.

17. Hall, *Hall*, pp. 241, 156.

18. Gillet, "Detailed History," 3:820, 851.

19. Rogers, "Charles Augustus Briggs, Conservative Heretic," pp. 409–10. This dissertation has a long chapter on the last two decades of Briggs' life, pp. 382–483.

20. Hall, *Hall*, p. 134.

21. Loetscher, *The Broadening Church*, p. 72.

22. Hall, *Hall*, esp. pp. 169–70, 176–98, 212–45; quotations on pp. 212–13, 230.

23. Ibid., p. 137.

24. Ibid., pp. 206–9; Minutes of the Board of Directors, January 26, 1905, March 13, 1906, November 10, 1908; Gillett, "Detailed History," 1: 384–90.

25. *The Laying of the Corner-Stone of the New Buildings of the Union Theological Seminary and the Inauguration of the Reverend Professor Francis Brown as President of the Faculty, November Seventeenth, 1908* (New York [1908]), p. 8.

26. Ibid., p. 26.

6. A Shift of Emphasis

1. Coffin, *A Half Century of Union*, pp. 75–76; Gillett, "Detailed History," 2:477.

2. *The Laying of the Corner-Stone . . . and the Inauguration of the Reverend Francis Brown . . .*, pp. 35, 42, 44–45, 49.

3. *Classification of the Library of Union Theological Seminary in the City of New York, Prepared by Julia Pettee, Chief Cataloguer* (rev. ed., New York, 1967).

4. Stephen A. Schmidt, *A History of the Religious Education Association* (Birmingham, Ala., 1983), pp. 14, 33–39.

5. Bound typescript in the Union Library, "Dedication Ceremonies, November 28th, 1910," pp. 21, 50, 114, 134, 139, 142, 144, 153, 167, 184, 211–12.

6. Minutes of the Board of Directors, March 9, 1915.

7. Coffin, *A Half Century of Union*, pp. 183–85.

8. Jo Ann Ooiman Robinson, *Abraham Went Out: A Biography of A. J. Muste* (Philadelphia, 1981), p. 16.

9. Briggs to Dom. Laurentius Janssens, February 19, 1907, Briggs Transcripts, 10: 450, #7024; on the later years of Briggs' career, see Rogers, "Charles Augustus Briggs: Conservative Heretic," pp. 382-490.

10. William Adams Brown, "A Century in Retrospect," *One Hundredth Anniversary, 1836–1936*, pp. 28–29.

11. As quoted by Coffin, *A Half Century of Union*, p. 95.

12. Robert Moats Miller, *Harry Emerson Fosdick: Preacher, Pastor, Prophet* (New York, 1985).

13. The extensive papers of the Union School of Religion in the Seminary Archives have been arranged with a finding aid by Ruthmary Pollack (1982), to whose work on this matter and on the history of women at Union I am indebted.

14. Gaius Glenn Atkins, *Religion in Our Times* (New York, 1932), p. 156.

15. Paul H. Varg, *Missionaries, Chinese, and Diplomats: The American Protestant Missionary Movement in China, 1890–1952* (Princeton, 1958), p. 56.

16. William Adams Brown, *A Teacher and His Times*, p. 131; see. pp. 126–133 for the context, and Coffin, *A Half Century of Union*, pp. 160–68.

17. C. Allyn Russell, "Mark Allison Matthews: Seattle Fundamentalist and Civic Reformer," *Journal of Presbyterian History* (Winter 1979) 57:446–66.

18. *Minutes of the General Assembly, 1915*, p. 148. The incident has been compactly summarized by Loetscher, *The Broadening Church*, pp. 99–100; see also Minutes of the Board of Directors, November 11, 1913, March 10, 1914.

19. As quoted by Gillett, "Detailed History," 2:447.

20. Minutes of the Board of Directors, November 12, 1912, January 9, 1917.

21. *Memorial Service in Honour of the Rev. Francis Brown* (New York, 1916), p. 19.

22. *Mutchmoor: The Memoirs of James Ralph Mutchmoor* (Toronto, 1963), pp. 27, 30.

23. Minutes of the Board of Directors, November 14, 1916, November 13, 1917; Coffin, *A Half Century of Union*, p. 103.

24. File, "Protests and Petitions, 1917–1949," Seminary Archives.

25. Minutes of the Board of Directors, May 15, 1915, November 9, 1915, November 14, 1916, May 15, 1917; Coffin, *A Half Century of Union*, pp. 186–87; Gillett, "Detailed History," 2:716–717.

26. William Summerscales, *Affirmation and Dissent: Columbia's Response to the Crisis of World War I* (New York, 1970), p. 68; for a full discussion of that complex case which precipitated the resignation of historian Charles A. Beard from the university see pp. 72–102.

27. The letter was slightly edited and published as a pamphlet, *Union Theological Seminary & Christian Ethics: An Open Letter, Thomas C. Hall to William Kingsley* (n.p., 1920).

28. Arthur C. McGiffert, "The Seminary and the War," *Union Theological Seminary Bulletin* (November 1917) 1(1):3–5.

29. John F. Piper Jr., *The American Churches in World War I* (Athens, Ohio, 1985), pp. 35–37; on Fosdick see pp. 62–64 and his *The Living of These Days: An Autobiography* (New York, 1956).

30. Minutes of the Board of Directors, October 3, 1918, November 12, 1918, May 13, 1919.

31. "Inauguration of President McGiffert," *Union Theological Seminary Bulletin* (July 1918) 1(5):16–18, 22, 24, 27, 29–32, 36.

32. Coffin, *A Half Century of Union*, p. 100; see Eugene P. Link, *Labor-Religion Prophet: The Times and Life of Harry F. Ward* (Boulder, Col., 1984).

33. As quoted by Coffin, *A Half Century of Union*, pp. 113, 110.

34. Schmidt, *History of the Religious Education Association*, pp. 85–86; Minutes of the Board of Directors, November 14, 1922; William R. Hutchison, *The Modernist Impulse in American Protestantism* (Cambridge, Mass., 1976), pp. 156–158; Coffin, *A Half Century of Union*, pp. 88, 106, 188.

35. Robert L. Kelly, *Theological Education in America: A Study of One Hundred Sixty-One Theological Schools in the United States and Canada* (New York, 1924), p. 83.

36. Minutes of the Board of Directors, November 14, 1922.

37. Brochure, *Plans for Expansion*, Seminary Archives, esp. p. 4. A petition for a refectory signed by 129 students was attached to the board minutes for May 18, 1920.

38. Kelly, *Theological Education in America*, p. 195.

39. William Adams Brown, *The Church in America: A Study of the Present Condition and Future Prospects of American Protestantism* (New York, 1922), p. 119; on the Interchurch World Movement see Eldon G. Ernst, *Moment of Truth for Protestant America: Interchurch Campaigns following World War One* (Missoula, Mont., 1974.) I have written on the spiritual difficulties of the 1920s in "The American Religious Depression, 1925–1935,"

Church History (1960) 29:3–16, and in A Christian America: Protestant Hopes and Historical Realities (2d ed., New York, 1984), esp. ch. 7.
    40. Minutes of the Board of Directors, January 13, 1925.
    41. Report of the Faculty to the Board of Directors, 1921 (New York, 1921). Such annual reports were published in pamphlet form, 1910–1925, Seminary Archives.
    42. Kelly, Theological Education in America, p. 88.
    43. Interview with John C. Bennett, January 2, 1984, Claremont, Cal.
    44. As quoted in William G. Chrystal, ed., Young Reinhold Niebuhr: His Early Writings, 1911–1931 (St. Louis, 1977), p. 149.

7. Advance Through Storm
    1. Alumni Bulletin of Union Theological Seminary (December, 1926–January, 1927) 2:47.
    2. The title of the chapter is adapted from the title of the 7th volume of Kenneth S. Latourette's "A History of the Expansion of Christianity," Advance Through Storm (New York, 1945).
    3. On Coffin's life, see Morgan P. Noyes, Henry Sloane Coffin, and his chapters on aspects of his career in Reinhold Niebuhr, ed., This Ministry: The Contribution of Henry Sloane Coffin (New York, 1945), pp. 1–22; and in Coffin, A Half Century of Union, pp. 116–33.
    4. Alumni Bulletin (October–November, 1929) 2:19–20.
    5. Van Dusen, in Niebuhr, ed., This Ministry, pp. 29–30.
    6. Alumni Bulletin (December, 1926–January, 1927) 2:53-61.
    7. Edith Hunter, Sophia Lyon Fahs: A Biography (Boston, 1966), esp. ch. 16.
    8. Minutes of UTS Alumni Club, (Union Seminary Archives), Book 3, entry for May 27, 1929.
    9. On the founding and early years of the School of Sacred Music, see Skinner, Sacred Music at Union Theological Seminary, pp. 27–62; Coffin, A Half Century of Union, pp. 170–75; Noyes, Coffin, pp. 189–91.
    10. See Miller, Fosdick, pp. 150–73. 200–13.
    11. Gillett, "Detailed History," 3:1083–84; Minutes of the Board of Directors, November 9, 1926; Hunter, Fahs, pp. 155–61; Noyes, Coffin, pp. 183–84.
    12. Coffin, A Half Century of Union, p. 153.
    13. A full-length study of Van Dusen is by Dean K. Thompson, "Henry Pitney Van Dusen: Ecumenical Statesman" (Ph.D. dissertation, Union Theological Seminary, Richmond, Va. 1974).
    14. Sherwood Eddy, Eighty Adventurous Years: An Autobiography (New York, 1955), pp. 126–27; Noyes, Coffin, pp. 191–93.
    15. Coffin to Niebuhr, December 2, 1929.
    16. There are many books and articles about Niebuhr; see, e.g., June Bingham, Courage to Change: An Introduction to the Life and Thought of Reinhold Niebuhr (New York, 1961); Charles W. Kegley and Robert W. Bretall, eds., Reinhold Niebuhr: His Religious, Social, and Political Thought (New York, 1956); Ronald H. Stone, Reinhold Niebuhr: Prophet to Politicians (Nashville, 1972); Richard W. Fox, Reinhold Niebuhr: A Biography (New York, 1985); Robert McAfee Brown, ed., The Essential Reinhold Niebuhr: Selected Essays and Addresses (New Haven, 1986).
    17. Minutes of the Board of Directors, November 11, 1930.

18. Ibid., January 13, 1931; January 12, 1932; May 17, 1932; November 15, 1932; November 13, 1934.

19. Ibid., November 11, 1930; January 13, 1931; November 10, 1931; November 15, 1932; Student Conferences Box, Union Seminary Archives.

20. Eberhard Bethge, *Dietrich Bonhoeffer: Man of Vision, Man of Courage* (New York, 1970), esp. ch. 5; quotations from pp. 114, 113, xix.

21. Niebuhr, ed., *This Ministry*, p. 35.

22. Doris Webster Havice, *Roadmap for a Rebel* (New York, 1980), pp. 46, 60.

23. Minutes of the Board of Directors, November 13, 1934, January 8, 1935, March 12, 1935.

24. Noyes, *Coffin*, pp. 200–203.

25. There are many books and articles on Paul Tillich; e.g. see Charles W. Kegley and Robert W. Bretall, eds., *The Theology of Paul Tillich* (New York, 1952); Wilhelm and Marion Pauck, *Paul Tillich: His Life & Thought*, Vol. 1, *Life* (New York, 1976); for shorter accounts see Wilhelm Pauck, "Paul Tillich: Heir of the Nineteenth Century," in his *From Luther to Tillich: The Reformers and Their Heirs* (San Francisco, 1984), pp. 152–209; Lewis A. Coser, "Paul Tillich (1886–1965): Refugee Theologian à la Mode Américaine," in his *Refugee Scholars in America: Their Impact and Their Experiences* (New Haven, 1984), pp. 313–19; Coffin, *A Half Century of Union*, pp. 134–40.

26. Minutes of the Board of Directors, January 14 and March 10, 1936.

27. Ibid., January 10 and March 10, 1934; Noyes, *Coffin*, pp. 203–6; letters of Coffin to Stewart Meacham et al, April 7, 1934, To the students, May 23, 1934.

28. Hubert C. Herring, "Union Seminary Routs Its Reds," *The Christian Century*" (June 13, 1934) 51:799–801; "Correspondence," ibid. (June 27, 1934), 865–66.

29. "The Undercurrent" (November 9, 1934) 1:1.

30. John C. Bennett, "Exponent of Social Christianity," in Niebuhr, ed., *This Ministry*, pp. 88–89; interviews with Roger L. Shinn, April 4, 18, 1985.

31. James H. Robinson, *Road Without Turning* (New York, 1950), pp. 205–10; Robert S. Cocks to the author, June 22, 1985.

32. E.g., for short accounts with good bibliographical references see H. Shelton Smith, Robert T. Handy, and Lefferts A. Loetscher, *American Christianity: An Historical Interpretation with Representative Documents* (2 vols.; New York, 1960–63), ch. 20, edited and introduced by Smith, "The Post-Liberal Theological Mind," 2:426–504; Sydney E. Ahlstrom, *A Religious History of the American People* (New Haven, 1972), ch. 55, "Neo-Orthodoxy and Social Crisis," pp. 932–48. A treatment that focuses on Union is by John C. Bennett, "Change and Continuity in the Theological Climate at Union Seminary," *Union Seminary Quarterly Review* (1963) 18:357–67.

33. Reinhold Niebuhr, *Reflections on the End of an Era* (New York, 1934), pp. 171–72, 202.

34. Harry F. Ward, *Our Economic Morality and the Ethic of Jesus* (New York, 1929), and *In Place of Profit: Social Incentives in the Soviet Union* (New York, 1933); Link, *Labor-Religion Prophet*, p. 141. For an interpretation of Ward quite different from Link's, see Ralph L. Roy, *Communism and the Churches* (New York, 1960).

35. George D. McClain, "FBI File Reveals 'War' On Religious Dissenters," *Social Questions Bulletin* (March–April 1983) 73:1–2.

36. As quoted by Bingham, *Courage to Change*, p. 286.

37. Edward Fuller, *Brothers Divided* (New York, 1951), p. 122. Link, *Labor-Religion Prophet*, pp. 147–48, 245–46 discusses the tensions between Ward and Niebuhr.

38. Coffin, A *Half Century of Union*, p. 101; Elizabeth Dilling, *The Red Network: A "Who's Who" and Handbook of Radicalism for Patriots* (Kenilworth, Ill. 1934), p. 232.

39. As quoted by Link, *Labor-Religion Prophet*, p. 244.

40. The sermon is reprinted in the Centennial brochure: Union Theological Seminary, *One Hundredth Anniversary*, see esp. p. 21. Niebuhr's quotation is from Noyes, *Coffin*, pp. 193–94.

41. Henry P. Van Dusen, "The Premises of Theology and the Task of Preaching," *Religion in Life* (Spring 1937) 6:180–90.

42. Quotations from Minutes of the Board of Directors, May 19, 1936, and George B. Ford, A *Degree of Difference* (New York, 1969), p. 126.

43. Quotations from a carbon of the original in folder, "Protests and Petitions, 1917–1949," Union Seminary Archives, which differs slightly from the version in Coffin, A *Half Century of Union*, pp. 192–94.

44. Minutes of the Board of Directors, May 21, 1940.

45. Noyes, *Coffin*, pp. 212–19; Mark L. Chadwin, *The Hawks of World War II* (Chapel Hill, 1962), pp. 48–71.

46. The faculty resolution is from Coffin, A *Half Century of Union*, pp. 197–98; Walter Russell Bowie's remark is in his autobiography, *Learning to Live* (Nashville, 1969), p. 232.

47. Don Benedict, *Born Again Radical* (New York, 1982), p. 49; see pp. 30–54.

48. For this experience see Roger L. Shinn, *Wars and Rumors of War* (Nashville, 1972), esp. Part I.

49. Cyril C. Richardson, "The Seminary and Civil Defense," *Alumni Bulletin* (March 1942) 17:2.

50. Noyes, *Coffin*, pp. 226–32.

51. Henry Sloane Coffin to Reinhold Niebuhr, July 16, 1938; June 17, 1942; May 26, 1942; Niebuhr to James B. Conant, October 17, [1942]; November 9, 1942; February 15, 1943 (copies in the possession of the author through the courtesy of Carl Hermann Voss).

52. Quotations from Niebuhr, ed., *This Ministry*, pp. 35, 120, 128.

8. Ecumenicity and Expansion

1. *UTS Journal* (April, 1975), p. 20.

2. Union Theological Seminary, *The Inauguration of the Reverend Henry Pitney Van Dusen, S.T.D. as President of the Faculty* [New York, 1945], pp. 10, 31, 34.

3. Minutes of the Board of Directors, January 13, 1948.

4. Ibid., November 22, 1949, January 13, 1948; Archive Box, "Union Theological Seminary—President. Selection of President (1962–63)," UTS Archives; Thompson, "Van Dusen," p. 57.

5. William E. Hordern, in Harold E. Fey, ed., *How My Mind Has Changed* (Cleveland, 1961), p. 147; Frederick Buechner, *Now and Then* (San Francisco, 1983), p. 8; John Knox, *Never Far From Home: The Story of My Life* (Waco, 1975), pp. 122–23; F. W. Dillistone, C. H. Dodd: *Interpreter of the New Testament* (Grand Rapids, 1977), p. 171.

6. Minutes of the Board of Directors, October 25, 1960.

7. Ibid., May 23, 1950; Minutes of the Executive Committee of the Board of Directors, July 24, 1950; Minutes of the Faculty, May 10, 1950.

8. Minutes of the Board of Directors, January 10, 1961.

9. Ibid., October 24, 1950; October 25, 1955; October 25, 1960.

10. Van Dusen, "Afterword," in Coffin, *A Half Century of Union*, p. 241.

11. Buechner, *Now and Then*, p. 20. Muilenburg was the prototype of Kuykendall in Buechner's novel, *The Return of Ansel Gibbs* (New York, 1958).

12. Jaroslav Pelikan, ed., *Interpreters of Luther* (Philadelphia, 1968), preface.

13. Coser, *Refugee Scholars in America*, p. 317; Wilhelm and Marion Pauck, *Paul Tillich: His Life and Thought*, 1, *Life*, p. 248.

14. Nathan A. Scott Jr. *Reinhold Niebuhr* (Minneapolis, 1963), p. 45.

15. The addresses were published in *Union Seminary Quarterly Review* (1962–63) 18:295–305; 306–19; quotations on pp. 305, 308.

16. Kenneth Scott Latourette, *Beyond the Ranges: An Autobiography* (Grand Rapids, 1967), p. 151.

17. Van Dusen summarized an extensive evaluation of the program for the board; see Minutes of the Board of Directors, October 21, 1958.

18. Yorke Allen Jr., *A Seminary Survey* (New York, 1960), p. 577.

19. Minutes of the Faculty, October 19, 1952.

20. Van Dusen, in Coffin, *A Half Century of Union*, p. 245.

21. The story is told in a typescript in the Union Archives: Frederick Fox, "Truth . . . Unity . . . Love: A Century and a Quarter of Union Theological Seminary in the City of New York, 1836–1961," following p. 32.

22. The paper was published in *Union Seminary Quarterly Review* (January 1954) 9:31–34. For the larger picture, see John G. Van Dusen, "Morningside Heights, Inc." (senior thesis, Princeton University, 1954) copy in Union Library.

23. Bruce Kenrick, *Come Out the Wilderness: The Story of East Harlem Protestant Parish* (New York, 1962), p. 66. The files of the EHPP are now in the Union Archives.

24. Buechner, *Now and Then*, pp. 28–29.

25. As quoted in Thompson, "Van Dusen," p. 13.

26. Minutes of the Board of Directors, October 25, 1948. There were a number of articles on the First Assembly of the WCC in *Union Seminary Quarterly Review* (November, 1948), vol. 4.

27. Ch. 14 of Thompson's "Van Dusen" is entitled "Van Dusen's Ecumenical Finale: Working for New Delhi, 1961"; Van Dusen's *One Great Ground of Hope: Christian Missions and Christian Unity* (Philadelphia, 1961), published shortly before the Third Assembly, provides the background and rationale for the merger of the two councils.

28. Minutes of the Board of Directors, January 9, 1961.

9. Turmoil and Transition

1. Archive box: "UTS—President. Selection of President (1962–63)."

2. Mark Juergensmeyer, interviewer, *Conversations with John Bennett: Reflections on His Life and on the Career of Christian Ethics* (Berkeley: Graduate Theological Union, 1982), p. 86.

3. The address was published in pamphlet form: *Union Seminary Quarterly Review* (May, 1964) 19 (4, part 2):397–408; quotations on pp. 406, 407. It was also privately published in a "program supplement": *The Inauguration of John Coleman Bennett as President of Union Theological Seminary in the City of New York, April 10, 1964*, pp. 16–27.

4. *The Inauguration of John Coleman Bennett*, p. 5.

5. *Conversations with John Bennett*, pp. 72–75.

6. *The Inauguration of John Coleman Bennett*, p. 14.

7. The address was reprinted in Niebuhr's *Pious and Secular America* (New York, 1958), pp. 86–112, quotation at p. 108.

8. David Langston and William McKeown, *The Student Movement at Union Theological Seminary, 1963–1969*, a pamphlet written in cooperation with the Department of Ministry of the National Council of Churches, May, 1971, p. 1.

9. Walter R. Stroebel, "Personal and Academic Problems of Bachelor of Divinity Degree Candidates at a Large Metropolitan Theological Seminary" (Ed.D. dissertation, Teachers College, Columbia University, 1965), p. 80.

10. James H. Cone, *My Soul Looks Back* (Nashville, 1982), p. 52.

11. Tom F. Driver, "Prisoner of War: Vinny McGee," *UTS Journal* (October 1971), pp. 7–9.

12. Union Theological Seminary . . . February 5–8, 1967, "A report of an evaluation visit by a team representing the Commission on Institutions of Higher Education of the Middle States Association of Colleges and Secondary Schools, the American Association of Theological Schools, and the National Association of Schools of Music." A bound copy of the extensive mimeographed materials prepared for the evaluation, "A Report from Union Theological Seminary" (December 1966), is in the library.

13. Minutes of the Board of Directors, October 24, 1965.

14. *Crisis at Columbia: Report of the Fact Finding Commission Appointed to Investigate the Disturbances at Columbia University in April and May 1968* (New York, 1968), p. 10; the three issues are discussed on p. 75. See also Jerry L. Avorn, et al., *Up Against the Ivy Wall: A History of the Columbia Crisis* (New York, 1969), and Langston and McKeown, *The Student Movement at Union*, pp. 9–14.

15. The major resources for the history of the Union Commission are two bound volumes of mimeographed materials in the library, "The Minutes, Documents, Working Papers, and Reports of the Union Commission, 1968–1969"; a typescript by Jeffrey C. Slade, "A History of the Union Commission" (a draft copy is in the author's possession); and a pamphlet, *What's Ahead at Union Theological Seminary: The Report of the Union Commission, 1969* (New York, 1969), usually referred to as "the yellow book."

16. *Conversations with John Bennett*, p. 101.

17. Folder 4, Archive box: "Selection of President (1), 1968–1970."

18. Langston and McKeown, *The Student Movement at Union*, pp. 20–23; *Conversations with John Bennett*, pp. 90–93; interviews with John C. Bennett, January 2, 1984, and with Lawrence N. Jones, April 30, 1984; Minutes of the Board of Directors, May 15, 20, June 4, 1969; Minutes of the Union Assembly, April 1, 1970.

19. *Conversations with John Bennett*, pp. 95, 97.

20. Minutes of the Union Assembly, March 4, 1970.

21. Minutes of the Board of Directors, March 17, 1970; President's Newsletter (7), March 24, 1970.

22. Minutes of the Board of Directors, March 8 and October 25, 1966, May 23, 1967, January 14, 1969.

23. Minutes of the Union Assembly, May 5 and 6, 1970.

24. Reinhold Niebuhr, "John Coleman Bennett: Theologian, Churchman, and Educator," in Edward LeRoy Long Jr. and Robert T. Handy, eds., *Theology and Church in Times of Change* (Philadelphia, 1970), p. 236.

25. *Conversations with John Bennett*, p. 6.

26. Ibid., pp. 89, 76.

27. Minutes of the Board of Directors, January 19, 1971.

28. Mimeographed "Report of the Planning Group, Part I, Recommendations,"

pp. 1, 2, 5, 7. A copy of the report is bound with the Minutes of the Board of Directors, May 30–31, 1972; others are in the library. See also Minutes of the Union Assembly, May 15, 17, and September 13, 1972.

29. The paper and the responses were published under the heading "Collegiality: An Initial Exploration," *Union Seminary Quarterly Review* (1973) 28:285–98; quotations on pp. 287, 291, 294; see also Minutes of the Faculty, November 16, 1972, April 25 and May 14, 1973. A personal account of some of the episodes of these years which shows how deep tensions in the faculty were can be found in Tom F. Driver, *Patterns of Grace: Human Experience as Word of God* (San Francisco, 1977), ch. 3.

30. Minutes of the Union Assembly, October 24, 1973.

31. Minutes of the Executive Committee of the Board, January 10, 15, and 28, 1974; Minutes of the Union Assembly, February 20 and April 17, 1974.

32. Minutes of the Executive Committee of the Board, June 4, 1974; *New York Times*, Wednesday, June 5, 1974; Minutes of the Board of Directors, October 23–24, 1973, June 25, 1974.

33. *Conversations with John Bennett*, pp. 102–3.

34. Minutes of the Board of Directors, October 22–23, 1974; Shinn's report is appended; quotations on pp. 4, 17.

35. Ibid., February 4, 1975.

36. Ibid., June 3, 1975.

37. Ibid., July 10, 1975.

38. Ibid., June 3, 1975.

10. Reaffirmation

1. Donald W. Shriver, Jr., "The Heart's Love Uttered with the Mind's Conviction," *Union Seminary Quarterly Review* (Fall 1976), 32:10–15.

2. Linda J. Clark, "Music at Union," *Union News* (March 1976), pp. 1, 3–4.

3. Robert McAfee Brown, *Creative Dislocations—The Movement of Grace* (Nashville, 1980), pp. 41–44.

4. Donald W. Shriver Jr., "An Educational Research Program. Why?" *Union News* (October 1976), p. 2.

5. ATS/MSA team, "Report of a Visit to Union Theological Seminary, New York, November 6–9, pp. 1, 14; a summary appeared in *Union News* (Spring 1978), pp. 1–2.

6. Marvin J. Taylor, "A Theological Faculties Profile: 1981 Data Compared with the 1971 Study," *Theological Education* (Autumn 1982) 19:138.

7. *Union News* (1979 #2), p. 2; *Union News* (September 1984), p. 10; see also *Auburn News*, published since 1977.

8. "The Report of the Committee on Educational Excellence in the 1980's" (February 17, 1981), quotations on pp. 2, 13, 16.

9. Minutes of the Board of Directors, February 17, 1981.

10. The committee report was discussed in considerable detail from the viewpoint of students in their newsletter of that period, "Balaam's Ass" (April 6, 1981), pp. 1–9.

11. Minutes of the Board of Directors, February 28, 1984; April 17, 1984; January 14, 1985.

12. Cone, *My Soul Looks Back*, p. 73.

13. *New York Times*, Sunday, May 30, Sec. E, p. 5; *Christian Century*, 99 (July 7–14, 1982), 773.

14. Minutes of the Board of Directors, February 6, 1979; April 16–17, 1979; *Union News* (1979 #2), p. 4.

15. *Union News* (January 1985), p. 5; ibid. (September 1985), p. 3

16. Ibid.; Minutes of the Board of Directors, April 22, 1985.

17. As quoted in "Balaam's Ass" (September 1984), p. 1.

18. Bound typescript in the Union Library, "Dedication Ceremonies, November 28th, 1910," p. 222.

19. Timothy Light, in a letter to the author, February 8, 1985.

Bibliographical Note

The bibliographical resources relevant to Union's history are vast but often diffuse. Many prominent Union figures have extensive bibliographies of their own, not only including books and articles they have written but biographies and essays about them, some of which are listed in the notes for each chapter. The papers of a number of these persons are kept in the seminary archives in the Burke Library, along with extensive other publications and records such as catalogs, alumni/ae directories and bulletins, reprints of inaugural addresses, student newsletters, promotional materials, audio tapes, and photographs. Here also are kept formal records of the Board of Directors, the Faculty, and other seminary organizations, and they are referred to where appropriate in the notes. Histories of Union have been prepared by Edwin F. Hatfield, *The Early Annals of Union Theological Seminary in the City of New York* (New York, 1876), included also as part of a *General Catalogue of Union Theological Seminary in the City of New-York, 1836–1876* (New York, 1876); George Lewis Prentiss, *The Union Theological Seminary in the City of New York: Historical and Biographical Sketches of its First Fifty Years* (New York, 1889), and *The Union Theological Seminary in the City of New York: Its Design and Another Decade of Its History* (Asbury Park, 1899); Charles R. Gillett, "Detailed History of the Union Theological Seminary in the City of New York: Containing all of the items of importance found in the Archives, the Minutes and other records of the

Board of Directors, of the Faculty, and of the various Committees of both bodies" (3 vols., typescript, n.d. [1937?]; and Henry Sloane Coffin, *A Half Century of Union Theological Seminary, 1896–1945: An Informal History* (New York, 1954). William Adams Brown gave many historical addresses about Union, concluding with his address at the Centennial, "A Century in Retrospect," published in the pamphlet, *Union Theological Seminary: One Hundredth Anniversary, New York, May 16–19, 1936* (New York, 1936) pp. 26–38. Other publications that provide useful information about aspects of Union's history include an unpublished typescript by Frederick Fox, "Truth . . . Unity . . . Love: A Century and a Quarter of Union Theological Seminary in the City of New York, 1938–1961" (New York, n.d. [1961?]; Milton M. Gatch, "Maintaining Academic Quality in Economic Gridlock," *Theological Education* (Autumn 1982) 19:89–98; a pamphlet by David Langston and William McKeown, *The Student Movement at Union Theological Seminary, 1963–1969* (New York, n.d. [1969?]; Ellouise W. Skinner, *Sacred Music at Union Theological Seminary, 1936–1953: An Informal History* (New York, 1963); and Walter R. Stroebel, "Personal and Academic Problems of Bachelor of Divinity Degree Candidates at a Large Metropolitan Seminary" (Ed.D. dissertation, Teachers College, Columbia University, 1965). The files of the *Union Seminary Quarterly Review* contain a number of articles which help to illumine Union's history; some have been referred to in the notes. There are entries on Union in various studies of theological education; for example: Robert L. Kelly, *Theological Education in America: A Study of One Hundred Sixty-one Theological Schools in the United States and Canada* (New York, 1924); Mark A. May and William Adams Brown, *The Institutions that Train Ministers*, vol. 3 of a series on *The Education of American Ministers* (New York, 1934); Claude Welch, *Graduate Education in Religion: A Critical Appraisal* (Missoula, Montana 1971).

One of the most crucial episodes in Union's history, the trials of Charles A. Briggs, has produced a large body of primary and secondary sources of its own; especially important for the larger history are Channing R. Jeschke, "The Briggs Case: The Focus of a Study in Nineteenth Century Presbyterian History" (Ph.D. thesis, University of Chicago, 1966); Max Gray Rogers, "Charles Augustus Briggs: Conservative Heretic" (Ph.D. thesis, Columbia University,

1964), and his "Charles Augustus Briggs: Heresy at Union," in George
H. Shriver, ed., *American Religious Heretics: Formal and Informal
Trials* (Nashville, 1966), pp. 89–147; see also Lefferts A. Loetscher's
informative study, *The Broadening Church: A Study of Theological
Issues in the Presbyterian Church since 1869* (Philadelphia, 1954).

References to Union in autobiographical writings are es-
pecially helpful in disclosing the atmosphere of a particular period of
Union's life. For example: Don Benedict, *Born Again Radical* (New
York, 1982); *Conversations with John Bennett: Reflections on his Life
and on the Career of Christian Ethics*, interviewed by Mark Juer-
gensmeyer (Berkeley, 1982); Walter Russell Bowie, *Learning to Live*
(Nashville, 1969); Robert McAfee Brown, *Creative Dislocation—The
Movement of Grace* (Nashville, 1980); William Adams Brown, *A
Teacher and His Times: A Story of Two Worlds* (New York, 1940);
Frederick Buechner, *Now and Then* (San Francisco, 1983); James H.
Cone, *My Soul Looks Back* (Nashville, 1982); Harry Emerson Fos-
dick, *The Living of These Days: An Autobiography* (New York, 1956);
Doris Webster Havice, *Roadmap for a Rebel* (New York, 1980); Carter
Heyward, *A Priest Forever* (New York, 1976); John Knox, *Never Far
from Home: The Story of my life* (Waco, Texas 1975); *Mutchmoor:
The Memoirs of James Ralph Mutchmoor* (Toronto, 1963); *Road
Without Turning: The Story of Reverend James H. Robinson, An Au-
tobiography* (New York, 1950); and Paul Tillich, *On the Boundary:
An Autobiographical Sketch* (New York, 1966).

Some of the biographical studies that include informative
insights into the story of Union are: Eberhard Bethge, *Dietrich Bon-
hoeffer: Man of Vision, Man of Courage* (New York, 1970); June
Bingham, *Courage to Change: An Introduction to the Life and Thought
of Reinhold Niebuhr* (New York, 1961); Richard Wightman Fox,
Reinhold Niebuhr: A Biography (New York, 1985); Basil Douglas Hall,
The Life of Charles Cuthbert Hall; "One Among a Thousand" (New
York, 1965); Edith Hunter, *Sophia Lyon Fahs* (Boston, 1966); Eu-
gene P. Link, *Labor-Religion Prophet: The Times and Life of Harry
F. Ward* (Boulder, Colorado, 1984; Robert Moats Miller, *Harry
Emerson Fosdick: Preacher, Pastor, Prophet* (New York, 1985); Mor-
gan Phelps Noyes, *Henry Sloane Coffin: The Man and His Ministry*
(New York, 1964); Wilhelm and Marion Pauck, *Paul Tillich: His
Life and Thought*, Vol. 1, *Life* (New York, 1976); David S. Schaff,

The Life of Philip Schaff: In Part Autobiographical (New York, 1897); George H. Shriver, *Philip Schaff: Christian Scholar and Ecumenical Prophet* (Macon, Georgia, 1986; Lewis French Stearns, *Henry Boynton Smith* (Boston, 1892); and Dean K. Thompson, "Henry Pitney Van Dusen: Ecumenical Statesman" (Ph.D. dissertation, Union Theological Seminary, Richmond, Virginia, 1974).

Index

Academic standards, 58, 94-96, 111-12, 124, 128-29, 287, 294-95, 309
Academic year, 40, 60, 203, 300
Accreditation: 1967, 272-73; 1977, 326-27
Adams, William, 29, 44-45, 51-55, 59-60
Allen, Horace T. Jr., 277
Andover Theological Seminary, 3, 11, 13-14, 22, 92
Association of Theological Schools, 153, 213, 233, 234; see also Accreditation
Auburn Theological Seminary, 4, 45; located at Union, 198-99, 222, 226, 287, 309, 326; Auburn Affirmation, 162
Ault, James M., 222, 266, 270

Bachman, John W., 242
Baillie, John, 173-74, 254-55
Baker, Robert S., 250, 298
Baldwin, John Center, 34; see also Endowed chairs
Barnes, Albert, 5
Barrick, William F., 270
Bates, M. Searle, 240, 244
Beach, Robert F., 221, 308, 311
Benedict, Donald L., 202, 252
Bennett, John C.: as faculty member, 176, 187-88, 196, 206, 216-17, 220, 231, 233-
34, 251, 255; as acting president and president, 257, 260-73, 281-84, 287, 289-90, 293; retirement, 291, 305
Berg, Earl F., 249-50, 298
Bergland, James W., 270, 300, 309
Bethge, Eberhard, 178, 319, 333, 335
Bewer, Julius A., 107, 140, 204
Biblical field, 10-14, 39, 50, 53-55, 96, 99-100, 107-8, 147, 149, 166, 182, 205-6, 222, 228-30, 263-64, 287-88, 295, 319-20
Bilderback, Carolyn, 330
Birch, George W.: 79, 81, 83-84, 87-88, 113
Black, Hugh, 107-8, 133, 174, 182
Black Panthers, 285
Blacks at Union: students, 41, 178-79, 188-89, 209, 252, 265-66, 281-82, 323, 341; faculty, 266-67, 282, 296-97, 341
Board of Directors: formation, 6-9, 11, 18; and Presbyterian reunion (1869–70), 45; prominent members, 58, 218-19; and Briggs case, 74-75, 77, 79, 82, 90; interdenominationalized, 114, 137; tenured professor dismissed, 141-42; tension with students, 281-82, 286-87; see also Divestment, Endowed charis, Finances, Governance since 1967
Bonhoeffer, Dietrich, 177-78, 287, 319
Boorman, James, 20-21, 33-34
Bowen, George, 16, 23

372 INDEX

Bowie, Walter Russell, 184, 201, 222, 242, 254
Briggs, Charles A., 41-42, 53-55, 60-93, 95-100, 102, 108-10, 112-14, 128-29, 131-32, 353n9, 354n1
Briggs, Emilie Grace, 97-98
Briggs, Julia Valentine, 126
Britton, Blanche M., 221, 313
Brown, Francis: as faculty member, 54-55, 75-76, 96, 100, as acting president and president, 115, 118, 121-25, 128, 130, 132-33, 136-37; illness and death, 138-39, 147; quoted, 345-46
Brown, James, 34, 52, 99, 102
Brown, John Crosby, 58, 83, 87, 99, 102, 112, 115-16, 118, 155
Brown, Raymond E., 263-64, 295, 309
Brown, Robert McAfee, 217, 233, 318, 321-22
Brown, Sydney, 318, 321-22
Brown, Thatcher M., 194, 218
Brown, William Adams: on Briggs, 63, 87, 90; as faculty member, 99-100, 109, 128, 130, 136, 139, 143, 167, 172-74; at Centennial, 132, 194-96; as acting president, 139, 156; retirement, 182; William Adams Brown Ecumenical Library, 243
Brunner, Emil, 189, 254
Buechner, Frederick, 216, 229, 253, 334
Burke, Walter, 312, 335, 340
Butler, Charles, 33, 70, 83, 87, 90-91, 102, 131
Butler, Nicholas Murray, 141, 194
Buttrick, George A., 237, 253-54
Buyske, Donna, 345

Carmody, Francis, 108, 172-73
Casteel, John L., 205-6, 240, 242
Cavert, Samuel McCrea, 131, 143, 195, 255, 259
Chapel, 14, 40, 110-11, 126-27, 133-34, 165, 170, 250-51, 288-89; 330-33
Christianity and Crisis, 200
Chong, Frank, 293
Civil Rights Vigil, 266
Civil War, 41-42, 47, 50
Clark, Linda J., 319, 330, 332
Clarke, L. Mason, 140-41
Coe, George A., 125-26, 130, 134, 149-50

Coffin, Henry Sloane, x, 39, 92, 100, 106, 110-11; as faculty member, 107, 133-34, 143; as president, 159-72, 174-81, 184-88, 192-201; retirement, 205, 207-9, 211
Coffin, William Sloane, 268
Cohen, Gerson, 335
Collegiality, 296, 302-3, 364n29
Columbia University, 61, 96, 117-21, 126, 129-30, 136, 141-42, 164, 167-68, 204-5, 214, 224, 238, 249, 273-74, 328
Cone, James H., 267, 309-10, 314, 341
Corwin, Virginia, 179
Cox, Mary Jordan, 340-41
Craig, Rena S., 222
Curriculum, 3-4, 40-41, 59-60, 95-97, 108-9, 151-53, 164, 198, 227-28, 234, 260, 269-70, 273, 275-78, 352n10
Curry, A. Bruce Jr., 173

Davies, William D., 230
Davison, Walter S., 199
Dawe, Donald G., 235
Degrees: seminary, 97, 109, 152, 170, 223, 238, 294, 298; joint with Columbia, and Teachers College, 167-68, 238, 328
Depression, 159, 175-77, 179-80, 184
Dickinson, Clarence, 168-70, 204, 208, 249
Dickinson, Helen, 168-70, 208, 249
Divestment, 268-69, 343-45
Dodge, William E., 55, 83, 114
Dodge, William E. Jr., 56, 58, 83
Dodson, Jualynne E., 330, 337
Dorner, Isaac, 48, 53, 73
Driver, Tom F., 246-47, 309
Dulles, John Foster, 218, 255
Dyer, Randolph H., 220, 300

East Harlem Protestant Parish, 252-53
Ecumenism, 91-92, 104, 112, 114, 131, 170, 195-96, 213-14, 218, 231, 240-41, 243, 254-56, 260, 318, 342
Eddy, Sherwood, 101, 175
Educational excellence, committee on, 336-39
Elliott, Harrison S., 150, 238
Endowed chairs, historic, Baldwin, 34; Briggs, 132; Brown, 34; Butler, 131; Coffin, 208; Danforth, 249; Davenport, 33-34; Dickinson, 249; Dodge, 114; Fosdick, 241; Hark-

ness, 154, 168; Hartley, 106; Jesup, 58, 108, 114; Luce, 240; Niebuhr, 233; Roosevelt, 31; Skinner and McAlpin, 53, 58; Tangeman, 287; Washburn, 34—in 1980s: Beaird, 330; Engle, 330; John D. Rockefeller Jr., 330

Enrollment, 14-15, 41-42, 47-48, 60, 98, 111-12, 129-30; 139, 144, 153-54, 166, 176, 203-4, 214-15, 223, 265, 291, 323, 337, 340, 356n2

Evangelical Alliance, 55, 92

Evangelical, evangelicalism, *see* Theological currents

Evans, Clarke, 344

Faculty: founding to 1910, 11-12, 20-21, 40, 54, 75-76, 100-102, 108-9, 112-14; 1910 to 1986, 139-40, 131, 157, 167, 204-5, 219-20, 270, 291-92, 299, 302-3, 308, 311-12, 318-21, 338-40

Fagnani, Charles P., 99-100, 109

Fahs, Sophia Lyon, 166, 172, 204

Fahs, Charles H., 171

Fellowship of Reconciliation, 179, 190, 200

Fellowship of Socialist Christians, 190

Field work (later field education, professional development), 8-9, 40, 60, 109-10, 151-52, 239-40, 269-70

Finances, 19-20, 31-34, 52, 56, 118, 126, 152-57, 168, 170, 176, 182, 204, 208, 215, 284, 292, 295, 305-8, 328-30, 335-41; *see also* Endowed chairs; Student fees

Finkelstein, Louis, 264

Fisher, A. Franklin, 178

Fleming, Daniel J., 135-36, 202, 204

Florovsky, George, 243, 255

Forbes, James H., 318-19, 330, 344

Ford, George B., 196

Fordham University, 262-63

Fosdick, Harry Emerson, 110-11, 133-34, 143, 145, 171, 194, 200, 236-38, 241, 308

Frame, James E., 100, 149, 182

"Free University" at Union, 1968, 274-75

French, Richard F., 287, 298, 302

Fuller, Reginald A., 287-88, 309

Fund for Theological Education, 223-24

Fundamentalist-Modernist controversy, 136-37, 162, 172

Gatch, Milton McCormick Jr., 327-28, 344

General Theological Seminary, 18, 129

Gilkey, Charles W., 161

Gillett, Charles R., 59, 90, 122, 138, 172, 352n15

Gordon, David, 345

Governance since 1967, 270, 274-78, 284, 303-6, 313; *see also* Union Assembly, Union Commission

Great Awakening: first, 1; second, 1, 26

Grant, Frederick C., 182, 203, 206, 227

Green, William H., 67, 77

Greenawalt, Jack C., 248, 270-71, 309

Greene, Amy, 345

Guido, Judith Cooper, 329

Gutiérrez, Gustavo, 319

Hahn, Raymond Jr., 300, 308

Haines, Richard T., 6, 19

Hall, Charles Cuthbert, 102-118, 125, 128, 135, 171; Barrows Lectures, 115-16

Hall, Thomas C., 106-7, 125, 140-43, 147

Handy, Robert T., 230-31, 293, 296, 306, 309, 326-27

Hargraves, J. Archie, 252

Häring, Bernard, 263

Harkness, Edward S., 154, 168

Harris, Erdman, 173

Harrison, Beverly Wildung, 260, 295, 309, 314, 322, 337

Harsh, Robert, 289

Hartshorne, Hugh, 134, 150

Harvin, Henrietta, 313

Hastings, Thomas S., 54, 61, 75-76, 83, 90, 95, 97-98, 100-2, 104, 107

Havemeyer, Rosalind E., 251, 293, 306, 311-12

Havice, Doris Webster, 179

Hawk, David R., 268

Hayes, Ardith S., 320, 337

Hendrickson, John H., 287, 309

Herring, Hubert C., 186-87

Herriott, Frank, 180-81, 202, 239

Heschel, Abraham Joshua, 264-65

Hickman, Charles L., 250

Historical field, 21-22, 29-31, 37-38, 51, 55, 96, 100, 107, 173, 181, 199, 206-7, 230-31, 266-67, 288, 319-20, 327, 338

Hitchcock, Roswell D., 19, 37-38, 41, 45, 52, 54-57, 61
Hodge, Archibald A., 64-66, 85, 89
Hodge, Charles, 35, 43-44, 64-65, 82, 85, 89
Hoekendijk, Johannes C., 272, 309
Holbrook, Charles H., 135
Hoon, Paul W., 237, 251, 309
Hordern, William E., 216
Horn, Robert L., 235
Hornbeck, David, 268
Hume, Robert E., 131, 135-36, 148, 204-5
Hyslop, Ralph D., 244
Hyun, Younghak, 342

Iglehart, Charles W., 207, 240
Imes, William Loyd, 209
Interchurch World Movement, 155, 358n39
Interpreter's Bible, 253-54
Interreligious Foundation for Community Organization, 281-82
Inter-Seminary Theological Education for Ministry, 301
Irwin, John N. II, 218-19, 229, 256, 281, 293

Jackson, F. J. Foakes, 132, 172
James, Arthur C., 154, 168
James, D. Willis, 45, 56, 58, 83, 90, 114, 116-18, 126
January Lectures, 250-51; see also Monday Lectures
Jeffery, Arthur, 205
Jesup, Morris K., 58, 83
Jewish Theological Seminary of America, 199-200, 264-65, 335
Johnson, Thomas S., 340
Jones, Lawrence N., 266-67, 282, 287, 293, 296, 309-10
Juergensmeyer, Mark, 291

Kachel, A. Theodore, 274-75
Kelly, Robert L., 151, 154
Kennedy, Edwin O., 221, 223
Kennedy, William B., 321, 344
King, Martin Luther Jr., 261, 273
Kingsley, Ezra M., 81
Kingsley, William M., 141-42, 194
Knight, James A., 248
Knox, George William, 106, 114, 116, 122, 131, 135, 148
Knox, John, 206, 217, 227, 254, 261, 287

Koenig, John T., 319
Koyama, Kosuke, 321-22, 342
Kraeling, Emil, 147, 204
Kroner, Richard, 205, 231
Küng, Hans, 263

Lampe, Joseph J., 79, 85, 88
Landes, George M., 230, 309
Lane Theological Seminary, 4, 45, 100
Lasserre, Jean, 178
Latourette, Kenneth Scott, 244
Leatherwood, Thomas O., 266
Lee, Robert, 240
Lehmann, Paul L., 177, 235-36, 267, 287, 302, 308, 314
Leiper, Henry Smith, 131
Library: University Place, 14, 18, 35, 53; Park Avenue, 56-59, 117, 124; Broadway, 124-25, 147, 206, 221, 224, 273, 311, 333-35; see also Missionary Research Library
Library of Christian Classics, 254
Light, Timothy, 346-47
Lincoln, C. Eric, 267, 309
Lindsay, Mary, 277
Logan, Willis, 289
Loomis, Earl A. Jr., 247-48
Loetscher, Lefferts A., 44, 73, 86
Lotz, David W., 288, 309
Luce, Henry R., 218
Luce, Henry W., 90, 101
Lyman, Eugene W., 148-49, 166, 182, 204, 222, 234
Lyman, Mary Ely, 166, 222, 242, 251
Lynn, Robert W., 239-40, 309

McAlpin, David H., 53, 58, 59
McAuley, Thomas, 6-7, 11, 18, 20
McCook, John J., 77, 79, 81, 83, 87-89
McCormick Theological Seminary, 4, 66, 129
McCormick, Wendy, 344
McCracken, Robert J., 238
McGee, Vincent F. Jr., 268
McGiffert, Arthur C.: as president, 42, 121, 139, 143-47, 150, 152-53, 155-57, 159, 167; as professor, 100, 107, 113-14, 117, 132, 136, 173
McGiffert, Arthur C. Jr., 8, 143, 351n8, 354n10
McNeill, John T., 206-7, 230, 254
Macquarrie, John, 235-36, 267, 284

Maguire, John D., 279-80
Maloy, Robert F., 311, 334
Markley, Lucy, 206, 224
Martin, J. Alfred Jr., 249
Martinez, Sergio Arce, 342
Martyn, J. Louis, 230, 302, 309
Mason, Erskine, 2, 6, 11
Mathews, Charles E., 222, 240, 251
Matthews, Mark A., 136-38
M.Div. Design Team, 297, 301
Methodist Federation for Social Service, 147, 191
Meyers, Eleanor Scott, 339
Missionary Research Library, 170-71, 243
Mission emphasis, 16-17, 23, 39, 101, 115, 135-36, 154, 196, 240, 244
Moffatt, James, 172-73, 182, 206
Monday Lectures, 287, see also January Lectures
Morgan, Edwin D., 52, 56
Morningside Heights, Inc., 252, 362n22
Morrow, Dwight, W., 167, 195
Morrow, Elizabeth Cutter, 195, 251
Morse, Christopher, 310
Mosley, J. Brooke, 286-87, 293-96, 301-6
Muchmoor, James, 139, 143
Muilenberg, James, 217, 228-30, 287
Music program, 21, 40-41, 108, 319, 332; see also School of Sacred Music
Muste, Abraham J., 130

Neale, Robert E., 248, 309
Neander, August, 11, 26, 48
Nelson, C. Ellis, 239, 269, 272, 283, 293, 309
New York University, 14, 61, 96, 108, 129
Nichols, Robert Hastings, 199, 204, 206
Niebuhr, H. Richard, 189, 234
Niebuhr, Reinhold, 157, 174-76, 181, 183, 189-90, 192, 195-96, 199, 202-3, 206, 208-9, 216, 220, 232-34, 255, 264, 267, 288, 324, 359n16
Nordheimer, Isaac, 13
Norris, Richard A. Jr., 320
Noyes, Morgan P., 92, 237

Office of Education Research, 324-26
Ogden, Robert Curtis, 128, 141
Oxford Life and Work Conference, 196

Parker, Grace Keefer, 342
Parker, Joel, 20
Parkhurst, Charles H., 61, 120
Parlin, Charles C., 218, 255
Parrish, Walter, 344
Patton, Francis L., 44, 66, 77
Patton, William, 6, 8
Pauck, Wilhelm, 217, 230, 254, 261, 288
Pelikan, Jaroslav, 328, 333
Pellauer, Mary D., 320
Pellegrom, Daniel E., 274
Pesante, Georgina, 328-29
Peters, Absalom, 6
Pettee, Julia, 124-25
Pitkin, Horace T., 101, 135
Planning Group, 295-300, 305
Porter, Hugh, 249-50
Portland Deliverance, 82, 89
Post, Avery, 268, 304
Powers, Charles W., 268, 277
Practical field, 11, 20-21, 38-39, 52-54, 96, 102, 107-8, 133-34, 173, 184, 199, 206, 222, 236-50, 311, 319-20, 339. See also Field work, Mission emphasis, Music program, Psychiatry and religion program, Religious education, School of Sacred Music
Preamble to the Constitution, 6-9, 11, 186, 351n9
Prentiss, George L., ix, 22, 31-33, 38, 47, 51-54, 69-70, 75, 91, 100-2, 135
Presbyterianism: Old School-New School tensions, 2, 4-5, 19; reunion of 1869-70, 42-47, 61-67, 353n23; Briggs trials and aftermath, 69-95, 112-14; since 1910, 136-38, 162, 198-99, 207
Presbyterian Review, 64-65
Presidential search committees: 1916-17, 139; 1926, 159; 1945, 211; 1962-63, 259-60; 1968-70, 279-80, 285-86; 1974-75, 312
Princeton Theological Seminary, 3-4, 8, 11, 22, 44-45, 54, 64-67, 77, 85
Professional development, see Field work
Program of Advanced Religious Studies, 223, 243-44, 272
Psychiatry and religion program, 247-48

Quigley, John L., 270-71

Ranck, Henry, 91
Rauschenbusch, Walter, 130

Read, David H. C., 211-12
Reed, Frank O., 308
Reeve, John Bunyan, 41
Refectory, 14, 40, 60, 111, 153-54, 166-67, 204, 295, 324, 332
Religious drama, 246-47
Religious education, 125-26, 134, 149-50, 238-39, 325
Richardson, Cyril C., 202-3, 217, 227, 230, 254, 260-61, 308-9, 320; Memorial Lectures, 333
Riverside Church, 171-72, 213, 281
Robarts, William M., 311
Roberts, David E., 182, 202, 231, 247
Roberts, Samuel K., 311, 318
Robinson, Edward, 10-14, 18, 20-1, 39-40, 70
Robinson, James H., 188-89
Robinson, Thomas L., 320
Rockefeller, John D. Jr., 138, 154, 171; see also Endowed chairs
Rockefeller, John D. III, 241
Rockwell, William W., 107, 114, 124, 206
Roosevelt, James, 31
Rosborough, Bonnie, 329
Ross, George A. Johnston, 133, 140, 172
Rowthorn, Jeffery W., 276, 298, 302

St. Vladimir's Russian Orthodox Seminary, 243
Sanders, James A., 287-88, 303, 309
Saucer, Bobby Joe, 297
Schaff, Philip, 35, 38, 47-51, 54-56, 59, 75-76, 80, 91, 353n3
Scherer, Paul, 217, 237, 251, 254
Schmidt, Stephen, 150
School of Sacred Music, 168-70, 179, 218, 249-50, 273, 287, 298-99, 319; see also Music program
Schram, William C., 279
Scott, Ernest F., 149, 174, 182
Scott, Nathan A., 232
Seaver, Robert E., 242, 246-47, 277, 306, 309, 329-30, 335
Selective Service Act, 1940: 200-1
Settlement house movement, 100-1; see also Union Settlement
Shedd, William G. T., 39, 44, 54, 74-76, 79, 85, 98

Sheppard, Gerald T., 319
Sherrill, Helen H., 222, 260
Sherrill, Louis J., 238-39
Shinn, Roger L.: as student: 198, 202; as faculty member, 234-35, 260, 265, 267, 309-10, 326; as acting president, 306-8, 313
Shriver, Donald W. Jr., x, 312-13, 315-18, 323-27, 332, 336-37, 344
Skinner, Thomas H., 21, 31, 33, 38, 51, 53
Skirvin, Sidney D., 270, 309, 326, 329
Slade, Jeffrey, 277
Slavery, 9, 17, 41-42, 55
Smart, James D., 242, 308
Smith, Henry Boynton, 21-22, 25-31, 33-38, 41-44, 48, 51, 53, 55, 58, 72-73, 98, 352n8
Smith, Henry Preserved, 147
Smith, Timothy H., 269
Snyder, T. Richard, 301
Social Creed of the Churches, 147
Social gospel, 61, 105, 109-10, 130, 147-48, 165, 224
Sockman, Ralph W., 154, 238, 255
Sölle, Dorothee, 311, 314, 319, 337, 339
Soup kitchen, 345
Speers, T. Guthrie Jr., 304
Spoor, Richard, 334
Stanton, Norman D., 329
Stearns, Lewis French, 98
Steffensky, Fulbert, 319
Steimle, Edmund A., 237, 309
Stinnette, Charles E., 248
Stoerker, Mildred B., 313, 326
Strong, Benjamin, 218
Stuart, Moses, 11, 13, 39
Student enrollment, 14-16, 41-42, 47-48, 60, 98, 111-12, 129-30, 139, 144, 153-54, 166, 176-78, 203-4, 214-15, 223, 265, 291, 323, 337, 340, 356n2
Student fees, tuition, financial aid, 14, 60, 111-12, 130, 152-53, 225, 265, 284, 308, 337-38
Student Interracial Ministry, 265-66
Student life: University Place, 14, 16, 34, 39-40, 42, 60; Park Avenue, 61, 90, 111-12; Broadway, 130, 140, 177-78, 184-89, 197-98, 222-25, 265-76, 281, 286-87, 344-46; see also Blacks at Union, Women at Union
Students, graduate, 108-9, 129, 146, 152, 177-78, 224, 298, 328

Student Volunteer Movement, 101, 135
Summer session, 130, 295
Support staff members, cited: James Anderson, 221; Elizabeth M. Barclay, 251; Robert E. Broadwell, 284, 313; George Bayley, 221; Joseph S. Gallagher, 33; Elizabeth Jones, 313; Emmanuel Romero, 221; Norah Wünsche, 313
Sutz, Erwin, 178
Swander, J. Phillip, 242
Swift, Arthur L., 151, 239-40

Tangeman, Robert S., 249, 287, 299
Taylor, Knowles, 1, 5-6
Tefferteller, Ralph, 187
Temple, William, 216
Terrien, Samuel L., 205, 217, 230, 254, 305-6
Thelen, Mary Frances, 179
Theological currents, 4-5, 26-31, 35-37, 43-44, 65-67, 112, 122-24, 136-37, 155-56, 162, 172, 175-76, 189-90, 194-95, 314, 351n5, 360n32
Theological field, 11, 22-23, 35-37, 96, 98-99, 106-7, 147-49, 173-76, 181-82, 205, 231-36, 260, 267, 310-14, 320-21, 338-39
Theological university, 104-6, 108, 121, 132, 164
Tholuck, Friedrich, 26, 48, 51
Thompson, Dean K., 195
Tillich, Paul, 181-83, 196, 203, 216-17, 231-33, 267, 288, 360n25
Trible, Phyllis, 320, 337
Tryon, Harold H., 108, 143, 203-4
Tully, Mary A., 239, 247, 308

Ulanov, Ann B., 272, 309, 337
Union Assembly, 283-85, 289-90, 293-304, 326
Union Commission, 275-82, 290, 299, 363n15
Union Medal, 333, 335
Union School of Religion, 134, 166, 171-72, 357n13
Union Seminary Book Service, 171, 335
Union Seminary Quarterly Review, 198, 220, 289
Union Settlement, 101, 109, 218
Union Theological Seminary: name, 7, 18-19; Centennial, 132, 193-96; founding, ix, 1-2, 5 (see also Preamble to the Constitution); on University Place, 14-15, 34, 56; seal, 347, 349; on Park Avenue, 56-58, 60, 111, 117; on Broadway, 117-20, 126-28, 154-55, 166-67, 170-71, 208, 215, 226, 243, 250, 256, 330-35

Van Dusen, Henry P.: as faculty member, 174, 176, 178, 180, 195-96, 200, 209; as president, 211-28, 231-33, 240, 243, 251, 254-57, 259-62, 283
Van Dyke, Henry Jackson, 98-99
Van Dyke, Henry, 86, 98
Van Ess, Leander, 18
Van Ness, Peter H., 339
Vatican II, 196, 262
Vietnam War, 266-68, 273-74, 289-90, 343
Vincent, Marvin R., 55, 75-76, 90, 100, 149
Visser 't Hooft, W. A., 255

Wainwright, Geoffrey, 321
Walton, Janet, 332, 337
Ward, Harry F., 141, 147-48, 190-93, 204, 206, 360n34
Warfield, Benjamin B., 65-66, 82, 89
Warford, Malcolm, 324-26
Washington, James M., 319
Webber, George W., 222, 240, 252-53
Weinstein, Marcia, 295, 309
West, Cornel, 320
Westminster Confession, 2, 5, 7, 9, 43-44, 50, 58-59, 65, 74, 76, 83-85, 104, 137, 351n3, 354n22
Wetzel, John W., 173
Wheeler, Barbara G., 300, 336
White, Charles T., 166, 202, 220
White, Gaylord S., 110, 136, 143, 150-51, 166, 172, 174
White, Henry, 6, 11, 20, 22-23, 31
Williams, Daniel Day, 233-34, 247, 256, 267, 284, 298, 303, 309
Williams, Russell S., 252
Wilson, James Patriot, 31, 35
Wilson, John F., 336
Wink, Walter, 288, 309
Women at Union, 60, 97-98, 163, 166, 179, 222-23, 251, 260, 292, 296-97, 322-23, 337, 341

Women's Center, 292, 322
Women's Committee, 251
Woodstock College, 263-64
Worcester, John H. Jr., 99
World Missionary Conference, 1910, 170, 196
World War I, 139-44

World War II, 159, 179, 197, 199-204
Worship, *see* Chapel services

Young, William C., 81

Ziprik, Mr. and Mrs. Fred, 335